# The People's Bible

# 2 Chronicles

## Paul O. Wendland

NORTHWESTERN PUBLISHING HOUSE
Milwaukee, Wisconsin

Second edition, 2002

Cover art by Frank Ordaz.

Interior illustrations by Glenn Myers.

Covers of first edition volumes and certain second edition volumes feature illustrations by James Tissot (1836–1902).

Library of Congress Card 97-76164
Northwestern Publishing House
1250 N. 113th St., Milwaukee, WI 53226-3284
© 1998 by Northwestern Publishing House
Published 1994
Printed in the United States of America
ISBN 0-8100-1170-0

# CONTENTS

## ILLUSTRATIONS

# CHARTS, DIAGRAMS, AND MAPS

# EDITOR'S PREFACE

The People's Bible is just what the name implies—a Bible for the people. It includes the complete text of the Holy Scriptures in the popular New International Version. The commentary following the Scripture sections contains personal applications as well as historical background and explanations of the text.

The authors of The People's Bible are men of scholarship and practical insight, gained from years of experience in the teaching and preaching ministries. They have tried to avoid the technical jargon that limits so many commentary series to professional Bible scholars.

The most important feature of these books is that they are Christ-centered. Speaking of the Old Testament Scriptures, Jesus himself declared, "These are the Scriptures that testify about me" (John 5:39). Each volume of The People's Bible directs our attention to Jesus Christ. He is the center of the entire Bible. He is our only Savior.

The commentaries also have maps, illustrations, and archaeological information when appropriate. All the books include running heads to direct the reader to the passage he is looking for.

This commentary series was initiated by the Commission on Christian Literature of the Wisconsin Evangelical Lutheran Synod.

It is our prayer that this endeavor may continue as it began. We dedicate these volumes to the glory of God and to the good of his people.

# INTRODUCTION TO 2 CHRONICLES

## *Purpose*

History is not happenstance. What we read in our newspapers, hear on our radios, and see on our television sets is not just the dreary, daily catalog of man's inhumanity to man. God is still in charge and working in all these things—working in judgment and above all in grace. His purpose is to work out in time the saving of those he chose in Christ before time began. This, in a nutshell, is the Chronicler's message.

There is no need to repeat everything that was said to introduce the first book of Chronicles. What follows is intended to prepare the reader for understanding the second volume of the Chronicler's work.

The Chronicler wrote for the community of God's people who had returned from exile in Babylon to the land of Judah, beginning with the decree of Cyrus in 537 B.C. They had come to rebuild the temple and to reestablish themselves in the land. In doing this, they faced many difficulties. The greatest of these were spiritual. The work on the temple had not gone as quickly as they might have hoped, since the people had become bogged down in their own affairs (Haggai 1). As they considered the size and beauty of the structure they were working on, many felt it was not at all as glorious as they might have expected the house of the Lord to be (Haggai 2). In view of the magnificent promises of restoration God had made to his people through the prophets Isaiah and Ezekiel, these small beginnings must surely have seemed "like nothing" (Haggai 2:3). God's people were tempted to become discouraged and disillusioned.

With the passing of time, there were other fights and fears that put pressure on the restored community, within and without. For example, they had incurred the resentment of the surrounding people when—out of a proper zeal for the purity of God's house—the people of Judah steadfastly refused to let outsiders work alongside them in the temple project (Ezra 4:1-5). Until Jerusalem's wall was rebuilt through the providential help of Nehemiah, they could not be secure from such outside interference.

Yet the enemies without were not as bad as the enemies within. When the initial call to return to Jerusalem had been issued to the exiles, a relatively meager number of Levites, or temple workers, responded to it. This lack of enthusiasm for the things of God demonstrated itself in other ways as well. Instead of resisting the pressure to let the outsiders join them, often the returned exiles simply caved in and let non-Jews become part of the community. They intermarried with them (Ezra 9). In one case a prominent outsider was given a room even within the sacred temple grounds (Nehemiah 13:7). The desire for racial and cultic purity was not racism on the part of pious Jews. It was rather a confession of faith in God's promise to bless all nations through the seed of Abraham (Genesis 22:18). Similarly, a lack of zeal for this kind of holiness demonstrated a lack of faith in God's promises and a waning of their spiritual strength. They were assimilating into the ways of the world. They were becoming just like everybody else.

The prophet Malachi identified that same spiritual torpor by pointing out his people's sins. They were (1) a tendency toward religious formalism (when worship becomes a matter of going through the outward motions), (2) growing doubt about God's justice, and (3) lack of support for God's work. Even the priests were lazy and uncaring in the way they taught and applied God's Word. Over the years the exiles who had returned from Babylon became deficient in their hope toward God and listless in love toward their neighbor. It would not be overstating the case to say that the returned exiles were in imminent danger of losing their sense of identity as God's people and had even begun to wonder whether the true God were truly to be found by means of the temple and worship in it.

In response to this deep spiritual sickness, God inspired the Chronicler to write his message. Unlike a prophet, whom we might expect to speak with vivid imagery, fiery thunderings of law, and soothing applications of gospel, the Chronicler speaks in more measured accents. It was his task to retell history from God's point of view. He does not so much make specific applications of his message as let his audience draw its own conclusions from the material he presents.

For example, in response to his people's identity crisis, the Chronicler in his first book showed by means of genealogies how they were the descendants of Israel, the nation God selected out of all other nations to be his very own. In ending his second volume with the exiles' return, he showed his people that their roots went deep into a glorious past and that their community was the continuation of the kingdom of David and Solomon. In response to their lack of interest in the temple and its services, the Chronicler highlighted the work of these two greatest kings of Israel in building the temple. These kings had been chosen and inspired by God for this work, and God's blessing had rested upon it. In a similar way, the Chronicler's generation could be sure that they had been chosen to rebuild the temple. No less did God's blessing rest upon them.

In dealing with his people's disobedience to God's law, the writer emphasized God's response of punishing those in times past who thought they knew better than God how to make their way through life. He demonstrated also how obedience to God's will brought with it God's gracious blessings.

Finally, to shore up their sinking hope, the Chronicler held before his people a carefully drawn picture of David and Solomon. He emphasized the positive aspects of the reigns of these two righteous kings, who served the Lord by devoting their lives to the building of his house. As such, they served to foreshadow the coming of the Lord's Anointed, the Son of David, whom the Lord would set "over [his] house and [his] kingdom forever" (1 Chronicles 17:14). There was no son of David ruling over Judah at the time when the Chronicler wrote, and the country had been reduced in status from a kingdom in its own right to a mere backwater province in the great Persian Empire. Even so, God's Word could not fail; the Lord's Anointed would come to rule over God's kingdom and to build God's house.

### Important themes

Since the last two topics mentioned are of particular importance in understanding the Chronicler's second book, we now will deal with them in greater detail. We consider both the Chronicler's portrayal of David and Solomon and his emphasis on God's response—in blessing and in judgment—to his people's moral behavior.

### The ideal king

Anyone even slightly familiar with the account of the lives of David and Solomon found in 2 Samuel and in 1 Kings is bound to ask, "Why are the accounts so different?" This is particularly true in the case of Solomon. In 1 Kings we can divide Solomon's life into two phases. There was his wise, early rule, during which he built God's house, followed by his later, sinful rule, during which his many wives turned his heart away from the Lord to serve idols. The writer of Kings evaluates Solomon's reign by saying, "So Solomon did evil in the eyes of the LORD; he did not follow the LORD completely, as David his father had done" (1 Kings 11:6). In 2 Chronicles there is no mention of the many wives, not a word about Solomon's idolatry. From start to finish, Solomon's reign is presented as a positive example of what a righteous king of Israel does. This is so much the case that the Chronicler can compare the behavior of the people under later kings to the standards set by both David *and* Solomon: "They strengthened the kingdom of Judah and supported Rehoboam son of Solomon three years, walking in the ways of David and Solomon during this time" (2 Chronicles 11:17). Those who have read 1 Chronicles know that a similar culling out of the more negative aspects of David's reign occurred in the Chronicler's presentation of the life of that great king.

What are we to make of this? First, let us note that the Chronicler was fully aware of another side to the story he was telling. For example, although he does not tell the story of David and Bathsheba, he certainly knew about the case (1 Chronicles 3:5). For this reason we can exclude from consideration the suggestion some negative Bible scholars have made that the inspired author had rewritten history with a lack of concern for facts.

It is much more in harmony with the rest of God's Word to assume, as this writer does, that the Chronicler was shaping and selecting his material to revive the hopes of God's people and to offer fresh encouragement to them to look forward with eager longing to the coming of the Messiah.

Some have theorized that the Chronicler wrote into a situation where the previously eager hopes for a swift arrival of the chosen King had lapsed into a despair of his ever coming. These hopes, they say, had been aroused by the pronouncements of Haggai in connection with Zerubbabel (Haggai 2:23) and confirmed by Zechariah's oracle dealing with Joshua, the high priest (Zechariah 6:12,13).

We, with vision clarified by the New Testament's bright light, properly understand those particular prophecies as applying to Jesus of Nazareth, and we realize that the prophets were speaking symbolically (Zechariah 3:8) when they used the names of Zerubbabel and Joshua in making their messianic predictions. At the same time, we can see how easy it would have been for those who lived before the time of fulfillment to become confused and to have supposed that the prophets had been speaking of things God intended to do through those two particular men. If this line of thinking is true, then we can readily see how God's people could have had the fervor of their messianic hope chilled by the passing of those two men from the earthly scene without the ushering in of the promised kingdom.

We have to confess that we simply do not have enough precise historical information about the exact setting of the Chronicler's message. Attempts such as these to reconstruct it must remain no more than educated guesses. What we can say is that the ideal king, as he emerges from the accounts of David and Solomon, is one who shows himself completely devoted to the true worship of God and to the building of God's house.

One of David's first official acts as ruler over all Israel is to bring the ark into the center of the kingdom, to his new capital at Jerusalem. He himself, a man whose hands are stained with blood, is unable to build the temple. Yet his life is dedicated to the success of the project his son, a man of peace, will complete. David secures the borders of the Holy Land by subduing all the enemies of God's people. He organizes priests and Levites, temple musicians and gatekeepers, government officials and army chieftains—all around the worship of the one true God. Each one serves the greater purpose in his own way. This task completed, he commissions his son Solomon—at first in private and then in the presence of all the people—for the great undertaking of building God's house. He provides physical resources and pledges his personal fortune for the project. Whatever he could do, he did.

Second Chronicles paints a correspondingly positive picture of Solomon. Solomon's first official act is to ask God for the wisdom to carry out the great enterprise. His alliance with Hiram and his great wealth give him all the physical resources needed to complete it. The temple's construction and the great day of its dedication form the capstone of Solomon's career. From the unlikely lips of Gentiles, God ordains the type of praise that fits such a king: "Praise be to the LORD your God, who has delighted in you and placed you on his throne as king to rule for the LORD your God. Because of the love of your God for Israel and his desire to uphold them forever, he has made you king over them, to maintain justice and righteousness" (9:8; see also 2:11).

On occasion the ideal king, as the Chronicler presents him to us through David and Solomon, serves the people not only as their shepherd and ruler but as their priest and prophet as well. By this we mean that at times the Chronicler shows David and Solomon serving almost in a priestly role as an intermediary between the people and their God (1 Chronicles 16:2; 2 Chronicles 6:3,12,13). At other times the Chronicler shows David and Solomon carrying out the prophetic function of being a spokesman for God and speaking by inspiration

(1 Chronicles 28:12; 2 Chronicles 7:12-22). In this way the writer helps his people understand that the Messiah to come will be one who serves as God's representative in all three offices: Prophet, Priest, and King.

### *Immediate blessings and punishments*

In keeping with his general idea that God directs, shapes, and rules over the history of this world, the Chronicler puts a decided emphasis on the truth that "a man reaps what he sows" (Galatians 6:7). We could list examples of this almost without end. It is easiest to see in connection with the lives of the kings. Faithfulness brings God's blessings. Stubborn disloyalty to Israel's Lord calls down his swift judgment. So David experiences God's wrath because, in sinful pride, he wanted to find out the extent and power of his kingdom. Brushing aside Joab's warning, he wants to know the number of his fighting men (1 Chronicles 21). Solomon, on the other hand, receives wealth and glory in response to his humble prayer for wisdom (2 Chronicles 1). Throughout 2 Chronicles, long life and wealth will be presented as God's response to kings who obey him, while sickness and trouble come to kings who disobey him.

Is this still God's way of dealing with his people? Would we be correct in pointing to the wealthier in our congregations as those who enjoy these marks of God's favor because of their faithfulness, while those troubled by ill health or poverty are being chastised for lack of obedience? Without attempting to present all that the Bible has to say on the matter of temporal blessings or punishments, there are a few observations we might make to keep our thoughts headed in the right direction.

In the days before the coming of Christ, God still treated his people as minor children, as Paul says in Galatians 3:23,24; 4:1. In that time of shadows before the full dawn of faith, the hope of God's people was directed by God's Word to attach itself to more physically perceptible things: the land of Israel, the temple at Jerusalem, long life, and prosperity. The best example of this is the Fourth Commandment, offering children long life in "the land the LORD your God is giving you" (Exodus 20:12) as a consequence of giving parents their rightful due. In a similar way, God threatened his Old Testament people with physical punishments if they failed to honor his covenant of law (Deuteronomy 30:15-20).

At the same time, God also inspired books like Job to be written. They served as a corrective for those in Old Testament times who thought too simply about such matters and imagined God to be a mere heavenly paymaster, dispensing good and ill in response to every deed. God taught Job that a human being's perspective is too limited to take in all of God's reasons for acting as he does and that ultimately we cannot—by means of pure reasoning power alone—justify the ways of God to men. In a similar vein, Psalm 73 pointed out that a child of God could only begin to understand the final destinies of believer and unbeliever (hidden as they are sometimes underneath the apparent injustices of this world) when he turned to the God who revealed himself through his appointed means (verse 17). The wicked might sometimes appear to prosper, but their prosperity would be swept away as a mere fantasy on judgment day. Likewise, a believer might suffer in this world, but his sufferings could not compare with the glory God would give him in the end (Psalm 73:16-26). In all of this we remember that the child of God in any age has always been saved in precisely the same way: "Abram believed the LORD, and he credited it to him as righteousness" (Genesis 15:6).

As New Testament believers, we live in the full light of God's grace revealed in the face of Jesus Christ. We know our God as the one who punished all our sins in Christ's body. After he had suffered all, he could say in triumph at the end, "It is finished!" The entire world has been reconciled to the Father in him (2 Corinthians 5:19). No wrath whatsoever remains for those who receive this message of forgiveness by putting their trust in him. On the other hand, those who reject this message have placed themselves outside God's grace and can expect nothing but God's righteous anger upon everything they do (Mark 16:16; John 3:18).

Saying this, however, does not mean that all of God's blessings and all of God's punishments are simply deferred until judgment day. Jesus himself promises that "all these [earthly] things will be given" to those who put the kingdom first (Matthew 6:33). Sin still has its consequences also in this present life. Even believers experience the loving chastisements of God that purify them of the unbelief remaining within them (1 Peter 1:6,7). Only faith can see these things as expressions of God's love; the unbelieving part of us feels nothing but the pain (2 Corinthians 12:7; Hebrews 12:10,11). Yet this faith is so powerful that it can even free our hearts to "rejoice in our sufferings" (Romans 5:3), since it is confident that our heavenly Father has in mind nothing but our good through them.

In addition, no wicked person ought to believe the lie that God has forgotten how to punish sin in this life nor think it the height of sophistication to believe in a God who smiles fondly at those who do as they please. Ananias stands in Scripture as a witness against these ideas (Acts 5:1-11). We don't have to look far in our own corrupt society to see those who "received in themselves the due penalty for their perversion" (Romans 1:27). Long ago Paul wrote, "God cannot be mocked" (Galatians 6:7). Those words remain as true as ever.

We live in a society that has conceived great contempt for God and his moral will. People have convinced themselves that there is no hell and that God—if he does anything at all in this life—merely showers down treats from heaven for the kiddies. They cannot believe that God would ever punish anyone for anything in the here and now. And when life is over, everyone expects to be embraced by the light. After all, no postmodern God could ever bring himself to design hell, much less put anyone there.

Christians need to tell the world that all these earthly "truths" are damnable lies that give impenitent sinners a false sense of security. It could well be that the Chronicler was writing to people who had begun to delude themselves in the same way. It could be that their lack of response and commitment was an outgrowth of that kind of stubborn unbelief that says, "The LORD does not see; the God of Jacob pays no heed" (Psalm 94:7).

In understanding the Chronicler's message to his own people, therefore, we will keep in mind the times and the era during which he wrote. He taught the people of Israel that God had not forgotten either his threats or his promises uttered as part of the covenant of Sinai. We will not be surprised at the immediacy with which God responded to these children of his during the time of their minority. As those who live after Christ, we don't expect God always to act toward us in quite the same way. We fix our eyes on the heavenly city and the life that is hidden with Christ in God.

At the same time, we will pay careful attention to what the Chronicler is saying to us here. We will avoid spiritualizing the message of the New Testament to such a degree that we forget about God's power in our present, everyday lives. We will not act as if God's blessings, judgments, and chastisements were so deferred as to render him practically irrelevant to the world in which we now live. We will continue to assert to society a truth it would prefer to forget: God is still in control, and he will be God whether it wants him or not. We still live in a moral universe in which people reap what they sow.

## Theme and outline

Theme: "Yours, O LORD, is the kingdom."
(1 Chronicles 29:11)

I. An overview of God's kingdom from the beginning to the restoration (1 Chronicles 1:1–9:44)*

II. God establishes his kingdom in Israel under David (1 Chronicles 10:1–29:30)*

III. God exalts his kingdom under Solomon (2 Chronicles 1:1–9:31)

   A. God gives Solomon the gifts of wisdom and splendor (1:1-17)

   B. Solomon builds a house for the Lord (2:1–7:22)

     1. Solomon makes provisions for building the temple (2:1-18)

     2. Solomon builds God's house (3:1-17)

     3. Solomon makes the furnishings and decorations for God's house (4:1–5:1)

     4. Solomon completes the work of David (5:2–7:22)

       a. The ark is placed in the sanctuary (5:2-13)

       b. God lives among his people—his glory fills the temple! (5:13,14)

       c. Solomon speaks a personal hymn of praise to God, the fulfiller of promises (6:1-11)

       d. Solomon's prayer of dedication (6:12-42)

       e. God dedicates the temple with fire and in glory (7:1-3)

---

*Parts One and Two were discussed in *1 Chronicles*.

f. All the people worship God through sacrifices and song (7:4-10)

g. God's answer to Solomon's prayer of dedication (7:11-22)

C. Solomon in all his splendor (8:1–9:31)

1. The splendor of Solomon's trading and building (8:1-6)

2. The splendor of Solomon's workforce (8:7-10)

3. The splendor of Solomon's worship (8:11-16)

4. The wealth of the nations is his (8:17,18)

5. The queen of the South gives testimony to God's king (9:1-12)

6. Summary of Solomon's wealth (9:13-28)

7. Solomon's death (9:29-31)

IV. God preserves his kingdom in Judah until the return from exile (10:1–36:23)

A. God's kingdom under Rehoboam (10:1–12:16)

1. Pride goes before a fall: The northern tribes rebel (10:1–11:4)

2. True Israel rallies around the Lord (11:5-16)

3. Rehoboam blessed for early faithfulness (11:17-23)

4. Rehoboam chastised for later unfaithfulness (12:1-11)

5. Rehoboam's restoration—for Jerusalem's sake (12:11-16)

B. God's kingdom under Abijah (13:1-22)

1. Abijah's speech to the northern army: "The LORD is our God" (13:1-12)

2. The Lord grants victory to Judah (13:13-22)

C. God's kingdom under Asa (14:1–16:14)

    1. Asa relies on the Lord and is delivered (14:1-15)

    2. Asa responds to God's Word and renews the covenant (15:1-19)

    3. Asa relies on man, rejects God's Word, and is chastised (16:1-14)

D. God's kingdom under Jehoshaphat (17:1–20:37)

    1. The Lord is with Jehoshaphat, and he prospers (17:1-19)

    2. An alliance with evil: Jehoshaphat escapes with his life (18:1-34)

    3. Jehoshaphat appoints judges for the Lord (19:1-11)

    4. God fights for his people against an unholy alliance (20:1-30)

    5. Summary of Jehoshaphat's reign and an unhappy postscript (20:31-37)

E. God's kingdom under Jehoram (21:1-20)

    1. A bleak summary of his reign: "He walked in the ways . . . of Ahab" (21:1-7)

    2. God judges Jehoram (21:8-20)

        a. God whittles him down to size (21:8-11)

        b. God pronounces judgment on Jehoram through Elijah (21:12-15)

        c. God carries out his verdict (21:16-20)

F. God's kingdom under Ahaziah (22:1-9)

    1. Listening to the counsel of the ungodly, sitting in the seat of the scornful (22:1-6)

    2. Becoming like chaff that the wind drives away (22:7-9)

G. God's kingdom under the usurper Queen Athaliah (22:10–23:21)

    1. A direct assault on the kingdom (22:10-12)

    2. God preserves his kingdom by the decisive actions of Jehoiada and Jehosheba (23:1-21)

H. God's kingdom under Joash (24:1-27)

    1. A good beginning: the temple restored (24:1-16)

    2. A bad ending: Joash "[does] not remember the kindness" of Jehoiada (24:17–27)

I. God's kingdom under Amaziah (25:1-28)

    1. A good beginning: his heart is open to advice from the Lord (25:1-12)

    2. A bad ending: his heart is led away to idols and closed to the good words of God (25:13-28)

J. God's kingdom under Uzziah (26:1-23)

    1. He remembers his name ("The LORD is my strength") and becomes powerful and prosperous (26:1-15)

    2. He forgets who he is, and pride leads to his destruction (26:16-23)

K. God's kingdom under Jotham: he begins well and sticks to it! (27:1-9)

L. God's kingdom under Ahaz: a promoter of evil (28:1-27)

    1. He leads the way into idolatry (28:1-4)

    2. God hands him over to Aram and Israel (28:5-8)

    3. The men of Israel act more justly than the men of Judah (28:9-15)

    4. Ahaz seeks help that is no help (28:16-21)

    5. All his troubles lead him to do more evil rather than repent (28:22-27)

M. God's kingdom under Hezekiah, a second Solomon: reform and renewal (29:1–32:33)

    3. Manasseh humbles himself, seeks the Lord's face, and is restored to Jerusalem (33:12,13)
    4. Manasseh's fruits of repentance (33:14-20)
    5. Amon's unfaithfulness and death (33:21-25)

O. God's kingdom under Josiah: one last reform (34:1–35:27)
    1. A faithful king purges land and temple (34:1-13)
    2. The Book of the Law is found; the king's repentance (35:14-21)
    3. God's response through Huldah: peace for Josiah's time, but after him, the deluge (34:22-28)
    4. The covenant is once more renewed (34:29-33)
    5. A Passover celebration without equal (35:1-19)
    6. King Josiah's untimely death (35:20-27)

P. God's kingdom under wrath and grace (36:1-23)
    1. Increasing defiance to the Lord and the Lord's response (36:1-10)
    2. King Zedekiah ushers in the end (36:11-19)
    3. Yours, O Lord, is the kingdom (36:20-23)
       a. God graciously preserves a remnant of his people (36:20)
       b. The land enjoys its sabbath rests (36:21)
       c. God moves Cyrus to issue a proclamation: "Return and rebuild!" (36:22,23)

"The book of Chronicles (which is, in fact, a summation of the entire Old Testament) is a book of such great importance that someone can only make a fool out of himself if he pretends to know the Scriptures without it."

—Saint Jerome
(*Ad Paulinum,* Ep. 53, 8)

# PART THREE

# God Exalts His Kingdom under Solomon
## (1:1–9:31)

### Structure of the account

When we pick up a Bible today, we scarcely notice the great amount of work that has gone simply into the display of the text as we see it before us. For example, we might find it difficult to believe that there was a time when even chapter divisions did not exist in the sacred writings, much less division into verses. The truth is that these conveniences represent additions made by the hands of later editors who wanted to make specific texts easier to locate. More recent editors have done a great deal of work in formatting the text into larger divisions of thought—sections and paragraphs, complete with headings. All this was done in an effort to make the Bible easier for us to read.

We have become so used to these features that sometimes we may have to remind ourselves that none of them existed in the text as it was originally inspired. All the same, we ought not to think that ancient writers had no resources available to them for showing the larger divisions of thought into which they wished to divide their accounts. A good example of this is a pyramidlike arrangement that some scholars have seen in the first nine chapters of 2 Chronicles.

The following is an illustration of that arrangement, somewhat simplified:

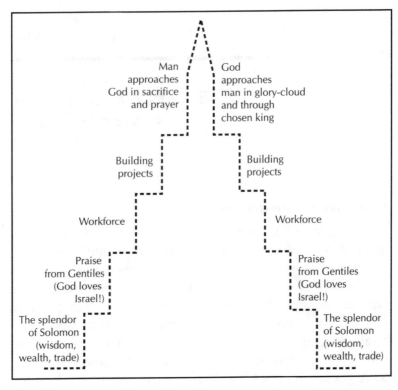

## The structure of 2 Chronicles 1–9[1]

Like bookends, accounts of Solomon's preeminence in wisdom, wealth, and trade flank the entire section (1:1-17; 9:1-28). Rising one step, there are corresponding accounts of heathen rulers offering their praise to the Lord for giving Israel a king like Solomon (2:11; 9:8). Moving one step further, we have two descriptions of Solomon's workforce (2:17,18; 8:7-10). Major building projects of Solomon's reign are given next (3:1–5:1; 8:1-6). At the apex of the pyramid, given the place of emphasis at the center of the account, we find the story of the dedication of the temple. Solomon comes into God's presence through animal sacrifice, praise, and prayer (5:2–6:42); God "responds" with fire from heaven, the appearing of the glory-cloud that signaled the Lord's gracious presence, and a special revelation to Solomon, corresponding to the prayer the king had offered (7:1-22).

Even though we will not be following this structure in our reading of the text, we mention it here for two reasons. First, we need to understand the basic unity of the first seven chapters of 2 Chronicles. These chapters form the capstone of the entire book, and they demonstrate the importance of the temple in the worship life of God's Old Testament people. Second, taking note of this structure helps us gain an appreciation for the skill and care with which the Chronicler wrote. Sections that may strike us as repetitious or verses that appear to be out of place only seem so to our modern eyes and ears. Judged by their own standards, the ancients were masters in shaping their material for the readers.

### *God gives Solomon the gift of wisdom*

**1** Solomon son of David established himself firmly over his kingdom, for the LORD his God was with him and made him exceedingly great.

**2**Then Solomon spoke to all Israel—to the commanders of thousands and commanders of hundreds, to the judges and to all the leaders in Israel, the heads of families—**3**and Solomon and the whole assembly went to the high place at Gibeon, for God's Tent of Meeting was there, which Moses the LORD's servant had made in the desert. **4**Now David had brought up the ark of God from Kiriath Jearim to the place he had prepared for it, because he had pitched a tent for it in Jerusalem. **5**But the bronze altar that Bezalel son of Uri, the son of Hur, had made was in Gibeon in front of the tabernacle of the LORD; so Solomon and the assembly inquired of him there. **6**Solomon went up to the bronze altar before the LORD in the Tent of Meeting and offered a thousand burnt offerings on it.

With a few broad strokes, the Chronicler sets the scene and prepares us for the building of the temple under Solomon. Just as one of David's first official acts had been to put God's worship at the center of his kingdom by bringing the ark to Jerusalem, so his son Solomon began his rule by seeking the Lord first at the high place of Gibeon. Just as David had acted as a leader in worship for all Israel, so Solomon gathered the whole assembly to accompany him.

In case one might ask why Solomon would make the six-mile journey to Gibeon instead of staying in Jerusalem, we are told that Solomon went to Gibeon because the Tent of Meeting was there. This was another name for the traveling sanctuary, or tabernacle, that Moses had made. It had been at the center of camp life during the time of Israel's wilderness wanderings. For many years it also had been the spot where the ark of the covenant was housed, until its removal during the final days of Eli and his sons (1 Samuel 4:1-11). After various wanderings, the ark had come to rest in Jerusalem, being placed in the temporary dwelling David had built for it (verse 4; see also 1 Chronicles 15,16). An additional reason for going to Gibeon to inquire of the Lord is mentioned. The bronze altar that Moses' master craftsman Bezalel had made was also to be found there.

It was fitting for Solomon to begin his rule by offering sacrifices at the older holy place. He was going to build a new temple to replace the old tabernacle and bring the ark, altar, and sanctuary together again into one permanent shrine at Jerusalem. He would carry out his work following the inspired plans of his father, David (1 Chronicles 28:11-19), just as Bezalel had followed the inspired plans of Moses (Exodus 39:42,43). He would be given the gift of wisdom to carry out his task, just as Bezalel had received wisdom from the Lord (Exodus 36:1). It appears likely that Solomon took a direct hand in fashioning the bronze altar of sacrifice for the temple—another similarity to Bezalel (Exodus 38:22; 2 Chronicles 4:1; 7:7). In drawing these parallels between the old and the new, between David and his son Solomon and between Solomon and Bezalel, the Chronicler emphasizes the continuity between past and present, the sure purposes of God in all the changing scenes of life.

Coping with change is difficult in any age. We happen to live at a time when new becomes old at a dizzying rate. In all of these changes, let us keep in mind the one who remains "the same yesterday and today and forever" (Hebrews 13:8). He is no shifting shadow but rather the firm rock of our salvation, giving stability to our present and certainty to our future.

### Solomon asks God for wisdom

**⁷That night God appeared to Solomon and said to him, "Ask for whatever you want me to give you."**

**⁸Solomon answered God, "You have shown great kindness to David my father and have made me king in his place. ⁹Now, LORD God, let your promise to my father David be confirmed, for you have made me king over a people who are as numerous as the dust of the earth. ¹⁰Give me wisdom and knowledge, that I may lead this people, for who is able to govern this great people of yours?"**

**¹¹God said to Solomon, "Since this is your heart's desire and you have not asked for wealth, riches or honor, nor for the death of your enemies, and since you have not asked for a long life but for wisdom and knowledge to govern my people over whom I have made you king, ¹²therefore wisdom and knowledge will be given you. And I will also give you wealth, riches and honor, such as no king who was before you ever had and none after you will have."**

**¹³Then Solomon went to Jerusalem from the high place at Gibeon, from before the Tent of Meeting. And he reigned over Israel.**

God appeared to Solomon that night and made him a wonderful offer. Think of it: the almighty God came to a human being and threw open the treasure houses of heaven by asking him to choose for himself any gift he might like to have. Truly a mark of God's special favor! Yet what difference is there between Solomon and any believer? We have in our constant possession the Savior's promise, "You may ask me for anything in my name, and I will do it" (John 14:14). Commenting on this passage, Luther says, "We know, of course, what we must ask God for. We must ask not only for this beggarly earthly pittance, that is, for all the needs of this temporal life; but we should pray for deliverance from all present and future misery, from sin, death, and the grave, and that we may be made just, holy, free, alive, and glorious."²

Solomon had two requests. In the first he took the promise of God and asked the Lord to speak his amen to it: "Let your promise to my father David be confirmed." This was the promise God had made to establish an enduring dynasty for David, a promise that included the prediction that David's son would build a house for the Lord (1 Chronicles 17:10-14; 22:7-10). Prayer based on the Word of God contains its own assurance that God will answer, since the child of God knows heaven and earth will dissolve before God ever goes back on one of his words. Second, Solomon asked God, "Give me wisdom and knowledge, that I may lead this people, for who is able to govern this great people of yours?"

In one sense a person could say that God had given Solomon wisdom even before he had asked for it. He was a living example of one who carried out our Savior's encouragement

Solomon is made king

to "seek first his kingdom and his righteousness, and all these things will be given to you as well" (Matthew 6:33). From the beginning Solomon wanted to dedicate himself to the Lord and seek the Lord's gracious presence. One thousand sacrifices and a journey to Gibeon provide evidence enough of that. As Solomon wrote in another place, "The fear of the LORD is the beginning of wisdom" (Proverbs 9:10).

This beginning of wisdom led Solomon to recognize the immensity of the task laid upon him. In humility he understood that the task of leading God's people in building the temple was quite beyond his ability. He knew that he was king over Israel by the will and gift of God. He understood that if he were to have godly success in carrying out his duties as king, God would have to give him the strength.

Humility is not so much a denial that we have abilities as it is the spiritual insight to see all our abilities as God's gift. God has placed what we have into our hands. Humble people see that if God takes away his creative, sustaining power, all their efforts will accomplish nothing. They depend completely upon their God to "establish the work of [their] hands" (Psalm 90:17).

The fear of the Lord seeks out the wisdom only God can give. In a world in which we are surrounded by deception, we want the power to see things as they really are, to be able to judge everything by the Word and to let the Word be the sole measure of who we are and how we are to live. We humbly ask God to free us from the lies of the devil, the empty delusions of this unbelieving world, and the fog caused by our sin that clouds our thinking (Genesis 3:5,6; Psalm 51:5,6; 90:10,12).

Specifically, no doubt, Solomon had in mind for God to grant him the ability to serve under God as king over God's people and the practical wisdom required for such a great project as the construction of God's temple. These were the specific tasks he had received from God through his father, David (1 Chronicles 22:9,10). He knew that he was "young and inexperienced" (1 Chronicles 22:5) and would require a special gift of God in order to demonstrate the skills normally possessed only by those older and wiser in the ways of life. It was a standard perception among God's Old Testament people that wisdom was normally to be found among those who had more than a few years to their credit and was seldom seen in the young (Job 32:7-9).

Each Christian has an office given to him or her by God. God has appointed us by Baptism to serve him as his royal representatives in this world (1 Peter 2:9). In addition, he has committed a specific calling in life to each of us. He has made us husbands, wives, parents, children, workers, or employers. What a disaster it is for the Christian life when we view these tasks as merely ordinary, the stuff of everyday existence, and fail to see in our daily lives the power and purpose of God at work over all! Instead of seeing our lives as commonplace, let Solomon teach us true reverence for God—the beginning of wisdom. Then we will regard our lives as charged with the holy, as the arena for God's activity, as the place where God does his work through us. May we approach our God-given duties with equal reverence, requesting from him the insight to do them according to his will.

In response to Solomon's request, God not only gave him wisdom but all the other good things of life as well. Wealth would be his, "such as no king who was before you ever had and none after you will have." In the history of God's people, Solomon would provide the standard by which earthly splendor would be defined. A description of it is given in the following verses.

## The splendor of Solomon

¹⁴**Solomon accumulated chariots and horses; he had fourteen hundred chariots and twelve thousand horses, which he kept in the chariot cities and also with him in Jerusalem. ¹⁵The king made silver and gold as common in Jerusalem as stones, and cedar as plentiful as sycamore-fig trees in the foothills. ¹⁶Solomon's horses were imported from Egypt and from Kue—the royal merchants purchased them from Kue. ¹⁷They imported a chariot from Egypt for six hundred shekels of silver, and a horse for a hundred and fifty. They also exported them to all the kings of the Hittites and of the Arameans.**

We will take a closer look at the splendor of Solomon in the larger section devoted to it at the close of the account of Solomon's reign (9:13-28). Its function here is to emphasize God's immediate response to Solomon's prayer, according to God's promise.

The key features of Solomon's glory were his military power, his wealth, and his trading empire. The *bounty* of God's blessing is clearly seen. Solomon's holdings in chariotry—the high-tech weaponry of the day—were vast. Precious metals became as common as stones in Jerusalem. Even taking into account what seems to be a case of over-statement (a common biblical figure of speech meant to emphasize the great quantities involved), Solomon must have ushered in an era of prosperity for Israel without par-allel in its history. The reference to cedars as opposed to sycamore-figs is also to be understood as descriptive of Israel's affluence under Solomon. A relatively rare and pre-cious wood like cedar became as common and ordinary in Solomon's Jerusalem as sycamore-figs were in the foothills of Israel. A Roman emperor once boasted, "I found Rome a city of wood, and I left it a city of marble." The Chronicler is making a similar assertion here with respect to Solomon. The crucial difference, of course, is that instead of a powerful man making a boast based on his own ability, here we have a humble believer exulting in the power of his God, who does such good things for his people.

These verses likewise describe Solomon to us as a merchant-prince, sending his agents throughout the ancient Near East in a bustling import-export trade. Then, as now, one of the most highly profitable and sought-after commodities was weaponry. Any kingdom hoping to compete in the power politics of the region had to be equipped with horses and chariots. Solomon was strategically located to serve as the middleman between Kue and Egypt (see map), making trades also with the Hittites and Arameans to the north and west of him. The profit in being a middleman comes from the markup: buying low and selling

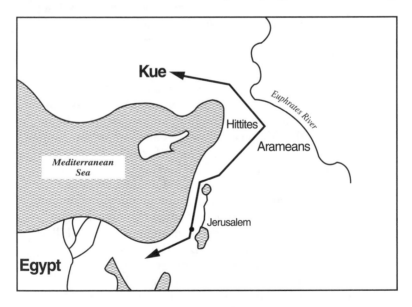

Solomon, the merchant-prince

high. In this way, no doubt, Solomon amassed a great deal
of his wealth.

### *Solomon builds a house for the Lord*

*Solomon makes provisions for building the temple*

**2** Solomon gave orders to build a temple for the Name of
the LORD and a royal palace for himself. ²He conscripted
seventy thousand men as carriers and eighty thousand as
stonecutters in the hills and thirty-six hundred as foremen
over them.

³Solomon sent this message to Hiram king of Tyre:

"Send me cedar logs as you did for my father
David when you sent him cedar to build a palace to
live in. ⁴Now I am about to build a temple for the
Name of the LORD my God and to dedicate it to him
for burning fragrant incense before him, for setting
out the consecrated bread regularly, and for making
burnt offerings every morning and evening and on
Sabbaths and New Moons and at the appointed feasts
of the LORD our God. This is a lasting ordinance
for Israel.

⁵"The temple I am going to build will be great,
because our God is greater than all other gods. ⁶But
who is able to build a temple for him, since the heavens, even the highest heavens, cannot contain him?
Who then am I to build a temple for him, except as a
place to burn sacrifices before him?

⁷"Send me, therefore, a man skilled to work in gold
and silver, bronze and iron, and in purple, crimson
and blue yarn, and experienced in the art of engraving, to work in Judah and Jerusalem with my skilled
craftsmen, whom my father David provided.

⁸"Send me also cedar, pine and algum logs from
Lebanon, for I know that your men are skilled in cutting
timber there. My men will work with yours ⁹to provide me
with plenty of lumber, because the temple I build must

**be large and magnificent. ¹⁰I will give your servants, the woodsmen who cut the timber, twenty thousand cors of ground wheat, twenty thousand cors of barley, twenty thousand baths of wine and twenty thousand baths of olive oil."**

On top of the extensive preparations already made by his father, David, for building the temple (1 Chronicles 22:2-19), Solomon added his own. His first order of business was to determine the number of workers he had and to organize them. Since the information in verse 2 is repeated with more detail at the end of the chapter, we will discuss it there. For those who are interested in such things, the repetition of a verse in two distinct places is a common feature of Hebrew style, serving to "enclose" the account and mark it as a unit. The second item on Solomon's agenda was to renew the treaty of cooperation his father, David, had enjoyed with Hiram, king of Tyre (1 Chronicles 14:1).

The official correspondence gave Solomon an opportunity to confess his faith in the Lord. He pointed to the ambitious nature of the project he was about to undertake. David needed Hiram's help to build a palace for himself. How much more then was Hiram's assistance needed to build a house for God. It was to be a "great" project, since it was for the God who was "greater than all other gods." By this last phrase, Solomon did not mean to imply that heathen gods were real; he only meant to underscore the incomparable nature of Israel's God.

In fact, Solomon says, no one is really capable of building a house for God. "Who is able to build a temple for him?" It's the same as if he had said, "I have been specially selected by God to build his house. Extensive preparations have been made. In fact, the entire kingdom with all its wealth of people and resources have been marshaled for the purpose of carrying out this task. Yet this is still not enough to build the temple in a way that matches the great glory of our God." God is great and deserves our best gifts. But even when he receives our best, we still have not given him anything truly worthy of his infinite dignity. What we offer God is received by him on the strength of his love and by the certainty of his promise to look with favor on our offerings—not because of the intrinsic worth of what we give.

In his letter Solomon continued to confess his faith by saying, "The heavens, even the highest heavens, cannot contain him." The truth that God is an infinite Spirit incapable of being confined to any place (John 4:24) was well known to God's Old Testament people. Therefore, this house was not to be thought of in crude terms as the physical dwelling place of God's entire being. Rather, it was the place where God would put his name (verses 4,6; see also Deuteronomy 12:11). This was just an Old Testament way of saying, "This is the place where God has chosen to reveal himself as our gracious God and Savior. Here he is pleased to come to us, and here he invites us to draw near to him. Though God is everywhere, we cannot grasp him everywhere. In this place he promises to come to us in a way that we sinful human beings can manage."

God remains the great initiator of our worship. He must first come to us and reveal himself to us, or we would never be able to approach him in the right way. None of our praises could ring true or be pleasing to him. We see this spiritual truth illustrated in the building of the temple. Solomon was not the one who chose to build God a house. God chose the place for it (1 Chronicles 21, especially verse 26), selected the man for it (1 Chronicles 22:9,10), made the plans of how to do it (1 Chronicles 28:19), and provided the resources to build it (1 Chronicles 29:14). God even made it clear to the Israelites exactly how and when they were to approach him. They had not invented their religion, nor did they hit upon their own way to honor God. Their form of worship had been provided by God as "a lasting ordinance for Israel."

We live in an age when people are busily trying to make their own connections to God. Even if they refuse to name "God" as the object of their quest, they are still searching for a way to gain access to something higher than themselves. They wander aimlessly in all sorts of directions, "harassed and helpless, like sheep without a shepherd" (Matthew 9:36). They try to touch God in nature, although he has never promised to be found by them there. They worship the beauty in things instead of the One who gave all things their beauty. They worship reason and intellect, forgetting him who gave us our ability to think and our power to understand. They may put forth tremendous efforts, daring to do great things—astounding things—all in a desire to please God. Yet these are things God never commanded them to do. They may turn to look inside themselves—deep within their innermost core—in an effort to find and release some spark of divine power. What else can they discover there but an image of themselves and another empty hope?

We will find God only where he has promised to be found. He must come to us and offer himself to us before we can approach him and offer him anything. The good news that initiates our worship is this: God did come to us in Christ and offers himself to us through his Son. Jesus said, "I am the way and the truth and the life. No one comes to the Father except through me" (John 14:6).

With this letter Solomon proposed a treaty to Hiram in which he requested Hiram's help in two matters. He wanted Hiram to send him a master craftsman capable of working

33

with many different kinds of material who would work alongside his own "skilled craftsmen." He also wanted Hiram to send from Lebanon—a country rich with a wealth of timber—the various kinds of wood needed to build the temple. In return, he pledged to send Hiram the provisions necessary to feed the woodcutters and a labor force from Israel to assist them.

Some see a contradiction between the quantities of provisions promised here and the ones listed in 1 Kings 5:11. A closer reading of the two texts reveals, however, that the contradiction is more imagined than real. In the case of 1 Kings, we have supplies Solomon gave to Hiram "as food for his household" (1 Kings 5:11). Here in 2 Chronicles, the supplies are earmarked for "the woodsmen who cut the timber." The supplies promised in 2 Chronicles appear to be more of a one-time deal, whereas the ones mentioned in 1 Kings 5:11 were given "year after year" as part of an ongoing treaty obligation. It is safe to say that each biblical writer selected his material from the official records in whatever way best served his own purpose. In 1 Kings the writer wishes to emphasize the ongoing, peaceful relationship between Solomon and Hiram (see 5:12); the Chronicler, on the other hand, remains devoted to his theme of building the temple.

Those whose consciences are bound by the Word of God know that it is not right to practice religious fellowship in defiance of that same Word or to act as if we are joined in a religious association with people who do not teach the whole truth of God's Word (Romans 16:17; Titus 1:16; 2 John 9-11). That being said, at times we can misuse these fellowship principles, as if the grace of God by which we enjoy his truth has put us into such a superior position over against the rest of the world that we could not possibly want to cooperate with anyone on any venture nor learn about any matter from anyone outside our fellowship. As long as the truth of God is not at stake nor any false religious unity implied, we do well to recognize the same truth that wise Solomon did. Complete wisdom and skill does not reside in our fellowship alone. Solomon needed the skills acquired by the people of a heathen city to build a house for the one true God. We too may well have need of the gifts God has given to others. They may use them in unbelief to their own destruction. We press them into service for the gospel. How else could children of God think? After all, we know our Father as one who "causes his sun to rise on the evil and the good, and sends rain on the righteous and the unrighteous" (Matthew 5:45). Since he scatters his gifts far and wide with a lavish hand, we are not surprised to find them even in the unlikeliest of places.

**¹¹Hiram king of Tyre replied by letter to Solomon:**

**"Because the Lord loves his people, he has made you their king."**

**¹²And Hiram added:**

**"Praise be to the Lord, the God of Israel, who made heaven and earth! He has given King David a wise son, endowed with intelligence and discernment, who will build a temple for the Lord and a palace for himself.**

**¹³"I am sending you Huram-Abi, a man of great skill, ¹⁴whose mother was from Dan and whose father was from Tyre. He is trained to work in gold and silver, bronze and iron, stone and wood, and with purple and blue and crimson yarn and fine linen. He is experienced in all kinds of engraving and can execute any design given to him. He will work with your craftsmen and with those of my lord, David your father.**

**¹⁵"Now let my lord send his servants the wheat and barley and the olive oil and wine he promised, ¹⁶and we will**

**cut all the logs from Lebanon that you need and will float them in rafts by sea down to Joppa. You can then take them up to Jerusalem."**

A comparison of Hiram's reply in 2 Chronicles with its parallel in 1 Kings 5:7-9 makes it clear that the Chronicler has preserved a more complete version of the official correspondence. Particularly striking is the expansion of the section praising Israel's king and Israel's God, along with the additional section mentioning Huram-Abi.

The prophets had so shaped Israel's hope that God's people lived in expectation of the day when the gentile nations would praise the one true God. That day would come, they knew, as part of the glorious rule of King Messiah (Isaiah 11:10-16; 49:22,23; Zechariah 8:8-13; Malachi 1:11). In Hiram's reply to Solomon, we see the Chronicler present to us a foreshadowing of that age, both in the praise Hiram offers Solomon and in the way Hiram refers to Israel's God.

Hiram called Solomon's rule a sign that God "loves his people." In a similar way, we Gentiles now praise God for exalting his Son, Jesus, at his right hand as our glorious King. He rules there "for the church" as an eternal sign of God's love for us (Ephesians 1:22). Hiram also acknowledges Israel's God as the one "who made heaven and earth," the Creator-God who gave "King David a wise son, endowed with intelligence and discernment, who will build a temple for the LORD." In a similar way, we praise God for Jesus, "in whom are hidden all the treasures of wisdom and knowledge" (Colossians 2:3). When we recognize him as the King who died out of love for us, we have no fear in placing our lives under his wise governance and direction.

Some may ask whether Hiram, in the original historical context, had come to believe in the Lord as the only true God. It is difficult to answer the question conclusively simply on the basis of these words. It could be argued that here we have nothing more than a case of diplomatic finesse, of fine talk calculated to engender goodwill. We have other examples in Scripture of unbelievers saying spiritual things that are nonetheless true (John 11:49-52).

On the other hand, the sudden flowering of the Israelite kingdom must have had a great impact on all the rulers in the vicinity. Connecting a nation's power with the power of that nation's god was a common enough equation in ancient thought. In addition, Hiram had worked closely with David even before he came under the influence of David's son. The testimony of those two men may well have borne fruit in the heart of the king of Tyre. In either case it makes no difference as far as the Chronicler's main point is concerned. Hiram's remarks served to point to the time when the Gentiles would—in the full joy of faith—acknowledge Israel's God and Israel's King as their own.

In response to Solomon's request, Hiram sent Solomon a craftsman by the name of Huram-Abi. It is possible to render his name in a slightly different way by translating it as "Huram, my master craftsman." The list of his job skills includes the same abilities that were seen in Bezalel, Oholiab, and the craftsmen who worked on the tabernacle at the time of Moses (compare verse 14 with Exodus 28:6-8; 31:1-11; 36:8-38). Huram-Abi, just like his ancient predecessors, was a man who had received the gift of wisdom. The NIV's rendition, "a man of great skill," flattens out the more generous praise of the Hebrew, "a man of wisdom and knowing understanding." The piling on of synonyms makes it clear that this Huram-Abi was the top man in his field. Another similarity to one of his predecessors can be found in the fact that, like Oholiab, he could claim descent from the tribe of Dan (compare verse 14 with Exodus 31:6).

On this last point we have a slight puzzle to unravel. In 1 Kings 7:14 Huram-Abi is described as being from the tribe of Naphtali, not of Dan. For those who have read the People's Bible commentary on 1 Chronicles, it might be useful to remember something we learned there about Hebrew genealogical references. The idea of strict descent and relationship by blood is not always in the foreground. Sometimes the phrases "the father of" and "the son of" indicate a looser connection of some type, such as the founder of a guild or the inhabitant of a certain village (see commentary on 1 Chronicles 2:5-9). So here we may say that Huram-Abi could trace his roots back to two tribes: Naphtali and Dan. The exact nature of those two connections remains unknown to us. Some have suggested that his mother was from Dan while his father was from Naphtali. The reference to his father being "from Tyre" would then be explained as indicating his place of residence, not his racial origin. Even though the precise understanding of this phrase may elude us, we may assert with a great deal more confidence that the Chronicler's chief reason in pointing out Huram-Abi's background to us is to draw another parallel between him and Oholiab.

A permanent temple in Jerusalem may replace a movable tabernacle in the wilderness. Moses may die and be succeeded by other leaders like David and Solomon. A man like Oholiab may receive the gifts to work for God's glory in his generation, and many years later another like Huram-Abi will take his place. The names, the places, the outward forms of things may change. But God's enduring purpose remains the same throughout all generations.

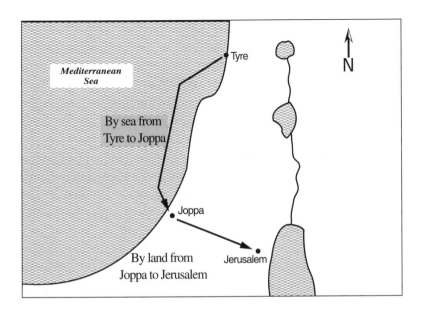

Importing timbers from Lebanon to Israel

In concluding his letter of acceptance, Hiram accepted Solomon's offer of provisions and promised to cut for Solomon "all the logs from Lebanon that you need." He proposed to make the task of transporting the huge timbers a somewhat easier one by floating them part of the way by sea (see map). That way they could avoid the rugged hill country of southern Lebanon and northern Israel.

## *Importing timbers from Lebanon to Israel*

[17]**Solomon took a census of all the aliens who were in Israel, after the census his father David had taken; and they were found to be 153,600. [18]He assigned 70,000 of them to be carriers and 80,000 to be stonecutters in the hills, with 3,600 foremen over them to keep the people working.**

A project like the temple required not only a tremendous expenditure of money but a stupendous physical effort as well. These verses give us some idea of the size of Solomon's labor force. As indicated, the core of Solomon's work force was made up of the "aliens who were in Israel." These were permanent residents of the land who had been permitted to survive the conquest of Canaan under Joshua. They had been pressed into service as woodcutters and water carriers for the Israelites and for the sanctuary. Some of them survived the exile and voluntarily returned to rebuild the temple. They are the "temple servants" mentioned in 1 Chronicles 9:2.

Here their work was carried out under compulsion, however, under the supervision of Israelite foremen. In 1 Kings 5:16 only 3,300 supervisors are listed, in contrast to the 3,600 mentioned here and in verse 2. This discrepancy might be due to an error during the copying of the text or due to the Chronicler's inclusion of some other people involved in supervising the work who were not included by the writer of 1 Kings (for example, some of the officials mentioned in 1 Kings 9:23).

In addition to the forced-laborers mentioned here, we know from the book of Kings that Solomon enlisted full-blooded Israelites to work alongside the resident aliens in what seems to have been some type of national service program (see 1 Kings 5:13,14). Some measure of the scope of this enterprise can be taken from the tens of thousands of laborers involved in it. The Chronicler's overall message is clear and summed up for us in Solomon's words, "The temple I am going to build will be great, because our God is greater than all other gods" (2:5). With preparations complete, Solomon is now ready to begin.

## Solomon builds God's house

### The temple site

**3** **Then Solomon began to build the temple of the Lord**
**in Jerusalem on Mount Moriah, where the Lord had**
**appeared to his father David. It was on the threshing floor of**
**Araunah the Jebusite, the place provided by David. ²He began**
**building on the second day of the second month in the fourth**
**year of his reign.**

With all that has been said so far about the importance
of the temple in the life of Israel and as the centerpiece of
the Chronicler's history, a person might expect the holy
writer to have given us the longest and most detailed scriptural account of the way this house for the Lord was built
and furnished. What a surprise it is to discover, then, that
the Chronicler's version of Solomon's greatest achievement
is, in reality, much *shorter* than the parallel description we
find in 1 Kings chapters 6 and 7. This is no doubt due to
the fact that the Chronicler's original readers consisted of
people who had to "make do" with a temple far more
modest in its construction. The reader might wish to consult the discussion on the first page of the introduction.
The spiritual meaning of the temple for God's people was
of far greater significance to the holy writer and his audience than its physical appearance.

That being understood, however, we are not to think that
the Chronicler here merely gives us the Reader's Digest™
condensed version of Kings. In the very first verse he departs
from the earlier account by emphasizing two key events from
the past that were associated with the temple site. To begin
with, we are told that the temple was built at the same place
where Abraham had been willing to offer his "only son"
Isaac in sacrifice at God's command (Genesis 22:2). This is

the only place in Scripture where the connection between the temple mount and Abraham's sacrifice is explicitly made for us. The Chronicler's readers would have remembered that the Angel of the Lord prevented Abraham at the last moment from carrying out his act of supreme devotion. Perhaps even more significantly, on that mountain the Lord provided Abraham with a ram to be offered in Isaac's place (Genesis 22:13). Leaping over several centuries, the Chronicler also reminds us here of the time when an angel of the Lord appeared to David. On that occasion the angel had been God's agent in bringing a virulent plague on Israel, killing tens of thousands. Just before the angel struck Jerusalem, David hurried outside the city to intercede for his people. He met the angel at a site where a Jebusite man named Araunah had been operating a threshing floor (1 Chronicles 21). There David had offered sacrifices at God's command, and the Lord had answered his prayers with a rain of fire from heaven that consumed the offerings. Upon seeing all of this, David realized that God himself had selected Araunah's threshing floor to be the site for his house (1 Chronicles 22:1).

It is this continuity of location that would have been especially meaningful for the Chronicler's original readers, since it assured them that, though the outward trappings of their temple might not have been as impressive as those of Solomon's temple, they had built on the site God had clearly chosen as his own "to put his Name there for his dwelling" (Deuteronomy 12:5).

As people who worship God "in spirit and in truth" (John 4:24), we are not so much concerned about the specific site of our worship as God's Old Testament people were. All the same, we dare not think that the grace of God is free-floating—to be found by meditating under any spreading tree, invoking the name of any god, or associating ourselves with any group of people who might claim to worship God. God's grace is *located* where the pure gospel is proclaimed and the sacraments are rightly administered. When the called servant of the Word announces God's forgiveness, we can firmly believe that "our sins are thereby forgiven before God in heaven."³ When we are located on a site where all this holds true, we can be certain that our God has put his saving name there according to his promise, whether we are worshiping him inside a fine old church or in a hotel conference room before a makeshift altar.

## *The temple structure*

³The foundation Solomon laid for building the temple of God was sixty cubits long and twenty cubits wide (using the cubit of the old standard). ⁴The portico at the front of the temple was twenty cubits long across the width of the building and twenty cubits high.

He overlaid the inside with pure gold. ⁵He paneled the main hall with pine and covered it with fine gold and decorated it with palm tree and chain designs. ⁶He adorned the temple with precious stones. And the gold he used was gold of Parvaim. ⁷He overlaid the ceiling beams, doorframes, walls and doors of the temple with gold, and he carved cherubim on the walls.

⁸He built the Most Holy Place, its length corresponding to the width of the temple—twenty cubits long and twenty cubits wide. He overlaid the inside with six hundred talents of fine gold. ⁹The gold nails weighed fifty shekels. He also overlaid the upper parts with gold.

¹⁰In the Most Holy Place he made a pair of sculptured cherubim and overlaid them with gold. ¹¹The total wingspan of the cherubim was twenty cubits. One wing of the first cherub was five cubits long and touched the temple wall, while its other wing, also five cubits long, touched the wing of the other cherub. ¹²Similarly one wing of the second cherub was five

cubits long and touched the other temple wall, and its other wing, also five cubits long, touched the wing of the first cherub. ¹³The wings of these cherubim extended twenty cubits. They stood on their feet, facing the main hall.

¹⁴He made the curtain of blue, purple and crimson yarn and fine linen, with cherubim worked into it.

¹⁵In the front of the temple he made two pillars, which together were thirty-five cubits long, each with a capital on top measuring five cubits. ¹⁶He made interwoven chains and put them on top of the pillars. He also made a hundred pomegranates and attached them to the chains. ¹⁷He erected the pillars in the front of the temple, one to the south and one to the north. The one to the south he named Jakin and the one to the north Boaz.

**4** He made a bronze altar twenty cubits long, twenty cubits wide and ten cubits high. ²He made the Sea of cast metal, circular in shape, measuring ten cubits from rim to rim and five cubits high. It took a line of thirty cubits to measure around it. ³Below the rim, figures of bulls encircled it—ten to a cubit. The bulls were cast in two rows in one piece with the Sea.

⁴The Sea stood on twelve bulls, three facing north, three facing west, three facing south and three facing east. The Sea rested on top of them, and their hindquarters were toward the center. ⁵It was a handbreadth in thickness, and its rim was like the rim of a cup, like a lily blossom. It held three thousand baths.

⁶He then made ten basins for washing and placed five on the south side and five on the north. In them the things to be used for the burnt offerings were rinsed, but the Sea was to be used by the priests for washing.

The Chronicler may have abbreviated this account from its counterpart in 1 Kings, and yet from a modern point of view—impatient as we are with verbal descriptions of any kind—our eyes may still droop because of too much infor-

mation. A further factor complicating our complete understanding of these verses is the uncertainty we have concerning the precise meaning of some of the words. Finally, there
are textual problems and discrepancies with the parallel
account in Kings—particularly in connection with some of the
dimensions of the temple and its furnishings—that are difficult
to solve in any definite way. It is said that one of the reasons
some orthodox Jews oppose rebuilding the temple today is
that they want to avoid the possibility of breaking any one of
God's instructions. This could happen if they would—even
inadvertently—interpret one of these verses incorrectly. Be
that as it may, we still have sufficient information given us
here to grasp the essentials of the temple structure.

Instead of getting bogged down in detail, let us try to
gain an understanding of the overall temple structure by
imagining the impact it would have made on Israelites who
were visiting it for the first time. If they approached
Jerusalem by taking the road up from Jericho, the sign to
them of their imminent arrival would have been that rise of
land known to us as the Mount of Olives. After climbing to
its summit, they could see the city spread out before them.
Across a deep ravine (later called the Kidron Valley) the city
of David would lie to the south and the temple mount to
the north. After crossing the ravine and entering the city,
they would come into the temple complex by way of the
east gate, where the official gatekeepers would be standing
on duty to ensure that no ritually impure or unclean person
tried to get in (1 Chronicles 26:1-19).

Once inside they would find themselves in the "large
court" (4:9), at the far end of which was a low wall made
of cedar and stone (1 Kings 6:36) standing between them
and the temple itself. This wall marked the beginning of
the courtyard of the priest. The two courtyards were con-

nected by doors overlaid with bronze. The wall also prevented non-Levitical worshipers from coming any closer to the temple proper. We have to understand, of course, that the temple was not a church in the sense of being a building *inside which* people gathered. It was rather a site chosen by God and set apart for him. There the invisible God promised to "be found" by his people—in a holy place where they could draw near him through sacrifice, address him in prayer, and praise him in song. The house itself, however, was closed to all but to those whom God had chosen to serve as priests.

Even from their vantage point in the outer court, no doubt our visitors could see the large bronze altar where the various sacrificial offerings were made to the Lord. Its base was as wide as the main temple chambers themselves—a full 30 feet! From the visitor's perspective, the altar was framed by the two large ornamental pillars that had been set in front of the temple's portico, or entry-porch. These were imposing enough to have been given their own names. To the left of the altar the visitors could see *Jakin* ("He establishes"), to the right *Boaz* ("In him is strength").

The house of God itself was probably built upon a base raised up several feet from the courtyard of the priests on which it stood. The dimensions of its entryway and its two interior rooms are given in 2 Chronicles 3:3,4. These areas were called the Portico, the Holy Place (also referred to as the main hall—3:5), and the Most Holy Place (also known as the inner sanctuary—5:7,9). It's worth noting that the latter two rooms were twice the size of those found in the tabernacle. The Chronicler is still making the point that this house had to be great "because our God is greater than all other gods" (2:5).

At the southeast corner of the temple, the huge bronze "Sea," perched on the backs of twelve bull statues, was visible to our imaginary visitors. As its name suggests, it was a reservoir for water and contained about 17,500 gallons. It was used, as the Chronicler tells us, "by the priests for washing"—no doubt a reference to the cleansing the priests had to receive before they could approach God's house (Exodus 30:17-21). In addition to the Sea, there were ten smaller basins for water set on ornate, movable stands, each with a capacity of 230 gallons. These were used for washing those portions of the sacrificial animals the Lord had designated for himself (4:6,14; 1 Kings 7:27-39; Leviticus 1:9).

## *The temple furnishings*

⁷He made ten gold lampstands according to the specifications for them and placed them in the temple, five on the south side and five on the north.

⁸He made ten tables and placed them in the temple, five on the south side and five on the north. He also made a hundred gold sprinkling bowls.

⁹He made the courtyard of the priests, and the large court and the doors for the court, and overlaid the doors with bronze. ¹⁰He placed the Sea on the south side, at the southeast corner.

¹¹He also made the pots and shovels and sprinkling bowls.

So Huram finished the work he had undertaken for King Solomon in the temple of God:

¹² the two pillars;
   the two bowl-shaped capitals on top of the pillars;
   the two sets of network decorating the two bowl-
      shaped capitals on top of the pillars;
¹³ the four hundred pomegranates for the two sets of net-
      work (two rows of pomegranates for each net-
      work, decorating the bowl-shaped capitals on top
      of the pillars);

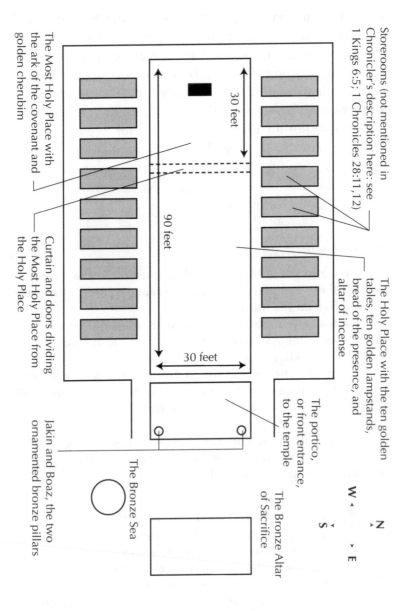

Solomon's temple

¹⁴ the stands with their basins;
¹⁵ the Sea and the twelve bulls under it;
¹⁶ the pots, shovels, meat forks and all related articles.

All the objects that Huram-Abi made for King Solomon for the temple of the LORD were of polished bronze. ¹⁷The king had them cast in clay molds in the plain of the Jordan between Succoth and Zarethan. ¹⁸All these things that Solomon made amounted to so much that the weight of the bronze was not determined.

¹⁹Solomon also made all the furnishings that were in God's temple:

the golden altar;
the tables on which was the bread of the Presence;
²⁰ the lampstands of pure gold with their lamps, to burn in front of the inner sanctuary as prescribed;
²¹ the gold floral work and lamps and tongs (they were solid gold);
²² the pure gold wick trimmers, sprinkling bowls, dishes and censers; and the gold doors of the temple: the inner doors to the Most Holy Place and the doors of the main hall.

5 When all the work Solomon had done for the temple of the LORD was finished, he brought in the things his father David had dedicated—the silver and gold and all the furnishings—and he placed them in the treasuries of God's temple.

Even more awe-inspiring than the things seen were the things that remained unseen, hidden behind the temple walls. The only way most Israelites could learn about the interior of the temple and its contents was by reading descriptions like the one we have before us. Only from them could one learn that once past the portico, the officiating priest entered a room gleaming with gold, glittering with precious stones, and fragrant with incense. This was the Holy Place. It was richly furnished with ten tables and ten lampstands (instead of the one table and one lampstand that had been sufficient for the tabernacle and its Holy Place—see Exodus 25:23-40).

Although all the tables were associated in some way with the 12 loaves called "the bread of the Presence," only one was used for displaying them (compare 4:19 with 1 Kings 7:48). Freshly baked each week, the loaves were set out in two rows of six (Leviticus 24:6), and they symbolized the gratitude the 12 tribes of Israel had for God's earthly blessings. In his sustaining presence the tribes lived; from him they received; to him they returned thanks for their daily bread. In the King James Version, these loaves are referred to as "shewbread." The NIV's more exact rendering of the original Hebrew alerts us to the fact that these loaves were to be placed continually in the presence of the Lord (Exodus 25:30).

The yellow glow from the lampstands together with the natural light from the clerestory windows above (1 Kings 6:4) combined to suffuse the interior with a gentle radiance. At the west end of the Holy Place, in front of the doors and the embroidered curtain that partitioned off the Most Holy Place, stood the golden altar of incense. Each morning and evening, the priest appointed for the day would go to it to burn the incense that signified the daily prayers of God's people (Exodus 30:7,8; Psalm 141:2; Luke 1:9; Revelation 8:3).

Restricted as the Holy Place was, the Most Holy Place was even more set apart from the common gaze of the congregation. What could be known about it could only be communicated to them through the Word. None of its contents could be seen from the larger chamber, with the exception of the tips of the poles used to carry the ark of the covenant to its permanent home (5:9). Apparently they were visible through small open spaces on either side between the doorjambs and the walls. For some reason these spaces were left uncovered even by the embroidered curtain (3:14). The ark and the room of gold containing it, however, remained concealed.

Only the high priest was allowed to enter there and then only once a year on the Day of Atonement (Hebrews 9:7). What is more, even he was not permitted to see the ark with unobstructed vision. Prior to his entering the Most Holy Place, he was to take some coals from the altar of burnt offering to use for burning incense within that sacred room. In this way the room would be so filled with smoke that the high priest would be unable to see the atonement cover (Leviticus 16:13).

This room was the beating heart of the temple, the center of the entire shrine. Solomon had overlaid the Most Holy Place, a perfect cube, with 23 tons of gold—a staggering amount! All the same, the room was still inadequate as a dwelling place for God. The heavens could not contain him, as Solomon readily admitted, and the whole earth was his (2:6; Psalm 24:1). Even so, God had promised Moses, "Before the ark of the Testimony—before the atonement cover that is over the Testimony—[there] I will meet with you" (Exodus 30:6). That is why we can say that God "lived" in the house built for him by Solomon according to his gracious promise. On the day of dedication, he would make it absolutely clear to all that he had condescended to adopt as his earthly throne the space above the atonement cover, between the cherubim (1 Chronicles 13:6).

Within the sanctuary the ark of the covenant was flanked by two freestanding statues that were meant to depict the heavenly creatures known to the Hebrews as cherubim. Richly overlaid with gold, the two statues were cast with wings outstretched in such a way that they overshadowed the entire room from end to end (3:10-13). These angelic beings are variously described for us in Scripture, so it is difficult to pin down exactly what Solomon's statues looked like.

"Cherubim and a flaming sword" were set to bar man's rebellious footsteps from returning to Paradise (Genesis 3:24). In the Psalms, David describes how he saw the Lord respond to prayer by parting "the heavens. . . . Dark clouds were under his feet. He mounted the cherubim and flew" (Psalm 18:9,10). Ezekiel's vision of the cherubim is the most extraordinarily ornate. Out of the darkness of a windstorm they came, looking like "burning coals" (Ezekiel 1:13) and with a form like "that of a man" (Ezekiel 1:5). They each had four faces—of a man, a lion, an ox, and an eagle. This last reference at once reminds us of the "four living creatures" around the throne of God in heaven, as described for us by John in the Bible's final book (Revelation 4:7,8).

Mysterious though they may be in many respects, we can at least say that cherubim are angels that stand in the presence of God, that are associated with God's throne, and that connote his supreme mastery over all his creatures. Whatever Solomon's cherubim may have looked like, we feel completely safe in declaring that they in no way could have resembled the pudgy-faced cupids of late-Renaissance paintings. Nor were they in any way like the little figurines some people of today collect. These were depictions of angels inspiring reverent awe. They were fit to adorn the earthly throne room of the almighty God and to stand in his presence.

There are a number of other items mentioned in this catalog that we have not discussed along the way: gold sprinkling bowls, pots, shovels, meat forks, pure gold wick trimmers, dishes, and censers. We have not spent much time either in looking at the various ornamental bas-reliefs and figures added to walls, curtain, and columns. Keeping in mind the Chronicler's basic message, we see that all these things serve to underscore the glory of Solomon's temple. Nothing but the best was used for the house of God, and nothing was overlooked. Gold was spread around in quantities that stagger the mind; the amount of bronze employed surpassed all quantification. Work completed, Solomon enhanced the glory of God's house still further by bringing the "things his father David had dedicated" to their proper home in the temple treasuries. These would have been the masses of silver, gold, and bronze that were taken in the warfare David had waged against the enemies of God's people (1 Chronicles 18:11).

This description of the beauty and grandeur of Solomon's temple would have had a bittersweet quality about it for the Chronicler's original readers. Certainly it would have filled them with wonder—just as it does us—to hear of the prodigious quantities of gold, silver, and bronze used in its construction. Yet reflecting on the glory that once had been could only show the deficiencies in the temple the exiles knew as their house of God. Those chastened believers, upon hearing this catalog of Solomon's temple furnishings, would be reminded of another place in Scripture where they could find a similar listing. However, there the list served to record the booty that triumphant King Nebuchadnezzar had carried off with him to Babylon. Along with these temple treasures, he took into exile the flower of God's people (2 Kings 25:13-21). All the gold in the world could not put an acceptable veneer over a people who had become detestable to their God through impenitent sinning. It was due to God's judgment on sin that his house no longer gleamed with quite the same luster as before.

This magnificent temple of Solomon was still glorious only with an earthly splendor. Such glory was bound to fade, to wither and fall "like the flowers of the field" (Isaiah 40:6). Even when it was first built, the temple remained a footstool fit for God only by grace, only because he had freely chosen to put his name there. In a similar way, the second temple, the temple rebuilt by those who returned, would remain God's house by grace alone. Whatever shortcomings they might perceive in their temple's outward appointments would be removed when suddenly "the Lord . . . [came] to his temple" (Malachi 3:1). Many years after this portion of Scripture was written, King Herod undertook a massively expensive renovation of the Lord's house. But all of Herod's glitter could never match the glory the King Messiah would bring once he graced the temple with his presence!

The final verse was intended to strike the reader's ear as well as his mind: "*Watishlam . . . Shlomoh*"—"*Complete* was all the work that the *Completer* [Solomon] had done" (literal translation of 5:1). In this way the Chronicler impresses on his readers one of the major themes in his account of the temple's construction. As the similar sounds indicate, we have a small play on words here that serves to remind the reader that it was Solomon, the man of peace, who had at last been enabled to complete what his father, David, "had it in [his] heart" to do (1 Chronicles 22:7). Ultimately, these words stand as a reminder of God's faithfulness. He had promised David a son to build his house. That son had come. That house had been built (1 Chronicles 17:11,12; 22:6-10).

### Significance of the temple for ancient Israel

Now let's pause for a moment to reflect on the meaning of the temple itself. What did it signify for God's Old Testament people? What meaning does it hold for us today? A closer look at some of the descriptive words and phrases used in this account will supply us with the answers to these questions. We have heard it called "the temple [literally: house] of the LORD" (3:1), "a place to burn sacrifices before him [literally: to his face]" (2:6), and "a temple for [God's] Name"

(2:4; 6:7). In chapter six Solomon asks that God would "hear from heaven" when prayer is directed to his temple (6:21).

All these expressions point to the same truth. At the temple, God lived among his people, doing it in a way that did not change or diminish in the least his nature as the infinite and almighty God. Here he revealed himself in grace. Here the Israelites could find him in a way poor sinners could grasp.

At the same time, one look at the temple would impress upon an Old Testament believer that here was a *holy* God, separate from sinners. Why else would there be a wall between the inner and outer courts? Why else would the Sea and the bronze altar of sacrifice stand in front of the temple? Why else would the ark be set in the most interior room of the temple? Why else would it be hidden behind doors and a curtain? Why else would only the high priest be permitted to enter the Most Holy Place, and only once a year at that? In a visual way, God was saying: "I cannot remain with sinners, and sinners cannot stand in my presence. Because I am holy, I must either consume them or purify them."

To reinforce this truth, only the chosen priests could serve in the inner court of God's house. The way to God for Israel led through priests, priests who were there to offer sacrifices. Before they could do that, however, they themselves had to undergo a cleansing bath with water from the Sea. Once they were cleansed, God graciously considered them fit to offer sacrifices. In those sacrifices God graciously counted an animal's life as a sufficient substitute for a human life made forfeit by sin. In his earthly dwelling place between the cherubim, God would look down at the tablets in the ark—tablets that accused and convicted humanity of sin—and see on the atonement cover the lifeblood of a substitute. That blood covered over the law's testimony to guilt and removed sin.

### Significance of the temple in the New Testament

From what has been said, any New Testament child of God can easily see the many parallels that exist between these Old Testament shadows and the reality that is Christ. The hold that the temple had on the minds of New Testament writers was so strong that it is often impossible to understand their line of thought without some knowledge of the temple's significance. We will look at only some of the most important ideas.

It is the gospel writer John who gives us the clearest parallel between the temple and Christ, the dwelling place of God housed in a human body. Already in verse 14 of his first chapter, he declares that Jesus, the Word, "made his dwelling among us." The term he uses for "dwelling" in the original is unmistakably reminiscent of the Old Testament *sanctuary*. Looking at Jesus, the disciples saw "the glory of the One and Only, . . . full of grace and truth."

Continuing in this same vein, we notice that Jesus himself offered the following sign to those who questioned his authority: "Destroy this temple, and I will raise it again in three days" (John 2:19). The unbelieving Jews thought he was speaking of the temple rebuilt by Herod over a period of 46 years. But John makes it clear to us that Jesus was speaking of "his body" (John 2:21). Consider what Jesus was saying. It took Solomon seven years to build his temple, the exiles who returned required 20 for theirs, and Herod's renovation took over 46 years before it was done. Jesus, on the other hand, would need only three days to raise his "temple." It was as if he had said: "A human being's greatest achievement is to build a mighty monument of wood, stone, and mortar. This task he is able to complete only at the expense of great time and effort. As God Almighty, I have the power to raise my own body within three days after it has been laid low in death."

That is why we, as New Testament believers, can be sure that in the risen Christ we have found our temple, the place where we meet our God. No other structure is needed. If people say—as, for example, the Mormons do—that we must build another house for the Lord, they insult the Father, who gave us his Son, and they despise the Savior, who raised a temple far greater than any man could match. The same is true of any who still regard specific patches of earthly real estate as being somehow holier in God's sight, who run to this shrine or that in the hope of getting closer to their God. Jesus is the "the way and the truth and the life" (John 14:6). No one comes to the Father except through him.

Even more commonly, New Testament writers refer to the church—in the sense of the community of believers—as being a temple in which "God lives by his Spirit" (Ephesians 2:22). Just as David's son Solomon had built God's house, so David's greater Son Jesus builds us as "living stones . . . into a spiritual house," as Peter tells us (1 Peter 2:5). When at last Solomon's Successor has completed his glorious work of building God's house, history will have achieved its purpose; faith will yield to sight, and we will all experience the perfect joy of living in God's presence forever.

This idea of believers being the temple of God on earth permeates all the writings of the New Testament. For this reason, when we become members of this family of faith, we are more than simply joined to an organization of people who happen to think alike or who share an earthly goal. Becoming one with this community bears an eternal significance. Those who belong to the church are saints—God's holy ones—who "were washed, . . . sanctified, [and] . . . justified in the name of the Lord Jesus Christ and by the

Spirit of our God" (1 Corinthians 6:11). Because I am a part of his church, God tells me, my whole life is seen as priestly service, a sacrifice of praise and thanksgiving that is offered to the one true God (Romans 12:1; 1 Peter 2:5). On the other hand, those solemnly declared to be cut off from the fellowship are "hand[ed] . . . over to Satan" (1 Corinthians 5:5). What the church does in Christ's name, Christ himself does, "for where two or three come together in my name, there am I with them" (Matthew 18:20). Through Word and sacrament, the assembled believers are assured of Christ's continued presence among them. God still lives among his people in the church!

Just as the community of believers together can be called "God's temple," so also the individual Christian is considered to be the dwelling place of God. In the most striking example of this, Paul uses the holiness of the temple as a mighty motivator for us to avoid sexual immorality: "Do you not know that your body is a temple of the Holy Spirit?" (1 Corinthians 6:19). Wherever Christ lives by his Spirit, there a believer prays with ardent desire, "Ah, dearest Jesus, holy Child, tear down every idol throne in my heart; root out all evil desire in me." Who would ever want to defile with immoral thoughts or impure actions a body whose heart Christ has consecrated for his very own?

In using the word *temple* then, New Testament writers build on the past to help believers understand the wealth of blessings we enjoy in Christ. But this is only the beginning of joy. A look at the ancient past also gives us a better grasp of our glorious future. In Revelation, John saw the full and final fulfillment of the temple. The Spirit granted him a vision of God's eternal dwelling place in heaven, the place Solomon's sanctuary was meant to reproduce on earth (Revelation 4; Hebrews 9:23,24). Our hearts thrill with happiness when we read John's description of it. Through his eyes we see God's dwelling set in the center of what will be our eternal home too, prepared for us by Christ.

In the New Jerusalem, God will live among his people with glory unconcealed (Revelation 21:22,23). Nothing impure will ever be found in that city, and then our hope for complete deliverance from sin and pain will at last be fully realized. Instead of the bronze Sea standing next to God's sanctuary, heaven holds a life-giving river "clear as crystal, flowing from the throne of God and of the Lamb" (Revelation 22:1). John makes no mention of any altar or sacrifice. We know why. The Lamb that was slain (Revelation 5:6) "by one sacrifice . . . has made perfect forever those who are being made holy" (Hebrews 10:14).

These brief paragraphs are intended only to whet the reader's appetite. They cannot delineate the length and breadth, the height and depth of the love of God as it is described for us whenever Scripture uses the earthly sanctuary of God's Old Testament people as a point of comparison.

## *Solomon completes the work of David*

In his next three chapters, the Chronicler tells the story of the temple's dedication. To help us get our bearings, it may be useful to see the entire account first in overview. The Chronicler divides his account into seven major parts. In the first we hear how the ark together with the ancient tabernacle and its holy articles were all moved to the new shrine Solomon had built (5:2-13). The second section relates how the glory of the Lord appeared within the temple (5:13,14). The third describes Solomon's response to this extraordinary sight and his blessing of the assembled Israelites (6:1-11). Then follows one of the key passages of Old Testament Scripture: Solomon's prayer of dedication (6:12-42). The final three sections speak of God's response in fire and glory to the sacrifices (7:1-3), Israel's joyful celebration in the days that followed (7:4-10), and the appearing of God to Solomon with an answer to his dedicatory prayer (7:11-22).

## *The ark is placed in the sanctuary*

²**Then Solomon summoned to Jerusalem the elders of Israel, all the heads of the tribes and the chiefs of the Israelite families, to bring up the ark of the LORD's covenant from Zion, the City of David. ³And all the men of Israel came together to the king at the time of the festival in the seventh month.**

⁴**When all the elders of Israel had arrived, the Levites took up the ark, ⁵and they brought up the ark and the Tent of Meeting and all the sacred furnishings in it. The priests, who were Levites, carried them up; ⁶and King Solomon and the entire assembly of Israel that had gathered about him were before the ark, sacrificing so many sheep and cattle that they could not be recorded or counted.**

⁷**The priests then brought the ark of the LORD's covenant to its place in the inner sanctuary of the temple, the Most Holy Place, and put it beneath the wings of the cherubim. ⁸The cherubim spread their wings over the place of the ark and covered the ark and its carrying poles. ⁹These poles were so long that their ends, extending from the ark, could be seen from in front of the inner sanctuary, but not from outside the Holy Place; and they are still there today. ¹⁰There was nothing in the ark except the two tablets that Moses had placed in it at Horeb, where the LORD made a covenant with the Israelites after they came out of Egypt.**

In many ways the completion of the temple must be regarded as the high point of the Old Testament. What God had predicted through Moses (Deuteronomy 12:10,11), what David had been barred from doing yet had spent his career preparing for as king, Solomon finally achieved. The first temple was under construction for seven years and was completed in the eighth month of Solomon's eleventh year as king (1 Kings 6:38). Evidently he was willing to wait for an additional 11 months before he dedicated it (compare 1 Kings 8:2 with 1 Kings 6:38). Perhaps he did this in order to have a sufficient period of time to plan and to prepare for a huge festal gathering of God's people.

"There is a time for everything . . . under heaven" (Ecclesiastes 3:1), including a time to celebrate in the presence of God. Without a doubt, the dedication of God's house was a perfect time for joyful celebration. To this earthly building were attached "the hopes and fears of all the years" (*Christian Worship* [CW] 65:1), as far as ancient Israel was concerned. It stood as a monument to the God who keeps his word and as a tangible sign to Israel that they were most certainly the Lord's people, the sheep of his pasture (Psalm 100:3).

Appropriately enough, Solomon chose the regular "festival in the seventh month" as dedication day. Its Hebrew name was *Succoth,* the Feast of Tabernacles in English. One of the three great festivals of the Israelite church year, Succoth served to remind God's people of the time when they had wandered in the desert and had lived in tents; at that time only God had been their dwelling place (Psalm 90). After the period of wandering, God had settled them in the spacious land he had promised to Abraham, Isaac, and Jacob. What better time to transfer the ark to its new home than during the festival that commemorated these events!

Though the people had found their earthly dwelling place in the Promised Land, for many years the ark had been denied a permanent address (1 Chronicles 17:5). It had been sheltered in tents and moved from place to place. During one dark period in Israel's history, the ark had passed into the hands of the Philistines, even spending a night inside a house dedicated to a heathen god (1 Samuel 4,5). But during David's reign, God had chosen the threshing floor of Araunah (1 Chronicles 21:22; 22:1) "as a dwelling for his Name" (Deuteronomy 12:11), and now Solomon had completed the temple on that same site. Bringing the ark at last to its home marked the culmination of Israel's exodus from Egypt. It signaled a people at rest from their enemies inside a holy land where they lived in the presence of their God.

The sacrifices mentioned as part of the procession were a lavish expression of Israel's utter dependence upon the good God who guarded every footstep. "Because of the LORD's great love we are not consumed, for his compassions never fail. They are new every morning" (Lamentations 3:22,23). Recipients of mercy this great do well to offer sacrifices beyond counting (compare 2 Chronicles 5:6 with Romans 12:1). In the original text, the verse describing the actual placement of the ark in the sanctuary conveys a sense of weightiness, of the last solemn steps before journey's end as a desired goal is finally reached. Beginning with an unusually full and dignified designation of the ark ("the ark of the covenant of the LORD"), the verse continues with a series of synonyms that increase in their specificity: "The priests brought the ark . . . into its place, into the inner sanctuary of the house, into the Most Holy place, to [the place] underneath the wings of the cherubim" (literal translation of verse 7). At the end a person can almost hear the priests put down their burden with a sigh of holy satisfaction.

As the "cherubim spread their wings over the place of the ark," the priests who had carried it removed themselves from the Most Holy Place. They left behind the poles they had used. From that time on, those poles would serve as the only visible indication to an observer in the Holy Place that the ark lay in the room beyond the doors and tapestry. This remark and the one immediately following ("There was nothing in the ark except the two tablets that Moses had placed in it at Horeb") must have been taken by the Chronicler from one of the sources he regularly used in writing his history (9:29). The ark, its contents, and its carrying poles had long since been lost by the time the exiles returned to Jerusalem to rebuild the temple.

In general, we may note several features of the Chronicler's presentation that distinguish it from its counterpart in 1 Kings. It is clearly our author's desire to draw a parallel between David bringing up the ark to Jerusalem (1 Chronicles 13,15,16) and Solomon placing the ark in its permanent home inside the temple. On both occasions the Israelite leaders are called together in solemn assembly, sacrifices are made during the procession, the role of Levitical musicians is highlighted, and the king pronounces a blessing on the assembled throng. On both occasions the theme of the Levites' song is the good God, whose "love endures forever" (compare 1 Chronicles 16:34 with 2 Chronicles 5:13).

By highlighting these similarities, the Chronicler reemphasizes in his telling of the story a fact he had plainly stated in verse 1: "*Complete* was all the work that the *Completer* [Solomon] had done" (a literal translation to bring out the play on words in the original). From the Chronicler's vantage point, the missions of David and Solomon were one and the same. The son was privileged to finish what his father had begun.

There is a discrepancy between Kings and Chronicles in their respective descriptions of this event. In 1 Kings 8:3 we read that "the *priests* took up the ark," while 2 Chronicles 5:4 tells us that it was the *Levites* who did so. One possible solution is to think of the ark being moved in two stages. At first the Levites carried it from David's city to the temple mount—a move of about three-quarters of a mile. After this the priests took over, carrying the ark the rest of the way into the temple itself. Both accounts plainly state that it was the priests who actually carried the ark into the shrine (verse 7; 1 Kings 8:6). This is not surprising, since the Levites were forbidden to enter the Most Holy Place (Numbers 4:20). An interpretation like this also fits in well with the Chronicler's normal practice of adding supplementary material that presents the Levites in a good light. In this case he had an opportunity to make it clear that the Levites had shared in the honor of carrying the ark at least part of the way on the dedication day of the first temple, an opportunity that would have been hard for him to pass up.

The flaw in this interpretation is that it seems to do injury to the native sense of the words as they stand in the book of Kings. Without the account of the Chronicler, anyone reading 1 Kings chapter 8 would think that it was the priests who had carried the ark all the way from David's City to the temple. If we simply let 1 Kings chapter 8 stand as it is, we might solve the problem by suggesting that the Chronicler is using the word *Levite* in a broader way than he usually does. Normally when referring to the Levites, the Chronicler has in mind the members of that tribe who were *not* priests. But in this case he changes his usual practice and calls the priests who carried the ark that day, Levites. Now it would be perfectly correct to call any one of the priestly sons of Aaron a Levite, since every one of them was born into Levi's tribe. At the same time, this somewhat unusual diction does leave us asking the question, Why would the Chronicler want suddenly to alter his normal manner of speaking?

An answer can be found by considering what the standard operating procedure was for moving the ark. Normal practice, as prescribed by Moses, was for the nonpriestly Levites to carry out this job (Numbers 3:31; 4:15). There had, however, been at least one other time when the priests were called upon to carry the ark. This occurred when Joshua first led the Israelites across the Jordan River into the Promised Land (Joshua 3:3). It seems reasonable to suppose that the priests were given the honor again at this time because the two occasions were felt to be of similar importance.

If we understand anything at all about the Chronicler's message, we know how much he wanted to emphasize the importance of worshiping the true God in the correct way. That is why it seems plausible that he would want to substitute "Levites" for "priests" in the verse mentioned above. After all, when he had written about David's first, abortive attempt to move the ark, the Chronicler had made the point that one of the key errors God's people had fallen into at that time was their failure to carry the ark "in the prescribed way" (1 Chronicles 15:13). Simply using the word *priest* here might appear to undercut that message. But calling the priests by their tribal name of Levites reminds the reader that this was an exceptional practice, and while it was in no way wrong, it was an exception all the same. Exceptions ought not to become rules.

This is not a bad lesson to teach this generation of believers also, for whom exceptional cases tend to become business as usual with blinding speed. The sinful world in which we live and move takes a positive delight in coloring outside the lines. How easy it is within such surroundings to use liberty as a pretext to justify outright sinning (Galatians 5:13). Even when no sin is involved, one ought to pause, at the very least, before plunging ahead in doing something outside of the norm.

In a culture in which change is cultivated almost for its own sake, a Christian needs to keep his or her head. Just because someone might say, "Well, it's not *forbidden* for us New Testament Christians," there's no cause to make the logical leap, "Therefore it is a good and whole-some thing to do!" The apostle Paul teaches us to ask in matters where God has not spoken absolutely: "Is this wise? Is it expedient? Is it loving? Does it edify my fellow Christians?" (1 Corinthians 10:23-33; 13:1-13).

**¹¹The priests then withdrew from the Holy Place. All the priests who were there had consecrated themselves, regardless of their divisions. ¹²All the Levites who were musicians—Asaph, Heman, Jeduthun and their sons and relatives—stood on the east side of the altar, dressed in fine linen and playing cymbals, harps and lyres. They were accompanied by 120 priests sounding trumpets. ¹³The trumpeters and singers joined in unison, as with one voice, to give praise and thanks to the LORD. Accompanied by trumpets, cymbals and other instruments, they raised their voices in praise to the LORD and sang:**

> **"He is good;**
> **his love endures forever."**

The Chronicler again sounds themes he has touched on before: "See the joy for all Israel," he says, "when it gathers together in worship of the one true God under its chosen king at the one place where God has promised to be found. Observe priest and Levite working together in harmony: both worshiping God in their own distinct offices yet each contributing to the perfect unity of the whole body. Note the dignity of Asaph, Heman, Jeduthun, and the other Levitical musicians as they offer praise to the LORD with voice and instrument." By telling the story, he is preaching a sermon to his own people on all these points: "Believer, see the spiritual importance of each of the gifts God gives! Understand how valuable each office is in the whole scheme of things! Keep the unity of the Spirit in the bond of peace."

The Chronicler highlights that unity in several ways. First he tells us that for the occasion, the priests suspended that priestly rotation of duties King David had set up (1 Chronicles 24:3). "All . . . consecrated themselves," the Chronicler says. Then again in describing the musical worship, he notes that the Levitical singers and priestly trumpeters "joined in unison, as with one voice." Finally he calls our attention to the way they were united in worship with that gathering of believers that neither time nor distance nor death can disperse. On dedication day they sang the same song David had taught the people to sing when the ark had been brought to Jerusalem: "Give thanks to the LORD, for he is good" (1 Chronicles 16:34). Israel would sing that song again when, many years later, King Jehoshaphat would lead the congregation out for battle (2 Chronicles 20:21). It's a song we will never stop singing, because "his love endures forever."

So many things can divide the church, like misunderstandings that so easily multiply among us—even when we share the same confession of faith. We have different gifts and different callings. We come from different backgrounds, races, and generations. The New Testament is full of warnings to Christians not to let envy, jealousy, and pride ignite quarrels among them. But how can God's people remain whole, one, and at peace with one another in a world where the devil and our sinful selves are constantly at work sowing seeds of mistrust and suspicion?

Unity is God's creation when, through the gospel, he makes each one of us personally certain of his great love for poor sinners. Even though God's love comes to people one by one, it embraces and unites us all—every child of Adam who stands in need of mercy. God's love does not obliterate our differences; it grasps us as we are, wherever we are. So when we become Christians, we do not stop being man or woman, father or mother, son or daughter, worker or supervisor. Our address may not change, and our abilities and aptitudes may still differ. But because of his great mercy, who we are and what we do matters to God, no matter what.

Even so, because his mercy endures forever, we know that each of us has become a vital part of something bigger. We have been woven into the fabric of God's eternal plan of love as it unfolds in history. We see that we live and breathe no more alone but with one heart, one mind, one Spirit, and one voice. We are God's people. He created us in Christ to carry out his single purpose of gathering all of his elect together, so that together we might sing the song of victory around his throne. Since he has joined us into one body, we know that we all need one another—not in spite of but rather because of our differences. What my brother or sister has will make up for what I lack. Whatever I have is God's gift to me to use in service for others. Only the mind of Christ—born in us by the gospel—can guide us into putting others before ourselves in this way. Only the Spirit of Christ can teach me to appreciate my brothers and sisters because of qualities and aptitudes I see in them that differ from my own. What serves to kindle envy and division among the children of this age ignites among Christians a more fervent love.

Created by God's gracious revelation of himself, this unity is a spiritual gift to be treasured and cultivated, not squandered and despised. In a world divided by deep fissures of sin and hatred, with our own souls the battleground of flesh against Spirit, it ought not to surprise any one of us to see the visible church—even our own fellowship—divided at times or to hear Christians bite and tear at one another in ways that cannot be justified. Sinful factionalism ought not to surprise us, but it should, nevertheless, grieve us, just as it grieves the Spirit within us, the Spirit of love God gave us. May we be conscious of our own weakness in this matter, and let the Chronicler teach us to pray, "How good and pleasant it is when brothers live together in unity!" (Psalm 133:1).

### God lives among his people—his glory fills the temple!

**Then the temple of the LORD was filled with a cloud, ¹⁴and the priests could not perform their service because of the cloud, for the glory of the LORD filled the temple of God.**

One of the spiritual gifts the Chronicler has to give us is the power to see the history of God's Old Testament people as a series of recurring patterns. In these patterns God shows his hand as the one who lovingly controls all our days. Half a millennium before the temple was dedicated, Moses consecrated the tabernacle in the desert of Sinai. At that time the Lord descended and revealed himself in a special way. His glory-cloud so filled the tabernacle that "Moses could not enter" (Exodus 40:35). We see the same pattern repeating itself at the dedication of Solomon's temple.

The heathen nations around Israel all had their physical representations of the gods they worshiped. If some Philistines wanted to ask their god Dagon for help, they could go to Dagon's temple, see the statue, and bow down to it in prayer. But to his own people God had said, "You shall not make for yourself an idol in the form of anything in heaven above or on the earth beneath or in the waters below. You shall not bow down to them or worship them; for I, the LORD your God, am a jealous God" (Exodus 20:4,5).

How, then, was Israel to "connect" with this invisible, ineffable God? It may be hard for us who live in the New Testament era to comprehend what a great temptation this posed for Old Testament children of God. After all, we have only to look at Jesus to find our God, and all Christians are familiar with the words our Savior spoke to Philip: "Anyone who has seen me has seen the Father" (John 14:9). But God is good. He did not let his ancient people struggle through the centuries without a visible sign of his presence. In his grace he met their need. Instead of an idol fashioned by human hands out of metal mined from the earth, God revealed himself in a bright, shining cloud. This manifestation of God the Old Testament writers simply call "the glory of the LORD."

Students of Scripture have described the cloud for us in various ways. Maimonides, the great Jewish scholar of the Middle Ages, defined it as "a certain created radiance that God caused to settle somewhere—as it were in a place of portent and miracle—to demonstrate his magnificence visibly."[4] August Pieper tells us that the glory of the Lord appeared as "a flare of fire enveloped in smoke or a cloud . . . at times . . . merely visible as a bright cloud or as a bare fire."[5] More important than catching its description is to grasp its meaning. The glory-cloud assured the wandering Israelites that their mighty God was near, guiding them and protecting them from danger (Exodus 14:19,20). It also revealed God's majestic holiness on earth in such a way that sinful humans could not fully bear the sight of it, even though they were not seeing the full and essential brightness of God in heaven. Notice how the glory-cloud kept Moses out of the tabernacle and how it prevented the priests from continuing their service in the temple (compare verse 14 with Exodus 40:35).

The special revelation of the glory of the Lord belonged to Israel as part of its unique heritage as God's chosen people. In this way God set them apart from all the other nations of the world. The heathens worshiped sculpted gods that could not save, that had mouths but could not speak, that had eyes but could not see (Psalm 115:5). Israel, however, could boast, "[Ours] is the adoption as sons; [ours] the divine glory, the covenants, the receiving of the law, the temple worship and the promises" (Romans 9:4). Israel's God was true; all other gods were lies. God's glory settled on the temple as a clear sign to Israel and to the entire world that he intended to be found there and nowhere else!

## Solomon's response and blessing

**6** Then Solomon said, "The LORD has said that he would dwell in a dark cloud; ²I have built a magnificent temple for you, a place for you to dwell forever."

³While the whole assembly of Israel was standing there, the king turned around and blessed them. ⁴Then he said:

"Praise be to the LORD, the God of Israel, who with his hands has fulfilled what he promised with his mouth to my father David. For he said, ⁵'Since the day I brought my people out of Egypt, I have not chosen a city in any tribe of Israel to have a temple built for my Name to be there, nor have I chosen anyone to be the leader over my people Israel. ⁶But now I have chosen Jerusalem for my Name to be there, and I have chosen David to rule my people Israel.'

⁷"My father David had it in his heart to build a temple for the Name of the LORD, the God of Israel. ⁸But the LORD said to my father David, 'Because it was in your heart to build a temple for my Name, you did well to have this in your heart. ⁹Nevertheless, you are not the one to build the

temple, but your son, who is your own flesh and blood—
he is the one who will build the temple for my Name.'
¹⁰"The LORD has kept the promise he made. I have
succeeded David my father and now I sit on the throne
of Israel, just as the LORD promised, and I have built the
temple for the Name of the LORD, the God of Israel.
¹¹There I have placed the ark, in which is the covenant of
the LORD that he made with the people of Israel."

The first words of Solomon expressed his awe at what
he had just witnessed. After all the meticulous preparations by himself and his father David, after all the effort
and skill that had gone into building the temple over
these last seven years, Solomon recognized that, in the
end, it was the work of God alone to complete and to
dedicate his house. Nothing a human being does can
bring God down to us. We might paraphrase Solomon as
saying in the first two verses: "My Lord, you gave your
word to Israel that you would reveal yourself in this
glory-cloud [see Exodus 19:9; Leviticus 16:2]. As for me, I
have built this magnificent house for you. But you are not
here because my great works have called you down. It is
only by your gracious promise that you are found here!"
God showed his favor to believers also in this respect: he
permitted them to take part in work that, properly speaking, belongs to him alone.

We note the way Solomon also spoke about the perma-
nence of the temple. It is a place where God dwells forever.
The returned exiles could find comfort in these words, even
though their house was by no means as magnificent as the
one Solomon had built. The sacredness of the site did not
depend on dressed stone and gold leaf but on the firm
promise of God. We too find comfort in them, especially as
we hear them renewed for us in our Savior's promise,
"Surely I am with you always, to the very end of the age"

(Matthew 28:20). Temples built with human hands have all gone to ruin, but the presence of the Lord Christ in his temple, the church, endures forever.

Next Solomon turned away from the temple to the throng assembled in the great courtyard. Wanting no doubt to exist in anyone's mind about what had just occurred, Solomon blessed the people by singing God's praises and by reciting to them the promises of God.

Notice the following features of this inspired blessing. From beginning to end, it was centered on God, not on humankind. When Solomon mentioned David or referred to himself, it was always as someone who was what he was because of God's gracious choice. Contrast this with the way sinful humanity sings the praises of one of its own: "You are great because you have done so many good things; your actions merit our praise and even recommend you to God." We find none of that human-centeredness here.

There are some who teach that at different stages in history, God proposed different ways of saving humankind. The Israelites of old, they say, were saved by what was essentially a covenant of works; but in the New Testament, Christians are saved by grace through faith. This passage and others like it in the Old Testament (see Deuteronomy 7:7,8; 9:4-6) make it clear that the Israelites always understood themselves to be a people who could stand before God only on the basis of grace. It was God who brought them out of Egypt and called them to himself. It was God who selected Jerusalem as the dwelling place for his name. It was God who chose David to be the founder of a dynasty, and it was God who named David's son Solomon as the one who would build him a temple.

Notice also the way that God named names. God did not allow his saving will to float around in the mists of human imagination. He called Israel, Jerusalem, David, and Solomon all by name. God is pleased to reveal his grace at specific times to specific people. Similarly, we are able to say with the apostle Paul: "Praise be to the God and Father of our Lord Jesus Christ, who has blessed us in the heavenly realms with every spiritual blessing in Christ. For he chose us in him before the creation of the world to be holy and blameless in his sight. . . . In him we have redemption through his blood, the forgiveness of sins. . . . And he made known to us the mystery of his will" (Ephesians 1:3,4,7,9).

Think of all the people in this world today who grope aimlessly in the dark for something to believe in. They find it in a self-help book; they look for it in a charismatic teacher; they even ransack their own souls in the hope of unlocking hidden potential. We too were once in the very same predicament. But God set his heart on us from all eternity, forgave all our sins in the precious blood of his Son, called us by name in our baptisms, and made his love known to us through the preaching of the gospel. In the full assurance of faith, we can say, "God chose *me* to be his own, called *me* by the gospel of his Son Jesus." Far from being some vague warm, fuzzy feeling, God's love is specifically for me, located in his Son, and brought to me in the gospel.

Finally, an important feature in Solomon's initial blessing is the way he pointed to the connection between God's *Word* and God's *work*. "Praise be to the LORD, the God of Israel, who *with his hands* has fulfilled what he promised *with his mouth* to my father David." In the following verses, Solomon emphasized to his people in a very concrete way that God is faithful. What God says, God does. There are some commentators who wonder how verses that seem to deal primarily with the relationship of God to the temple and to the dynasty of David can be viewed as a pronouncement of blessing upon the people. In saying this they must leave out of their consideration the tremendous comfort a believer gains from the truth Solomon stressed here.

These were not personal blessings Solomon held up to provoke the wonder and envy of others who could never share them. God was pleased to bless Solomon for the sake of Israel and in the interests of saving all people. God does not simply keep the promises he makes to ancient patriarchs and Israelite kings. Whatever he says with his mouth to any believer, God will fulfill with his hands. God is faithful: he cannot disown himself (2 Timothy 2:13). To put your trust in his Word is to trust the most certain thing there is.

### *Solomon's prayer of dedication: the setting*

**[12]Then Solomon stood before the altar of the LORD in front of the whole assembly of Israel and spread out his hands. [13]Now he had made a bronze platform, five cubits long, five cubits wide and three cubits high, and had placed it in the center of the outer court. He stood on the platform and then knelt down before the whole assembly of Israel and spread out his hands toward heaven.**

Solomon's dedicatory prayer probably took place in the large outer courtyard that surrounded the temple complex. This was as close as the congregation of Israel—all who were not priests—could come. In the middle of this courtyard, Solomon had a bronze platform constructed for the occasion. We do not know its precise purpose. Did he go on top of it so that he could be better seen and heard by the people as he led them in prayer, or was the platform a special sign of royal respect for the Lord? It was probably a little of each. It is interesting to know that archaeologists have discovered pictures of near-eastern monarchs kneeling or standing in prayer upon similar platforms.[6]

Among the ancient Israelites, standing and kneeling were normal postures of prayer. Kneeling was, of course, a mark of particular humility and reverence, as well as being a way for the king to show his complete dependence upon the Lord. Instead of folding their hands as we do, people in those days lifted up their hands in prayer (Nehemiah 8:6; Psalm 141:2; 1 Timothy 2:8). It does not matter a great deal what form these outward preparations for prayer take, as long as they help a believer to hold the body in check while the heart readies itself to talk to God. "Real prayer is done as attentively as a good and diligent barber fixes his mind and eyes upon his razor and the hair, and does not forget where he cuts."[7]

There is no better place to see the difference between godly and worldly leadership than right here. Leaders of this world are full of their own visions. They like to be seen as men of action who know how to take charge of a situation and can bend it to their own will. Godly leaders want to be filled with the vision of God and let God's Word shape their hearts and minds and wills. They do not trust their own wisdom and have no confidence in their own power to change things for the better. Instead, they rely upon God, who alone can make things right. The worldly leader strikes the pose of a man who is ready for action. A godly leader often finds himself on his knees, hands held heavenward in prayer.

*Solomon's prayer of dedication: general prayer*
**¹⁴He said:**

> **"O LORD, God of Israel, there is no God like you in heaven or on earth—you who keep your covenant of love with your servants who continue wholeheartedly in your way. ¹⁵You have kept your promise to your servant David my father; with your mouth you have promised and with your hand you have fulfilled it—as it is today.**

¹⁶"Now LORD, God of Israel, keep for your servant David my father the promises you made to him when you said, 'You shall never fail to have a man to sit before me on the throne of Israel, if only your sons are careful in all they do to walk before me according to my law, as you have done.' ¹⁷And now, O LORD, God of Israel, let your word that you promised your servant David come true.

¹⁸"But will God really dwell on earth with men? The heavens, even the highest heavens, cannot contain you. How much less this temple I have built! ¹⁹Yet give attention to your servant's prayer and his plea for mercy, O LORD my God. Hear the cry and the prayer that your servant is praying in your presence. ²⁰May your eyes be open toward this temple day and night, this place of which you said you would put your Name there. May you hear the prayer your servant prays toward this place. ²¹Hear the supplications of your servant and of your people Israel when they pray toward this place. Hear from heaven, your dwelling place; and when you hear, forgive.

Good prayer is built on God's promises. First and Second Chronicles have many good prayers like this, and Solomon's is no exception. We may wonder why Solomon chooses to repeat some of the same words he had just spoken in response to the sight of God's glory-cloud again at the opening of this prayer (compare verse 15 with 6:4). One of the Chronicler's purposes is to paint for his readers a picture of how a faithful shepherd of God's people acts. Here he makes use of the opportunity to show the king as a man who lived from the words and promises of God. He not only used God's promises to interpret what he saw with his eyes, but he also used God's Word as the anchor of his hopes and the basis for his prayers.

God had promised David that a son of his would build a temple for the Lord and that David would "never fail to have a man to sit . . . on the throne of Israel" (verse 16; see also 1 Chronicles 17). In the prayer he made on the basis of these words, Solomon demonstrated his understanding that God's promise was not yet completely fulfilled, even though he had succeeded in building a house for the Lord. Ultimately, it would find perfect fulfillment in the coming of the Savior. In the meantime, every son and successor to Solomon and every worshiper who found the Lord at his temple would demonstrate that God had not forgotten his ancient word to David.

David and Solomon were also to be models of what God wanted to see in future kings of Israel. Never absolute monarchs, these men were meant to rule as those who themselves were ruled by the Word of God. God expected them to "walk before [him] according to [his] law." Viewed as a promise of the coming Savior, the covenant with David was pure grace, without any condition whatsoever attached to it. Viewed as a promise to those kings who would rule over ancient Israel, the covenant *was* conditional, bringing rewards when one of David's sons followed in his father's footsteps and punishments when they deviated from David's path (see also 2 Samuel 7:14-16).

Solomon's first request was a simple one: "Let your word . . . [to] David come true." There is no better prayer than this: Whatever I feel, whatever the unbelieving world says, whatever slander the devil speaks, or whatever ungodly suggestions he makes, may your Word be true, Lord—may your Word be true! I know that it will be true even if all people on earth and all demons below howl out against it. I know that it will be true even if my own treacherous, sinful heart whispers against it. But I ask that it will be true for me and that I may believe it with my whole heart.

In the concluding portion of the general part of his prayer, Solomon built his second request upon a consideration of the nature of God's presence in the temple. Anyone possessing even a passing acquaintance with ancient religions has to be amazed at the depth of insight Solomon demonstrated in these verses. In this age the heathen nations viewed their gods as localized beings who held sway over this village or over that mountain range. When they were worshiped in their temples at these particular locations, it was felt that these gods were bound to answer prayers favorably—almost as if they had to keep their part of the bargain—as long as their devotees said and did all the right things.

Solomon, on the other hand, understands that the Lord is utterly free, completely unbound, and absolutely independent of any location or human being. The temple is incapable of boxing him in. "The heavens, even the highest heavens, cannot contain you. How much less this temple I have built!" If God is to be found on earth with humans, it can only be on the basis of his promise, "this place of which you said you would put your Name there." If God is to live in communion with his people and answer their prayers, it must be on the basis of forgiveness, "Hear from heaven, . . . and when you hear, *forgive*."

Simply put, Solomon's second request was for this transcendent God to hear the prayers of the king and the people whenever they would seek him in the house where he had promised to be found. Let this house be dedicated as a place where God's people approach him through sacrifices for sin and where prayers might be directed for the Lord of heaven and earth to hear.

Every time a preacher of God's Word steps down from a pulpit, he understands with Solomon that he has not said all there is to say about God. This would still be true even if he were to preach every truth about God revealed in the Bible and if his congregation were to believe every word of his preaching. Instead, the more we learn about the Savior-God, the more we say in awe, "Truly you are a God who hides himself" (Isaiah 45:15). The height of God's love for us far exceeds our grasp. If we are unable to fully understand the earthly things God has freely given to us in his Son, how much less can we grasp heavenly things: the full glory of the infinite and almighty God (John 3:12)!

That is why we will have nothing to do with people who try to explain God to us in ways that seem reasonable and plausible as far as earthly logic is concerned. That is why we avoid speaking where God has not spoken or following our wandering thoughts wherever they might lead. We know what we know, and what we know is what God has said. That is why we cling all the more to his words of promise and his revelation of himself in Jesus. That is why we are glad to gather with those who come together in Jesus' name.

Our God is free. He is bound by no duty to us, nor does he need to repay us any debt. But he has graciously bound himself by his own word. "There am I in your midst," he says. There, where forgiveness is announced in his name. There, where flesh and blood is born again by water and the Spirit. There, where in bread and wine we receive his body and his blood. "For you," he says, "for the forgiveness of sins." By these means he meets with us in the only way we can meet with him: on the basis of his word of forgiveness.

*Solomon's prayer of dedication: first petition—oath-taking*

[22]**"When a man wrongs his neighbor and is required to take an oath and he comes and swears the oath before**

**your altar in this temple, [23]then hear from heaven and act. Judge between your servants, repaying the guilty by bringing down on his own head what he has done. Declare the innocent not guilty and so establish his innocence.**

Solomon here begins to spell out what he meant in his general request when he asked that the Lord would respond to prayers directed toward his house. Solomon uses a formula that he repeats seven times in the verses that follow: "When [there is some breach of faith] . . . and [there is repentance or recourse to the temple], then hear from heaven and [respond in the appropriate way, that is, with judgment, forgiveness, or help]." Examining these petitions one by one, we see that the king envisions the whole future prayer life of his people being regulated by God's decision to reveal himself at the temple.

The first petition has to do with oath-taking, a procedure that was part of the legal system of ancient Israel. Especially in doubtful cases where it would be the matter of one person's word against another, Moses made provision in his law for an accused person to be put under a solemn oath in the name of the Lord. This would have the effect either of bringing justice down upon the guilty or of clearing the name of one falsely accused. In times past this procedure had been carried out at the tabernacle (Exodus 22:7-15); now Solomon asks God to dedicate the temple for that same purpose.

We who worship in spirit and in truth simply want our yes to be yes and our no to be no (Matthew 5:37). Honesty and candor are to characterize us, for we know that whatever we say to our neighbors is also uttered in the presence of God (Matthew 12:36).

## Solomon's prayer of dedication:
### second petition—in times of national defeat

<sup>24</sup>**"When your people Israel have been defeated by an enemy because they have sinned against you and when they turn back and confess your name, praying and making supplication before you in this temple, <sup>25</sup>then hear from heaven and forgive the sin of your people Israel and bring them back to the land you gave to them and their fathers.**

The peaceful communion of God's people was disrupted not only when neighbor sinned against neighbor but also when the people sinned against their God. Israel was meant to keep itself consecrated to the Lord. National sin would bring disastrous consequences for the whole people (see Introduction: Immediate blessings and punishments, page 8). Solomon envisions a time when their faithlessness will bring on them the punishment God had threatened: "If you do not obey the LORD . . . , the LORD will cause you to be defeated before your enemies. . . . The LORD will scatter you among all nations" (Deuteronomy 28:15,25,64). Only God could restore them at such a time. So Solomon asks the Lord to be true to his promise and to allow himself to be found in his temple by a penitent nation.

At the time when Chronicles was written, its readers were still living with the consequences of the great scattering that had been the Babylonian exile. Those who had returned were few, and there were many Jews still living far away from "the land [God] gave to them and their fathers." As for those who had made the journey back, their hold on the land was weak; they were under constant threat of being attacked and carried off by the enemies surrounding them. Repeating Solomon's words was the Chronicler's gentle way of reminding them, "We may be weak, but we are not without resource. We have God's house where God has promised to live. He has promised to give this land not just to our fathers, but to us as well [compare verse 25 with 1 Kings 8:34]. Call on his name, and depend on his strength. He will revive us and bring back our scattered people."

We too live in evil days. In a land where public breaches of morality once brought the disapproving outcry of millions, few now manage to stifle their yawns as they watch the latest outrage revealed on television. Children hold parents in contempt, parents murder their own children, thugs rule the night, and drugs eat like cancer at the nation's soul. Who can question the fact that much of the evil has come to us as a consequence of our own lack of faithfulness to the Word? Those of us who are left are few in number, surrounded by so many enemies. But we are not without resource. "We are hard pressed on every side, but not crushed; perplexed, but not in despair; persecuted, but not abandoned; struck down, but not destroyed" (2 Corinthians 4:8,9). To us too the Chronicler speaks his word of encouragement: "Call on the name of him who rules all nations! In Christ, God has declared himself for us. Let us confess our sin and depend on his strength to revive us."

*Solomon's prayer of dedication:*
*third and fourth petitions—*
*in times of drought and disaster*

> [26]"**When the heavens are shut up and there is no rain because your people have sinned against you, and when they pray toward this place and confess your name and turn from their sin because you have afflicted them, [27]then hear from heaven and forgive the sin of your servants, your people Israel. Teach them the right way to live, and send rain on the land you gave your people for an inheritance.**

28"**When famine or plague comes to the land, or blight or mildew, locusts or grasshoppers, or when enemies besiege them in any of their cities, whatever disaster or disease may come, **29**and when a prayer or plea is made by any of your people Israel—each one aware of his afflictions and pains, and spreading out his hands toward this temple—**30**then hear from heaven, your dwelling place. Forgive, and deal with each man according to all he does, since you know his heart (for you alone know the hearts of men), **31**so that they will fear you and walk in your ways all the time they live in the land you gave our fathers.**

For ancient Israel the land was a sacred bequest from God, the inheritance from him. The pious believer of the Old Testament looked at the promise of the land as one aspect of that great cluster of promises that reached their apex in the promise of the Messiah (see Genesis 12,13). So one can readily see why it was important for the Israelites to retain a physical presence in the land. It was not only their homeland but also the cradle of King Messiah. That is why God's people simply had to lift up their eyes and look around at the landscape to see how affairs stood between them and their God. The land's physical condition reflected the people's moral condition.

Unlike Egypt with its complex system of irrigation ditches, Israel depended completely on rain to grow its crops. If the rain did not come, famine was the result. We live in a land where our surplus grain fills huge silos across great, wide prairies. For us famine is not much of a threat. But for people who had no alternative to watching their only food supply dwindle down to nothing in their grain bins, clouds darkening the sky were the most welcome of all earthly sights. They brought the promise of another harvest and another year of life. When they failed to come, Jeremiah graphically describes for us the result:

Judah mourns,
>   her cities languish;
they wail for the land,
>   and a cry goes up from Jerusalem.
The nobles send their servants for water;
>   they go to the cisterns
>   but find no water.
They return with their jars unfilled;
>   dismayed and despairing,
>   they cover their heads.
The ground is cracked
>   because there is no rain in the land;
the farmers are dismayed
>   and cover their heads.
Even the doe in the field
>   deserts her newborn fawn
>   because there is no grass.
Wild donkeys stand on the barren heights
>   and pant like jackals;
their eyesight fails
>   for lack of pasture. (Jeremiah 14:2-6)

Significantly, Jeremiah makes the same connection between drought and sin that Solomon does, continuing in the next verse, "Although our sins testify against us, O Lord, do something for the sake of your name. For our backsliding is great; we have sinned against you" (verse 7).

The fourth petition (verses 28-31) sums up all the ills common to humanity that can afflict people at any time and cause them to seek the Lord's help. We notice that there is no mention here as in previous verses of a specific sin being the cause of any one of them. The list of seven (famine, plague, blight, mildew, locusts, grasshoppers, siege) is not intended to exhaust the possibilities; rather, it is meant to emphasize that there is no trouble on earth beyond the scope of prayer. The trouble may affect many or be felt by one alone (note: "each one aware of his afflictions and pains"). King or noble, priest or Levite, rich or poor, man or woman—none is excluded from an audience with the Most High. "Each one" has equal privileges when it comes to "spreading out his hands toward this temple."

Also significant is the anticipated impact on God's people when God hears and answers the prayers of those in affliction. God's saving response empowers his people to live good and holy lives. It increases their reverent faith for God and their fervent love for one another.

Finally we note once again the basis for God's response to prayer. It is not the eloquence of the prayer itself nor the worthiness of the one who utters it. "*Forgive,* and deal with each man according to all he does, since you know his heart." Forgiveness is the essential prerequisite. Forgive us first; then consider the moral texture of our lives. We might paraphrase it in this way: "If you, O Lord, were to judge us strictly and consider our lives apart from the filter of your grace, none of our deeds could endure the light of your presence. We could have no hope ever of your help. But you do not examine only the visible side of things, as we do. We are easily impressed by great outward acts of piety, but you see into our hearts. You detect the faith your great love has planted there, a faith in our Savior that purifies all we do."

In these magnificent words, the Chronicler portrays Solomon to us as a king who encouraged his people to call on God in the day of trouble. In a similar way, we hear our

Savior encourage us to "ask and it will be given to you; seek and you will find; knock and the door will be opened to you. For everyone who asks receives; he who seeks finds; and to him who knocks, the door will be opened" (Luke 11:9,10).

*Solomon's prayer of dedication:*
*fifth petition—for the foreigner*

> [32]"As for the foreigner who does not belong to your people Israel but has come from a distant land because of your great name and your mighty hand and your out-stretched arm—when he comes and prays toward this temple, [33]then hear from heaven, your dwelling place, and do whatever the foreigner asks of you, so that all the peoples of the earth may know your name and fear you, as do your own people Israel, and may know that this house I have built bears your Name.

In typical Old Testament style, Solomon sees the kingdom of God being extended by people coming *in,* to the land and to the place where God has chosen to reveal himself. We might contrast this with the way we, on the basis of the Great Commission, tend to view the extension of the kingdom of God as a matter of missionaries going *out* into all the world to preach the good news about Jesus. Whatever the perspective, it amounts to the same thing whether we pray, "Lord, bring *in* all those whom you have chosen to be your own" or "Lord, let your gospel message be spread through*out* all nations." All this is a way of emphasizing that Solomon's petition here is simply filled with a zeal for missions.

Many commentators point out the significant omission here of any mention of sin or repentance leading to the foreigner's prayer. Instead, Solomon sees the foreigner's prime motivation as being the compelling power of "[God's] great name and [his] mighty hand and [his] outstretched arm."

If there is any distinction to be drawn between these expressions here, then "name" would be a reference to God's revelation of his true nature to Israel as the God of grace, while "mighty hand" and "outstretched arm" would refer more to God's concrete, historic, saving actions. Both point to the power of the gospel "for the salvation of everyone who believes" (Romans 1:16).

Solomon is not saying that foreigners have no need to repent. As one familiar with the sad truth about our fallen nature, he later said, "There is no one [literally, no human being] who does not sin" (6:36). Sin and repentance are not in view here because, throughout this prayer, Solomon has been thinking primarily of *Israel's* sin and *Israel's* need for repentance in the terms of the Sinai law covenant. Israel sinned when it broke the stipulations of that covenant. Its forms of repentance were also governed by the covenant, in which specific provisions were made for sacrifices to remove sin. In this sense a foreigner was unable to sin since he was not under *Israel's* law (see Romans 5:13). Nor would it be appropriate for him personally to offer sacrifices in the manner prescribed by Moses. Such sacrifices would be reserved for *Israel* to make.

Solomon asks the Lord to answer the prayers of those foreigners who have been drawn by the light of Israel's hope "so that all the peoples of the earth may know your name and fear you, as do your own people Israel, and may know that this house I have built bears your Name." In his own way, the Chronicler is reminding his people why God permitted them to return to the land and rebuild the temple. God wanted his saving purposes to be fulfilled. A truth like this was easy to forget when Judah's earthly power was at such a low ebb. After experiencing exile and the continued hostility of the surrounding nations, it must have been hard for the people to see non-Israelites as anything but enemies.

There really are so many reasons for perceiving a limit to the love of God and for saying, "Thus far—and no further!" But if we cease to be a light for the world, we cease to be God's people (Matthew 5:13,14). The church that has no sense of its gospel mission has no right to be called a church. God did not freely give us the gospel so that we would be content in serving only ourselves with it. "Freely you have received, freely give," our Savior says (Matthew 10:8). It took an infinite love to save sinners like you and me. How could any sincere heart, knowing this, want to set a limit on God's love? Instead, as those who have been grasped by God's grace, we are compelled to cry out in prayer with Solomon, "May your name be holy, and may all the peoples of the earth know your name as we do!"

*Solomon's prayer of dedication:*
*sixth petition—when Israel goes to war*

> ³⁴**"When your people go to war against their enemies, wherever you send them, and when they pray to you toward this city you have chosen and the temple I have built for your Name, ³⁵then hear from heaven their prayer and their plea, and uphold their cause.**

Many times nations at war claim that God is on their side, invoking his aid against their enemies. It would be a misreading of this petition to interpret Solomon's words as if they were an echo of this idea. The nation of Israel truly was a nation belonging to God in a way no other nation before or since could claim. Their battles were God's battles, provided that they were following God's will and God's way. Solomon prays for help when they are fighting wherever *God may send them,* not wherever they might want to go.

The battles in which we are engaged are not against flesh and blood but against the spiritual forces at work within and around us. If we are seasoned spiritual warriors, we should know well enough by now that, left to our own devices, we could not make a stand against the world with all its lies and false promises. We would be unable to overcome our sinful selves by our own strategies. The liar's power to entice us into sin—making evil look good and good, evil—is truly frightening. And who has not felt the poisonous despair coming from that serpent, who wants us to believe that forgiveness is for others, not for us, since our sin is far too bad for God to want anything more to do with us. "But for us fights the valiant one whom God himself elected," as Luther says (CW 200:2). And so we pray, "Uphold our cause, dear Jesus; trample Satan underfoot and bring us to victory."

### Solomon's prayer of dedication:
### seventh petition—when Israel mourns in captivity

**³⁶"When they sin against you—for there is no one who does not sin—and you become angry with them and give them over to the enemy, who takes them captive to a land far away or near; ³⁷and if they have a change of heart in the land where they are held captive, and repent and plead with you in the land of their captivity and say, 'We have sinned, we have done wrong and acted wickedly'; ³⁸and if they turn back to you with all their heart and soul in the land of their captivity where they were taken, and pray toward the land you gave their fathers, toward the city you have chosen and toward the temple I have built for your Name; ³⁹then from heaven, your dwelling place, hear their prayer and their pleas, and uphold their cause. And forgive your people, who have sinned against you.**

Solomon sees two possible states for the Israelites, two lands in which they can exist. The one is the land of captivity; the other is the Land of Promise. The land of captivity might be their state if they sin against God, causing God to give them up to their enemies. A life, one might call it, but hardly a life. There they live under their enemies' power, under another's control. The oppressive nature of that power is seen in the way Solomon repeats the word *captive* again and again.

But though the Israelites may serve their captors with their bodies, they need not serve with their minds. In the land of their captivity, they may have a change of heart (verse 37, literally: they may return to their true hearts) and turn to God in genuine prayer, acknowledging the perversity of their actions. In repentance they may turn again—heart, mind, and soul—to the land of promise, to Jerusalem, to the house built for God by Solomon. This is their homeland, their lasting city, where God dwells. Solomon prays, "When they turn to you like this, do not reject them. Do not abandon them to their exile. Forgive their sin and bring them home."

Our Lord once told a story about a son who left his home and went off to a far country looking for freedom. He didn't find it. Instead, he found himself held captive by wretched, unfulfilled desires for wretched, unfulfilling things: "He longed to fill his stomach with the pods that the pigs were eating, but no one gave him anything" (Luke 15:16). When he came to his senses (Luke 15:17, literally: when he came to himself), he wanted to go home again. Though he felt sure that he could never be reaccepted as a son, he hoped he might be received as a servant.

While he was still a long way off, his father saw him coming down the road. Unable to contain himself for joy, the father ran to his son, embraced him, and accepted him unconditionally—as his son again with full honors. In this portion of the parable, we see how Jesus expanded the essence of Solomon's prayer, filling it with a new and spiritual meaning. He was aiming to give comfort to the outcast, to every one who is exiled from God's people, has come to his senses, and longs for his true home again.

During Advent we sing of how we mourn in lowly exile here. This is not our home, because here nothing lasts, and far too often we find ourselves stumbling into sin again. "For there is no one who does not sin." Our true home can only be where our Savior is, a place where at last we will be free from all that torments us. Soon Jesus will come again to bring us home. That is why the church also sings, "Rejoice! Rejoice! Emmanuel shall come to you, O Israel!" (CW 23). We know that God will answer Solomon's prayer once more—and bring us back from exile.

### Solomon's prayer of dedication: conclusion

⁴⁰"Now, my God, may your eyes be open and your ears attentive to the prayers offered in this place.

⁴¹ "Now arise, O Lᴏʀᴅ God, and come to your resting place,
    you and the ark of your might.
May your priests, O Lᴏʀᴅ God, be clothed with salvation,
    may your saints rejoice in your goodness.
⁴²O Lᴏʀᴅ God, do not reject your anointed one.
    Remember the great love promised to David
        your servant."

Often at the ends of great pieces of music, there will be what is called a coda. The music gradually slows down. Major musical themes are sounded again. We might call Solomon's concluding words here a verbal coda. The tempo slows as he shifts into the rhythm of poetry (the words remind us of Psalm 132:8-10). He repeats his most important thoughts again.

It is also possible that we have here a verbal pattern sometimes used in ancient literature to mark off larger units of thought. Solomon had begun his prayer with a reference to the covenant God made with David (6:14-17). He went on to ask God to "put his Name" on the temple, as he had promised, and, on that account, to hold his eyes open to the needs of his people and to keep his ears attentive to their prayers (6:18-21). Solomon concluded his general prayer with an overarching plea for forgiveness (6:21). In these final verses we see a similar pattern, only in reverse order. There is a request for forgiveness, a prayer for God's open eyes, listening ears, and presence in the temple, and a request that God would "remember the great love promised to David." It's as if Solomon is going out the way he came in and bracketing his entire prayer with reminders of God's grace to poor sinners.

Solomon's conclusion contains many beautiful facets. We will examine only a few here. Consider, for a moment, the phrase "may your eyes be open and your ears attentive." This is clearly a thought dear to Solomon's heart, a fact we can infer not only from the way he repeats it but also from the way God himself uses the same phrase in his reply to Solomon in the next chapter (7:15). What a vivid way of speaking about God's active concern for his people! We are not dealing with an impersonal being high above who is indifferent to his people's fate. The true God is a loving Father who sees our needs and hears our prayers.

Look at Solomon's masterful allusion: "Arise, O LORD God, and come to your resting place." These words echo in part what Moses had said whenever the ark was to set out during the years that Israel wandered in the wilderness, "Rise up, O LORD! May your enemies be scattered; may your foes flee before you" (Numbers 10:35). But as we noticed before, this section is also Solomon's free paraphrase of snippets from Psalm 132. There, the psalmist celebrated David's vow not to rest until the ark had found a resting place of its own. And so with a single phrase, Solomon was able to connect the centuries and join together two key points in Old Testament history. It's as if he were saying, "What all Israel longed for during the many years of wandering and what my father, David, did his utmost to prepare for has now come to fruition. No more must God arise to scatter our enemies, those who would oppose our living in this land. Because he has given us rest, his ark may now arise and come to its rest in this house that I have built for God's Name."

A fruit of that rest is the joy God's people experience in the presence of their God. For obvious reasons Solomon's prayer focused on the times when God's people would fall on their knees in their need and ask for God's forgiveness and help. But forgiveness is only one aspect of a life lived in fellowship with God. Forgiveness always has in view the barrier of sin that must be removed before we can ever delight in a true fellowship with God. Stated positively, fellowship consists of the perfect joy we have when there is nothing standing between us and God, leaving us to bask in the light of his presence. Solomon strikes this important note at the end with the words, "May your priests, O LORD God, be clothed with salvation, may your saints rejoice in your goodness."

Solomon concludes with a reference to the covenant promise God made with David. In the book of Chronicles, it is the unconditional aspect of that promise that is emphasized (see 1 Chronicles 17). God's unconditional love is not merely the hope of Israel's king ("Do not reject your anointed one"); rather, the love promised to David is the basis for the hope of all Israel (see Isaiah 55:3). Even more so, it is the only hope for a world of sinners. Through David, God would send an eternal King to rule over all nations and deliver us from all our enemies. Because of his great love—a love revealed and promised to David—God sent his only Son into the world to die for us all. For us then "the great love promised to David" is the assurance that God hears our requests and will give us "whatever [we] ask in [Jesus'] name" (John 16:23).

One might think it strange to hear this emphasis on the Lord's Anointed, and on David the king, in a passage dealing with the temple. After all, for the Chronicler's first readers, only the temple was left. The earthly dynasty of David had long since disappeared as a visible sign of God's favor. Why emphasize something that was missing from Israel's life? Why else but to stir up in God's people a longing for the Messiah to come! Each one of God's promises would find its perfect fulfillment in him. In fact, this entire picture of Solomon—completing the work of David, building God's temple, interceding for his people in prayer—may also be seen as the Chronicler's depiction of the King who would be the incarnation of God's name, the fulfiller of all promises, the builder of a spiritual house to which we belong, and the one who intercedes for us in prayer (see John 17).

*God dedicates the temple with fire and in glory*

**7** When Solomon finished praying, fire came down from heaven and consumed the burnt offering and the sacrifices, and the glory of the LORD filled the temple. [2] The priests could not enter the temple of the LORD because the glory of the LORD filled it. [3] When all the Israelites saw the fire coming down and the glory of the LORD above the temple, they knelt on the pavement with their faces to the ground, and they worshiped and gave thanks to the LORD, saying,

**"He is good;
his love endures forever."**

God is certainly under no obligation to give signs and wonders to confirm his Word to those who doubt it (Luke 11:29). All the same, there were times when God did give his believers signs to confirm and strengthen the faith he had already worked in their hearts through the Word. When it happened, it was grace upon grace, gift piled high on top of gift. And whenever God did it, it was to show his people where they should look for their help in every time of need.

By the appearance of his glory-cloud, God had already confirmed that the temple was now his dwelling place on earth (5:13,14). Above and beyond that, however, God immediately responded to Solomon's prayer by sending down fire from heaven to consume the sacrifices that had been laid out and by again filling the temple with his glory. This time all the people of Israel clearly saw what had happened and, in awestruck wonder, they bowed low with their faces to the ground. Then they took up the refrain of grace that earlier had been sung by all the Levites: "He is good; his love endures forever" (5:13).

Some commentators suggest that the Chronicler is embroidering the account here, adding an extra appearance of the glory-cloud where the writer of Kings was content to mention only one. Others[8] see it as a feature of the Chronicler's style in which, by means of repetition, he essentially picks up the narrative he had interrupted in 5:14. What we have here, they say, is not two different appearances of the glory-cloud but rather a resumption of the earlier description of the same event. This second position seems possible, since it at least shows some respect for the truth of the biblical text.

What both of these interpretations overlook, however, is the different impact the glory-cloud had at this stage of the narrative. In its first appearance, the glory-cloud punctuated the entrance of the ark into the Most Holy Place, as if God were declaring in symbolic fashion, "I indeed dwell between the cherubim" (see Exodus 25:22). Here it gave God's visual assent to all that Solomon had requested in prayer and, by consuming the sacrifices with fire, confirmed this house as the correct place to offer them (6:12). In this way God made it unmistakably clear that he accepted the people's sacrificial service.

In a similar way, God had consecrated the tabernacle for sacrifice (Leviticus 9:23,24), had shown his approval of David's altar on the threshing floor of Araunah (1 Chronicles 21:26), and would confirm Elijah before the people as a genuine prophet of the only true God (1 Kings 18). We do not have to think too hard to come up with New Testament parallels either. There was the voice from heaven at Jesus' baptism and later at his transfiguration. In response to Jesus' request to glorify his name, the Father answered, "I have glorified it, and will glorify it again" (John 12:28). In answer to the believers' prayer for the power to give a bold witness in the face of their enemies' threats, we read, "After they prayed, the place where they were meeting was shaken. And they were all filled with the Holy Spirit and spoke the word of God boldly" (Acts 4:31).

In every case and in a way appropriate to each age, God was palpably confirming essentially the same truth: "I am present *here,* just as I said I would be! This is where you may find me. This is where I accept your sacrifices to atone for guilt. This is where I accept your sacrifices of thanksgiving and praise. When you pray to me at this place, I hear you; when you call out to me for help, I will answer your requests. I am not hard to locate, even though you may not see me." To us who live in the full light of Christ, God the Father says, "Here is my Son! In all his life, in all he said and did and suffered, you see me and know me. You know what my thoughts are toward you, and you see how great my love is for you. He is the sacrifice that removes the guilt of the world. Through him your entire life is an offering that pleases me, and whatever you ask me in his name, I am glad to give."

That is why we know that God is present wherever believers gather around Word and sacrament and that when we call on God's name, we are not speaking into thin air but to the God who is there. That is why we are so confident in Christ that our lives are pleasing to God. Our dear Father does not want us to spend our time on earth in an agony of doubt, uncertain as to whether he listens to us, unsure as to whether our lives please him. God's presence among us is not brought about by our great expectations. God does not draw near to us because we have lived so piously and well. God's presence does not depend on our sense of his being near. Our senses can deceive us; our own hopes rise and fall, and we are always far more conscious of our own sinful weakness than of God's great power. We could never be sure of God's presence if it depended on us in any way. To make us certain, the heavenly voice declares, "Here is my Son," and in the greatest of all confirmations of love, the Son was lifted high on a cross to draw all people to himself.

What more could we ask for? What more do we need? Christ crucified and raised to glory is God's most palpable proof of his great love. And so we are certain of his abiding presence among us wherever word of him rings out.

## All the people worship God through sacrifices and song

⁴Then the king and all the people offered sacrifices before the LORD. ⁵And King Solomon offered a sacrifice of twenty-two thousand head of cattle and a hundred and twenty thousand sheep and goats. So the king and all the people dedicated the temple of God. ⁶The priests took their positions, as did the Levites with the LORD's musical instruments, which King David had made for praising the LORD and which were used when he gave thanks, saying, "His love endures forever." Opposite the Levites, the priests blew their trumpets, and all the Israelites were standing.

⁷Solomon consecrated the middle part of the courtyard in front of the temple of the LORD, and there he offered burnt offerings and the fat of the fellowship offerings, because the bronze altar he had made could not hold the burnt offerings, the grain offerings and the fat portions.

⁸So Solomon observed the festival at that time for seven days, and all Israel with him—a vast assembly, people from Lebo Hamath to the Wadi of Egypt. ⁹On the eighth day they held an assembly, for they had celebrated the dedication of the altar for seven days and the festival for seven days more. ¹⁰On the twenty-third day of the seventh month he sent the people to their homes, joyful and glad in heart for the good things the LORD had done for David and Solomon and for his people Israel.

Here the Chronicler gives us one more of those snapshots out of his album entitled "Worship at its finest." Some we have seen already (1 Chronicles 13–16; 29); we will see more later. In this particular glimpse of ancient Israel at worship, we notice the vast scale on which everything was done. The number of sacrifices is astounding: "twenty-two thousand head of cattle and a hundred and twenty thousand sheep and goats." This exceeds all similar counts mentioned elsewhere (1 Chronicles 29:21; 2 Chronicles 1:6;

29:32; 30:24). But it is also a count entirely in keeping with a festival intended to inaugurate "a place to burn sacrifices" to the Lord (2:6).

To accommodate these huge quantities, Solomon pressed the temple courtyard itself into service "because the bronze altar he had made could not hold the burnt offerings, the grain offerings and the fat portions." Here it's worth saying that not all the sacrifices were "burnt offerings," sacrifices expressing the worshipers' total devotion to the Lord. This type of sacrifice was completely burned up. The other type mentioned—"fellowship offerings"—was partly consumed on the altar and partly eaten by the participants. As such it expressed the joyful fellowship between the believer and God. To ensure the full participation of all who had gathered was surely also one of the reasons prompting so many sacrifices.

Those assembled to dedicate the temple comprised a truly huge throng. At the height of the nation's earthly power, "all Israel" gathered together—"a vast assembly, people from Lebo Hamath to the Wadi of Egypt." This last expression is a geographical way of saying "from the farthest reaches of the land of Israel." The Chronicler points this out not only to mark the greatness of the occasion but also to show that the temple's dedication united all Israel in joint worship. It wasn't just the king who offered sacrifices; all the people did too.

There were a number of special touches to the event as well. Normally the Feast of Tabernacles was a seven-day festival, beginning on the 15th day of the seventh month and ending with a special assembly on the 22nd day (Leviticus 23:34-36). Solomon preceded these festal days by an additional week of celebration that began on the 8th day of the month. These earlier days were set aside to celebrate "the dedication of the altar." In effect, Solomon doubled the length of the holy celebration in the seventh month. We will see a similar extension of a festival's length in connection with Hezekiah's Passover (30:23). The Day of Atonement (Leviticus 16:29,30) must also have interrupted Solomon's first week of celebration, although the Chronicler does not mention it.

In addition to making sacrifices, Israel also worshiped the Lord with music and song. The Levites made use of "the LORD's musical instruments, which King David had made for praising the LORD and which were used when he gave thanks." There is a slight but significant inaccuracy in the NIV's rendition of that last phrase. Perhaps a better way to render those final words would be: "whenever David offered praises *by their ministry*" (New Revised Standard Version). The Levites were servants who represented and led the others in worship. When they praised the Lord, they were not simply doing it in their own name but on behalf of the king and the people. This would hold true also for the priests assigned to blow the trumpets.

In spite of its grand scale, this great convocation was orderly. Again, the NIV's translation, "The priests took their positions, as did the Levites," does not quite bring out the full force of the original. The Chronicler's point is that the priests and Levites did not abandon the roles assigned to them, even though it was a special occasion. Each group continued to serve in the duties Moses and David had assigned to them. The priests offered the sacrifices and blew the trumpets. The Levites had the privilege of leading the entire assembly in music and song, using the instruments David had designed for them. The priests did not envy the Levites; the Levites did not look down upon the ministry of the priests. In loving order, both worked together.

The prevailing mood of the entire 15-day celebration is contained in those words describing the congregation's state of mind after Solomon had sent them on their way. They were all "joyful and glad in heart for the good things the LORD had done for David and Solomon and for his people Israel." Order in worship need not result in listless boredom, just as spontaneity in worship cannot guarantee joy. Some worship is off the cuff and shows it!

We notice the Chronicler's hand here in the way he repeats himself in various ways. The themes of unity, order, and worship have all been sounded before. It is also a case of "déjà vu, all over again" to hear of Levitical musicians exercising a craft that harked back to David. Not only themes and topics but also characteristic words and phrases crop up over and over: "his love endures forever," "from Lebo Hamath to the Wadi of Egypt," and "all Israel," to mention only a few. Since we are at the high point of the book, it is probably worth reminding ourselves again of the reason for all this repetition.

First, the Chronicler was making sure that there were some vital connections being made in his listeners' minds. As David was, so was Solomon: both good kings whose devotion to worship laid the foundation for future generations. These connections were meant to give those who followed the firm assurance that they were the inheritors of an ancient and sacred tradition, ordained by God himself. The worship of God in his temple, so recently reestablished in the land of Judah, nevertheless had roots that went far back in time. It was founded on God's Word, that is, on what God had revealed through Moses and David as the way to approach him. That is why those of the Chronicler's generation could be assured that they were still God's people and that God— the God whose love endures forever—was still their God.

Second, David and Solomon would also be serving as the Chronicler's ideal and pattern of what a king of Israel should be like, as far as worship in the house of God was concerned. Future kings would either be praised or blamed to the degree that they conformed or did not conform to David and Solomon's example. These recurring patterns are ways the Chronicler has of impressing on us that the history of the world is not a random series of events but rather a river whose flow is directed and guided by God in the channels he chooses for it. The ultimate goal God has in mind for this river is to flow into the ocean that is Christ. All law is fulfilled by him, all promises come true in him, all humanity is represented in him, all sins are washed away in him, and all love is found in him.

Finally, the Chronicler's method of repetition points out what is perhaps a slightly different way of dispensing religious knowledge from that which we have grown used to. We in the West are accustomed to logical outlines, questions with answers, speeches in which the theme is openly stated and where no one is left in the dark as to the point of it all. It was the Chronicler's method—somewhat more commonly found in societies where the force of the oral word is strong—simply to tell the story, retell it, and then tell it again. By hammering away at these themes, this master craftsman of the holy writings (as we hope we have shown the Chronicler to be) has impressed his point on his readers without ever having to say, "Here's the point."

This method is different, yet not so foreign to us. We start out in all our schools teaching children the standard accounts of Bible history. Our Sunday schools follow a regular series of Bible stories portraying the life of Christ and major events from the Old Testament. Any pastor can tell you how difficult it is to teach the more abstract truths of the Catechism to children who have not had a firm foundation in those (simple?) Bible stories. Think of a pastor hard at work with his confirmation class. The students are all struggling to grasp the meaning of the passage "Christ died for the ungodly." Now go to the next room and watch the awestruck faces of the little ones as they hear the account of our Savior's passion told skillfully and lovingly by their Sunday school teacher. Remove the one, and you destroy the basis for the other. If his pupils do not have a firm grounding in Bible history, the pastor's discussion of Bible passages will seem lifeless, abstract, and even incomprehensible to his listeners. And this is true not because of the pastor's lack of ability but because of his pupils' lack of essential background! Repetition of these Bible stories by Sunday school teachers, parish school teachers, and Christian parents at home is a vital way of impressing the truths they contain on our young, and it goes a long way toward shaping a child's Christian identity.

Perhaps all this writer is trying to do is underscore one of the Chronicler's themes in this section: Sunday school teacher, pastor, father, mother—never underestimate the importance of your work! For the well-being of God's people, it is vital for us all to be found at our "positions" in the temple of God (7:6).

## God's answer to Solomon's prayer of dedication

¹¹**When Solomon had finished the temple of the LORD and the royal palace, and had succeeded in carrying out all he had in mind to do in the temple of the LORD and in his own palace, ¹²the LORD appeared to him at night and said:**

**"I have heard your prayer and have chosen this place for myself as a temple for sacrifices.**

¹³**"When I shut up the heavens so that there is no rain, or command locusts to devour the land or send a plague among my people, ¹⁴if my people, who are called by my**

name, will humble themselves and pray and seek my face and turn from their wicked ways, then will I hear from heaven and will forgive their sin and will heal their land. [15]Now my eyes will be open and my ears attentive to the prayers offered in this place. [16]I have chosen and consecrated this temple so that my Name may be there forever. My eyes and my heart will always be there.

[17]"As for you, if you walk before me as David your father did, and do all I command, and observe my decrees and laws, [18]I will establish your royal throne, as I covenanted with David your father when I said, 'You shall never fail to have a man to rule over Israel.'

[19]"But if you turn away and forsake the decrees and commands I have given you and go off to serve other gods and worship them, [20]then I will uproot Israel from my land, which I have given them, and will reject this temple I have consecrated for my Name. I will make it a byword and an object of ridicule among all peoples. [21]And though this temple is now so imposing, all who pass by will be appalled and say, 'Why has the LORD done such a thing to this land and to this temple?' [22]People will answer, 'Because they have forsaken the LORD, the God of their fathers, who brought them out of Egypt, and have embraced other gods, worshiping and serving them—that is why he brought all this disaster on them.'"

Verse 11 is the first time that the Chronicler mentions Solomon's other major building project—the royal palace. A section found in 1 Kings describing the magnificence of that palace (7:1-11) is entirely missing in this account. The Chronicler's editorial purpose seems clear enough. He has been set on keeping his readers' attention focused on the temple. A comparison of the two versions of God's reply to Solomon—found here and in 1 Kings 9:1-9—yields a similar conclusion. Though the differences are, in most cases, a matter of an occasional word or two, the Chronicler's shaping of this material has the effect of connecting Solomon's dedication prayer and God's reply much more closely to each other. Again, the purpose is to keep the account tightly focused on the temple.

The most obvious example of this is the section from verses 12 to 15, in which we find a great deal of material not mentioned at all in 1 Kings. For one thing, God summarizes the gist of Solomon's prayer in a more complete way. God has even shaped his reply by following a pattern similar to the one Solomon had used: "When there is [some act of God's judgment] and then [there is repentance, with the people turning to God for help]—then I will forgive and help." More than this, in verse 15 God goes on to echo Solomon's exact words: "My eyes will be open and my ears attentive to the prayers offered in this place" (compare with 6:40). Finally, the section from verses 19 to 22 has been edited to make God's threat apply more exclusively to the temple.

At the beginning of his response, God assures Solomon that he will indeed answer his penitent people's prayers. Words like these are meant to give us the heart to take our needs to God in prayer. Through the Word we understand that God hears us not because our words have been so finely crafted nor because we have proven ourselves worthy of an audience with so great a Lord. He hears us because he has promised he will. Luther once ended a prayer by saying, "It is not the worthiness of my prayer, but the certainty of your truth that makes me firmly believe that [your answer to my requests] will be and remain yes and amen."[9]

The kernel of God's message to Solomon is beautifully stated in verse 16: "I have chosen and consecrated this temple so that my Name may be there forever. My eyes and my heart will always be there." David and Solomon had labored many years to see it built, but the essential feature of the temple was God's choosing it as a place to reveal his gracious nature (Deuteronomy 12:5-7). God also promised that he would always have his heart set on the temple. Though the building made by hands has long since disappeared, God's promise did not fail. Again we hear God's own voice declare in the New Testament, "This is my Son, whom I have chosen; listen to him" (Luke 9:35). In Christ we find God's gracious heart laid bare.

What more did God have to do to assure Solomon and his people of his steadfast love? He had appeared once to the young king at Gibeon, twice in the glory-cloud at the dedication, and now once more in a vision at night. How many times does God have to demonstrate his goodwill before a person's doubt is overcome? In how many ways must he seek us out before we can be found? "In the past God spoke to our forefathers through the prophets at many times and in various ways, but in these last days he has spoken to us by his Son. . . . We must pay more careful attention, therefore, to what we have heard, so that we do not drift away" (Hebrews 1:1,2; 2:1).

We do not find the terms *law* and *gospel* in the Old Testament as we are familiar with them in our Lutheran churches. Yet the ideas those terms represent are embedded deeply in every page. And as in all of Scripture, it is important to distinguish law from gospel here. We notice some promises in God's reply to Solomon that are made in an absolute way, without condition. These are pure gospel. God is telling people what he will do for them. We notice other promises with conditions attached. These are pure law. God is telling people what he expects of them—the blessings they will receive if they obey and the punishments that will ensue if they disobey.

It is also important to remember that God's covenant with David (2 Samuel 7; 1 Chronicles 17) contained elements of both law and gospel. Some of the aspects of the covenant God made with David were God's way of renewing that ancient gospel promise he had once made to Adam and Eve. He simply attached that promise specifically to the house of David. The Savior would be born as a king in David's line. Other features of that covenant were God's way of applying the Mosaic Law to an Israel that had now settled in the land and had acquired for itself a king. Some of the terms God used might have changed, but the law covenant's essential nature had not. "*If* you obey me fully and keep my covenant, *then* out of all nations you will be my treasured possession" (Exodus 19:5). A great deal was riding on that *if*.

We have already considered verse 16 as being an excellent example of a gospel promise, made without condition. But when we look at the rest of the section—directed first to Solomon and then applied to all his successors on the throne—we will see that key word *if*. Whether the earthly dynasty of Solomon continues or not depends on his obedience to God's law. Whether the Israelite kingdom endures or not depends on the obedience and faithful worship of Solomon and all those who succeed him on the throne (verses 19-22—the *you* in these verses shifts into the plural). The consequences of that disobedience are clearly spelled out in verse 20: Israel will be uprooted from the land, and God will abandon his temple, even though he had it "consecrated for [his] Name."

In this section the Chronicler has let God himself give us the outline for the rest of his book. Israel and her kings will be unfaithful. They will worship other gods and disobey God's law. As a consequence, king and temple, people and land will all bear the marks of God's wrath. Some kings will lead the Israelites in penitently humbling themselves and in seeking the Lord again. God will hear and answer their pleas for forgiveness and will "heal their land." In the end, Judah will degenerate to a point where God will uproot his people from his land and reject Solomon's temple.

Particularly telling and vivid are God's final words describing the temple in its state of rejection. The rejection of his house will be so total, God says, that it will become proverbial for complete destruction. Other nations will use it as a way to mock what they saw as the pretentious claim of Israel to be God's chosen people. A temple that now inspires wonder with its magnificence will then appall with its desolation. People will ask why. The answer will come back, "Because they have forsaken the LORD." There is a solemnity and a tragedy about this passage that starkly depicts the futility of sin. In pursuit of the truth, people chase lies; they fashion a bleak desert and call it life.

The Chronicler wrote these words both to encourage and to warn the people of his own generation. A temple building alone was no guarantee of safety and well-being in the Land of Promise. As serious as God was in his promise of love, he was just as serious in his threats against those who despised his love by disobeying his law. Again the writer to the Hebrews drives it home for us who know Christ: "How shall we escape if we ignore such a great salvation?" (2:3).

A central issue in interpreting the next two chapters is the question of whether or not the Chronicler still sees his material as being directly related to the construction of the Lord's house. In other words, is the magnificence of Solomon, the king, in the foreground, or is the Chronicler emphasizing the faithfulness of Solomon who built the Lord's house? Perhaps we can split the difference and view chapter 8 as still being germane to Solomon's completion of the temple project while chapter 9 emphasizes the wisdom and magnificence of the Lord's Anointed. In any case, we should know by now that the temple and its services are never far from the mind of our writer.

### Solomon in all his splendor

*The splendor of Solomon's trading and building*

**8** At the end of twenty years, during which Solomon built the temple of the LORD and his own palace, ²Solomon rebuilt the villages that Hiram had given him, and settled Israelites in them. ³Solomon then went to Hamath Zobah and captured it. ⁴He also built up Tadmor in the desert and all the store cities he had built in Hamath. ⁵He rebuilt Upper Beth Horon and Lower Beth Horon as fortified cities, with walls and with gates and bars, ⁶as well as Baalath and all his store cities, and all the cities for his chariots and for his horses—whatever he desired to build in Jerusalem, in Lebanon and throughout all the territory he ruled.

All along the Chronicler has been painting for us a picture of Solomon as an ideal king and worthy successor to David. The final two chapters describing Solomon's reign will be no exception to this rule. Verses 1 to 6 depict Solomon as the maintainer and extender of the land in which the Lord had set his temple. In this he compares favorably with David, through whom the Lord provided Israel with rest from its enemies (1 Chronicles 17:9; see also Deuteronomy 12:10,11).

A great deal of Solomon's efforts were devoted to the extension of the city of Jerusalem, a city his father had captured (1 Chronicles 11:4-8). Solomon built his palace on the same hill as the temple, doing it in such a way that it adjoined the temple grounds to the south. The two buildings became one large building complex that, in all, took 20 years to complete.

Verse 2 seems to disagree with its parallel in 1 Kings, where we are told that Hiram received 20 cities in Galilee *from* Solomon, not that Hiram *gave* cities *to* Solomon (1 Kings 9:11). The deal came about, according to 1 Kings, because of what Solomon owed Hiram for all the building supplies he had received. The writer of Kings also informs us that Hiram was none too pleased with what he received in the bargain, calling the area "Cabul" (1 Kings 9:13), a word that we might freely translate as "like smoke." Hiram's hoped-for profits had vanished into thin air! The most plausible explanation for this "contradiction" is the one offered long ago by the Jewish historian Josephus. In 2 Chronicles we see how the bargain initiated in 1 Kings came around in a full circle: Hiram gave the cities he deemed worthless back to Solomon; Solomon then turned smoke into substance by colonizing the cities with Israelites. Again, the Chronicler's major desire here is to highlight Solomon's role in building up and extending the kingdom.

Solomon also consolidated Israel's authority over the trade routes of the Near East (see comments on 1:14-17). Control had to be reestablished over Hamath Zobah, first conquered during David's reign (compare verse 3 with 1 Chronicles 18:1-9). Fortifications were added to Tadmor, an important oasis on the desert road between Israel and Mesopotamia. Two cities, Upper and Lower Beth Horon, were also rebuilt with substantial fortifications. Located northwest of Jerusalem, they guarded one of the western approaches to Jerusalem. The Chronicler singled out these projects for special mention, a handful of examples from the list of "store cities and . . . cities for his chariots and . . . horses" that Solomon had a hand in building. The general impression conveyed

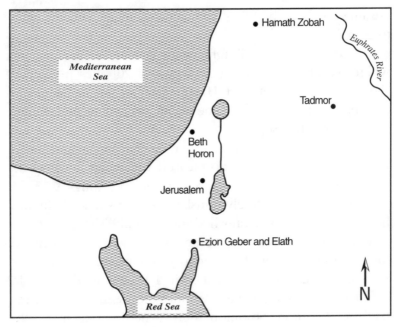

Solomon's activities

throughout is that Solomon was the kind of king who could build whatever he wanted, whenever he wanted. Thus the land enjoyed rest, and the house of the Lord was well protected during Solomon's watch.

### *The splendor of Solomon's workforce*

<sup>7</sup>**All the people left from the Hittites, Amorites, Perizzites, Hivites and Jebusites (these peoples were not Israelites), <sup>8</sup>that is, their descendants remaining in the land, whom the Israelites had not destroyed—these Solomon conscripted for his slave labor force, as it is to this day. <sup>9</sup>But Solomon did not make slaves of the Israelites for his work; they were his fighting men, commanders of his captains, and commanders of his chariots and charioteers. <sup>10</sup>They were also King Solomon's chief officials—two hundred and fifty officials supervising the men.**

Besides his work as warrior-king, David had expended a great deal of effort in organizing his kingdom for worship. The Levites had been divided up according to their families and clans and had been assigned their specific duties (1 Chronicles 23; 24:20–26:32). The priests had been organized into 24 courses to provide an orderly rotation in the officiants at daily worship (1 Chronicles 24:1-19). David also gave the army and the ruling officials their duty rosters and specific assignments (1 Chronicles 27). Our own ideas of separate spheres for "religious" and "secular" activities really did not apply to ancient Israel. In all those spheres of activity, David's motives were religious. He wanted to have a kingdom organized around the worship of the one true God.

In these and the following verses, we see how Solomon followed in his father's footsteps. He maintained the good order his father had established, and he expanded it where necessary. Solomon's assignment to the non-Israelite tribes still living in the land was, as we have already seen, to supply the work force necessary for his building projects (2:17,18). The reader is referred to comments made there for a fuller understanding of these tribes "remaining in the land."

Another reason the Chronicler mentions these people is to contrast their slavery to the glorious freedom enjoyed by the Israelites under Solomon. The Israelites, far from being Solomon's slaves, formed his military and governmental elite. In this way we again see Solomon carrying on the work of his father, using the organizational structure he had inherited. For believers of the Chronicler's era, these words would have had the effect of shoring up their courage and strength, since they now lived in much reduced circumstances. Not many noble, not many powerful—as the world counted power—were among the remnant that returned to

Israel. Yet they served their God and King. In the end, that is what made their service have priceless worth.

Undoubtedly there were also many in Israel who read these words while they themselves were serving as slaves in a foreign country. It must have thrilled them in spirit to hear of a time when Israelites, far from being slaves, had been free to serve their own king in their own land as "his fighting men, commanders of his captains, and commanders of his chariots and charioteers." In a much more profound way, the apostle Paul uses his gospel insight to transform the low status of a Christian slave into the high privilege of serving the Lord who became everyone's slave (Ephesians 6:5-8; Philippians 2:1-11).

The fact is that, because of our sinful flesh, we are still so prone to be impressed by names and titles and perquisites—all that glitters about earthly power. If, for one moment, God would cause the scales to drop from our eyes so that we could see everyone as he sees them, how strangely altered everything would seem! We might suddenly notice that aged grandmother painstakingly culling through the local newspapers for all the little triumphs recorded in them concerning children of the congregation. We would watch her as she carefully cuts them out and presents them to each child on Sunday, along with her warm smile of congratulation. Next to her we might catch a glimpse of countless thousands of others—nameless, faceless, and quite forgettable to us because all they do are the seemingly mundane tasks of life. Yet they would shine like the stars, because each one of those lives was, in fact, a faithful, daily offering of praise to Jesus. And all those who had shined so brightly before, we would barely be aware of—so unheroic, so trivial, and so earthbound their lives would seem by comparison.

## The splendor of Solomon's worship

### Purity in worship

**¹¹Solomon brought Pharaoh's daughter up from the City of David to the palace he had built for her, for he said, "My wife must not live in the palace of David king of Israel, because the places the ark of the Lᴏʀᴅ has entered are holy."**

A mark of how impressive the Lord's anointed king had become in the eyes of the surrounding heathen nations surely must be the fact that even so great a power as Egypt sat up and took notice of him. In the ancient world of power politics, nations made alliances with one another through marriage. While it is true that a ruler like Pharaoh must have had many daughters, the fact that he gave one in marriage to Solomon speaks volumes about his regard for the Israelite king and his desire to maintain friendly relations with Solomon.

For the Chronicler, however, questions of worldly honor were secondary to matters of cultic purity. He approves of Solomon's thinking it not right for a wife of his to live "in the palace of David king of Israel, because the places the ark of the Lᴏʀᴅ has entered are holy." Solomon's concern for keeping God's worship pure and undefiled matched that of his father, David. Again we see here how closely connected the king's palace was to the place of God's worship. Under his father, David, the ark had been placed very near David's house in the old city—in a spot David had prepared for it (1 Chronicles 15:1). But the two dwellings were not just part of one physical complex; they were also considered to be part of one spiritual context. If one was holy, the other was holy too; anything defiling one would defile the other.

Again, for us who grew up with a dividing wall of separation between church and state, ideas like this might be a

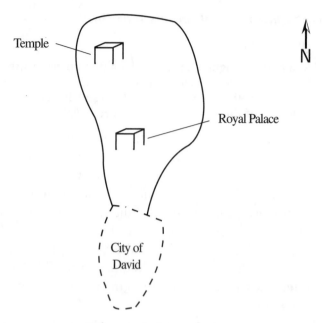

## Solomon's Jerusalem

little hard to understand at first. But we must remember that God's people Israel did not operate with the kind of division into sacred and secular which is so familiar to us. The king of Israel was, as we have seen, very much the spiritual leader of his people. His family had been chosen by God in a solemn covenant to rule not his own people but God's people. David's palace, therefore, was all part of the sacred precinct where "the ark of the LORD [had] entered." Therefore, Solomon had his wife moved from the palace to a special residence built just for her. Then the question of defilement would not arise.

Even more difficult to understand, perhaps, is the reason Pharaoh's daughter was seen as a source of defilement in the first place. The text simply gives Solomon's reason as being the fact that she was "his wife." While some have spoken of her gentile birth as being the main problem, more likely is the consideration that she was a woman. In the Law of Moses, God had made special provision for the separation and purification of women for the times when they were "unclean" (Leviticus 12). It was particularly in connection with the ark, we remember, that God had shown his wrath against David. He had not taken the proper precautions to keep the ark free from things that defile (see 1 Chronicles 13). David had learned his lesson (1 Chronicles 15:12-15), and Solomon was maintaining the concern his father had shown in keeping Israel's worship pure. Keep in mind too that people had died as a result of David's carelessness. In moving her away from the palace of David, Solomon was also showing the kind of love and care that any man should show for his wife.

We, of course, are not under laws of religious cleanliness. Yet it would be a mistake to think that God has lost interest in keeping his worship pure and undefiled. Scripture warns Christians against being defiled by hypocrisy and false doctrine (Matthew 16:12; Luke 12:1). Since we are holy people, God wants us to keep ourselves pure from giving our approval to evil deeds or from giving in to wicked thoughts. These corrupt our worship of him and render meaningless our professions of love for one another (1 Corinthians 5:5-7).

### Order in worship

**¹²On the altar of the LORD that he had built in front of the portico, Solomon sacrificed burnt offerings to the LORD, ¹³according to the daily requirement for offerings commanded by Moses for Sabbaths, New Moons and the three annual feasts—the Feast of Unleavened Bread, the Feast of Weeks and the Feast of Tabernacles. ¹⁴In keeping with the ordinance of his father David, he appointed the divisions of the priests for their duties, and the**

Levites to lead the praise and to assist the priests according to
each day's requirement. He also appointed the gatekeepers by
divisions for the various gates, because this was what David the
man of God had ordered. ¹⁵They did not deviate from the king's
commands to the priests or to the Levites in any matter, including that of the treasuries.

¹⁶All Solomon's work was carried out, from the day the foundation of the temple of the LORD was laid until its completion. So
the temple of the LORD was finished.

Solomon's worship on the great day of dedication was
not a flash in the pan. The Chronicler tells us that it was
the beginning of a regular, continuing order of worship at
the temple. Temple worship under Solomon was conducted in the *right way* ("commanded by Moses," "in
keeping with the ordinance of his father David"), at the
*right times* ("daily," "the three annual feasts"), by the
*right people* ("priests for their duties, and the Levites to
lead the praise and to assist the priests"). None of the
provisions of his father, David, were overlooked. Gatekeepers were appointed and assigned in divisions to their
various posts (verse 14; see also 1 Chronicles 26:1-19).
Even the matter of the temple treasuries received Solomon's careful attention (verse 15; see also 1 Chronicles
26:20-28). David's blueprint for worship in God's house
was faithfully carried out in every detail.

In this way Solomon fulfilled his mission in life, a mission God had given him long ago through his father,
David: "The LORD has chosen you to build a temple. . . .
Do not be afraid or discouraged, for the LORD God, my
God, is with you. He will not fail you or forsake you until
all the work for the service of the temple of the LORD is
finished" (1 Chronicles 28:10,20). God had kept his word
to his people. "The temple of the LORD was finished."
Solomon, the completer, had completed his task.

In his letter to the Ephesians, the apostle Paul gives us a "God's-eye view" of the church, that holy temple which the Son is in the process of building (Ephesians 2:21,22). We may rest assured that God's saving plans for it will not fail, since they are rooted in his will from all eternity and established by a covenant signed in the blood of his Son. This high and holy mission is carried out in time by other sons and daughters of the king. To them, in each generation, he entrusts his gospel word. It seems incredible to think, sometimes, that God could give such an important task and precious message to poor, frail sinners like you and me. Yet he does. And we don't carry out that work by staring idly into heaven (Acts 1:11). We do not bring it to completion simply by mouthing fine words and making a great fuss on a mission Sunday once a year. It will be brought to completion only through consistent and faithful service, carried out day after day by thousands upon thousands of his people. That's how it was with Solomon's temple. God has given us the vision of our goal through books like 2 Chronicles and Ephesians. He has assigned us each to our own particular post. Now he charges us to "Be strong and do the work" (1 Chronicles 28:10), certain of the power of him who will not fail us or forsake us.

### *"The wealth of the nations is his"*

**¹⁷Then Solomon went to Ezion Geber and Elath on the coast of Edom. ¹⁸And Hiram sent him ships commanded by his own officers, men who knew the sea. These, with Solomon's men, sailed to Ophir and brought back four hundred and fifty talents of gold, which they delivered to King Solomon.**

In spite of the English chapter division, it seems likely that the Chronicler intended these words to help smooth our transition from thoughts of worship to thoughts of the king. He is about to show us Solomon in all his splendor. The account of a voyage for gold looks ahead to that splendor about to be revealed. But it also casts a backward glance at a life centered on worship. You see, the last time the Chronicler mentioned gold from Ophir, he was talking about how David had amassed three thousand talents of it for use in God's house (1 Chronicles 29:4). The mention of gold also reminds us of Solomon's liberal use of it while building the temple (3:5-14).

Perhaps it is not too much to infer from this that the Chronicler is not at all interested in glorifying human beings by spinning yarns full of heroic quests, harrowing deeds, and fabulous fortunes lost and won. Instead, he's telling us about all that Solomon did for the sake of the Lord's house, and he's showing us how the Lord made Solomon great for the sake of his people Israel (9:8).

The Chronicler has already introduced Solomon to us as a merchant-prince (see 1:14-17 and commentary). We learn here that his joint ventures with Hiram branched out to the south and even launched out into the sea. He built up port and fortress facilities at Ezion Geber, located at the north end of the Gulf of Aqaba (see map on page 112). This gave Solomon access to the rich trade routes that led to Africa and southern Arabia and perhaps even extended as far as India. The name *Ophir* itself remains a puzzle; perhaps it was a puzzle also to the Chronicler's first readers. In any case it would have conveyed to them a sense of mystery and great wealth, filling them with awe as they pondered the extent of Solomon's reach in Israel's golden age.

### The queen of the south gives testimony to God's king

**9** When the queen of Sheba heard of Solomon's fame, she came to Jerusalem to test him with hard questions. Arriving with a very great caravan—with camels carrying spices, large quantities of gold, and precious stones—she came to Solomon and talked with him about all she had on her mind. ²Solomon answered all her questions; nothing was too hard for him to explain to her. ³When the queen of Sheba saw the wisdom of Solomon, as well as the palace he had built, ⁴the food on his table, the seating of his officials, the attending servants in their robes, the cupbearers in their robes and the burnt offerings he made at the temple of the LORD, she was overwhelmed.

⁵She said to the king, "The report I heard in my own country about your achievements and your wisdom is true. ⁶But I did not believe what they said until I came and saw with my own eyes. Indeed, not even half the greatness of your wisdom was told me; you have far exceeded the report I heard. ⁷How happy your men must be! How happy your officials, who continually stand before you and hear your wisdom! ⁸Praise be to the LORD your God, who has delighted in you and placed you on his throne as king to rule for the LORD your God. Because of the love of your God for Israel and his desire to uphold them forever, he has made you king over them, to maintain justice and righteousness."

⁹Then she gave the king 120 talents of gold, large quantities of spices, and precious stones. There had never been such spices as those the queen of Sheba gave to King Solomon.

¹⁰(The men of Hiram and the men of Solomon brought gold from Ophir; they also brought algumwood and precious stones. ¹¹The king used the algumwood to make steps for the temple of the LORD and for the royal palace, and to make harps and lyres for the musicians. Nothing like them had ever been seen in Judah.)

¹²King Solomon gave the queen of Sheba all she desired and asked for; he gave her more than she had brought to him. Then she left and returned with her retinue to her own country.

This remarkable chapter presents to perfection the Chronicler's idealized portrait of Solomon. Absent are any references to his many wives or to his idolatry; gone are the references to a rebellious spirit at work among nations subject to him and even among his own people Israel (1 Kings 11). Instead, we see in outline form a king who attracts the surrounding nations to the brightness of his rising (see also Isaiah 60). We see a king to whom the nations come bearing gifts yet leave taking with them more than they brought (see also Matthew 2:11; Luke 10:23,24). We see a king whose wealth, wisdom, and righteous rule put him in a class by himself (see also Isaiah 9:7). Using historical details taken from the life of Solomon, the Chronicler has, in fact, drawn his readers a picture of the Messiah-King. Though there are many parallel texts one could have used for this purpose, we will be interposing readings from one of the messianic psalms throughout this chapter's commentary, chosen because of its striking similarities.

"Since you have . . . asked for . . . wisdom . . . to govern my people . . . , wisdom . . . will be given you. And I will also give you wealth, riches and honor, such as no king who was before you ever had and none after you will have" (1:11,12). So God had promised to Solomon. And in chapter 9 we see every one of those words come true. Solomon was a king so wise in his rule, so glorious in his wealth that he defied comparison. His person and his court outstripped what had seemed at first to the queen to be nothing more than the most exaggerated rumors.

> May his name endure forever;
> > may it continue as long as the sun.
> > > (Psalm 72:17)

The queen of Sheba herself came from no underprivileged country. Located on the southern tip of the Arabian

Solomon and the Queen of Sheba

peninsula, Sheba was a land far more happy in its prospects than those areas of the arid interior. Through shrewd management of trade, Sheba had become famous for its wealth in gold, spices, and aromatic resins. Whether the queen had come in part to make a trade deal with Solomon is at best only grist for the mill of scholarly speculation. What is certain is that she had heard in her own country about Solomon's "achievements and . . . wisdom," and had been willing to make the long, hard journey to find out if what she heard was true. It is this willingness of hers that Jesus used as a striking point of contrast to the Pharisees' stubbornness in his own time. She had come "from the ends of the earth" to give Solomon a fair hearing. The Pharisees shut their ears to one in their own midst, even though he was far greater than Solomon (Matthew 12:42).

What she witnessed left her breathless in amazement. Altering Julius Caesar's words slightly, we could say of her, *"Venit, vidit, victa est*—She came, she saw, she was conquered." None of her searching questions caused Solomon any difficulty at all. She saw how his mind had given birth to beauty and order, to abundance among his people, and to splendor in his offerings to God. She gave her testimony, "Praise be to the LORD your God, who has delighted in you and placed you on his throne as king to rule for the LORD your God. Because of the love of your God for Israel and his desire to uphold them forever, he has made you king over them, to maintain justice and righteousness."

We notice how her praise is centered not on Solomon, but on Solomon's God. The kingdom is the Lord's (see 1 Chronicles 28:5; 29:11)! It is *his* throne and *his* rule. Solomon, as it were, acted only as God's regent. It is a mark of God's love for Israel that he chose someone like Solomon to act as his representative. God's purpose for Israel in sending this king was to uphold his people forever and to create through Solomon a dominion in which what is right and just prevails. At a time when the house of David was collapsing under the weight of its own sin—and bringing Judah down with it—Jeremiah foresaw a time when the Lord would "raise up to David a righteous Branch, a King who will reign wisely and do what is just and right in the land. In his days Judah will be saved and Israel will live in safety. This is the name by which he will be called: The LORD Our Righteousness" (Jeremiah 23:5,6).

Every dream a person has ever had to create a heaven here on earth has ended in the most dismal failure. More than just failures, some of the worst horrors of this century have been perpetrated in the hope of making a new society, a place where human dreams of justice and equity might prevail. Ask the living skeletons that crept out of concentration camps just how righteous Hitler's Thousand-Year Reich was. Pause awhile at the mass graves where millions of Stalin's victims lie buried, murdered for the Workers' Paradise. Even lesser hopes of merely holding back chaos and setting limits to evil have come at the price of many fields where "poppies grow, between the crosses, row on row." It is enough to make us run for cover anytime someone stands up for "the people" to make promises he'll never keep. It is enough to make us hang our heads in complete despair.

But the kingdom is still the Lord's. He still walks through the corridors of power, accomplishing his purposes. He still urges us to pray for the good of these shantytowns we find ourselves living in while we wait in exile here (Jeremiah 29:7). Far more than this: he *has* sent us the righteous King, him of whom the Chronicler and Jeremiah wrote. He came with such a hidden glory—gentle, and riding on a donkey. His throne on earth was a rough wooden cross.

When he held court on Golgotha, he looked out at hundreds who were abusing him, dozens who stood appalled, and one dying thief who believed in him. But by his death he removed our sin and all its wretched consequences. He won for us a place in that city where death is abolished, evil is removed, and God's own splendor is all the light we'll ever need (Revelation 21).

> He will judge your people in righteousness,
>> your afflicted ones with justice.
>
> The mountains will bring prosperity to the people,
>> the hills the fruit of righteousness.
>
> He will defend the afflicted among the people
>> and save the children of the needy;
>> he will crush the oppressor.
>
> He will rescue them from oppression and
>> violence,
>> for precious is their blood in his sight.
>
> All nations will be blessed through him,
>> and they will call him blessed.
>
> (Psalm 72:2-4,14,17)

## *Summary of Solomon's wealth*

¹³The weight of the gold that Solomon received yearly was 666 talents, ¹⁴not including the revenues brought in by merchants and traders. Also all the kings of Arabia and the governors of the land brought gold and silver to Solomon.

¹⁵King Solomon made two hundred large shields of hammered gold; six hundred bekas of hammered gold went into each shield. ¹⁶He also made three hundred small shields of hammered gold, with three hundred bekas of gold in each shield. The king put them in the Palace of the Forest of Lebanon.

¹⁷Then the king made a great throne inlaid with ivory and overlaid with pure gold. ¹⁸The throne had six steps, and a foot-

stool of gold was attached to it. On both sides of the seat were armrests, with a lion standing beside each of them. ¹⁹Twelve lions stood on the six steps, one at either end of each step. Nothing like it had ever been made for any other kingdom. ²⁰All King Solomon's goblets were gold, and all the household articles in the Palace of the Forest of Lebanon were pure gold. Nothing was made of silver, because silver was considered of little value in Solomon's day. ²¹The king had a fleet of trading ships manned by Hiram's men. Once every three years it returned, carrying gold, silver and ivory, and apes and baboons.

²²King Solomon was greater in riches and wisdom than all the other kings of the earth. ²³All the kings of the earth sought audience with Solomon to hear the wisdom God had put in his heart. ²⁴Year after year, everyone who came brought a gift—articles of silver and gold, and robes, weapons and spices, and horses and mules.

²⁵Solomon had four thousand stalls for horses and chariots, and twelve thousand horses, which he kept in the chariot cities and also with him in Jerusalem. ²⁶He ruled over all the kings from the River to the land of the Philistines, as far as the border of Egypt. ²⁷The king made silver as common in Jerusalem as stones, and cedar as plentiful as sycamore-fig trees in the foothills. ²⁸Solomon's horses were imported from Egypt and from all other countries.

The clear emphasis here is on Solomon's tremendous wealth. With loving care the Chronicler dwells on enumerating the king's riches, trying to give us a sense of them through a wealth of detail and repetition. The word *gold*, for example, is repeated 13 times. In addition, some of the vocabulary the Chronicler uses conveys a touch of the exotic. The words for "apes" and "baboons" in verse 21 are found so seldom in ancient Hebrew literature that translators are unsure how to render them. In the previous section, the word for the algumwood imported to Israel also fits into this same category. It was so rare that the Hebrews had no word for it; the word they used came from another language. Far-off lands and distant places are also suggested by the phrase "ships that could go to Tarshish" (see NIV footnote, verse 21). Tarshish was in Spain, the farthest destination imaginable to an ancient Israelite.

Besides his vocabulary, the Chronicler has other devices that he uses to put across the idea of Solomon's fabulous wealth. Consider his discussion of how the king displayed his treasure. He had decorative shields made, large ones out of beaten gold and smaller ones with gold plating. He built an extraordinarily ornate ivory throne, and he even had his ordinary household articles and drinking cups made from gold. In a reversal of the proverb, it seems that most of what glittered in Solomon's kingdom *was* gold. The quantities involved are emphasized both numerically and comparatively. Such was the prosperity in Jerusalem that silver became "as common . . . as stones," even losing its status as a precious metal. Finally, the Chronicler points to the various sources of Solomon's riches. Far from being tied to a single cash cow, some of Solomon's wealth came from his own trading ventures, some came from tariffs he imposed on merchants who used the major trade routes that crisscrossed the land, and the rest came from gifts and tribute.

In all of this, one of the Chronicler's major points is to show the rich blessings that come to God's people when king and people are united in a pursuit of righteousness. To put it somewhat differently, this picture of a golden age is not intended to evoke nostalgia but rather to inspire the zeal for righteousness in people who knew much poorer circumstances. When times are hard, earthly concerns have a way of crowding out things that are truly important. "Seek first the kingdom of God," the Chronicler is saying, "and all these other things will be added unto you."

> He will be like rain falling on a mown field,
>> like showers watering the earth.
> In his days the righteous will flourish;
>> prosperity will abound till the moon is no
>> more.
> Long may he live!
>> May gold from Sheba be given him.
> May people ever pray for him
>> and bless him all day long.
> Let grain abound throughout the land;
>> on the tops of the hills may it sway.
> Let its fruit flourish like Lebanon;
>> let it thrive like the grass of the field.
> (Psalm 72:6,7,15,16)

"King Solomon was greater in riches and wisdom than all the other kings of the earth. He ruled over all the kings from the River to the land of the Philistines, as far as the border of Egypt." More than any other, these two verses sum up the essence of the Chronicler's message here. Solomon, the king who built the temple, was supreme: supreme in wealth, supreme in wisdom, supreme in power. There was no other king who could compare, not only in Israel but in all the earth. He had brought the boundaries of the Promised Land to their ideal limits, as spoken of by God to Abram so many years before: "The LORD made a covenant with Abram and said, 'To your descendants I give this land, from the river of Egypt to the great river, the Euphrates'" (Genesis 15:18). By descriptions like these, the Chronicler kept his people's hope alive that one day the Messiah would come.

> He will rule from sea to sea
>> and from the River to the ends of the earth.

> May his name endure forever;
>> may it continue as long as the sun.
> All nations will be blessed through him,
>> and they will call him blessed.
>
> (Psalm 72:8,17)

### *Some concluding reflections on the Chronicler's picture of Israel's ideal king*

The completed picture of Solomon now takes its place in the gallery where the Chronicler's paintings of the good kings of Israel are shown. David's is the only other likeness hanging there so far. These first two will always have pride of place. None that come after will ever be able to match them in sharpness of detail and depth of treatment. Some will qualify only to have portions of their lives commemorated on these walls, while others will not make it at all. From this point on, the Chronicler will be measuring the other kings in terms of the qualities he has shown us in David and Solomon: Are they faithful to the law of the Lord? Do they honor and uphold the ministries of the prophets, priests, and Levites? Are they faithful to the worship of the one true God at his house, and do they lead Israel to join them in that worship? Those who do will be blessed, as Solomon and David were. Those who don't will quickly learn the hard way that God is not mocked.

Yet what can we say about the picture of the Messiah that we have seen foreshadowed in these two kings? Perhaps some of you have been wondering how so earthly a picture can correspond to so spiritual a King. In fact, if given a little thought, many of the details seem to be the direct opposite of the "reality . . . found in Christ" (Colossians 2:17). Solomon was wealthy beyond compare and lived his life in fabulous luxury. But what do we see in Jesus? He said of himself,

"Foxes have holes and birds of the air have nests, but the Son of Man has no place to lay his head" (Luke 9:58).

Jesus' words, even though they brought amazement to his fellow townsmen, brought very few of them to faith (Luke 4:22-30). He was considered wise by many for a time; yet the majority, in the end, "turned back and no longer followed him." The wisdom he spoke was too hard to hear (John 6:60,66). And more often than not, his message evoked the fury of his listeners rather than their admiration. His followers were not the mighty, the noble, the wealthy, the wise. Fisherfolk and tax collectors, former prostitutes and common people made up his loyal band. We could say he had a rich man's grave, like Solomon's, but only after he had suffered a slave's death on a cross.

We must remember that the Old Testament was a time when God treated his people like children and minors (Galatians 3:23,24; 4:1). This is just another way of saying that he accommodated himself to a way of thinking that was still immature, not fully developed. He worked through the formal, outward structures of a visible, earthly kingdom. He worked with a nation that was defined by race as well as by faith, a nation with its own particular land, its own God-given kings, customs, worship, and code of laws.

To say this, however, is not to say that the people did not yearn for a spiritual Savior or that they did not put their trust in the Promised One, who would bring them freedom from sin and death. The picture we have in Solomon and David is not the only picture of the Messiah we get in the Old Testament. God also told them about a Suffering Servant, one who would have no beauty or majesty to attract people to himself, one who would die alone and abandoned (Psalm 22; Isaiah 53). All this leads to the point that God's Old Testament people were saved in precisely the same way we are (John 8:56).

Nevertheless, we can learn from the Chronicler's presentation of David and Solomon that people before the coming of our Lord often spoke and thought of New Testament realities in Old Testament terms. When Christ came, not only Israel's language but all tongues were transformed, and the whole world's normal way of thinking turned upside down. Then, by the Spirit, we came to understand fully the truth of God's wisdom, a wisdom that seems like foolishness to humans. We came to see by faith a power overwhelmed by apparent weakness. We were moved by a beauty in our Savior that we saw precisely *then,* when his face was marred most cruelly by suffering. In short, by grace, through faith, we fully grasped the beauty, the power, and the wisdom of the cross (1 Corinthians 1,2).

These ancient pictures are also meant to tell us, just as the Chronicler intended them to tell his own people, that the best is yet to come. The promises have not yet come true in all their perfection, not, at least, in a way that we can see now. But one day we will. Jesus will return not as the Suffering Servant but as the Lord of glory. He will drive away the shadows that cloud our vision, pull away the shroud that covers mankind, and put an end to death's gloomy reign. Then every knee will bow to him and every tongue will confess him as Lord. "Of the increase of his government and peace there will be no end. He will reign on David's throne . . . establishing and upholding it with justice and righteousness . . . forever" (Isaiah 9:7).

### Solomon's death

**²⁹As for the other events of Solomon's reign, from beginning to end, are they not written in the records of Nathan the prophet, in the prophecy of Ahijah the Shilonite and in the visions of Iddo the seer concerning Jeroboam son of Nebat?**

**³⁰Solomon reigned in Jerusalem over all Israel forty years. ³¹Then he rested with his fathers and was buried in the city of David his father. And Rehoboam his son succeeded him as king.**

Here is one more stark reminder that Solomon was not yet the perfect fulfillment of the righteous King promised by God. "Solomon reigned . . . forty years. Then he rested with his fathers and was buried." This is where his story ends, until the One who was crucified, died, was buried, and rose again returns.

Here we also notice the difference in Israel's history from the histories of all other nations. Histories of the Greeks were written by the curious or by the politically savvy. Histories of the Romans were written by noble Roman senators. Modern histories are written by noted scholars. But the annals of Israel were written by prophets and seers. They not only saw what happened; they understood what it meant.

---

# PART FOUR

## God Preserves His Kingdom in Judah until the Return from Exile
(10:1–36:23)

### God's kingdom under Rehoboam

All along the Chronicler has shown himself as being aware that there was another side to the stories of David and Solomon besides the one he has given us. He has deliberately depicted them in their ideal forms to help his reader see the coming Messiah in their shape. He demonstrated, for example, how God was with Solomon until his mission was accomplished—"from the day the foundation of the temple of the LORD was laid until its completion" (8:16). However, he may well mean to imply with those same words his awareness that once Solomon had completed his mission, his heart began to grow cold toward his Lord. Certainly, as he tells the story of Rehoboam, the Chronicler expects the reader to be aware of the less positive facts from Solomon's later life. Not the least of these was the activity of Jeroboam.

The Chronicler assumes that we already know some details about Jeroboam's relationship to Solomon (see 10:2). First Kings tells us that Jeroboam had been one of Solomon's officials, "put . . . in charge of the whole labor force" of the northern tribes (1 Kings 11:28). Himself a man from the north, he was once met on a journey by Ahijah the prophet (the same man mentioned in 10:15). Ahijah told him that he would one

135

day become ruler of the ten northern tribes, leaving the house of David with only two (1 Kings 11:26-39). It seems that Jeroboam tried to exercise power before Solomon's death (13:6). His bid for the throne, however, was premature, and he was forced to run for his life to Egypt (1 Kings 11:40).

### Pride goes before a fall: the northern tribes rebel

**10** Rehoboam went to Shechem, for all the Israelites had gone there to make him king. ²When Jeroboam son of Nebat heard this (he was in Egypt, where he had fled from King Solomon), he returned from Egypt. ³So they sent for Jeroboam, and he and all Israel went to Rehoboam and said to him: ⁴"Your father put a heavy yoke on us, but now lighten the harsh labor and the heavy yoke he put on us, and we will serve you."

⁵Rehoboam answered, "Come back to me in three days." So the people went away.

That all is not well in the kingdom is signaled already by the fact that Rehoboam had to go to Shechem because "all the Israelites had gone there to make him king." Shechem was an ancient city with roots that went deep into the covenant history of God's people. There Abraham first received the promise, "To your offspring I will give this land" (Genesis 12:7). There Joshua renewed with Israel the solemn covenant of Sinai, according to specific provisions laid down in Deuteronomy (Joshua 24; Deuteronomy 11:26-30). All Israel had been willing to go down to Hebron to make David king (1 Chronicles 11:1-3). But they wanted David's grandson Rehoboam to come to them at Shechem, evidently as a reminder that they were willing to serve a king who ruled by covenant but not a tyrant who did as he pleased.

Here we first meet Jeroboam, who had returned from Egypt after Solomon's death to take part in the negotiations.

This too ought to have served to caution Rehoboam that the people were restless. Their grievance was that the king's yoke had grown too heavy for them to bear. As we have already noted, Solomon had put in place some kind of system of national service for Israel (see commentary on 2:17, page 40). He had not enslaved them, as the Chronicler also makes clear (8:9). Yet the people were feeling worn out by the system, just as Samuel had predicted they would (1 Samuel 8:11-18). The burden of taxation (1 Kings 4:7,22-28) coupled with the king's demands for labor seemed too high a price to pay for stability.

The Israelites were careful enough in the way they phrased their request. They made no threat to revolt if they didn't get their way (although it shouldn't have been too difficult for Rehoboam to read between the lines). They only asked Rehoboam to lighten their load. Rehoboam asked for some time to frame a reply, thus creating the expectation that he would give their request serious consideration.

**⁶Then King Rehoboam consulted the elders who had served his father Solomon during his lifetime. "How would you advise me to answer these people?" he asked.**
**⁷They replied, "If you will be kind to these people and please them and give them a favorable answer, they will always be your servants."**
**⁸But Rehoboam rejected the advice the elders gave him and consulted the young men who had grown up with him and were serving him. ⁹He asked them, "What is your advice? How should we answer these people who say to me, 'Lighten the yoke your father put on us'?"**
**¹⁰The young men who had grown up with him replied, "Tell the people who have said to you, 'Your father put a heavy yoke on us, but make our yoke lighter'—tell them, 'My little finger is thicker than my father's waist. ¹¹My father laid on you a**

**heavy yoke; I will make it even heavier. My father scourged
you with whips; I will scourge you with scorpions.'"**

"The way of a fool seems right to him, but a wise man
listens to advice" (Proverbs 12:15). Rehoboam could scarcely
stand in greater contrast to his father Solomon nor be more
complete a fool than he appears in this chapter. Solomon
had made it his first priority to seek the Lord, and when the
Lord promised to give him whatever he wished, Solomon
asked for wisdom. Rehoboam, however, has it all figured
out. He consults with two groups, the young and the old.
He's looking for the kind of advice in which people tell you
what you want to hear and confirm you in your own opinion, even if it might bring about disaster. The old men give
him good advice, but they tell him what he does not want
to hear. The young men, his peers in age, have a better
understanding of what Rehoboam wants but a much poorer
grasp on what the situation calls for. In contrast to the plain-
spoken comments of the elders, the young men's advice is
rich in rhetorical polish—the type that might appeal to a
king—but turns out to be empty-headed bombast. A "scor-
pion" is a whip with metal teeth, used for punishing the
lowest type of criminal. To threaten this kind of punishment
is not exactly good diplomacy.

We might pause here for a moment to reflect on our
own natures. How hard it is for us to humble ourselves
to ask for advice! And once we get it, how hard it is to
follow good advice, especially if it reveals to us something about ourselves we'd rather not know. It's easy to
see the foolishness of Rehoboam. For 40 years as crown
prince, he had been chomping at the bit for his share of
power, while living under his father's rule. Some of his
friends inflated his ego and tickled his ears with words
that told him how he could top his old man and show

everybody who's boss. What the old men said must have sounded like platitudes he had heard a dozen times before: "A gentle answer turns away wrath" (Proverbs 15:1). "Yeah, right!" youth says, "How can you old guys teach me anything?"

It's easy enough to see the foolishness of Rehoboam; it's a good deal harder to see our own. How often do we only pretend to ask for advice, when what we *really* want is for people to confirm us in our own desires? How easily we find reasons to discount someone else's helpful comments, all because they make us confront the sinful flaws in our own souls. How strong our walls of defense become, built up by self-love and complacency: "That can't be right; that's just not true." A word of warning is in place for us too as we remember what our Savior says about the person who builds on sand as opposed to the one who builds on the rock of his Word (Matthew 7:24-27). The only way we can ever be open to God's wisdom is when we first learn to despair of our own.

<sup>12</sup>**Three days later Jeroboam and all the people returned to Rehoboam, as the king had said, "Come back to me in three days." <sup>13</sup>The king answered them harshly. Rejecting the advice of the elders, <sup>14</sup>he followed the advice of the young men and said, "My father made your yoke heavy; I will make it even heavier. My father scourged you with whips; I will scourge you with scorpions." <sup>15</sup>So the king did not listen to the people, for this turn of events was from God, to fulfill the word the LORD had spoken to Jeroboam son of Nebat through Ahijah the Shilonite.**

<sup>16</sup>**When all Israel saw that the king refused to listen to them, they answered the king:**

> **"What share do we have in David,**
> **what part in Jesse's son?**
> **To your tents, O Israel!**
> **Look after your own house, O David!"**

**So all the Israelites went home. ¹⁷But as for the Israelites who were living in the towns of Judah, Rehoboam still ruled over them.**

The proverb we quoted earlier about the soft answer goes on to say that "a harsh word stirs up anger" (Proverbs 15:1). We can see the whole truth of that illustrated here. Instead of a judicious reply or some well-chosen words showing how carefully the king had considered their request, the expectant throng hears the nonsense that the young men had cooked up. The people in turn have a reply of their own to give. It is Israel's standard call to revolt: "To your tents, O Israel!" (see 2 Samuel 20:1). It too is framed with some care as a poetic reversal of a stirring profession of loyalty David once heard (1 Chronicles 12:18):

| | |
|---|---|
| "We are yours, O David! | "What share do we have in David, |
| We are with you, O son of Jesse! | what part in Jesse's son? |
| Success, success to you, and success to those who help you, | To your tents, O Israel! |
| for your God will help you." | Look after your own house, O David!"¹⁰ |

By the Lord's mercy, even though the majority of the northern tribes "went home," the kingdom of David was not consumed, and at least part of the northern tribes remained loyal to David's house. "But as for the Israelites who were living in the towns of Judah, Rehoboam still ruled over them."

Before moving on, our eyes are arrested by some words we read in verse 15: "This turn of events was from God, to fulfill the word the LORD had spoken to Jeroboam son of Nebat through Ahijah the Shilonite." All along this has been the Lord's doing! "But," we want to ask, "hasn't it been the result of Rehoboam's foolishness, depicted so vividly here? Didn't it happen because Israel had grown tired of the demands of its king? Doesn't some of the blame also belong to Jeroboam, who took advantage of the situation (see 13:7)?" "Yes, to all three questions," the Chronicler would answer, "and it was the Lord who ruled over it all." God's intent was to "humble David's descendants" (1 Kings 11:39). In particular, God had in mind to humble the current occupant of the throne, who when asked to rule as a king under covenant had haughtily asserted the rights of a tyrant.

**¹⁸King Rehoboam sent out Adoniram, who was in charge of forced labor, but the Israelites stoned him to death. King Rehoboam, however, managed to get into his chariot and escape to Jerusalem. ¹⁹So Israel has been in rebellion against the house of David to this day.**

While still at Shechem, Rehoboam committed one more blunder that nearly cost him his life. Completely misreading the seriousness of the situation, he sent out the leader of his national service, Adoniram, as if nothing had happened. Provoked by the king's casual indifference, the Israelites stoned the man. The king himself was forced to get back to Jerusalem as fast as his chariot would take him. The last sentence in verse 18 has more than a touch of irony to it. The king was a fool who would not take good advice. He talked tough but acted weak. The only time Rehoboam seemed resolute was when it came time to run back home.

Although Rehoboam had acted foolishly, he was still the Lord's anointed. That is the force of the Chronicler's final remark of the chapter. No matter how you cut it, the house of David was the house God had chosen to rule his people. He might have humbled them for a time by permitting the Jeroboams of this world to rule. The occupants of David's throne might have been utterly faithless to the Lord and undeserving. Yet God's grace had always been the determining factor in the choice of David and his successors (1 Chronicles 17), and man's faithlessness could not nullify God's promises (Romans 3:3,4). That is why Israel, that is, the ten tribes of the north, was in a state of rebellion ever since that time, as far as the Chronicler was concerned.

Unlike 1 and 2 Kings, from here on out the Chronicler will not give us a drama with two screens running side by side, the one showing Judah, the other showing Israel. Since the house of David is the only legitimate ruling house, it is only the kingdom of Judah that will be featured here. Our writer does not mean to imply by this that God has ceased to care about the ten tribes to the north—far from it! Again and again he will point out that Judah is inhabited not only by the tribes of Judah and Benjamin but by Israelites from the north as well. Verse 17 of the previous section is a prime example of this.

For the Chronicler it is not an issue of tribe nor even a matter of his national spirit triumphing over regional interests, as some have suggested. For the Chronicler the only questions worth asking are "Which ruling house has God chosen to rule over Israel forever?" and "Where is the dwelling place of God located and the city God has chosen?" He has spent the bulk of his book so far in establishing David's house and the temple in Jerusalem as the answers to those two questions. He's not about to change his mind on these points.

*Applying these verses to ourselves*

What an excellent story for the head of a household to tell his family around the supper table in a family devotion! You could combine it with the Fourth Commandment. You could talk about the need to respect elders and to listen to good advice. You could talk about the rivalry that sometimes exists between old and young because of sinful pride. You could talk about how headstrong and foolish we all often are and how we show it when we don't ask God first what he thinks or talk to him in prayer. But above all, tell the story! And don't forget to remind everyone of another king who, unlike Rehoboam, spoke the soft word of forgiveness in the face of man's anger (Luke 23:34). Don't forget to tell them of the One who invites all the weary and burdened to find rest in him. His yoke is easy; his burden is light (Matthew 11:28-30).

Those a little older might meditate on this story and consider the hidden yet glorious way God works his will through it all; people's rebelliousness, foolishness, and faithlessness do not overrule the plans of our God. And he is our God. His glory hidden on Calvary is proof enough of that. When our life appears to come apart at the seams, we can place ourselves with confidence into the hands of the master. He is at work in all things for our good.

**11** **When Rehoboam arrived in Jerusalem, he mustered the house of Judah and Benjamin—a hundred and eighty thousand fighting men—to make war against Israel and to regain the kingdom for Rehoboam.**

**²But this word of the LORD came to Shemaiah the man of God: ³"Say to Rehoboam son of Solomon king of Judah and to all the Israelites in Judah and Benjamin, ⁴"This is what the LORD says: Do not go up to fight against your brothers. Go home, every one of you, for this is my doing.'" So they obeyed**

**the words of the LORD and turned back from marching against Jeroboam.**

A king humiliated is a king who wants war, if he is in any way able to fight. It is not hard for us to understand the anger that moved Rehoboam to call out the troops. He wanted to regain his pride in battle and remove the injury of having over half of his kingdom taken away. What is more difficult to grasp is his immediate willingness to call the whole thing off at the word of a prophet. The fact that he *did* shows that he had learned at least something from the whole affair at Shechem. We can speculate about all kinds of less worthy motives, but the Chronicler's evaluation of Rehoboam's first three years (see 11:17) leads us to believe that God's Word through Shemaiah carried weight with both the king and his troops.

Shemaiah pointedly called Rehoboam the "king of *Judah*," in effect telling him of his new status. At the same time he reminded the king—and his troops—that Judah was more than just a tribal designation. According to Shemaiah, there were many "Israelites" who also had made their home in the territory of Judah. Most powerful were Shemaiah's two statements, "Do not go up to fight against your brothers. . . . This is my doing." The latter phrase confirmed Ahijah the Shilonite's message. The Lord had spoken; he would not change his mind. This was his final word on the matter. The former phrase reminded king and army what their anger and sense of injured pride was about to lead them into—civil war! These were not God's enemies they were fighting. These were their brothers. How could they hope for the Lord's help in such a cause? Demonstrating themselves truly wise, they went back home.

There are few things so dangerous as injured pride. Blood runs high, fists are clenched, faces twist with rage, and spiteful words are spoken. You see it all the time, everywhere you go: as you're driving, in the store, at the beach. It seems sometimes as if all the insulation has worn off the wiring of the world; we're shorting and sparking all over the place. It happens in families; it happens at work; it can even happen in the church—among those who call one another brothers and sisters. The lust for revenge can dress itself in many righteous-looking rags: "Our cause is just!" "They're just plain wrong!" "Look at what they did to me!" The lust for revenge comes in many costumes but remains the same beast.

For those who might still be stopped with a word, the apostle says, "Be kind and compassionate to one another, forgiving each other, just as in Christ God forgave you" (Ephesians 4:32). For those who might still be inclined to go their own way, he says, "If you keep on biting and devouring each other, watch out or you will be destroyed by each other" (Galatians 5:15).

### *True Israel rallies around the Lord*

*Rehoboam blessed for early faithfulness*

⁵Rehoboam lived in Jerusalem and built up towns for defense in Judah: ⁶Bethlehem, Etam, Tekoa, ⁷Beth Zur, Soco, Adullam, ⁸Gath, Mareshah, Ziph, ⁹Adoraim, Lachish, Azekah, ¹⁰Zorah, Aijalon and Hebron. These were fortified cities in Judah and Benjamin. ¹¹He strengthened their defenses and put commanders in them, with supplies of food, olive oil and wine. ¹²He put shields and spears in all the cities, and made them very strong. So Judah and Benjamin were his.

¹³The priests and Levites from all their districts throughout Israel sided with him. ¹⁴The Levites even abandoned their pasturelands and property, and came to Judah and Jerusalem because Jeroboam and his sons had rejected them as priests of

the LORD. [15]And he appointed his own priests for the high places and for the goat and calf idols he had made. [16]Those from every tribe of Israel who set their hearts on seeking the LORD, the God of Israel, followed the Levites to Jerusalem to offer sacrifices to the LORD, the God of their fathers. [17]They strengthened the kingdom of Judah and supported Rehoboam son of Solomon three years, walking in the ways of David and Solomon during this time.

[18]Rehoboam married Mahalath, who was the daughter of David's son Jerimoth and of Abihail, the daughter of Jesse's son Eliab. [19]She bore him sons: Jeush, Shemariah and Zaham. [20]Then he married Maacah daughter of Absalom, who bore him Abijah, Attai, Ziza and Shelomith. [21]Rehoboam loved Maacah daughter of Absalom more than any of his other wives and concubines. In all, he had eighteen wives and sixty concubines, twenty-eight sons and sixty daughters.

[22]Rehoboam appointed Abijah son of Maacah to be the chief prince among his brothers, in order to make him king. [23]He acted wisely, dispersing some of his sons throughout the districts of Judah and Benjamin, and to all the fortified cities. He gave them abundant provisions and took many wives for them.

That virtue has its rewards was far more than a cliché to the Chronicler. Because Rehoboam swallowed his pride, listened to the prophet of God, and called off the civil war, he was able, by God's blessing, to build up the strength of his house and his kingdom. It is also likely that the Chronicler was making a subtle comparison between the two first kings of a now-divided Israel. We note that the description of Rehoboam's success here matches—almost point for point— the account of Jeroboam in 1 Kings. If Jeroboam had some success in building cities (1 Kings 12:25), Rehoboam surpassed him (2 Chronicles 11:5-12). If Jeroboam had a disastrous impact on his kingdom's religious life, his sin, in turn, led directly to a strengthening of true worship in the kingdom of Judah (compare 1 Kings 12:25-33 with 2 Chronicles 11:13-17). Finally, if Jeroboam suffered loss in the size of his family, Rehoboam's family increased dramatically (compare 1 Kings 14:10-14 with 2 Chronicles 11:18-21).[11] Of course, this entire interpretation rests on the thought that the Chronicler could assume his readers were familiar with 1 Kings.

Whether this was in the mind of the Chronicler is hard to prove. What seems far more certain is that in all of his characterizations of the kings of Judah, he is presenting concrete examples of the two "ways" described for us in Psalm 1. The righteous man prospers; the wicked man does not (Psalm 1:3,4). While the Lord watches over the way of the righteous, the way of the wicked will perish (Psalm 1:6). Rehoboam obeyed God's Word. That is why he prospered (see Introduction: Immediate blessings and punishments, page 8).

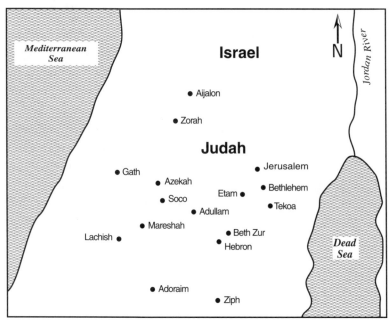

Rehoboam's fortified cities

Rehoboam's fortifications were a remarkable achievement in themselves. We can learn a great deal just by looking at a map of their placement in the kingdom.

The first thing we notice is how contracted the kingdom's borders are when compared to the expansive days of David and Solomon. This is very much a defensive posture. Rehoboam is fortifying only the heartland against an enemy that might approach from the south, east, or west. Students of ancient roads and trading routes inform us that these cities all guard strategic passes leading up into the Judean hills.[12]

The reason for this posture will become evident in the following chapter. David and Solomon had presided over a world in which both Egypt and the city-states of Mesopotamia were relatively weak. Toward the end of Solomon's rule, however, the situation changed dramatically. Sheshonq (called Shishak in our text) managed to gain control of both upper and lower Egypt, founding a new dynasty. He was unable to do much to Israel while Solomon was still alive, except to annoy him by giving political asylum to his rivals (1 Kings 11:14-40). But the man had ambition, and one of the ways ancient rulers satisfied their ambition for wealth was to mount expeditions of pillage and conquest. Once Solomon was out of the way and his kingdom was divided, it didn't take a doctorate in ancient political science to figure out where Shishak might want to throw his weight around. Rehoboam was using his head in falling back to defensible borders. That he was also anticipating siege warfare seems clear from the supplies he laid in store.

Rehoboam's second trophy of success was a revival of national religious life, brought about by Jeroboam's abandoning of the proper worship of the Lord. So disinterested is the Chronicler in the royal doings up north that he does not even mention Jeroboam's coronation as king of Israel. The only way we learn from him that Jeroboam has become king is by this reference to Jeroboam's revamping of religion, a measure meant to consolidate his hold on the Northern Kingdom. Since this is our first encounter with it in 2 Chronicles, a closer look at the so-called "sin of Jeroboam" (1 Kings 12:30; 15:26) would be beneficial.

First, Jeroboam set up two calf idols to prevent his people from going south to Jerusalem to worship the Lord. Jeroboam feared that, once there, his people might be tempted to transfer their affections to Rehoboam (1 Kings 12:26-29). The calves' selling point for his own people was that they offered a more convenient and accessible way to worship the God of Israel.

It is hard to believe that they were meant to be actual representations of the Lord. More than likely Jeroboam borrowed the idea from the Canaanite practice of using the backs of bulls as pedestals upon which to put the idol images of their gods. He did, however, exercise a little restraint by putting no image of the Lord on top of his calves. It was a distinction without much of a difference; he was still content to allow the people to imagine—in their own separate ways—what ought to be filling in that blank space. It is doubtful whether many even bothered after a time. The more they got used to it, the more they would just call the calf idol "Lord."

Either way, this was not God hidden deep within a Holy of Holies, behind doors and walls and a welter of restrictions. This was God brought out into the open. And so convenient too! Who needed Jerusalem when they had their own shrines so much closer? It is from the Chronicler that we learn that Jeroboam also instituted a form of goat worship. The only other certain reference in Scripture that we have to goat idols is the prohibition we find against it in Leviticus 17:7. We know nothing about what its worship entailed, although perhaps the Latin word used long ago to translate the Hebrew might give us a sense of it. Saint Jerome chose *daemon* (demon) to render it for his readers. In any case, it went beyond calf worship by deliberately representing a god in the form of a beast.

Not satisfied with this, Jeroboam wanted his own pet priests. When there is no real distinction or separation between religion and the state, it is important for a political leader (if he has no fear of God) to be able to control those who claim to connect with the divine side of things. Having the tribe of Levi in his midst must have made Jeroboam feel like his country was threatened by a fifth column. Their loyalties lay in Jerusalem. They would still be going to Jerusalem to serve during their allotted times. "That will never do," thought Jeroboam. So he "appointed his own priests."

In the end, the essence of idolatry is to make God more manageable somehow. This is not to say that unbelievers don't like their mysteries or that they don't come up with profound ways of speaking to humanity's fears and longings. They will contrive religious demands that are more than a little rigorous and gods that are more than a little frightening. The difference, however, remains in that a false god is someone with whom people can make deals. With the true God, that is not an option. Pagans don't claim that their gods come through for them every time, but they feel they can at least expect *something,* if they make enough sacrifices, say enough prayers, and prove themselves worthy.

With the true God, there are no deals, except the non-negotiable demands he makes in his law. With God there are no deals, except the unconditional promise he makes in his gospel. People by nature want nothing to do with the God who says, "I will have mercy on whom I will have mercy, and I will have compassion on whom I will have compassion" (Exodus 33:19). To trust such a God means to abandon all thoughts of controlling him or manipulating him.

In all this we cannot forget that the Chronicler's reference to Jeroboam has been no more than an afterthought. He simply assumed that a few words would give his readers the picture. His main desire has always been to show how Jeroboam's transgression translated into spiritual riches for Judah. Jeroboam's religious measures caused an exodus of priests and Levites. Even the natural hold "their pasturelands and property" might have exerted on them did not prevent them from leaving all behind to answer a higher, spiritual call. Zeal for the Lord's house compelled them (just as the love of Christ compels us). In Judah and Jerusalem, God— the true and only God—was still worshiped, and their services were still valued. And they were not alone. "Those from every tribe of Israel who set their hearts on seeking the LORD, the God of Israel, followed the Levites to Jerusalem to offer sacrifices to the LORD."

Nothing would have come of forcing Israel to submit except to make a brothers' quarrel turn bloody. Rehoboam may not have grasped the wisdom of the Lord's Word right away, but he did obey it. He then discovered, when he "walk[ed] in the ways of David and Solomon," that Israel freely came back to him and gave him its strength and support.

The Chronicler meant to inspire and encourage his people here. "Just think of it: not only Levites but also ordinary Israelites were willing to pull up stakes and move rather than be separated from the worship of their God." Today we listen to accounts from mission fields that speak of hardships overcome and sacrifices made—many by new converts eager to hear the Word of the Lord. They inspire us in a similar way. What we need to recognize in them more than anything is the power of God's love. It is so extraordinary, so amazing, that it can accomplish great things with ordinary people.

The final evidence of God's blessing upon Rehoboam's obedience is seen in the way his family grew so large. It is difficult to understand how God could have blessed him through the many wives that he had. But it seems clear enough that this is the overall thrust of verses 18 to 22. For a fuller discussion of this, the reader is encouraged to turn to the People's Bible commentary *1 Chronicles,* pages 159 and 160. For our purposes here, let us simply accept the Chronicler's point that God blessed Rehoboam with many children.

It is possible for even a foolish king to grow in wisdom with time, and, in some respects, prove himself wiser than the wise. The Chronicler closes out the chapter by pointing out a couple of areas where Rehoboam acted wisely. What is particularly interesting about these two examples is the fact that they concern areas where his grandfather David had *not* done so well. Although the Chronicler says nothing about it, he must have been aware of the many difficulties David had experienced because of rivalry among his sons and how David had also failed to settle the question of the succession in a timely way (see 2 Samuel 13–19; 1 Kings 1,2). Rehoboam, on the other hand, made it clear that Abijah was to succeed him, even though he was not the first-born. More than that, he separated his sons and gave them each responsibilities to keep them occupied and happy.

My mother used to say, "One swallow doesn't make a summer." We might say a similar thing here. Three good years don't make a good reign. Rehoboam may have been chastened after what happened at Shechem, but he still had a lot to learn. We find that out in the next chapter.

## Rehoboam chastised for later unfaithfulness

**12** After Rehoboam's position as king was established and he had become strong, he and all Israel with him abandoned the law of the LORD. ²Because they had been unfaithful to the LORD, Shishak king of Egypt attacked Jerusalem in the fifth year of King Rehoboam. ³With twelve hundred chariots and sixty thousand horsemen and the innumerable troops of Libyans, Sukkites and Cushites that came with him from Egypt, ⁴he captured the fortified cities of Judah and came as far as Jerusalem.

It is a tale that unfortunately has been told too many times. An erring believer is humbled. He repents. He seeks the Lord and begins to experience the Lord's strength again in his life. Then he forgets where his blessings come from; he forgets that "unless the LORD builds the house, its builders labor in vain" (Psalm 127:1). The Lord had helped Rehoboam establish himself in his kingdom, had helped him fortify his cities and, as if that were not enough, had built up the size and strength of his family too. Yet pride filled Rehoboam's heart again, and he began to glory in all his achievements, as if he had been the one to do them all. These were *his* sons, *his* fortresses—he now had the resources to protect himself and his people from any danger that threatened. We can almost hear him boasting along these lines. What is equally depressing in its frequency is the way the people of God blindly follow their leader into the ditch. It was not just the king who erred but "all Israel with him."

The Chronicler calls this behavior exactly what it is. He uses a very strong expression, "[They] abandoned the law of the LORD." We've met it before; we'll see it again. *Abandon* is obviously an important word in the Chronicler's religious vocabulary, one that he uses to show the way a person turns his back on something that he used to hold dear. It can be used in a positive sense, as when people show themselves to be willing to abandon things that might hold them back from worshiping the Lord. Mostly, however, it is used to refer to the way the people turn their back on the God they once held dear. In this way it is sometimes linked with the expression we find in 12:2: "They had been *unfaithful* to the LORD."

Both expressions depict the great divide caused by sin. Sin is turning your back on the God who loves you. Sin is disloyalty to the one who deserves your total devotion. There are only two ways. There is no middle ground. "He who is not with me is against me, and he who does not gather with me scatters," as Jesus put it (Matthew 12:30). We live at a time when people are trying to expunge the word *sin* from their everyday vocabularies. Word studies like these help to sharpen our consciences so that we again perceive sin in all its horror.

The emptiness of the things Rehoboam and Israel relied on is demonstrated by Shishak's invasion. All their mighty fortress cities fell down before the advance of Shishak's huge army. We are reminded of the phrase from the hymn, "The arm of flesh will fail you; Ye dare not trust your own" (CW 474:3). Rehoboam and the leaders of Judah understood well enough what had happened, but the prophet of the Lord was going to tell them what it meant.

**⁵Then the prophet Shemaiah came to Rehoboam and to the leaders of Judah who had assembled in Jerusalem for fear of Shishak, and he said to them, "This is what the LORD says, 'You have abandoned me; therefore, I now abandon you to Shishak.'"**

⁶The leaders of Israel and the king humbled themselves and said, "The LORD is just."

⁷When the LORD saw that they humbled themselves, this word of the LORD came to Shemaiah: "Since they have humbled themselves, I will not destroy them but will soon give them deliverance. My wrath will not be poured out on Jerusalem through Shishak. ⁸They will, however, become subject to him, so that they may learn the difference between serving me and serving the kings of other lands."

⁹When Shishak king of Egypt attacked Jerusalem, he carried off the treasures of the temple of the LORD and the treasures of the royal palace. He took everything, including the gold shields Solomon had made. ¹⁰So King Rehoboam made bronze shields to replace them and assigned these to the commanders of the guard on duty at the entrance to the royal palace. ¹¹Whenever the king went to the LORD's temple, the guards went with him, bearing the shields, and afterward they returned them to the guardroom.

By now we should be growing in our understanding of how important prophets were in the life of God's ancient people. In Chronicles we see them chiefly in the role of plain-speaking advisors to the kings of Judah. If we only had the Chronicler's account to go by, we might think that Shishak came on his campaign expressly to enrich himself at Judah's expense. In an Egyptian temple inscription, however, we get Shishak's own description of his invasion. On it the only towns of Judah mentioned as conquests were in the far south. Furthermore, the inscription reads as if Shishak's main target was the kingdom of Israel, not Judah.[13] People have their own readings of history. God sees things in a different light. What Shishak thought didn't matter. Shemaiah was there to report God's point of view.

Completely unintimidated by the titles or rank of those hiding in fear of Shishak, Shemaiah announced to them the wrath of someone much more important, whom they had forgotten to fear: "You have abandoned [the LORD]; therefore, [he] now abandon[s] you to Shishak." His announcement was met with a forthright confession: "The LORD is just," which they said in humble penitence. God justifies people when he declares them not guilty of sin. People glorify God when they stop making excuses for their behavior, accept responsibility for their sin, and declare that God has every right to punish them.

God told Shemaiah that he had set a limit to his anger and that he would not allow Shishak to capture Jerusalem. He would, nevertheless, allow Rehoboam and his people to feel the yoke of the Egyptians weighing down on them heavily. He wanted them to learn from experience the difference between serving other kings and serving God as king. The father of lies often makes people believe that serving the true God is a joyless, burdensome business. "Please yourself; do what you want!" he whispers. Those taken in by the lie learn by experience the difference between living in sin and living in grace. In a matchless phrase, Saint Augustine captures that difference for us. Describing his life when sin was his master, he says, "I became to myself a region of need."[14] Left to ourselves, we become deserts of desire, wastelands where we are filled with needs that are never satisfied.

The ceremonial shields that Solomon had made came down from the walls and were handed over as tribute to quench the king of Egypt's thirst for gold. How quickly Solomon's earthly splendor faded! His great empire was gone, his kingdom divided in two, and his gold carried off to buy the goodwill of another king. Not even "the treasures of the temple of the LORD" were allowed to remain. God was content with them as long as they were emblems of his people's devotion to him. Once they became symbols of pride, out they went!

It is difficult to know how to read the last two verses of this section. Are they a somewhat wistful depiction of tarnished glory? Probably. The best Rehoboam was able to manage—all that Shishak left him with—was bronze to use in place of gold. And this in a city where, only a few years before, silver had been as common as stones. *Sic transit gloria mundi*—so passes away the glory of the world.

### Rehoboam's restoration—for Jerusalem's sake

¹²**Because Rehoboam humbled himself, the LORD's anger turned from him, and he was not totally destroyed. Indeed, there was some good in Judah.**

¹³**King Rehoboam established himself firmly in Jerusalem and continued as king. He was forty-one years old when he became king, and he reigned seventeen years in Jerusalem, the city the LORD had chosen out of all the tribes of Israel in which to put his Name. His mother's name was Naamah; she was an Ammonite. ¹⁴He did evil because he had not set his heart on seeking the LORD.**

¹⁵**As for the events of Rehoboam's reign, from beginning to end, are they not written in the records of Shemaiah the prophet and of Iddo the seer that deal with genealogies? There was continual warfare between Rehoboam and Jeroboam. ¹⁶Rehoboam rested with his fathers and was buried in the City of David. And Abijah his son succeeded him as king.**

How should the Lord respond to this two-timing king, this two-time loser? "Because Rehoboam humbled himself, *the LORD's anger turned from him,* and he was not totally destroyed." God's thoughts are higher than our thoughts. We can barely find it in our hearts to forgive someone if they prove disloyal once. Rehoboam had let self-love crowd God from the throne in his heart twice, and twice God forgave him for it. But that's what he promised Solomon he would do: "If my people . . . humble themselves and pray and seek my face and turn from their wicked ways, then will I hear from heaven and will forgive their sin and will heal their land" (7:14). Rehoboam was permitted to continue as king.

This was certainly not done for the sake of Rehoboam. If verse 14 is anything to go by, his repentance was short-lived. The general evaluation of his character was that he was someone who had not set his heart on seeking the Lord. From beginning to end he had been too full of himself, too fickle and unstable in his attitude toward God. Since we all have a sinful self to contend with, we will do well to take warning from this and to pray with Luther, "Give us a firm resolve and ability not merely to begin being devout, but to continue boldly and to win."[15] If we stand firm in faith, it will only be because God has upheld us. Why, then, did God continue to let Rehoboam rule? For the sake of his promise, as we have seen, and because God wanted to demonstrate that Jerusalem was the city he had "chosen out of all the tribes of Israel in which to put his Name."

There was indeed "some good in Judah." The gold and the glitter were gone. But God's temple was still there, God's priests and Levites still served, and God's prophets still proclaimed the Word. In short, the grace of God was still working its miracles in the hearts and lives of his people. It may not look like much to the unbelieving world, but the kingdom of God is still the greatest kingdom around. It's not hard to find what's wrong with the church these days. People may stand up with passion and power and denounce all the ills that they see around them. We may find it hard to disagree; those problems are so readily apparent. But may God give us the eyes to look out and see the church bathed in the light of his grace. Then we might still find some good.

### God's kingdom under Abijah

The Chronicler deals with Abijah's brief rule in a way decidedly different from the way we see it handled in 1 Kings. First Kings 15:3 tells us that "he committed all the sins his father had done before him; his heart was not fully devoted to the LORD his God." The Chronicler, on the other hand, reports a stirring speech that Abijah gave to Israel, in which the king asserts God's promises to his people and their faithfulness to the Lord. Even more, the Chronicler records a stunning victory Abijah won over his rival Jeroboam, a victory the Lord granted in answer to prayer. What are we to make of this?

We remind ourselves, once again, that Chronicles was written to God's people at an entirely different time and for an entirely different purpose than the books of Kings and Samuel. Those books respond to the question, Why did the Lord bring judgment on his kingdom and his people? Chronicles speaks to the sins, fears, and insecurities of God's people as they tried to reestablish themselves in the land after returning from exile. These people were hurting. They needed reassurance that they were the people of God and that their worship was pleasing to him. Whenever he can, the Chronicler makes use of any information he has to make it clear to his people that God had not changed his mind, that their worship was still pleasing to him, and that they still enjoyed his favor, according to God's promise.

This incident from the life of Abijah was tailor-made to carry out the Chronicler's purpose. How could he *not* make use of it? Without contradicting in the least the evaluation of

Abijah given in 1 Kings, the Chronicler chose instead to present Abijah's brief shining hour on the day of battle. It is God's own word of reassurance meant to silence all the fears of his trembling people. When our own hearts trouble us and our own doubts and fears allow the world to come crashing in around us, we can do no better than to fortify ourselves with Abijah's defiant declaration of faith.

### Abijah's speech to the Northern army: "The LORD is our God"

**13** In the eighteenth year of the reign of Jeroboam, Abijah became king of Judah, ²and he reigned in Jerusalem three years. His mother's name was Maacah, a daughter of Uriel of Gibeah.

**There was war between Abijah and Jeroboam. ³Abijah went into battle with a force of four hundred thousand able fighting men, and Jeroboam drew up a battle line against him with eight hundred thousand able troops.**

Kings and Chronicles both agree that there was "war between Abijah and Jeroboam" (verse 2; also 1 Kings 15:6). A state of hostility had existed, in fact, ever since Rehoboam and the debacle at Shechem (see 10:15). It appears, however, that with the accession of Abijah to the throne, the war heated up from the occasional border skirmish to a full-scale invasion mounted by Judah against the North. But it was nowhere close to being an even matchup. Israel outnumbered Judah two to one.

**⁴Abijah stood on Mount Zemaraim, in the hill country of Ephraim, and said, "Jeroboam and all Israel, listen to me! ⁵Don't you know that the LORD, the God of Israel, has given the kingship of Israel to David and his descendants forever by a covenant of salt? ⁶Yet Jeroboam son of Nebat, an official of**

Solomon son of David, rebelled against his master. ⁷Some worthless scoundrels gathered around him and opposed Rehoboam son of Solomon when he was young and indecisive and not strong enough to resist them.

⁸"And now you plan to resist the kingdom of the LORD, which is in the hands of David's descendants. You are indeed a vast army and have with you the golden calves that Jeroboam made to be your gods. ⁹But didn't you drive out the priests of the LORD, the sons of Aaron, and the Levites, and make priests of your own as the peoples of other lands do? Whoever comes to consecrate himself with a young bull and seven rams may become a priest of what are not gods.

¹⁰"As for us, the LORD is our God, and we have not forsaken him. The priests who serve the LORD are sons of Aaron, and the Levites assist them. ¹¹Every morning and evening they present burnt offerings and fragrant incense to the LORD. They set out the bread on the ceremonially clean table and light the lamps on the gold lampstand every evening. We are observing the requirements of the LORD our God. But you have forsaken him. ¹²God is with us; he is our leader. His priests with their trumpets will sound the battle cry against you. Men of Israel, do not fight against the LORD, the God of your fathers, for you will not succeed."

Abijah decided to even the odds by telling Israel what the fighting was all about. Jeroboam and Israel were taking their stand against the Lord and against his anointed: "Don't you know that the LORD, the God of Israel, has given the kingship of Israel to David and his descendants forever by a covenant of salt?" Whatever the exact point of using the word *salt* is, in this context it must mean an irrevocable covenant (see Numbers 18:19 for a similar use). They were in a state of rebellion against God's own order. To think that Jeroboam, Solomon's slave and descended from nobody, had plotted against Solomon, the son of David! The whole idea was repugnant.

Even more vile were Jeroboam's actions against Rehoboam "when [Rehoboam] was young and indecisive and not strong enough to resist." While Abijah is certainly trying to put the best face on his father's conduct, he does not distort the truth by absolving Rehoboam of all responsibility. To call a 40-year-old man "young and indecisive" is not a song of praise. His proud words and bumbling actions had shown an instability of character that Jeroboam should have recognized. But instead of strengthening the position of the Lord's anointed when he was weak, Jeroboam took advantage of that weakness by gathering a band of "worthless scoundrels" against him.

Now Jeroboam was facing another son of David on the field of battle. What advantages did the Israelites bring to the conflict? True, their army was vast. True, they had their gods on display. But take a closer look. What were those gods, really, but "golden calves that Jeroboam made to be [their] gods"? Next to them, whom do we see as priests—sons of Aaron perhaps? Not at all! "Whoever comes to consecrate himself with a young bull and seven rams may become a priest of what are not gods." For all their numbers, the Israelites were still led by a slave in revolt, under the protection of gods that did not exist, and served by priests with no credibility. They had abandoned their true king, abandoned their true God, and forced their true priests out.

As for little Judah, what strength did it have? Abijah recounts the glorious promises of God that the Israelites had so lately spurned. Lovingly he dwells on the individual features of their temple worship, as if to set a rich feast of good things before the starving. Their worship was offered in the right place, by the right people, at all the appointed times.

To use Abijah's own words, the essential conflict was between those who "resist the kingdom of the LORD" and those who could say, "God is with us; he is our leader." There can be no success for those who set themselves against the God of their fathers.

At a somewhat similar critical time in the life of the early New Testament church, God's people gathered for prayer. Peter and John had just been examined before the high council of the Jewish leaders. They had been told not to preach anymore in the name of Jesus, a name hated by those who preferred to worship their own conception of God. They had been threatened with punishment if they continued to speak about what they had seen and heard in Jesus. We might ask what God's people prayed for under those circumstances. Did they pray for protection? for escape from their enemies? Not at all! They prayed instead for the ability to speak the Word of God boldly even in the face of so massive a threat (Acts 4:29)—to speak as we hear Abijah speaking to Israel on the brink of battle.

> Why do the nations conspire
>     and the peoples plot in vain?
> The kings of the earth take their stand
>     and the rulers gather together
> against the LORD
>     and against his Anointed One.
> "Let us break their chains," they say,
>     "and throw off their fetters." (Psalm 2:1-3)

We could perhaps assume that after such a stirring speech, Israel simply would have abandoned its cause as lost. But we would be wrong. Those who hold great power—as measured in human terms—are rarely frightened into submission by a recitation of God's Word and will, and those whose strength is evident are seldom intimidated by those whose strength is hidden. While Abijah was preaching a sermon, Jeroboam was getting ready to destroy him and his army.

### The Lord grants victory to Judah

¹³Now Jeroboam had sent troops around to the rear, so that while he was in front of Judah the ambush was behind them. ¹⁴Judah turned and saw that they were being attacked at both front and rear. Then they cried out to the LORD. The priests blew their trumpets ¹⁵and the men of Judah raised the battle cry. At the sound of their battle cry, God routed Jeroboam and all Israel before Abijah and Judah. ¹⁶The Israelites fled before Judah, and God delivered them into their hands. ¹⁷Abijah and his men inflicted heavy losses on them, so that there were five hundred thousand casualties among Israel's able men. ¹⁸The men of Israel were subdued on that occasion, and the men of Judah were victorious because they relied on the LORD, the God of their fathers.

¹⁹Abijah pursued Jeroboam and took from him the towns of Bethel, Jeshanah and Ephron, with their surrounding villages. ²⁰Jeroboam did not regain power during the time of Abijah. And the LORD struck him down and he died.

²¹But Abijah grew in strength. He married fourteen wives and had twenty-two sons and sixteen daughters.

²²The other events of Abijah's reign, what he did and what he said, are written in the annotations of the prophet Iddo.

Before they even knew what was happening, Judah had been outflanked. Abijah may have been a great preacher, but he was not much of a general. Unbeknownst to Abijah, Jeroboam had sent a detachment of troops to ambush Judah from behind, while he and the main body of his troops remained to tackle Abijah's army head-on. Trapped, Judah "cried out to the LORD." The priests sounded the battle alarm by blowing on their trumpets. In so doing they were keeping the word of Moses, who said, "When you go into battle in your own land against an enemy who is oppressing you, sound a blast on the trumpets. Then you will be remembered by the LORD your God and rescued from your enemies" (Numbers 10:9).

At the critical moment, just as Judah was raising the war cry and all seemed to be lost, the Lord intervened, and the battle was won. "God routed Jeroboam and all Israel before Abijah and Judah." The weaker side proved stronger because they put their trust in God, not in themselves. Israel suffered staggering losses. According to the Chronicler, 500,000 men fell—over half of its own army, and more than the entire army of Judah! Whether we view this number as an actual head count or as a rough estimate, we know that what we have is a decisive victory. After such a shattering defeat, it is not surprising to us to read that Jeroboam failed to regain his military strength as long as Abijah lived. Though he survived Abijah by about a year, Jeroboam's death, when it came, was sudden—a sign of God's judgment on him.

> The One enthroned in heaven laughs;
>     the Lord scoffs at them.
> Then he rebukes them in his anger
>     and terrifies them in his wrath, saying,
> "I have installed my King
>     on Zion, my holy hill." (Psalm 2:4-6)

Abijah consolidated his victory by capturing some key cities and villages, thereby moving Judah's border well north into what had been Israelite territory. Most notable among the towns captured was Bethel, one of Jeroboam's centers of worship for his calf idols (1 Kings 12:32). The Lord continued to bless Abijah while he lived, giving him many sons and daughters.

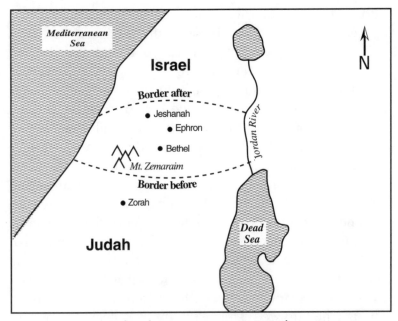

Abijah's victory over Israel

In a similar way, God answered those early Christians who had so earnestly asked him to consider the threats of their enemies and to give them the power to go on preaching about Jesus. "After they prayed, the place where they were meeting was shaken. And they were all filled with the Holy Spirit and spoke the word of God boldly" (Acts 4:31). Many of them were persecuted for it; some of them lost their lives. But all were contending for the only kingdom that lasts.

### Applying these verses to ourselves

The question here is one of legitimacy. We might put the argument in the mouth of an opponent of Abijah. "How can you think so highly of yourself, Abijah, with more than half your kingdom gone? Don't your palace guards now march with little bronze shields where great Solomon once walked through halls hung with gold? Do you really mean to say that you preside over God's kingdom? that you are the Lord's man, anointed to sit on his throne? Are you trying to tell us that what we worship is nothing?

"Aren't you forgetting that you stand here now only because Shishak spared your father? What about the gods of Egypt? Didn't they have to be made merciful to your people through treasure dedicated to the Lord, the one you say is with you?"

No doubt an opponent living at the Chronicler's time could have said: "Little Judah, little, little Judah! How can you give yourself such airs? What are you now but a tiny backwater province of the great Persian empire? Can you really mean to say that your God is the only God of all the earth? that your temple (and that too—how little!) is the only place to meet this God, this exclusive God who you claim chose you and yet who let you go off as captives and slaves to the bidding of the king of Babylon? How can you say this and keep a straight face!"

So too in our own day, there are millions desperately seeking spirituality, each claiming to have found it, or at least to have found *something*. Then we come along, proclaiming the exclusive claim to the only name given to humanity for its saving. "Do you really mean to say," our enemy might ask, "that you alone have the truth? that you alone have found the way? that you alone have life? Do you put down every other way and deny our truths, saying our gods are no gods and that our angels are demons? Just who elected you prophets, who made you priests, and who chose you to be kings of all the world?"

Here let each Christian learn to say with complete confidence: "Though I am nothing, and came from nothing, and would be nothing if left to myself, I know a King who came down from heaven. He loved me with all his heart and laid down his life on the cross for a beggar like me. He chose me from all eternity. He made me his own in time. He anointed me to be his priest and his prophet. He exalted me to rule with him at God's right hand as king. All things must now serve me, as I draw my life from him. I am absolutely sure of all this because he clothed me with himself at my baptism and wrapped me in the pure splendor of his name. He buried my sin deep within his own death and grave. He also feeds me daily on the rich pastures of his Word, and I come to him regularly at the appointed celebrations of his Holy Supper. There I feast on his forgiveness as I receive his body and blood. I am what I am because he is what he is, and he graciously gives himself to me."

We are not to judge truth on sight and sound and sense, on how many believe it, on how reasonable it seems, or on how great a show it makes. Like Abijah, we have no personal strength of which we can boast, but we have God's Son, and he is for us. In him we trust; of him we boast. He has pledged himself to us in his Word; there he's made his choice clear.

### God's kingdom under Asa

The portrait of Asa is a troubling one. The Chronicler meant it to be. On the one hand, the Chronicler reserves for Asa descriptive phrases that he applies only to godly kings (verse 2). Yet on the other hand, Asa sins foolishly in ways comparable to wicked kings (16:9,10).

He is, for example, a king who brings rest to the land as David did, standing at the head of God's army. He leads his people in worship much as David and Solomon did before him, and as Jehoshaphat, Hezekiah, and Josiah will later. He embarks on a program of cleansing the land from idolatry and teaching the people the law of the Lord. He renews the covenant in a solemn assembly. He listens to the Word of the Lord through the prophets, seeks the Lord in prayer, and relies on the God of his fathers in a holy war against tremendous odds.

Then comes "the rest of the story," as they say. Instead of relying on the Lord, he makes an unholy alliance with a heathen ruler to reduce the power of the Northern Kingdom. He refuses to accept a prophet's warning and does not seek the Lord when struck down with illness. His kingdom is chastised with the scourge of war, and he becomes an oppressor of his own people.

The contrast can hardly be more stark. In some ways it is similar to certain Hebrew proverbs we may have learned along the way. Two pithy statements are placed side by side—each with similar phrasing yet each one saying the opposite of the other.

> Do not answer a fool according to his folly,
> or you will be like him yourself.
> Answer a fool according to his folly,
> or he will be wise in his own eyes.
> (Proverbs 26:4,5)

The obvious question is, Which one is correct? And the obvious answer is, Both! Real people and genuine truths are rarely simple. There is often more than one answer to a question, and there is often more than just one way to characterize a person. The Chronicler means to jog us out of complacency and self-satisfaction (the besetting sins of the righteous) by painting for us a portrait of a king who did so well yet stumbled so badly.

It is worth making one more observation before we read the Chronicler's account of Asa. In our own age of doubt and confusion, a writer might enjoy portraying the king for us as a deeply ambiguous character. "See how 'conflicted' he was! How hard were his choices, how difficult for him to fight his way through to some kind of truth." You know the routine, if you've read any modern authors lately. This is not the Chronicler's style at all. The truth about one human life may have more than one aspect to it, and those aspects may involve deep contradictions, yet there is no question at all for the Chronicler about the truth itself. A king either does what is good and right or he acts foolishly (compare 14:2 with 16:9).

## *Asa relies on the Lord and is delivered*

**14** And Abijah rested with his fathers and was buried in the City of David. Asa his son succeeded him as king, and in his days the country was at peace for ten years.

²Asa did what was good and right in the eyes of the LORD his God. ³He removed the foreign altars and the high places, smashed the sacred stones and cut down the Asherah poles. ⁴He commanded Judah to seek the LORD, the God of their fathers, and to obey his laws and commands. ⁵He removed the high places and incense altars in every town in Judah, and the kingdom was at peace under him. ⁶He built up the fortified cities of Judah, since the land was at peace. No one was at war with him during those years, for the LORD gave him rest.

⁷"Let us build up these towns," he said to Judah, "and put walls around them, with towers, gates and bars. The land is still ours, because we have sought the LORD our God; we sought him and he has given us rest on every side." So they built and prospered.

⁸Asa had an army of three hundred thousand men from Judah, equipped with large shields and with spears, and two hundred and eighty thousand from Benjamin, armed with small shields and with bows. All these were brave fighting men.

In the beginning there is nothing bad to point to in Asa's actions as king. Putting first things first, he (1) cleanses the land of "foreign altars and the high places," (2) commands Judah to "seek . . . the God of their fathers," and (3) encourages his people to build up the land. To a king and a people who seek him, God's response is equally unequivocal. The Lord gives them rest; the people build, and they prosper.

Since the Chronicler will continue to mention the high places as a threat to the true worship of God, it might be good to pause here to gain some idea of what they were. For various reasons the ancient people of Canaan often associated hills and prominent features of the landscape with the worship of their gods. God's people, however, were instructed by Moses to worship the Lord only at "the place the LORD your God will choose from among all your tribes to put . . . his dwelling" (Deuteronomy 12:5). The idolatrous impulse splits the one true way of worship into many ways, the one true God into many gods. The Lord did not want this impulse to rule his people.

After the Philistines had destroyed the tabernacle at Shiloh (referred to indirectly in Scripture at Psalm 78:60; Jeremiah 7:12,14; 26:6,9), there evidently was some worship of the true God at various high places (1 Samuel 9:13; 10:5; 2 Chronicles 1:3). But once Solomon's temple was built, God made it clear that he wanted his people to seek him there, as we have seen. It did not take long, however, for the cancer of idolatry to work its insidious way into the heart of the kingdom. Surprisingly, Solomon himself was the ruler who could claim the dubious "first" of worshiping again at high places other than the temple mount. That alone was bad enough, but what made it so much worse was his worship there of foreign gods (1 Kings 11:7). Even a pretense of worshiping the Lord had been dropped! The division of the

171

Lord's kingdom into two parts naturally gave idolatry a tremendous boost as Jeroboam's sin (see page 149) made its impact felt. By the time of Asa, it is clear that high place worship—not only of the Lord but also of foreign gods—had become an established feature of the religious landscape, North and South.

Asa dedicated himself to rooting out idolatry early on in his rule. The sacred stones that he smashed were probably a type of incense altar.[16] The Asherah poles were associated with the goddess of happiness, the wife of Baal in the Canaanite pantheon. As vigorous as his efforts were, the power and resiliency of idol worship are revealed in a comment we read later: "[Asa] did not remove the high places from Israel" (15:17). This is probably best understood in the light of verses 2 to 5 of our current chapter: he removed those high places dedicated to the worship of *foreign gods;* he did not, however, remove those dedicated to the worship of the *Lord.* All in all, his was a noteworthy effort, but it fell short of completely eradicating this scourge from the land.

God blessed his efforts by giving the land prosperity and rest from war. It is clear enough from the context that the peace Judah enjoyed was only a relative one. They still had to contend with their hostile neighbors to the north (probably less so in the years immediately following Abijah's smashing victory). And they were soon going to have to contend with another threat from the south. The surprising recurrence of terms for "rest" throughout this entire section (verses 5-7; see also 15:15) lets us know that, from the Chronicler's point of view, tranquillity and peace were the key blessings enjoyed during the good period of Asa's reign. God's people had entered that rest through "[seeking] the LORD," that is, through faith in him (verse 7; see also Hebrews 4:3). Rest was not won through their own efforts. Security was not a product of bricks and mortar, nor was a large citizen army any guarantee of tranquillity. These were all blessings given to the one who learned to say with David, "I will lie down and sleep in peace, for you alone, O LORD, make me dwell in safety" (Psalm 4:8).

No state of peace and tranquillity endures long for any country in this world. All we can know are relative periods of calm. America herself is quite unusual in this respect: she has enjoyed freedom from wars ravaging her own soil for over one hundred years. Lately, however, we see our cities turning more and more into battlegrounds. The terrorist's efforts tear holes in the earth and leave scars on our hearts. Gangs seem to kill at random sometimes. Maybe our time of earthly peace likewise has run its course, as we the people seek from created things a gift found only in God. Yet a rest remains for the people of God. "I have told you these things, so that in me you may have peace. In this world you will have trouble. But take heart! I have overcome the world" (John 16:33). We thank you, dear Jesus! Root out the idols in our hearts and grant us your peace!

**⁹Zerah the Cushite marched out against them with a vast army and three hundred chariots, and came as far as Mareshah. ¹⁰Asa went out to meet him, and they took up battle positions in the Valley of Zephathah near Mareshah.**

**¹¹Then Asa called to the LORD his God and said, "LORD, there is no one like you to help the powerless against the mighty. Help us, O LORD our God, for we rely on you, and in your name we have come against this vast army. O LORD, you are our God; do not let man prevail against you."**

**¹²The LORD struck down the Cushites before Asa and Judah. The Cushites fled, ¹³and Asa and his army pursued them as far as Gerar. Such a great number of Cushites fell that they could not recover; they were crushed before the LORD and his forces.**

**The men of Judah carried off a large amount of plunder. ¹⁴They destroyed all the villages around Gerar, for the terror of the LORD had fallen upon them. They plundered all these villages, since there was much booty there. ¹⁵They also attacked the camps of the herdsmen and carried off droves of sheep and goats and camels. Then they returned to Jerusalem.**

Just who this Zerah was, no one knows for sure. As a Cushite he would have called the upper Nile region his home, an area that is now the northern Sudan. We may also deduce from 2 Chronicles 16:8 that Libyan troops as well as Cushites formed a substantial wing of his army. Putting these facts together, many suggest that he was the commander of Egypt's army, sent on his mission by Pharaoh Osorkon I. A ruler in the so-called Libyan dynasty, Osorkon is said to have wanted to duplicate the feat of his father Sheshonq (Shishak) and gain plunder at Judah's expense. This guess seems as educated as any. What we do know is that Zerah attacked from the south, advancing from the coastal highway into the Judean foothills through the Valley of Zephathah, near Mareshah (see map on page 147). This is where Asa and the army of Judah made a stand.

Vastly outnumbered and completely outclassed (bow, spear, and shield are no match for chariotry), it seemed that Judah's army would be slaughtered by its enemies. By now we should recognize the kinds of battles the Chronicler likes to depict. Physical supremacy is never the issue in them. If the Chronicler's battles were to be settled in earthly terms, the opposing army should have easily won out every time over the Lord's little flock. But they were not so much a physical contest as they were spiritual warfare. The kingdoms of this world are setting themselves up in opposition to the Lord; it is his army they defy and his anointed they seek to conquer.

As his people's representative, Asa prayed to the Lord in a way that made the issues clear. "There is no one like you," he began. The faithful in Israel never grew tired of saying how unique their God was. The other gods of other nations could only "help" when those who served them already had armies strong enough to win on their own. Only the true God helped the powerless win victories over impossible odds. "There is no one like you to help the powerless against the mighty."

Deeply embedded in the books of Moses was the truth that God takes up the cause of those who have no one else to depend on. He forbids his people from harming the widow and the orphan (Exodus 22:22). He makes provision for them in the distribution of the tithe offering (Deuteronomy 14:28,29) and wants no one to exclude them from celebrating the harvest festival (Deuteronomy 16:11). He warns against taking advantage of them by legal trickery (Deuteronomy 24:17), and he instructs his people not to harvest their fruit trees and grain so thoroughly that none is left for the poor to glean (Deuteronomy 24:19-21). It is this truth that led Luther to remark, "Christ has such a kingdom that he wills to help poor wretched people. . . . Without him not all the world with all its might and means can help. . . . It is his kingdom to preach the gospel to the poor. . . . For to the great and holy he cannot come. They do not wish to be counted sinners, and therefore do not need his gospel."[17]

Asa counted himself and his people in the company of those who have nothing in the world to count on when he said, "There is no one like you to help the powerless. . . . Help us . . . for we rely on you." It is the same as if he had said: "If you don't help, we must remain helpless. My citizen armies—however many men strong—cannot win this fight. My fortress cities provide no true refuge, no strength. You, and you only, are our refuge and strength." Eyes that have spiritual sight see things for what they are. A person who truly sees has looked within and found nothing there to rely on. That person has sized up the enemy and knows the impossibility of standing against him. Above all, such a person has turned to God and has found in him a place of rest for an anxious heart.

We have this certainty of God's help in every trouble, in every battle of body and mind, because we have the Lord's promise. We dare not hope because of what we are; we only dare to hope because of what he is: "In your name we have come against this vast army. O LORD, . . . do not let man prevail against you." God promised his ancient people, "I will be your God" (Exodus 6:7). Jesus says to all his disciples, "My Father will give you whatever you ask in my name" (John 16:23). God has put his name on the line and staked his reputation on saving us. Our Savior-God has so identified himself with our struggles and conflicts that those who oppose us oppose him. We are his army and so do battle under his banner. Let every baptized believer be sure of this: God has put his name on us; we never fight alone, for we are his!

For the Chronicler, the real questions are always settled before the contest. "Will God's people lean on their own understanding, or will they depend upon their God?" Once this spiritual contest has been decided, what the world might see as the actual battle becomes no battle at all. "The LORD struck down the Cushites before Asa and Judah. The Cushites fled, and Asa and his army pursued them as far as Gerar. Such a great number of Cushites fell that they could not recover; they were crushed before the LORD and his forces." What remains for God's people is to pick up the pieces the enemy has left behind and to plunder the territory.

The Chronicler recorded this battle so that the flock of God's own might have reason to hope in all their struggles. Gently he leads them to see that the real issues they face are never those earthly questions that usually stand at the top of people's anxiety lists: "What shall we eat; what shall we drink; how are we ever going to make it?" The genuine struggle always takes place on a spiritual plane. Do these earthly concerns lead me to try in some desperate way to save myself, relying on whatever resources I possess to surmount the difficulty at hand? Or do they teach me again to despair of myself and lean upon my gracious God? The Chronicler speaks to us here too so that "through endurance and the encouragement of the Scriptures we might have hope" (Romans 15:4).

### Asa responds to God's Word and renews the covenant

**15** The Spirit of God came upon Azariah son of Oded. **²He** went out to meet Asa and said to him, "Listen to me, Asa and all Judah and Benjamin. The LORD is with you when you are with him. If you seek him, he will be found by you, but if you forsake him, he will forsake you. ³For a long time Israel was without the true God, without a priest to teach and without the law. ⁴But in their distress they turned to the LORD, the God of Israel, and sought him, and he was found by them. ⁵In those days it was not safe to travel about, for all the inhabitants of the lands were in great turmoil. ⁶One nation was being crushed by another and one city by another, because God was troubling them with every kind of distress. ⁷But as for you, be strong and do not give up, for your work will be rewarded."

Asa and his victorious troops are met by the prophet Azariah as they return from the field of battle. This is the first of two prophetic messages Asa will receive. In this place God means to encourage Asa and all the people of Israel so that they continue to rely on him; later he will rebuke and warn Asa because Asa failed to depend on him. Completely under the sway of the Spirit, the prophet first stresses the great spiritual lesson to be learned from what had just occurred. The true God *is* a very present help in trouble. He is faithful; he keeps his word. Those who trust in him, who rely on him as their God, will find answers to their problems.

On the other hand, when God's people abandon him, they are turning their backs on the only true hope they have, and God will forsake them in anger. When people make idols out of earthly things, they must understand the true nature of the deed. To fashion other hopes in this way is to reject God's offer to help; persisting in this provokes God's wrath. He will give people up to dream their own dreams and to find comfort in their own hopes. Then they will discover if they have built on something worthwhile or not.

After stating this principle, Azariah recounts the history of God's people as an instructive example of the principle in action (verses 3-6). While this appears to be a summary of the experience of God's people particularly during the period of the judges (compare verses 3,4 with Judges 3:7-9), it is stated in a way that is general enough to be applicable at all times. These are the sorts of conditions that prevail whenever and wherever people do not welcome the rule of the Lord's Anointed nor listen to his Word.

How accurately the prophet portrays the hopeless and chaotic state of God's people (and of all people) when they try to get along without the true God and his Word! There is no peace, no security. No one can walk outside nor is there any safety to be found in going back home, so great is the turmoil. Apostasy leads to anarchy! When his people do not serve him in joy, God lets them taste the bitter results of their self-seeking ways. "God was troubling them with every kind of distress." This is God's judgment on people who prefer darkness to light, who give in to the kingdom of this world as it thrusts itself forward to rival God's gracious rule in their hearts.

Paul could write of a time when his Christian readers were "without hope and without God in the world" (Ephesians 2:12). They were under the rule of every demon and spiritual tyrant that existed. But God, in his mercy, had worked a new birth of freedom in their hearts: he graciously joined them to his own people in Christ and gave them peace through his blood. Ever since then the western world has been able to walk in the light of the Lord. Yes, there have been famines of the Word here and there, and the gospel rain shower has moved from one country to the next, but there have always been those in the West who have clung to God's Word and put their hope in the Lord's anointed King. It seems as if the great apostasy has come, at least among us. Preferring darkness to light, our nation is discovering just how deep that darkness can be.

Is this the final crescendo of evil before the end? Or will there still be those who will turn to the Lord in their distress, seek him, and find him? As far as our own country in general is concerned, God alone knows. As for us, "we will not fear, though the earth give way and the mountains fall into the heart of the sea" (Psalm 46:2). We know that heaven and earth may pass away, but our Savior's gracious words will not pass away. It is for us to "[stand] firm to the end," as our Savior commands (Matthew 24:13), to "be strong and . . . not give up," as his prophet states here (verse 7).

However chaotic things might appear, we can do far more than simply "rage against the dying of the light." Christ has given us his mission. The gospel must be preached to all nations (Matthew 24:14). That means we have work to do, and whenever the devil says, "Why bother? It's hopeless!" or whenever our fearful and despairing hearts tempt us to give up, we can look into the empty tomb and see the victory promised there. This victory is not only intended to bring us joy when the Lord's perfect day arrives; it's meant to give us new strength right now. Didn't the Lord's apostle tell us (in words similar to Azariah's), "Stand firm. Let nothing move you. Always give yourselves fully to the work of the Lord, because you know that your labor in the Lord is not in vain" (1 Corinthians 15:58)?

**⁸When Asa heard these words and the prophecy of Azariah son of Oded the prophet, he took courage. He removed the detestable idols from the whole land of Judah and Benjamin and from the towns he had captured in the hills of Ephraim. He repaired the altar of the Lord that was in front of the portico of the Lord's temple.**

**⁹Then he assembled all Judah and Benjamin and the people from Ephraim, Manasseh and Simeon who had settled among them, for large numbers had come over to him from Israel when they saw that the Lord his God was with him.**

**¹⁰They assembled at Jerusalem in the third month of the fifteenth year of Asa's reign. ¹¹At that time they sacrificed to the Lord seven hundred head of cattle and seven thousand sheep and goats from the plunder they had brought back. ¹²They entered into a covenant to seek the Lord, the God of their fathers, with all their heart and soul. ¹³All who would not seek the Lord, the God of Israel, were to be put to death, whether small or great, man or woman. ¹⁴They took an oath to the Lord with loud acclamation, with shouting and with trumpets and horns. ¹⁵All Judah rejoiced about the oath because they had**

sworn it wholeheartedly. **They sought God eagerly, and he was found by them. So the LORD gave them rest on every side.**

**16King Asa also deposed his grandmother Maacah from her position as queen mother, because she had made a repulsive Asherah pole. Asa cut the pole down, broke it up and burned it in the Kidron Valley. 17Although he did not remove the high places from Israel, Asa's heart was fully committed to the LORD all his life. 18He brought into the temple of God the silver and gold and the articles that he and his father had dedicated.**

**19There was no more war until the thirty-fifth year of Asa's reign.**

The word of the prophet achieved God's purpose in Asa's heart: "He took courage," and his response was swift and dramatic. For the second time, he embarked on a search-and-destroy mission against idols. This time he included in his purge the towns that he had captured from the Northern Kingdom (Ephraim). Though this was the second time he had to do it, and though worship of the Lord persisted at the high places, it seems clear enough that these facts say less about the strength of his resolve than they do about the attraction idolatry holds for the human heart. His response was not merely a negative one against idols. He also took the positive steps of repairing the altar of burnt offering and summoning his people to a great festival of covenant renewal.

Asa experienced blessings similar to the ones enjoyed by Rehoboam (11:13-17). His faithfulness to the Lord had attracted the attention of some believing northerners, so that "large numbers had come over to him from Israel when they saw that the LORD his God was with him." As compelling as the philosophies of this world may seem at times, nothing compares with the compelling power of God's love. So it was that Asa was able to summon together a group truly representative of all Israel for the festival he had in mind.

He held it, the Chronicler tells us, in "the third month of the fifteenth year" of his reign. This would mean that he celebrated it in association with the Feast of Weeks, or Pentecost (Leviticus 23:15-22). This also enables us to date Zerah's invasion with some degree of accuracy to the year 897 B.C., since we are told it was at this same festival that "they sacrificed . . . seven thousand sheep and goats from the plunder they had brought back." Even assuming some delay between the invasion and the celebration, this would still put the Cushite's incursion somewhere late in Asa's 14th year of rule or very early in his 15th.

The theme of the festal gathering was "Seek the LORD, the God of [our] fathers, with all [your] heart and soul." Its purpose was to allow a new generation of believers to affirm publicly their desire to remain in the covenant that God had made with the people of Israel on Mount Sinai. This was not the first time Israel had done so. A person could say that the entire book of Deuteronomy is a form of covenant renewal, carried out under the leadership of Moses as the new generation of Israelites (born after God's meeting with Israel at Sinai) was about to enter the Promised Land. Joshua ratified this covenant with due reverence once the initial phase of conquest was over (compare Joshua 8:30-35 with Deuteronomy 27), renewing it again at the end of his life (Joshua 23,24). Asa's renewal was not the last time the Israelites would recommit themselves to worshiping the Lord. We will see it occurring again during the reigns of Hezekiah and Josiah.

The serious resolve with which Asa and his people approached the day is seen in a number of features that follow. Lavish sacrificial offerings are made. Those unwilling to commit themselves exclusively to the Lord are put to death, regardless of their sex or social standing. This was in keeping with the covenant stipulations found in

Deuteronomy 13:6-9. A solemn oath of loyalty is taken, accompanied by shouts and sounds of trumpets. That this is no mere outward show becomes clear from verse 15: they take the oath *joyfully, wholeheartedly,* and *eagerly.* And Asa is a leader in more than just words. He takes action against idolatry within his own household, deposing his grandmother Maacah from her high position and publicly destroying her "repulsive Asherah pole." Finally, he brings gifts to the temple, the articles of silver and gold that he and his father had dedicated to the Lord.

We might ask what purpose these covenant renewals served. Often they took place when Israel's transgressions had reached a point at which a person could say that the covenant had already been broken. The reforms of Hezekiah and Josiah are clear examples of this. In the case of the reaffirmation that took place near the end of Joshua's life, the reason there seems to be more the passing of an era. There was a new generation coming to adulthood, the first born in the Land of Promise. Soon their great leader Joshua—who could personally recall Sinai—would pass from the scene. Joshua wanted to know whether this new group would remain committed to serving the Lord. The one theme common to every covenant renewal, however, is the idea that the true worship of the true God is not a given. Just because fathers believed, it was no guarantee that their children would be faithful. A covenant renewal, then, was an important way for a new generation of believers to say that they stood exactly where their faithful fathers had stood.

We have similar occasions within our own lives and in every church year; we call them confirmations, Reformation rallies, and (if it's not stretching a point) installations. On all three occasions we have opportunity—sometimes individually and sometimes as a group—to say, "We want to seek the God of our fathers and to worship him only." No doubt customs like these will continue long after this writer has passed from the scene. One can only hope and pray that, within the Lutheran church, these times of solemn recommitment will be more than mere outward show. It is vitally important for each generation to make the precious, saving truths of God's Word their own.

"They sought God eagerly, and he was found by them," the Chronicler says. The fact is, we must confess that our own treacherous hearts so often lead us astray. So often we have provoked the Lord with our idols, our own prideful visions of what we are and what we can do. It's a wonder God still talks to us at all—so unreliable have we been, so unworthy of the name son or daughter. Whenever we read passages in which themes of commitment and loyalty loom large, we soon find ourselves back in that place described earlier by Asa: I am powerless, Lord, help me! (14:11). The truth is—and it's a galling truth, but we had better admit it— there is always something lacking in our commitment, in our dedication, in our resolve to seek the Lord. Thanks be to God that nothing is ever lacking—nothing at all—in his commitment, his dedication, his resolve to save us.

### A brief detour into biblical chronology

Before we move on to the next phase of Asa's life, we need to deal with two questions that are bound to trouble the careful reader of Scripture. The first difficulty involves the twin time references given to us, one in the last verse of this chapter and the other in the first verse of the next. We are told both that Asa had peace "until the thirty-fifth year of [his] reign" and that in Asa's "thirty-sixth year," King Baasha of Israel tried to push the border southward again, toward Judah. The problem is that 1 Kings 15:33 tells us that Baasha became king "in the *third* year of Asa" and that he "reigned *twenty-four* years." It seems impossible for both statements to be true. King Baasha would have been long gone by Asa's "thirty-sixth year."

At one time there were numerous difficulties involved in unraveling the dates of the various kings of Judah and Israel. It was hard to give a sensible explanation that took into account all the scriptural evidence. Then, in 1965, a man by the name of E. R. Thiele came out with a book entitled *The Mysterious Numbers of the Hebrew Kings,* in which he solved many of these problems. He began with the assumption that the numbers given in the scriptural dating were accurate, and that the writers of Chronicles and Kings were anything but bad historians who did not concern themselves with working out inconsistencies in their sources.

Some of his best solutions were the following: (1) There were often periods of co-regency, when father and son ruled together. During such a time, both kings counted the years as their years of rule. (2) Sometimes scribes dated according to an accession-year system, in which the first *partial* year of a king's rule was counted only as an accession year and was not included in his total. Only *full* years (calculated from new year to year's end) would be included in the final tally of years ruled. (3) Sometimes scribes did not follow this accession-year system, and then all years—full and partial— would count as years and be included in the total. To get a more in-depth look at some of the problems involved in dating, and at Thiele's solutions, borrow Thiele's book from the local library or consult a larger Bible dictionary.

Thiele's work is widely accepted among conservative Bible scholars today, and he is named here for the sake of readers who have an interest in such things. Unfortunately, none of the solutions mentioned help us with the problem we have, which is, How could Baasha be alive in Asa's 36th year when he died ten years earlier? Thiele suggests that if these two numbers were calculated from the year the united kingdom was split in two, then the problem disappears. The date of Baasha's hostile actions toward the South then falls around 894 B.C., well within the realm of possibility. Many difficulties remain with this "solution," however. It is doubtful whether it represents the last word.

The reader may take along from this discussion the following points: (1) At one time most of the numbers of the Hebrew kings involved problems of explanation. (2) Someone came along who trusted the text and proposed solutions that were not only ingenious but also compelling. They are widely accepted today. (3) Thiele's solution for our own particular problem is more ingenious than compelling, yet (4) no doubt other ones will come along. Until then we take comfort from the thought that many Bible difficulties once considered insoluble have been satisfactorily resolved. This one will be too—if not now, then later when what is partial will give way to the perfect (1 Corinthians 13:9,10).

If we are accused of having blinders on when dealing with the sacred text and of operating with obvious biases in our interpretative method, we freely admit it. There is no such thing as dispassionate scholarship, that is, not in the sense that anyone can approach any text free from bias. Our bias is simply that the Lord Christ, who reveals himself in Scripture, has confiscated our hearts, minds, and wills. He's done this with the compelling power of his love. We've come to trust his voice and to believe that he does not lie. We reject as an idolatrous worship of the human intellect any method that, in effect, puts the sacred Scriptures at arm's length and allows people to sift through them for things that they find appealing. We, on the other hand, will continue to approach them expecting to hear nothing less than God's authentic voice ringing out clearly in every word.

The second question regarding this section on Asa's rule will be given only the briefest mention here. It belongs more to a study of human nature than it does to the category of biblical inconsistencies. We are referring to the Chronicler's remark that "Asa's heart was fully committed to the LORD all his life." This seems hard to reconcile with the following chapter, in which Asa's times of peace will turn to war, his reliance on God will become a reliance on man, and his eager acceptance of the prophetic Word will become hostile rejection. Saddest of all, perhaps, is the description we will find of a man who stubbornly refuses to seek the Lord. It is enough to say here that we will come back to this question once we have thoroughly discussed the next chapter.

### Asa relies on man, rejects God's Word, and is chastised

**16** In the thirty-sixth year of Asa's reign Baasha king of Israel went up against Judah and fortified Ramah to prevent anyone from leaving or entering the territory of Asa king of Judah.

²Asa then took the silver and gold out of the treasuries of the LORD's temple and of his own palace and sent it to Ben-Hadad king of Aram, who was ruling in Damascus. ³"Let there be a treaty between me and you," he said, "as there was between my father and your father. See, I am sending you silver and gold. Now break your treaty with Baasha king of Israel so he will withdraw from me."

⁴Ben-Hadad agreed with King Asa and sent the commanders of his forces against the towns of Israel. They conquered Ijon, Dan, Abel Maim and all the store cities of Naphtali. ⁵When Baasha heard this, he stopped building Ramah and abandoned

his work. ⁶Then King Asa brought all the men of Judah, and they carried away from Ramah the stones and timber Baasha had been using. With them he built up Geba and Mizpah.

⁷At that time Hanani the seer came to Asa king of Judah and said to him: "Because you relied on the king of Aram and not on the LORD your God, the army of the king of Aram has escaped from your hand. ⁸Were not the Cushites and Libyans a mighty army with great numbers of chariots and horsemen? Yet when you relied on the LORD, he delivered them into your hand. ⁹For the eyes of the LORD range throughout the earth to strengthen those whose hearts are fully committed to him. You have done a foolish thing, and from now on you will be at war."

¹⁰Asa was angry with the seer because of this; he was so enraged that he put him in prison. At the same time Asa brutally oppressed some of the people.

¹¹The events of Asa's reign, from beginning to end, are written in the book of the kings of Judah and Israel. ¹²In the thirty-ninth year of his reign Asa was afflicted with a disease in his feet. Though his disease was severe, even in his illness he did not seek help from the LORD, but only from the physicians. ¹³Then in the forty-first year of his reign Asa died and rested with his fathers. ¹⁴They buried him in the tomb that he had cut out for himself in the City of David. They laid him on a bier covered with spices and various blended perfumes, and they made a huge fire in his honor.

Perhaps troubled by the droves of his own people attracted by Asa's commitment to the Lord (15:9), King Baasha of Israel decided to move against his brothers to the south and create the Old Testament equivalent of the Berlin Wall. His motive was the same as that of the communists in East Germany. He wanted to squeeze off easy communication and travel between the two countries.

Asa's next move is puzzling—puzzling to a believer, that is. But to anyone schooled in the art of practical politics, it is perfectly understandable. Essentially Asa bribed Ben-Hadad, the ruler of Aram-Damascus, to break his alliance with Israel, to form an alliance with him instead, and to harass the Israelite king. Asa calculated that if Baasha was forced to deal with an Aramean threat at his back, he would be compelled to pull back from his hostile activity along Judah's borders. To sweeten the size of the bribe, Asa removed the treasures of the Lord's temple that he had so recently placed there (verse 2; compare with 15:18).

If success is measured only by whether a policy achieves its goals, we can then say that Asa succeeded. Ben-Hadad dispatched his troops to wreak a little havoc in the northern cantons of Israel. Naphtali was brought low. Baasha was forced to abandon his fortification project entirely. Asa's policy also produced a windfall: the timbers and stones left by Baasha's men were put to good use in building up Asa's own fortifications at Geba and Mizpah. There the border would remain for the rest of the period of the divided kingdom. A hardheaded politician might have said: "Good work, Asa! A bloodless victory."

The clear-eyed prophet, however, viewed things differently. Hanani the seer came to administer a sharp rebuke to the king by setting the matter into its spiritual context. As Lord of all, God knows more than the art of what's "practical." Whenever we argue practicalities, we do well to remember that we are discussing them only from a human standpoint. God makes those who rely on him masters of the impossibilities and enables them to do far more than they could have imagined. In striking a deal with Ben-Hadad, Asa had thought small and had sold himself (and God) short. Had he relied instead on the Lord, he would have mastered both Baasha and the king of Aram.

Asa's own past spiritual experience should have taught him this, the prophet continued. The odds had been decidedly against him when he had taken on the Cushites and Libyans. But human odds don't matter for the one who knows where his help comes from. "When you relied on the LORD, he delivered them into your hand." And God's help is not limited to one place, one time, one battle. God is on the lookout at all times and in all places to give strength to those who put their whole trust in him. The Lord's rebuke, when it came, was as sharp and direct as Nathan's once was to David (see 2 Samuel 12:7): "You have done a foolish thing." (Remember, in the Bible foolishness is more than just stupidity; it is willful disregard for God's clear revelation, as its use in this context plainly shows.) The announcement of sin's consequence, when it came, was equally direct: "From now on you will be at war."

What a shock! There you are, floating along on a sea of well-being, thinking everything is fine, when suddenly you discover it's anything but fine. "Floating along" is the right expression for it, since this is just the sort of thing that happens when we forget how powerless we are by nature, when we ignore the warnings in Scripture that tell of the might of our enemies arrayed against us. The storm of evil is always raging, inside and outside of us, even when we feel ourselves to be inside the placid eye. When things are going smoothly, we are especially likely to forget how desperate our situation would be if God would ever withdraw his help. Then above all we need to pray: "Lord, lead me not into temptation! Help me from feeling a worldly sense of security. Keep me from complacency!"

Here too we might note the bluntness of the Lord's spokesman. So much is written these days about the "people skills" pastors need to have. "Let them learn to be tactful. Teach them good communication skills and how to avoid putting unnecessary roadblocks in the way of understanding." This writer could not agree more with those who speak of the importance of all these things. There certainly is no virtue in being rude and impolite. When, however, it comes down to announcing God's judgment on sin, we must be careful not to expect the impossible. "Law brings wrath," the apostle says (Romans 4:15). If everyone loves the pastor because he is so tactful that he never tells it like it is, then he's ceased to be God's spokesman, and he's not doing his people much good. When tact masks the severity of God's law to a sinner who needs to hear it, give me a man who's blunt!

It is a great pity that Asa did not respond to the prophet's plain-speaking ways with a forthright confession, as David his father had. Instead, we see him react in a way common to those who don't like the message God sends them. They become angry with the messenger. So angry did Asa become, in fact, that he put Hanani in prison. The Hebrew word for prison connotes some sort of physical torture—"a twisted place," literally. Perhaps this refers to the practice of holding prisoners in uncomfortable positions— limbs distorted—in devices like stocks. Jeremiah, we know, suffered a similar fate (Jeremiah 20:2). Asa, the first king to begin a reformation at the encouragement of a prophet, also becomes the first king mentioned in Scripture to physically abuse a prophet.

His anger was not satisfied with the torture of a man of God. He also "brutally oppressed" some of his own people, very likely those who had sided with the prophet. This too represents a complete turnaround from the man we saw in chapter 15. There he led the people as a true shepherd in the spirit of David; here we see the spirit of a cruel tyrant.

Though the two are not specifically connected in our text, the sickness that struck Asa in his 39th year was probably the Lord's way of reminding him of his sin and showing who was in charge. It is described for us as a foot disease that struck him with uncommon severity. But just as he had shown himself to be uncompromising in his stance toward idolatry, so he also demonstrated his stubbornness toward the Lord when he became sick. "He did not seek help from the LORD, but only from the physicians."

Before we interpret that last remark as the Chronicler's slam against doctors, we should understand that what is under condemnation is Asa's failure to seek the Lord. His reliance upon doctors represented for him an unwillingness to depend on God. Where that is not an issue, there is no sin. But if we should confuse the doctor with God and assume that God cannot help us—only the doctor can—then we commit the sin of Asa. Quite apart from all this, it is also possible that these physicians made use of superstition and idolatry to work their cures, methods that are completely illegitimate.

What concerns us most about Asa is whether or not he died in the faith. It is quite possible that you will not agree with the answer you are about to read. That is perfectly acceptable. Fortunately, none of us has been given the task of determining another's eternal destiny after death. We are all perfectly happy to leave that matter in the Lord's hands. Yet since it seems that the text itself raises the question, it is worth making an attempt, at least, to answer it, with the full understanding that we have not settled the matter.

We begin with the evidence of verse 17 from the previous chapter. The words seem clear enough, "Asa's heart was fully committed to the LORD all his life" (see also 1 Kings 15:14). And this is not an isolated instance of a positive evaluation. The Chronicler later uses Asa as one of those benchmark kings whose behavior stood as an example to his successors (see 20:32; 21:12). We might add to it the pomp and circumstance that attended his funeral. A special bonfire, laced with spices, was set ablaze in his honor (the exact significance of which remains unclear). This was not the sort of thing that accompanied the funeral of lesser kings (see 21:19,20). Apparently, in the judgment of the people themselves, this had been a good king, one whose death merited lament. Finally, the parallel account in 1 Kings 15:9-24 views Asa as one of the kings who "did what was right . . . as his father David had done" (1 Kings 15:11). It is the Chronicler alone who mentions the dark turn Asa's life took toward the end. On the basis of this evidence, we prefer to see Asa as a believer, a believer who fell grievously and publicly but who died in faith nevertheless.

Do you remember those two proverbs we considered at the beginning of Asa's account? Both of them were true. Yet the whole truth was found in neither one alone. Sometimes it's best to say nothing when you hear foolish talk. Sometimes you have to speak up. Like the two proverbs existing in tension with each other, so were the two phases of Asa's life. Here was a king who had accomplished good things for his people in holding off the great ocean of idolatry that threatened to sweep them all away. But he acted foolishly in relying on Ben-Hadad, in rejecting the Word of the Lord, in abusing his people, and in stubbornly refusing to seek the Lord's help in his illness.

Unlike God, we can assess people's spiritual state only by what we see and hear. We might ask, Did Asa's evil toward the end completely negate the evidence for good we see at the beginning and throughout most of his life? It seems that the Chronicler's answer is, No, it does not. We can describe the sins of his latter days, perhaps, as being a fall similar to David's with Bathsheba. A fall from grace, but not a fall beyond hope of recovery. We might conceive of it as something brought on by the suddenness of his rebuke and by the rush of anger he felt at being humiliated. As time went on, it could well have been that, feeling trapped by shame, he built his own wall of pride around himself, a wall that—somewhere deep down—he still knew to be hollow. At the very end, that sense of hollowness ripened, through God's grace, into genuine penitence. More than one person has finally seen things clearly in the light of approaching death.

Unconvinced? We have no quarrel. You are free to differ. We can all agree that the Chronicler's presentation gives no aid or comfort to those who would postpone repentance. The somber hues in which the Chronicler paints the portrait of Asa's final years stand out all the more when set against the brightness of his beginning. Those good years and the sudden way he fell ought to teach us all to work out our own salvation in fear and trembling (Philippians 2:12). If such a good king could stumble, what about us?

### God's kingdom under Jehoshaphat

In the Chronicler's account of Jehoshaphat, the first thing the reader becomes aware of is its sheer length when compared with the parallel account in 1 Kings. Our writer has devoted almost as much space to Jehoshaphat as he does later to good King Hezekiah. By contrast, in 1 Kings, Jehoshaphat rates a scant ten verses. The reason for this seems to be the desire of the inspired writer of 1 Kings to concentrate on the ministry of Elijah, which took place in the North. As we have seen, the Chronicler's heart has always been set upon the Southern Kingdom, that kingdom where the Lord caused his name to dwell and his anointed one to rule.

As with Asa before him, we have a king here who is a mixture of both good and bad, although the contrast between the two is less stark in Jehoshaphat's case. Through skillful combination of light and shade, the Chronicler paints a portrait for his people of a king whose good points are there to strengthen their hope and to present them with a godly pattern to follow. His weaknesses, on the other hand, are set before them as warning signs: Here, O Israel, are paths to avoid if you want to live in God's peace and avoid his wrath (19:1,2,10).

If there is an overarching theme uniting all the chapters that describe Jehoshaphat's reign, it would be that God opposes every evil alliance. A believer aligned with the Lord will know God's peace and reap great blessings (chapter 17). When he walks as one with the wicked—no matter how shining its path may seem—he is deceiving himself and headed for disaster (chapter 18). Good judgment comes from officials who care about God's judgment (chapter 19). God is just and protects his people from every evil confederation (20:1-30). God is just and opposes the marriage of light with darkness (20:37).

### *Jehoshaphat's first and best ally: the God of his fathers*

**17** Jehoshaphat his son succeeded him as king and strengthened himself against Israel. ²He stationed troops in all the fortified cities of Judah and put garrisons in Judah and in the towns of Ephraim that his father Asa had captured.

³The LORD was with Jehoshaphat because in his early years he walked in the ways his father David had followed. He did not consult the Baals ⁴but sought the God of his father and followed his commands rather than the practices of Israel. ⁵The LORD established the kingdom under his control; and all

**Judah brought gifts to Jehoshaphat, so that he had great wealth and honor. ⁶His heart was devoted to the ways of the LORD; furthermore, he removed the high places and the Asherah poles from Judah.**

It seems at first that Jehoshaphat saw matters clearly. He refused to have dealings with the Northern Kingdom and instead "strengthened himself against Israel." He saw to it that there were protective garrisons stationed not only in the cities of Judah but "in the towns of Ephraim that his father Asa had captured." Jehoshaphat's motive in all this was not military but spiritual. He was aware of the increasing popularity of Baal worship to the north, and he wanted nothing to do with it.

In marrying off his son Ahab to Jezebel, the powerful daughter of the king of Tyre, King Omri of Israel had unwittingly introduced a new element into the spiritual mix of his country. Idolatry had flourished unofficially for a long time already in Israel. Even in the official worship of the Lord, there was that odd blend of truth and lies we've heard about, with its calf idols and priests from nowhere (13:8,9). What Jezebel, the wife of Ahab, did was to give official sanction in Israel to the worship of her hometown god, the idol Baal. Not only did her husband allow her to worship her false god, but he also built Baal an altar and a temple in Israel's capital city, Samaria. Even worse, by his example of joining his wife in worshiping her imported god, Ahab led so many in Israel to bow the knee to Baal that the prophet Elijah at one time thought he was the only believer left in Israel (1 Kings 16:29-33; 19:10).

Jehoshaphat's steadfastness is emphasized with verses of nearly poetic quality that may be better appreciated in literal translation:

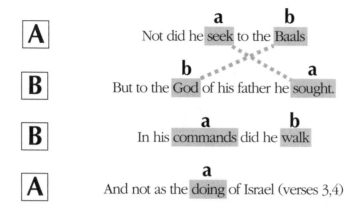

The first sentence is marked the way it is to illustrate that it is a chiasm (pronounced KEYE-asm). This is just a way of saying that it is written in two word pairs, with the second pair nested inside the first. The ancients called it a chiasm because the *X* formed by joining each word pair together looked to them like the Greek letter *chi*. What is more, each negative statement ("Not did he . . .") is matched by a corresponding positive statement (". . . did he . . ."), with the two positive statements again chiastically nested in the center, as if framed by the two negative ones.

Perhaps this little foray into ancient Hebrew style is less than appealing to you, and you wonder what the point of it all can possibly be. Studies like this are useful because they are one way we have of detecting where the original writer was placing emphasis. Whenever you have speech as carefully constructed as this, the careful reader knows that the writer wants to call particular attention to the message the words convey. You can look at it as a sort of ancient exclamation point that matches the steadfastness of the king's conduct with an elegance in describing it.

What were the results of Jehoshaphat's devotion to the Lord? "The LORD was with [him]." God allied himself with

Jehoshaphat and made the king's cause his own. And whenever the Lord does that, good things happen. God showered his blessings upon the king. The Lord himself saw to it that the kingdom was under Jehoshaphat's firm control. His subjects brought him gifts as a mark of their devotion. This last phrase, by the way, is a very unusual expression. Scripture often mentions that subject nations brought tribute gifts to the king of whatever nation held power over them. But it is hardly ever said that the people of Judah and Israel brought gifts to their own kings. The only other case we have of it is in 1 Samuel 10:27, where we are told that some troublemakers refused to bring Saul gifts.[18] Again, the point here is that by using this unusual expression, the Chronicler is calling attention to the extraordinary nature of this act, as if he were urging us to notice this unique affection that existed between this king and his people. What great blessings God showered on Jehoshaphat!

Even though "he had great wealth and honor," success did not turn his heart away from seeking the Lord. Once again we have a striking choice of words here. For the Hebrew represented by the NIV's "devoted to," the Chronicler uses a verb that Scripture most often employs in a bad sense. Literally it means "to be high, to be exalted." When applied to a person's attitude, it becomes the common Hebrew expression "to be haughty, to be proud." That's the meaning one would normally expect to attach to it. But the Chronicler confounds his readers' expectations and uses the word in a positive sense instead. In its effect the entire sentence is similar to one of those pointed sayings we have in our own language that come with a surprise ending, for example, "You have to be *cruel . . .* to be *kind*" or "She didn't know *what to do with him* anymore . . . so she *married him.*" So here the Chronicler says, "His heart became *proud . . . in the* LORD." The power of surprise causes the reader to stop and think of what an unusual king Jehoshaphat was.

Instead of allowing these blessings to become idols drawing him away from the Lord, Jehoshaphat's honor and wealth served to renew his sense of God's grace and goodness all the more. And he responded, "[removing] the high places and the Asherah poles from Judah." This was truly a king remarkable for his piety. So many times fame and fortune make people too great in their own estimation to have any more time for the God of their fathers. We almost expect them to say, "Ah yes, I used to believe all that, but now things are different. I just don't need God anymore." But Jehoshaphat's eye wasn't dazzled. His heart wasn't turned. Wealth does not have to spell the end of a person's relationship with God.

**⁷In the third year of his reign he sent his officials Ben-Hail, Obadiah, Zechariah, Nethanel and Micaiah to teach in the towns of Judah. ⁸With them were certain Levites—Shemaiah, Nethaniah, Zebadiah, Asahel, Shemiramoth, Jehonathan, Adonijah, Tobijah and Tob-Adonijah—and the priests Elishama and Jehoram. ⁹They taught throughout Judah, taking with them the Book of the Law of the Lord; they went around to all the towns of Judah and taught the people.**

Luther once wrote, "As there is no fire without heat and smoke, so there is no faith without love. . . . But since God does not need our work . . . , the Christian makes haste to give himself wholeheartedly to his neighbor, serving and helping him freely." These are apt words to describe the faith of a king who was not satisfied with fortifying his kingdom merely against the enemies outside. He also had to help his people become strong on the inside. This picture of a teaching king is almost without parallel in the Old Testament. We

199

think, of course, of David and the way he taught Israel to praise the Lord with inspired words fitted to music. We remember Solomon's marvelous example and prayer on the day of the temple's dedication. But Jehoshaphat goes beyond this. He organizes a delegation of his own officials, specially chosen Levites and priests, and sends them out "to all the towns of Judah" to do their work among the people.

The composition of this delegation is interesting in itself. It is well known that God had given the priests primary responsibility for teaching people "the Law of the LORD" (see also Leviticus 10:11; 2 Chronicles 15:3; Jeremiah 18:18; Haggai 2:11). But here we see not only the Levites but even the king's officials joining together with the priests on the same teaching mission. As we have observed before, it helps to remember that some of the clear lines Americans draw between the sacred and the secular were not as much of a concern to ancient Israel. For them, "the Book of the Law of the LORD" (the Torah, or first five books of Moses) was the Bible, constitution, civil and criminal law code, and worship manual rolled into one. Theirs was the kingdom of God, and their king, the Lord's anointed. Keeping this in mind, it is not surprising at all to see a group like this at work. No doubt each member of the delegation concentrated on teaching whatever was appropriate to his own office.

In this way Jehoshaphat demonstrated himself to be a truly pastoral king. It is one thing to try to protect your people from outside dangers; it is another thing to pull down all the physical images and disgusting idols inside your own kingdom. But keeping worldly influence at bay and smashing stones and pillars will not protect anyone from the worldly power at work inside each one of us, the power of our own sinful selves. Only the Word of God can pull down idols from the high places of our hearts.

We need God's law to smash the idols of pride, to remove the high places dedicated to wealth and power, and to hew down the disgusting images of selfishness, greed, and illicit sexuality. But more so, we need God's promises in Christ to give us comfort and rest from our anxious and accusing conscience and to fortify us with joy and power through his matchless grace. How like Christ does Jehoshaphat show himself to be! And how like himself does our Savior urge us in turn to be, freely giving to others as we freely have received from him.

And the more we try to give God's love away, the more we will discover ourselves on the receiving end. "You can't outgive God" was one stewardship principle Jehoshaphat found to be abundantly true in his own life.

¹⁰**The fear of the Lord fell on all the kingdoms of the lands surrounding Judah, so that they did not make war with Jehoshaphat. ¹¹Some Philistines brought Jehoshaphat gifts and silver as tribute, and the Arabs brought him flocks: seven thousand seven hundred rams and seven thousand seven hundred goats.**

¹²**Jehoshaphat became more and more powerful; he built forts and store cities in Judah ¹³and had large supplies in the towns of Judah. He also kept experienced fighting men in Jerusalem. ¹⁴Their enrollment by families was as follows:**

> **From Judah, commanders of units of 1,000:**
> **Adnah the commander, with 300,000 fighting men;**
> ¹⁵**next, Jehohanan the commander, with 280,000;**
> ¹⁶**next, Amasiah son of Zicri, who volunteered himself for the service of the LORD, with 200,000.**

¹⁷**From Benjamin:**
> **Eliada, a valiant soldier, with 200,000 men armed with bows and shields;**
> ¹⁸**next, Jehozabad, with 180,000 men armed for battle.**

**¹⁹These were the men who served the king, besides those he stationed in the fortified cities throughout Judah.**

God shows himself to be a tremendous and resourceful ally. Jehoshaphat has fortified cities and garrisons? Very well, God will put the "fear of the LORD" upon the enemy nations that surround Judah. This is not the fear of trusting reverence and respect; this is the sheer terror and panic that comes upon those who realize that they are up against supernatural powers far too strong for them. It is the secret weapon in the Israelite arsenal (Exodus 15:16; Joshua 2:9; 1 Chronicles 14:17; 2 Chronicles 14:14; 20:29). Their enemies' terror of getting on the wrong side of the Lord, however, means the blessing of peace for God's people, a security far more lasting than any offered by wall and fortress.

But God did more than put fear into the hearts of the Gentiles. He also moved some of them to draw close to his anointed one, bearing gifts. The Philistines, once the great enemies of Israel, now came bringing silver and gold. The Arabians also came with their flocks and their herds. Here again it is not hard to see in the Chronicler's description of Jehoshaphat the shadow of Israel's coming Messiah as depicted by Old Testament prophecy (Psalm 72:10; compare with Isaiah 60:6; Matthew 2:11).

Being the kind of ally he is, God was still not satisfied. He continued to add grace upon grace, blessing upon blessing. "Jehoshaphat became more and more powerful." God enabled him to build more forts and cities with supplies for time of siege. He also accommodated himself to his ancient people's need to see tangible signs of his protection by giving Jehoshaphat an army so huge that it would have been madness to attack him. If we add up the figures on the right side of our text, we arrive at the astonishing total of more than a million men from Judah and Benjamin. And these did not include "those he stationed in the fortified cities throughout Judah." Jehoshaphat never could have amassed such power if the Lord had not been with him.

It is time now to consider the larger question of where this chapter fits into the thread of the Chronicler's discourse on Jehoshaphat. He has drawn for us the picture of a faithful king, a pastoral king, a king who depended upon God's promises and who therefore could count on God as his ally. The tremendous outpouring of blessings that he received—wealth, fame, his subjects' love, freedom from war, fortified cities, many troops—moved him to boast in the Lord rather than in his own power or strength. We have also duly noted the shadow of the Messiah in the Chronicler's portrayal of Jehoshaphat.

But as soon as we say all this, we come face-to-face with the inexplicably great power of sin as it works in us. This was a good king, a pious king, a devout king. And this king had it all—with God as his ally. What possible reason could he have had, then, for "ally[ing] himself with Ahab by marriage" (18:1)? This question is one that the Chronicler wants us to consider as well.

A person simply can't argue with the worldly sense of such an alliance. Why should Judah and Israel continue to bleed each other dry in a fruitless war of attrition when there were so many enemies outside their borders against whom they could unite? Ahab had a lot going for him as an ally. He had pretty much been able to fight off his greatest regional rival, Ben-Hadad of Damascus (1 Kings 20). Not only that, but he—in a coalition with several other regional powers— had made a good showing of himself against the rising strength of Assyria. In 853 B.C. Ahab and the others with him fought Shalmaneser III of Assyria to a standstill in the battle of Qarqar, thus putting a temporary hold on Shalmaneser's ambitions for Palestine. But the Assyrians had not ceased to exist, and Ben-Hadad was still a threat. East of the Jordan, the Moabites were making rebellious noises, and one could never be sure of the Edomites to the south. Besides, there was always the crocodile along the Nile (Egypt) to think about. In a frightening world like that, it would be good for Ahab and Jehoshaphat to count each other as friends.

Besides the military reason, there were also economic incentives. Ahab was an ally of Tyre. Jehoshaphat controlled Edom—at least the port city of Ezion Geber (see 20:35-37). Trade between the Mediterranean and the East could open up again, just as in the days of Solomon. The direct benefi- ciaries of this trade would be, of course, the two kings through whose territories it passed—Jehoshaphat and Ahab.

Without a doubt, an alliance with Ahab had a lot to recommend it from a worldly point of view. It seems such a good idea, in fact, that an unspiritual person has to won- der about Jehoshaphat's wisdom in being so standoffish at first. Why continue the failed policy of Rehoboam, Abijah, and Asa?

Because it was a sin to cut a deal with a man like Ahab, that's why! This was the Chronicler's reply. No amount of hype or economic boosterism could change that plain truth. The association with Israel and the house of Omri would bring near ruination upon Judah and the house of David. And, as we have already seen, God had given substantial blessings to Jehoshaphat *without* an alliance with Ahab. Jehoshaphat really did not need Ahab's help. But he wanted it anyway, and so he married his son to Ahab's daughter. The deal was done. Again we ask, Why?

That's just the way sin is. It makes no sense for people to prefer darkness to light. It makes no sense for people to trap themselves inside self-destructive ways of life. It makes no sense for people to resist the good God who made them. But they do it all the same. Does this give us some idea of what we're up against when we confront the power of the sin inside us all? Athletes often say, "I just need to keep my focus," as they get ready to compete in a big event. They mean that they need to concentrate all their inner powers on the challenge at hand. One slip, one moment when the mind wanders, can mean the difference between glory on the winner's stand or sorrow in the locker room.

In spiritual matters it will not help much to focus on one's inner powers or on the task at hand, except to assess the former as inadequate and the latter as impossible. By nature we have no focus: sin makes our minds wander from one wretched thing to the next. Even Christians must admit that we are easily pulled away from our God, attracted by the latest thing that glitters. Heedlessly we wander off into the desert of need, where one craving gives birth to another in an endless succession of desire. Deeply conscious of our own lack of strength, we can only turn to our God and ask, "Lord, in love, help me keep my focus. Help me fix my heart on you and run away in horror from anything that would divide me from your love."

### *Jehoshaphat makes an alliance with evil— but escapes with his life*

From time to time, Scripture invites us to make a journey into the underground world of evil, where darkness pretends to be light, where your greatest enemy comes across as your best friend, and where lies act like the truth. God wants us to look closely at scriptural situations where the reality of sin can be seen very clearly, so that we might gain insight into our own daily struggles, where our vision is often far less clear.

**18** Now Jehoshaphat had great wealth and honor, and he allied himself with Ahab by marriage. ²Some years later he went down to visit Ahab in Samaria. Ahab slaughtered many sheep and cattle for him and the people with him and urged him to attack Ramoth Gilead. ³Ahab king of Israel asked Jehoshaphat king of Judah, "Will you go with me against Ramoth Gilead?"

Jehoshaphat replied, "I am as you are, and my people as your people; we will join you in the war." ⁴But Jehoshaphat also said to the king of Israel, "First seek the counsel of the LORD."

As Luther once remarked, "The disaster of unbelief began with a small and innocent-looking doubt." What applies to unbelief is often also true with lapses into great sin. Sin seems so small and innocent in its first appearance. In Jehoshaphat's case it seemed to be only a marriage matter. Didn't kings often make alliances through marriage? Hadn't there been enough conflict already between Israel and Judah? Why not make peace and seal the deal by marrying off his eldest son, Jehoram, to Athaliah, Ahab's daughter?

Then the bill comes due. "Some years later," Ahab had a problem. Could his new relation by marriage help out? It seems that Ben-Hadad of Aram-Damascus had reneged on one of his treaty promises and had refused to return to Ahab the strategic town of Ramoth in Gilead, which had been captured earlier by the Arameans (see 1 Kings 20:34). Ahab invited Jehoshaphat to Samaria and put on a tremendous feast for him to entice him into joining in an expedition against Ramoth Gilead. The NIV's translation "urged" is a bit too weak to convey the flavor of the Hebrew word. "Incited" or "tempted" would have been better, and "seduced" is none too strong. The word appears in such contexts as Deuteronomy chapter 13, "If your very own brother . . . *entices you,* saying, 'Let us go and worship other gods' . . . do not yield to him or listen to him" (verses 6,8).

Was Jehoshaphat dazzled by Ahab's festive display of affection? Or was it that he felt duty-bound to honor his own treaty commitment? Who can ever say for sure what a person's excuse will be for giving into temptation. Every sinner finds a fig leaf. The fact is, Jehoshaphat's expression of commitment to his ally could not have been more wholehearted: "I am as you are, and my people as your people; we will join you in the war." It is important to take note of the way Jehoshaphat completely associated himself with his ally's schemes and plans. He kept no spiritual distance whatever. It is only *after* committing himself that he asked Ahab to "first seek the counsel of the LORD." Perhaps he did this to soothe a nagging conscience. He should have done it long before. Now he could only look for the Lord's counsel with desperate hope that plans he had already hatched would coincide with the Lord's will. Hardly the spirit of prayer!

⁵So the king of Israel brought together the prophets—four hundred men—and asked them, "Shall we go to war against Ramoth Gilead, or shall I refrain?"

"Go," they answered, "for God will give it into the king's hand."

⁶But Jehoshaphat asked, "Is there not a prophet of the LORD here whom we can inquire of?"

⁷The king of Israel answered Jehoshaphat, "There is still one man through whom we can inquire of the LORD, but I hate him because he never prophesies anything good about me, but always bad. He is Micaiah son of Imlah."

"The king should not say that," Jehoshaphat replied.

⁸So the king of Israel called one of his officials and said, "Bring Micaiah son of Imlah at once."

Who were these "prophets" that Ahab called in? The text indicates that they were prophets who truly believed they were speaking for the Lord, prophets who had escaped the sword of Jezebel (1 Kings 19:14). Perhaps the reason for their escape was their willingness to speak smooth words that the king liked to hear. Yet Zedekiah's later outrage against Micaiah seems genuine enough (18:23), and Zedekiah's words imply that he was one who felt himself to be under the control of the Spirit of the Lord. In the end it does not matter what their own feelings told them; they were still false prophets. False prophets can tell lies most sincerely, being utterly convinced that every word they say is true. That is precisely the power of the lie: it seems so very true.

Four hundred men spoke with one voice, "Go . . . for God will give it into the king's hand." Yet Jehoshaphat was not satisfied. He had enough spiritual discernment to know that something in their message just did not seem right. "Is there not a prophet of the LORD here whom we can inquire of?" he asked. These men did not sound to him like the Lord's prophets. There was something oddly disquieting about their total agreement, in their servile affirmation of the plans of men. Could there be someone else who also spoke for the Lord?

Ahab's reply is revealing. Yes, there *was* someone else. A man (notice that Ahab won't call him a prophet directly) whom he hated. Why? "He never prophesies anything good about me, but always bad." His answer not only shows how much people dislike to hear hard truths about themselves (as we have observed already in the case of Asa), but it also shows how they try to discount and subvert the truth of the message by implying that it arises out of some personal rancor on the messenger's part. "Micaiah? Oh, well, how can you believe him? He always has something bad to say about me. He just hates me, so I hate him back!"

It is useful to notice the methodology of the devil so that we can better take our stand against his schemes (Ephesians 6:11). At one time, for example, the admonition of a congregation's pastor or its elders was taken very seriously. Now people just blow it off as a matter of personality conflict and legalism. "I just don't know about that pastor. He didn't try to understand my problem. He kept rehashing the same old thing, like some parrot. For some reason he has it in for me." Not only do we see this method at work in congregations, but we also see it at work nationally as people's hearts grow increasingly cold to the Word of God. People who speak out against abortion or homosexuality are attacked as "fanatics from the Christian Right" and "homophobes." It all boils down to the same thing as Ahab's discounting of Micaiah: "I hate him. He never says anything good about me."

Again we see Jehoshaphat's conscience at work. He will not accept the reply of his ally. "The king should not say that," is his answer. A rather weak, milk-and-water rebuke, wouldn't you say? "Come, come," "Tut, tut," "Now, now"— once you've allied yourself to evil, pathetic little bleats of protest like these are about all your conscience can manage. But to satisfy his partner, Ahab has someone fetch the son of Imlah.

**⁹Dressed in their royal robes, the king of Israel and Jehoshaphat king of Judah were sitting on their thrones at the threshing floor by the entrance to the gate of Samaria, with all the prophets prophesying before them. ¹⁰Now Zedekiah son of Kenaanah had made iron horns, and he declared, "This is what the LORD says: 'With these you will gore the Arameans until they are destroyed.'"**

> ¹¹**All the other prophets were prophesying the same thing. "Attack Ramoth Gilead and be victorious," they said, "for the LORD will give it into the king's hand."**
>
> ¹²**The messenger who had gone to summon Micaiah said to him, "Look, as one man the other prophets are predicting success for the king. Let your word agree with theirs, and speak favorably."**
>
> ¹³**But Micaiah said, "As surely as the LORD lives, I can tell him only what my God says."**

With the deft strokes of a master storyteller, the writer sets the scene for the approaching confrontation between truth and error. First, he gives us a clear picture of the stage on which it will take place. The two kings are decked out in all their royal regalia, sitting in state on their thrones in the great open space near the gates of Samaria. It is all very impressive to the eye.

Surveying the scene further, we see a throng of prophets completely filling that open space, each one prophesying loudly, all saying the same thing. Our eyes are taken by one of them, Zedekiah, by name. He looks every inch a prophet. And he sounds like a prophet too. In true prophetic style Zedekiah uses a visual aid to lend force to his message. With iron horns on his head, he imitates the action of an enraged bull and says, "With these you will gore the Arameans until they are destroyed." Of course, he introduces his oracle by saying, "This is what the LORD says." Great stuff, powerful stuff!

Meanwhile, where is Micaiah, son of Imlah? He's on his way, having a nice conversation with the court official who had gone to fetch him. The court official is full of friendly advice: "Why make it hard on yourself, Micaiah? You could be the closing act! You could bring down the house! Everyone is predicting success for this expedition.

You just walk in there and say the same thing as everybody else—in your own inimitable style, of course!" Within these shadowlands of image and pretense, the bold words of a prophet sound out at last: "As surely as the LORD lives, I can tell him only what my God says."

**¹⁴When he arrived, the king asked him, "Micaiah, shall we go to war against Ramoth Gilead, or shall I refrain?"**

**"Attack and be victorious," he answered, "for they will be given into your hand."**

**¹⁵The king said to him, "How many times must I make you swear to tell me nothing but the truth in the name of the LORD?"**

**¹⁶Then Micaiah answered, "I saw all Israel scattered on the hills like sheep without a shepherd, and the LORD said, 'These people have no master. Let each one go home in peace.'"**

**¹⁷The king of Israel said to Jehoshaphat, "Didn't I tell you that he never prophesies anything good about me, but only bad?"**

Does God owe the truth to those who despise it? "Do not give dogs what is sacred; do not throw your pearls to pigs," our Lord once said (Matthew 7:6). Often, in judgment, God will "drive a man as he finds him." Ahab had shown that he was far more pleased with hearing comforting lies. Since this was true, Micaiah quickly responds to Ahab's initial query by merely repeating the glib and pleasant lie Ahab was used to hearing by now: "Attack and be victorious . . . for they will be given into your hand."

Yet there must have been something wrong in the way he said it, some lack of sincerity in his voice that informed the king that he was hearing a lie, purposefully and sarcastically uttered. Kings want their courtiers to be good liars; it takes all the fun out of flattery if it sounds as such. "How many times must I make you swear to tell me nothing but the truth in the name of the LORD?" Ahab angrily demands. It almost sounds as if these two men have been down this road before, as if Micaiah has always delivered the truth in this roundabout way to the king. He would start out making a mockery of the smooth lie by imitating it, yet with a catch of irony in his voice. In this way he would goad Ahab into demanding a truth he really did not want to hear. Whether this was Micaiah's standard operating procedure or not, it comes close enough to describing the truth of what happened on this day.

Only after Ahab demands sincerity does he get it. And when Micaiah speaks honestly at last, he shows himself to be as different as can be from the other prophets. He does not introduce his first message with words like "This is what the LORD says." There are no visual aids, no running back with horns of iron on his head.[19] He simply sees, and what he sees, he tells: "I saw all Israel scattered on the hills like sheep without a shepherd, and the LORD said, 'These people have no master. Let each one go home in peace.'" All Israel without a master to lead and guide them, shepherdless sheep wandering aimlessly over the hills—this is to be the awful aftermath of the approaching battle. The Lord takes pity on the sheep, even if no one else will. "Let each one return home safely," he says.

Notice that "all Israel" is being talked about. Most commentators apply these words simply to Ahab's death. Once he is dead, they say, the Northern Kingdom will have lost its leader. What they say is true enough, but we might go a step further. Judah too is to be involved in this battle. It is the North and the South *together* that make up "all Israel," if we understand this term according to the Chronicler's ordinary usage. By striking a deal with evil, hasn't Jehoshaphat ceased to be a true shepherd of his people, the kind of shepherd he used to be when he sent out teachers of the Word among them? Yes, he lives; yes, he rules—but he is not truly tending to the needs of the Lord's flock and therefore has ceased to deserve the title "shepherd." No doubt Micaiah intended these words to be a strong rebuke not only for Ahab but also for Jehoshaphat.

Similarly, Jesus looked out upon the Israel of his own day. Teachers and would-be prophets were there in abundance. Some took the sheep to pastures of legalism, where the strict carrying out of laws and traditions was to be their salvation. Others took the sheep to the pastures of worldliness, where the final judgment and resurrection were denied and where people were taught to forge a type of suitable compromise with the world. Then there were some who advocated revolution—violent men who, in the name of God, wanted to create a heaven on earth and didn't care whom they killed to make it happen. There were many teachers, many would-be shepherds, but when Jesus saw the crowds, "he had compassion on them, because they were harassed and helpless, like sheep without a shepherd. Then he said to his disciples, 'The harvest is plentiful but the workers are few. Ask the Lord of the harvest, therefore, to send out workers into his harvest field'" (Matthew 9:36-38).

What sincere observer has any doubts that the visible church and the world of sinners around us are in much the same condition as the ones Jesus detected in the sheep of his day? Many would-be teachers are everywhere, but few legitimate shepherds can be found. Pray for faithful workers; then get out there yourself to speak the truth in love!

Realizing the danger that the prophet's words posed for his precious alliance, Ahab quickly tried to undercut them. "What did I tell you, Jehoshaphat? This guy hates me! Why should you listen to the words of one so obviously prejudiced against me?" But Micaiah is undeterred. He has something even more striking to say.

> **[18]Micaiah continued, "Therefore hear the word of the Lord: I saw the Lord sitting on his throne with all the host of heaven standing on his right and on his left. [19]And the Lord said, 'Who will entice Ahab king of Israel in attacking Ramoth Gilead and going to his death there?'**
>
> **"One suggested this, and another that. [20]Finally, a spirit came forward, stood before the Lord and said, 'I will entice him.'**
>
> **"'By what means?' the Lord asked.**
>
> **[21]"'I will go and be a lying spirit in the mouths of all his prophets,' he said.**
>
> **"'You will succeed in enticing him,' said the Lord. 'Go and do it.'**
>
> **[22]"So now the Lord has put a lying spirit in the mouths of these prophets of yours. The Lord has decreed disaster for you."**

Now at last Micaiah makes the standard announcement of a prophetic message from the Lord: "Hear the word of the Lord . . ." But when it comes, the message is anything but standard. It is not an announcement of what *will* happen when the kings go up against Ramoth Gilead. Instead, it is an explanation of something that is *in the process of happening* as the two kings are considering their plans and listening to various prophets before them. And, once again, Micaiah announces it as something that he has seen, a vision given to him by the Lord.

"I saw the Lord sitting on his throne with all the host of heaven standing on his right and on his left." We are given one of those rare glimpses into the throne room of God. What makes it even more remarkable is that, on this occasion, the vision of God's heavenly throne room is announced before two earthly kings as they sit on their thrones. The two scenes have been deliberately set side by side before the reader (compare verse 9 with verse 18) to drive home the truth that "Many are the plans in a man's heart, but it is the LORD's purpose that prevails" (Proverbs 19:21). No matter what decision these two kings would arrive at on the threshing floor, it is God who has the last word.

Through Micaiah's vision God was telling Ahab that he had already reached his decision and that the farce playing itself out before the two kings was his own doing. God had determined to "entice Ahab king of Israel in[to] attacking Ramoth Gilead" so that he would die there. God had asked those assembled in his court to volunteer their own ideas for carrying out his determination. Various suggestions were offered until one of those who were there came forward and offered to "be a lying spirit in the mouths of all his prophets." God gave his permission. "Go and do it," he said and gave his assurance that the mission would be successful.

Is God the author of lies? Never! He gives off a light of truth more constant than the sun (James 1:17). But this was one of those times when God had decided to drive a man as he had found him. Ahab was determined to shut his heart to the Word, much preferring pleasant lies. In judgment, therefore, God handed him over to be ruled by those lies he had set his heart on hearing. "To the pure you show yourself pure, but to the crooked you show yourself shrewd" (Psalm 18:26). What makes this passage so pointed is that here God even tells Ahab that he has determined to send lies to deceive Ahab. He couldn't have made it more plain: "Your four hundred prophets are all telling you untruths!" Yet Ahab is still deceived.

What a statement this makes about our own perverse generation! No question at all, people are hungry for truth today.

They run everywhere, hoping to find something to hang their hearts on. In the process they become credulous fools who are willing to believe anything but the simple, saving truths of Scripture. A mysterious bright, shining light at the end of death's dark corridor, aliens from outer space, magic crystals and harmonic forces, psychic hotlines—all these they swallow with incredible ease. But one mention of sin, judgment, and the grace of a Savior who died for all, and their eyes glaze over. "Oh no, not *that* again!" And it's back again to their crystals.

Understand that more is at work here than mere credulity. What a frightening thing it is to read in Scripture that "God sends [people] a powerful delusion so that they will believe the lie" (2 Thessalonians 2:11). This spells God's judgment for those who refuse to "love the truth and so be saved" (2 Thessalonians 2:10). When God speaks to us in his Word, he is utterly serious, and he is absolutely in earnest when he says, "Therefore consider carefully how you listen. Whoever has will be given more; whoever does not have, even what he thinks he has will be taken from him" (Luke 8:18).

**²³Then Zedekiah son of Kenaanah went up and slapped Micaiah in the face. "Which way did the spirit from the LORD go when he went from me to speak to you?" he asked.**

**²⁴Micaiah replied, "You will find out on the day you go to hide in an inner room."**

**²⁵The king of Israel then ordered, "Take Micaiah and send him back to Amon the ruler of the city and to Joash the king's son, ²⁶and say, 'This is what the king says: Put this fellow in prison and give him nothing but bread and water until I return safely.'"**

**²⁷Micaiah declared, "If you ever return safely, the LORD has not spoken through me." Then he added, "Mark my words, all you people!"**

Zedekiah, the prophet with the iron horns, got angry, as well he might have. After all, it's not every day that someone tells you that you've got it absolutely wrong. Remember, he had his reputation as a certified prophet of the Lord to think about. Besides this, he was convinced that he had been speaking as one under the influence of some kind of spirit. It had to be the Lord's. It certainly could not be the same spirit that spoke through Micaiah. Zedekiah knew that God does not talk out of both sides of his mouth. So by what authority could Micaiah say, "Thus says the LORD!" and then call him a liar! "Just how did the LORD's Spirit leave me and go to you!" might be an idiomatic rendering of his words in verse 23. He didn't expect an answer. Convinced he was right, he thought the answer was obvious. God's Spirit could not have left him. God's Spirit had not spoken through Micaiah.

He didn't expect an answer, but Micaiah gave him one anyway. Even though he had been publicly humiliated—slapped on the cheek—he did not cry out in anger or make any threats. He simply gave Zedekiah his own personal prophecy to think about: "You will find out on the day you go to hide in an inner room." What was this all about? We do not know precisely. But we do know what Zedekiah would find out. Micaiah was saying that someday Zedekiah would find himself hiding away inside an inner room in danger of his life. At that time Micaiah's prophecy would come back to him, and he would suddenly realize that Micaiah had spoken as a true prophet all along and that he himself had been under the influence of a lying spirit, just as Micaiah had said.

Growing tired of the game, King Ahab had Micaiah taken back into custody. This time he was to be kept in prison and given nothing but enough to survive on. Whether he had been held in a prison before or not is hard to determine. He certainly had not been Ahab's honored guest! Here we get a measure of Micaiah's courage, a courage born of faith in the one true God, who would keep him safe in every trial. Even though he had been somewhat under arrest before, he had not minced his words when speaking before kings. Even though he knew well enough that telling hard truths to a king was dangerous, he held nothing back.

When Micaiah heard the words of Ahab that tried to give the lie to his own ("Put this fellow in prison . . . until I *return safely*"), he spoke out again, loud and strong, "If you ever return safely, the LORD has not spoken through me." This was probably enough to put the seal on his death sentence, enough to earn him a burial in an anonymous grave. But the souls of God's people were at stake. The little flock had to know which was the voice of their true shepherd. So he spoke the truth and accepted the consequences: "Mark my words, all you people!"

The world has always been helped along by truth-tellers, honest folk who—even if they are not Christians—will say what is right, whatever the cost. But the world—and especially the Lord's church in it—will die without its prophets, without people who are willing to give themselves to proclaiming God's truth to every nation, calling sinners to repentance and pointing them to their Savior Jesus. This is the only message that can save people from the wrath of God that is coming. But it is not a message people like to hear, especially in an age that much rather prefers the pleasant lie. And it seems to be getting less popular by the minute. Will there still be those in this next generation whose lips—cleansed by the coal of truth from God's altar—will say: "Here am I. Send me!" (Isaiah 6:8)? Pray it will be so.

Those with an eye for patterns in history will have noticed an amazing affinity between Micaiah the prophet and our

Lord Jesus Christ, especially as we see the latter on trial for his life. Jesus also took his stand in the middle of liars, to be judged by those who preferred shadows to substance (Matthew 26:59,60). Likewise his frustrated judge also finally had to demand to hear a truth from him that he did not really want to hear (Matthew 26:62-65). Jesus was publicly slapped and humiliated as well (Matthew 26:67,68). And even though he knew the truth would be denied, even though he knew it would become the basis of his false condemnation, he too spoke of seeing another tribunal that would sift through the evidence of every idle word spoken by sinners. Before this judgment seat his captors would be condemned, and he would shine like the sun. "In the future you will see the Son of Man sitting at the right hand of the Mighty One and coming on the clouds of heaven" (Matthew 26:64).

These things are written for our strength and comfort during those moments of despair in this fallen world when we are close to believing that the truth cannot prevail against the power of the lie. God is in charge of all things, and he even weaves from human deceits the whole, strong cloth of his eternal truth: "All [this had] taken place that the writings of the prophets might be fulfilled" (Matthew 26:56).

**²⁸So the king of Israel and Jehoshaphat king of Judah went up to Ramoth Gilead. ²⁹The king of Israel said to Jehoshaphat, "I will enter the battle in disguise, but you wear your royal robes." So the king of Israel disguised himself and went into battle.**

**³⁰Now the king of Aram had ordered his chariot commanders, "Do not fight with anyone, small or great, except the king of Israel." ³¹When the chariot commanders saw Jehoshaphat, they thought, "This is the king of Israel." So they turned to attack him, but Jehoshaphat cried out, and the LORD helped him. God drew them away from him, ³²for when the chariot**

commanders saw that he was not the king of Israel, they stopped pursuing him.

**<sup>33</sup>But someone drew his bow at random and hit the king of Israel between the sections of his armor. The king told the chariot driver, "Wheel around and get me out of the fighting. I've been wounded." <sup>34</sup>All day long the battle raged, and the king of Israel propped himself up in his chariot facing the Arameans until evening. Then at sunset he died.**

The issues had been made plain because the Lord had made them so. Against better knowledge, then, Jehoshaphat "went up to Ramoth Gilead," together with his ungodly ally, Ahab, selling his own soul into service to the lie. Ahab, troubled by the prophet's words, tried to look for a way around them. Clearly, if he was to die, he had to be recognized. Therefore, he could evade the prophet's word by disguising himself. Better still, Jehoshaphat should continue to "wear [his] royal robes" so that he might be mistaken for Ahab. In this way Ahab would be doubly protected. A brilliant scheme! It couldn't miss! Why Jehoshaphat should have been so easily persuaded to serve as Ahab's patsy is hard to say. Perhaps he thought it was beneath his dignity to play silly games of subterfuge, and simply went into battle wearing his royal insignia as he had intended all along.

The deceiver's ploy met with some success at first. Ben-Hadad had given his charioteers strict orders to focus their attack purely on King Ahab. Tricked into believing that Jehoshaphat was Ahab, they pursued him. All seemed lost; the situation was hopeless. Jehoshaphat was bound to die under the onslaught of Aramean chariots. At the brink of death, he cried out to the Lord in penitent faith, and the Lord was his ally again. The word translated "drew away" in this verse is the same Hebrew word ("urged") we discussed previously under verse 2 (page 206). The writer wants us to make the connection here. The Lord had outfoxed the schemer Ahab. The Lord exposed his ruse to the Arameans, and once the chariot commanders realized that they had the wrong man in their sights, "they stopped pursuing him."

The amazing grace of our Lord is seen in all its glory here. A king on whom the Lord had lavished his love had been faithless. The king had turned away from his best ally and had spurned the warning of the Lord's spokesman in Samaria. Heedlessly, foolishly, he had walked into danger; yet when the waters threatened to cover him, he cried out to the Lord in prayer, and the Lord answered him. The miracle of forgiveness is nowhere better seen than in the words "and the LORD helped him." There is no better commentary on this passage than these words from Psalm 130:

> Out of the depths I cry to you, O LORD;
>   O Lord, hear my voice.
> Let your ears be attentive
>   to my cry for mercy.
>
> If you, O LORD, kept a record of sins,
>   O Lord, who could stand?
> But with you there is forgiveness;
>   therefore you are feared.
>
> O Israel, put your hope in the LORD,
>   for with the LORD is unfailing love
>   and with him is full redemption.
> He himself will redeem Israel
>   from all their sins. (verses 1-4,7,8)

The final settling of accounts with the schemer comes almost as an afterthought. For the one who had wished to survive the battle by remaining anonymous, the Lord appointed a random death by an unnamed bowman. An Aramean took aim and shot an arrow "at random"—"in all his innocence" as the Hebrew literally reads. That is, he had no intention whatsoever in his mind of killing a specific individual like the king of Israel. He just fired away, and his arrow just happened to pierce the scales of Ahab's coat of armor. The wound was mortal, and for all Ahab's courage in facing the Arameans till the end of day, his life still ebbed away until it ended at the setting sun. He could not cheat the Lord's sentence of death. Anyone who thinks that all this "just happened" has not been paying attention. God always has the last word, and there is not a schemer alive who can evade his appointed hour.

The chapters probably should have been divided *after* verse 1 of chapter 19, "Jehoshaphat king of Judah returned safely to his palace in Jerusalem," since the word *safely* is an obvious echo of the prophet's earlier warning to Ahab, "If you ever return *safely*, the LORD has not spoken through me" (verse 27). At the time the prophet had left the fate of Jehoshaphat unmentioned. By this God was giving him opportunity to turn back again in faith to him and, as we have seen, this is exactly what happened in Jehoshaphat's hour of need. He turned, he cried out, and the Lord let him live.

Yet this is not quite the end of the matter, as far as either the Lord or Jehoshaphat was concerned. This will become clear as we read the rest of chapter 19.

## *Jehoshaphat appoints judges for the Lord*

### God impartially assesses his king

**19** **When Jehoshaphat king of Judah returned safely to his palace in Jerusalem, ²Jehu the seer, the son of Hanani, went out to meet him and said to the king, "Should you help the wicked and love those who hate the LORD? Because of this, the wrath of the LORD is upon you. ³There is, however, some**

**good in you, for you have rid the land of the Asherah poles and
have set your heart on seeking God."**

Although the theme of "judging" stands out in this
chapter, the Chronicler has not abandoned his other
theme of "alliances—good and bad." It is verse 2, in fact,
that clarifies for the reader the entire issue of making
alliances with evil. The prophet Jehu frames it for his
king as an either/or proposition. "Should you help the
wicked and love those who hate the LORD?" What often
happens in this matter is that the father of lies masquerades as an angel of light (2 Corinthians 11:14) and
attempts to induce spiritually minded people into diluting
the severity of the law with the compassion of the
gospel. The result is the loss of both. Let us examine the
context of the prophet Jehu's words to avoid making this
same error ourselves.

To play devil's advocate again, we might say: "What
made Jehoshaphat's alliance with Ahab so wrong? After all, it
was not an alliance with an outright heathen, like Asa's was
with Ben-Hadad. Come to think of it, Solomon enjoyed a
good working relationship with Hiram of Tyre. So why was
it so crucial for Judah to avoid making common cause with
its brother to the north? For all its problems, God still recognized the Northern Kingdom as his own people—separated
from the house of David, true, but still his own. And isn't it a
harsh and loveless thing to be so judgmental of those who
one could say had been misguided from birth? They didn't
choose to be born in the kingdom with the calf idols. How
would they ever come to know better if Judah did not asso-
ciate with them?"

Now let's examine the assumptions underlying those
words. First of all, God was not condemning every kind of
working relationship with other groups of people, even with

223

the outright heathen. Rather, he had in mind those kinds of associations in which God's people make no effort to keep their *spiritual* distance. Listen to Jehoshaphat's words again from chapter 18: "I am as you are, and my people as your people" (18:3). During the same time when Elijah, at the risk of his life, had been working to stem the rising tide of Baalism, Jehoshaphat undercut Elijah's testimony by marrying his son off to Ahab's daughter. It was as if he were saying, "You know, we may have our differences, but they're not all that important. What's a little Baal worship between brothers? I know you have to please your wife. And as for that calf idol thing—well, I'm sure your heart's in the right place at least. Maybe we can talk about that some other time."

Second, to insist that maintaining spiritual contact was the only *real* way to help the erring folk of the North disregards the ongoing testimony of the temple worship in Jerusalem. It's the same as saying that the way of life of God's people in the South was not a powerful witness to God's people in the North. This line of thought assumes that only ongoing dialogue within the context of some kind of religious association qualifies as testimony and that any attempt to witness while keeping one's spiritual distance falls under the category of being judgmental. But King Abijah had already made the issue clear to the North (chapter 13). There could be no question as to which kind of worship was legitimate and which was not. Many had heard that testimony and had responded in faith. They were willing to leave their ancestral home and hearth in the North to be near the courts of the Lord.

Finally, we must ask, "Is it really love—love born of the gospel—that allows people to continue in error without any attempt to make the issues clear for them? Is it really love to muddy the waters for upcoming generations so that they will have less ability to discern light from darkness and truth from error?" This writer grew up as a member of a generation that was taught to sing, "All you need is love." Deceived, we thought it was true. That is, we believed in this ill-defined, mushy tolerance that could go along with all kinds of immorality under the banner of love. After all, it was the age of different strokes for different folks, right?

In the end, however, that kind of love leaves you with nothing, with less than nothing. "Only the false gods survived to ensure our ruin," as one writer so aptly put it.[20] One look at the lives of so many flower children crushed by evil, one look at the awful aftermath of the '60s, and we will not call it love to tolerate evil. "Should you help the wicked and love those who hate the LORD? Because of this, the wrath of the LORD is upon you." There is no doubt at all where God stands on this matter. Jehoshaphat knew. He had felt God's wrath in that battle when he saw the Aramean chariots heading straight for him.

Yet Jehoshaphat also experienced in that same crisis God's unyielding love, which will not let his own destroy themselves. God granted Jehoshaphat a change of heart and escape from death. Now he was listening again to God's prophet, who put his actions under scrutiny to let him know how he then ought to spend the rest of his rescued life. "There is, however, some good in you, for you have rid the land of the Asherah poles and have set your heart on seeking God." Humbly penitent, Jehoshaphat resolved again to walk with the only reliable ally he had.

*Jehoshaphat lives as he is named and establishes the Lord's justice*

**⁴Jehoshaphat lived in Jerusalem, and he went out again among the people from Beersheba to the hill country of Ephraim and turned them back to the LORD, the God of their**

fathers. ⁵He appointed judges in the land, in each of the fortified cities of Judah. ⁶He told them, "Consider carefully what you do, because you are not judging for man but for the LORD, who is with you whenever you give a verdict. ⁷Now let the fear of the LORD be upon you. Judge carefully, for with the LORD our God there is no injustice or partiality or bribery."

⁸In Jerusalem also, Jehoshaphat appointed some of the Levites, priests and heads of Israelite families to administer the law of the LORD and to settle disputes. And they lived in Jerusalem. ⁹He gave them these orders: "You must serve faithfully and wholeheartedly in the fear of the LORD. ¹⁰In every case that comes before you from your fellow countrymen who live in the cities—whether bloodshed or other concerns of the law, commands, decrees or ordinances—you are to warn them not to sin against the LORD; otherwise his wrath will come on you and your brothers. Do this, and you will not sin.

¹¹"Amariah the chief priest will be over you in any matter concerning the LORD, and Zebadiah son of Ishmael, the leader of the tribe of Judah, will be over you in any matter concerning the king, and the Levites will serve as officials before you. Act with courage, and may the LORD be with those who do well."

The name Jehoshaphat means "The Lord judges." Whether it is simply coincidence or whether the Lord had given his parents some special knowledge ahead of time about their child, it certainly seems as if Jehoshaphat's life matches his name. The entire section is prefaced by what seems to be a summary verse: "He went out again among the people from Beersheba to the hill country of Ephraim and turned them back to the LORD, the God of their fathers." This judicial reform was a continuation of that pastoral duty Jehoshaphat had begun to carry out in chapter 17. It involved his entire kingdom, south to north, and had as its goal his people's spiritual good. It could well be that Jehoshaphat also wanted to deal with some problems of idolatry in his kingdom that had come up as a result of his close association with Ahab.

A close reading of this chapter informs us that Jehoshaphat planned for a system of justice with at least two levels. The first level operated locally in the "fortified cities" that the king and his predecessors had built all over Judah. The second level was centrally situated in Jerusalem and served the entire system by providing courts of appeal. There were two chief justices appointed for each of the two types of cases that could arise. One was in charge of matters "concerning the LORD"; the other, over matters "concerning the king."

We notice that Jehoshaphat's plan was very much in agreement with Moses' prescriptions in Deuteronomy. There God both provided for the establishment of local courts in every town and granted the right of appeal to a higher, centralized court for those cases that would prove to be too difficult for the local judges to handle (Deuteronomy 16:18; 17:8). Jehoshaphat assigned to the Levites the role of court officials. The word used for *official* may imply that they served as organizers of the court's docket or as a kind of ancient court stenographers, although the exact nature of their duties remains unclear.

As absorbing as some of these details may be, we are far more interested in what Jehoshaphat said to his newly appointed judges. Here we can observe the mind behind the reform and what he hoped to accomplish with it. Clearly, we see a man who has learned his lesson and who has listened to the rebuke of the Lord's prophet. The supreme goal of this reform is a spiritual one: "You are to warn [your fellow Israelites] not to sin against the LORD; otherwise his wrath will come on you and your brothers." This is the voice of experience talking (compare verse 10 with verse 2).

Jehoshaphat is saying, "In this kingdom, justice means more than being fair with one another or being legally in the right. We are God's people. He wants us to seek him in faith, to live devout and holy lives before him in reverent fear, and to shun with horror anything that might defile us before him who is holy. We are to remember that God's wrath breaks out against those who do wrong."

In Chronicles we have seen the term *fear of God* being used in two distinct senses. A fear of being punished for having crossed the line is something found even in the conscience of the heathen. You don't have to be a believer in the Father of our Lord Jesus Christ to slow down on the freeway when you see a state trooper. But a fearful sense of having sinned against the Savior-God and an ensuing horror of doing anything God hates—this kind of fear occurs only in believers, those whose hearts the Spirit has taught to trust in the God who forgives sin. The first kind of fear (found also in unbelievers) we might call *dread;* the second—combining elements of reverence, awe, and trust—we might even read as an Old Testament synonym for *faith.*

In the kingdom of Judah, there were always both believers and unbelievers living side by side—both spiritual children of Abraham and children of Abraham whose relationship to their father was merely a physical one. Jehoshaphat had the combined task of regulating a community of believers and of ensuring peace within an earthly society, one with the same challenges as any earthly kingdom. Jehoshaphat could hope that a true fear of God (understood in that second sense mentioned above) would rule the hearts of his people and be seen in their daily lives. But if that kind of fear was absent, then he could at least count on the law— with its threats and punishments—to keep the unruly hearts of people in line through sheer dread of God's wrath.

To apply this to the present day, we need only consider the following points. There is such a beast in the heart of every sinful human being that no orderly society can exist on earth without this sense of dread. When a society starts losing the sense of dread, there is no bridle on earth left that will keep people from running in any direction they please. Dread keeps the lid on evil. Yes, it is true that only a genuine fear of God can join people together into an eternal community of faith. But a dread of God's punishment will at least keep things on earth quiet enough for us to preach the gospel. It may not be the final good we would want for all people, but it is a provisional good for our societies that is certainly worth praying about and working toward (1 Timothy 2:1-4).

Many have observed something profoundly troubling about the current scene in America. Our future as a society does not look bright, not only because there has been a tremendous decline in the number of Christians in it but also because we, as a country, seem to have lost our sense of dread. Anyone who might suggest in public that "[God's] wrath will come" upon a person who did wrong would be laughed to scorn. This was not always so. Thomas Jefferson (who, as far as we can tell, was no Christian) once wrote, "Indeed, I tremble for my country when I reflect that God is just; that his justice cannot sleep forever."[21] If we care about our earthly country, we have a lot to pray about and a great deal of work to do.

Returning to our text, we notice that there are several essential qualities Jehoshaphat wants to see in his judges. The first is "the fear of the LORD," which we would understand in the deeper sense of a believer's reverence. The second is faithfulness, and the third is decisiveness. Jehoshaphat wants his judges to operate with the bold faith that they serve as the Lord's representatives with the Lord as their constant ally. The whole of any believer's life is lived in the presence of God, but a judge is one who has the calling to sit in the Lord's seat, judging "for the Lord." Since judges are believers, the image of their Father will be seen in them when they carry out their calling. As God plays no favorites, neither will they. As unthinkable as it would be for God to act unjustly or to take a bribe, so unthinkable must it be for them.

Faithfulness means taking each case seriously, whether it involves "bloodshed or other concerns of the law, commands, decrees or ordinances." This is the law of the Lord; to break it is to sin against him and incur his wrath. No matter of the law, therefore, is a small matter. Finally, decisiveness is necessary in a person who is asked to apply the law to people's lives. Judges cannot dither; they must act. And when they act in the fear of God, let them humbly trust in the promise that the Lord is their ally and will be with those who do well.

We have already observed what kind of application these verses might have for Christians who live in an earthly society. They also hold a special meaning for Christians as people called to share the gospel with all nations. It is found in the phrase, "With the Lord our God there is no . . . partiality." This idea of God's absolute impartiality is rooted in the conviction that God is completely just. It contains a striking picture. The word *partiality* is a rendering of Hebrew words that might be represented more literally with the English "receiving of faces." God does not look at a person's social status, sex, or age before he decides what to do.

Early in the life of the New Testament church, when it had still not fully grasped the truth that the gospel is for all people, it was hard for Jewish Christians to reach out to the gentile world with the saving message of Jesus. Centuries of law, custom, and habit prevented Jewish believers from any easy association with non-Jews. It took a special vision from the Lord to convince Peter, for example, that he could go into the house of the Roman Cornelius to preach the gospel to him and not become unclean by doing so. After the Lord had convinced Peter of this, however, and Peter found himself facing a group of Gentiles who were waiting for him to speak, this ancient principle of God's law came back to him. Only then he understood it in a more profound way: "I now realize how true it is that God does not show favoritism but accepts men from every nation who fear him" (Acts 10:34,35).

In our relationship to God, no one stands any higher in God's esteem than another because of race, social standing, or sex. The gospel of Jesus teaches us to believe that the love of God recognizes no borders, is blinded by no prejudice, and is impressed by no pedigree. "There is neither Jew nor Greek, slave nor free, male nor female, for you are all one in Christ Jesus" (Galatians 3:28). Since this is how our Father looks at us, he has every right to expect his people to have the same regard for one another. "My brothers, as believers in our glorious Lord Jesus Christ, don't show favoritism" (James 2:1). We are grateful for James' reminder that the gospel is not only for those who look like us, talk like us, and act like us, but for all people everywhere. We should not require any more special revelations before we put this into practice in mutual love.

### God fights for his people against an unholy alliance

Some time after he had shored up the spiritual defenses of his people, Jehoshaphat heard of a new and deadly threat.

**20** **After this, the Moabites and Ammonites with some of the Meunites came to make war on Jehoshaphat.**

**²Some men came and told Jehoshaphat, "A vast army is coming against you from Edom, from the other side of the Sea.**

It is already in Hazazon Tamar" (that is, En Gedi). **³Alarmed, Jehoshaphat resolved to inquire of the** LORD**, and he proclaimed a fast for all Judah. ⁴The people of Judah came together to seek help from the** LORD**; indeed, they came from every town in Judah to seek him.**

**⁵Then Jehoshaphat stood up in the assembly of Judah and Jerusalem at the temple of the** LORD **in the front of the new courtyard ⁶and said:**

Three traditional enemies of God's people—the Moabites, Ammonites, and Meunites—had banded together in an unholy alliance against Judah. Verse 10 identifies the Meunites more exactly as men from Mount Seir in Edom. They were attacking from an unexpected quarter. Usually Judah had to fend off her enemies from the south, the north, or the west. Her southeastern flank was relatively safe, protected as it was by the forbidding shores of the Dead Sea and the rock cliffs of the Judean wilderness. Yet somehow without being detected, this vast army had managed to get past the Dead Sea. Now they were at En Gedi, from which there was a mountain pass leading directly into the heartland of the Judean hill country. By the time Jehoshaphat heard the news, his enemies were already poised to strike.

Little wonder that Jehoshaphat was alarmed! Without warning this vast army appeared on his doorstep; he was left with precious little time to prepare. But though God's people may at times be struck with fear because of the magnitude of the threats they face, they know what to do with their fears. So it was with Jehoshaphat. He did not—as a worldly king would—begin by calling out his troops for battle. Instead, he mustered his spiritual strength by declaring a national fast and by calling for a solemn religious gathering of the people. He knew that Judah's help would come from "the LORD, the Maker of heaven and earth" (Psalm 121:2).

After Jehoshaphat and the people had gathered at God's house, the king stood up to lead his people in prayer. The Chronicler once again permits us to hear the words of God's king praying on behalf of his people:

> "O LORD, God of our fathers, are you not the God who is in heaven? You rule over all the kingdoms of the nations. Power and might are in your hand, and no one can withstand you. ⁷O our God, did you not drive out the inhabitants of this land before your people Israel and give it forever to the descendants of Abraham your friend? ⁸They have lived in it and have built in it a sanctuary for your Name, saying, ⁹'If calamity comes upon us, whether the sword of judgment, or plague or famine, we will stand in your presence before this temple that bears your Name and will cry out to you in our distress, and you will hear us and save us.'
>
> ¹⁰"But now here are men from Ammon, Moab and Mount Seir, whose territory you would not allow Israel to invade when they came from Egypt; so they turned away from them and did not destroy them. ¹¹See how they are repaying us by coming to drive us out of the possession you gave us as an inheritance. ¹²O our God, will you not judge them? For we have no power to face this vast army that is attacking us. We do not know what to do, but our eyes are upon you."

¹³All the men of Judah, with their wives and children and little ones, stood there before the LORD.

We notice that Jehoshaphat begins his prayer by *confessing his faith* in the Lord. He is the only true God in heaven. Every other god is an idol. The true God has graciously bound himself by solemn promise to be the God of Abraham, Isaac, Jacob, and their descendants. Though from Jehoshaphat's point of view the attack of this vast army may have been sudden and unexpected, he knows that such is not the case as far as the Lord is concerned. "Power and might" are in God's hands. God controls and directs the affairs of men. Clearly this matter also is under his command.

The king then proceeds to *remind God of his promises.* God himself had promised this land to Abraham and his descendants by saying, "All the land that you see I will give to you and your offspring forever" (Genesis 13:15). God fulfilled that promise by driving out the inhabitants of the land and settling his people Israel in it. The tender relationship that existed between God and his people was also emphasized by the presence of the temple. The temple was God's sanctuary, the place where he had put his name. As we have seen before, this expression means that the temple was the place where God had chosen to reveal himself as the God of grace. At the temple God's people could approach him in prayer and find him. This was God's promise.

Weaving God's promises into our prayers is a good practice for us to follow as well: "Lord, you said this. You cannot lie. I ask that it may be for me just as you have said." And when we approach him in Christ, we are certain that God hears us.

In verses 10 to 12, King Jehoshaphat *points out the specific need* with which he and his people have come: "Our enemies have united against us and are bent on driving us out of our land." His cry for help may strike us as being a somewhat curious way to express oneself in prayer: "O our God, will you not *judge* them?" Yet it springs from the conviction that it is God who draws the maps and sets the boundaries among men and nations. And he does this as the God who is absolutely fair and completely impartial.

God had assigned Moab, Ammon, and Edom the territories they now possessed. While the Israelites were on their way to the Promised Land, God had expressly told them, "Do not provoke [the Edomites, Ammonites, and Moabites] to war, for I will not give you any of their land [east of the Jordan]" (Deuteronomy 2:5). Israel had obeyed. God then settled his people in the land west of the Jordan that he had determined to give them as an inheritance, or permanent possession. This invasion, therefore, was completely unjust, and by it these enemies were defying God's Word. The situation simply cried out for God to pronounce judgment on those who would defy his will.

In much the same spirit we pray "Thy will be done," by which we ask God to destroy every evil plan or unholy alliance of the devil, the world, and our sinful nature. We ask him to execute judgment upon anyone who openly defies God's Word or tries to keep God's saving will from being carried out.

Jehoshaphat concludes by confessing the weakness they all feel and their utter dependence on God. "We have no power. . . . We do not know what to do." These words at first might sound like a hopeless cry from someone who has given up. But when put together with the last phrase, "our eyes are upon you," they become a beautiful prayer of faith. It's as if he said: "This battle is beyond us; we cannot cope. But we look to you, whose power and wisdom are infinite." In a similar way, Luther speaks of praying in times of trouble: "God [wants] you to pour out your trouble before him, and not let it lie upon yourself . . . so that in the end you make ten, or even a hundred calamities out of one. He wills that you should be too weak to bear and overcome such trouble, in order that you may learn to find strength in him, and that he may be praised through his strength in you. Behold, this is how Christians are made!"[22]

God's king in this way expresses the earnest longing of all the people. Men, women, children, and babies stand there in the presence of the Lord. All eyes are on him, expecting an answer to their prayer. Notice, however, that the king does not presume "to show God the goal and to determine the time and the manner [in which] . . . they wished to be helped. . . . Those who truly wait upon God ask for grace, and they leave it free to God's good pleasure how, where, and by what means He shall help him. They do not despair of help, yet they do not give it a name."[23] Such is the confidence Christians have every time they look to God in prayer. Our Father will hear us not because our prayer is so worthy but because his promise is so certain.

For Jehoshaphat and the assembly, God immediately gives a name to the kind of help he intends to give.

**[14]Then the Spirit of the LORD came upon Jahaziel son of Zechariah, the son of Benaiah, the son of Jeiel, the son of Mattaniah, a Levite and descendant of Asaph, as he stood in the assembly.**
**[15]He said: "Listen, King Jehoshaphat and all who live in Judah and Jerusalem! This is what the LORD says to you: 'Do not be afraid or discouraged because of this vast army. For the battle is not yours, but God's. [16]Tomorrow march down against them. They will be climbing up by the Pass of Ziz, and you will find them at the end of the gorge in the Desert of Jeruel. [17]You will not have to fight this battle. Take up your positions; stand firm and see the deliverance the LORD will give you, O Judah and Jerusalem. Do not be afraid; do not be discouraged. Go out to face them tomorrow, and the LORD will be with you.'"**

The Spirit of the Lord came upon Jahaziel the Levite with a special revelation for all. The Spirit moved him to declare in some detail how the Lord would answer them and come to their rescue. God directed them to march out against their enemies until they met in a mountain pass. Then the Lord showed his great love by telling them, in effect: "Don't worry about this particular battle. This one is mine; I'll take care of it. You won't have to fight at all. All I ask is that you take up the position assigned to you, stand firm, and watch me win the victory for you."

It is important for us to note here that God always answers our prayers, although those answers may not always come with the speed of Jehaziel's reply. We pray to a Father who loves us as his dear children for Jesus' sake. *For Jesus' sake* means that there is nothing more certain in heaven and earth than our Father's love, and it is on the bedrock of this certainty that we base our prayers. Because of it we know, for example, that God doesn't know how to give us bad gifts, and if we do ask for something that might hurt us, God will answer our request with a loving no before giving us something far better and finer. That is also why, when we are making our requests known to God in those areas where we have no clear word of God to guide us, we pray in the full joy of faith, "Your will be done!" We know that even if God doesn't do what we want at the time, what he wants and gives us will be for our eternal good.

Above all, we look to God's promises in Scripture to find solid answers to our prayers. What God promises, he delivers. When God gives a clear and universal promise, there is no need to pray "if it be your will," for God has already expressed his saving will in the promise. We think here especially of his promises to forgive all sin, to give his Spirit, to remain with us and let nothing separate us from his love, and to give us strength to overcome when life's trials threaten to overwhelm us. When asking for any of these things, we say "Amen" in the full conviction that God will give us what we ask, since Jesus says that the Father will not respond to our cry for bread by giving us stones.

This response of joyful faith to God's promise is exactly what we see in Jehoshaphat and the people of Judah.

**¹⁸Jehoshaphat bowed with his face to the ground, and all the people of Judah and Jerusalem fell down in worship before the LORD. ¹⁹Then some Levites from the Kohathites and Korahites stood up and praised the LORD, the God of Israel, with very loud voice.**

**²⁰Early in the morning they left for the Desert of Tekoa. As they set out, Jehoshaphat stood and said, "Listen to me, Judah and people of Jerusalem! Have faith in the LORD your God and you will be upheld; have faith in his prophets and you will be successful." ²¹After consulting the people, Jehoshaphat appointed men to sing to the LORD and to praise him for the splendor of his holiness as they went out at the head of the army, saying:**

**"Give thanks to the LORD,
for his love endures forever."**

Jehoshaphat recognized that he had heard the living voice of God, who simply used Jahaziel the prophet as his instrument to speak his Word. The entire assembly bowed down low in reverent awe at the God who promises such great things to his people. Loud songs of praise from the Levite choir broke the worshipful silence at last.

This same spirit of worship was maintained the following day as God's people marched out for battle. The king took the lead in encouraging the people to trust the Lord and to trust his prophets. The king saw to it that the songs of praise begun in the temple continued as they marched. Men were appointed to sing the victory song of faith, "Give thanks to the LORD," before the victory was even realized. What God promises is as good as done even before it actually happens.

What a sight God places before our eyes here! An entire nation marches out to a battlefield against very real enemies armed with swords, shields, slings, and spears. Yet Jehoshaphat's people look more like a congregation leaving church than an army going to war. All the same, the army of God is marching out fully equipped. They have the sword of the Spirit, the shield of faith, and an attitude of prayer in their hearts.

In a similar way, we may approach our entire lives as one undivided act of worship. The high points come at our formal services, when we gather together as God's people. We come to seek the Lord in prayer and to draw strength from Word and sacrament. We leave prepared to do battle with our enemies, those who seek to destroy our spiritual life. Our victory is assured by the words we have heard. Then as God gives us daily victories over sin and Satan, we have fresh reasons to gather together in praise and prayer. His mercy endures forever.

**²²As they began to sing and praise, the Lord set ambushes against the men of Ammon and Moab and Mount Seir who were invading Judah, and they were defeated. ²³The men of Ammon and Moab rose up against the men from Mount Seir to destroy and annihilate them. After they finished slaughtering the men from Seir, they helped to destroy one another.**

**²⁴When the men of Judah came to the place that overlooks the desert and looked toward the vast army, they saw only dead bodies lying on the ground; no one had escaped. ²⁵So Jehoshaphat and his men went to carry off their plunder, and they found among them a great amount of equipment and clothing and also articles of value—more than they could take away. There was so much plunder that it took three days to collect it. ²⁶On the fourth day they assembled in the Valley of Beracah, where they praised the Lord. This is why it is called the Valley of Beracah to this day.**

**²⁷Then, led by Jehoshaphat, all the men of Judah and Jerusalem returned joyfully to Jerusalem, for the Lord had given them cause to rejoice over their enemies. ²⁸They entered**

**Jerusalem and went to the temple of the LORD with harps and lutes and trumpets.**

**²⁹The fear of God came upon all the kingdoms of the countries when they heard how the LORD had fought against the enemies of Israel. ³⁰And the kingdom of Jehoshaphat was at peace, for his God had given him rest on every side.**

The battle itself was somewhat anticlimactic. "The LORD set ambushes," the Chronicler tells us. This phrase is best explained by the following verses, which describe the enemy alliance falling to pieces and the former allies fighting among themselves. In the same way, all must perish who defiantly set themselves against the Lord and against his anointed (Psalm 2). When the people of Judah arrived at the place where they could look down into the mountain passes that lead up from the Dead Sea area, they discovered that there was no army left to fight. The truth of the phrase "the battle is the LORD's" became part of their living experience. The only thing left for them to do was to pick up the plunder: the equipment, clothing, and valuables strewn over the battlefield. It took them three days to do it—a fact that speaks volumes as to how rich and extensive the booty was and how complete the victory. On the fourth day they gathered to thank God for the victory and its fruits. A valley that could have been the scene of a terrible defeat for Judah had become the Valley of Beracah. *Beracah* is a Hebrew word meaning "praise." They gave the valley a new name to remind themselves that their God had given them another reason to praise his saving name.

Following their on-site thanksgiving service, the company returned joyfully to Jerusalem to praise the Lord in his temple. The first service was spontaneous, a person might say. The second was more formal. The king and his people wanted to do things properly and to praise the Lord with all the resources at their disposal, "with harps and lutes and trumpets."

The response of the enemies of God's people was quite different. In verse 29 we are told that the "fear of God" came upon them. This refers once again to that supernatural and paralyzing dread God would put into the hearts of the people and nations that surrounded Israel, causing them to leave God's people alone. The result for God's kingdom under Jehoshaphat was that the Lord's own were able to live undisturbed lives in peace and safety.

## Summary of Jehoshaphat's reign and an unhappy postscript

<sup>31</sup>So Jehoshaphat reigned over Judah. He was thirty-five years old when he became king of Judah, and he reigned in Jerusalem twenty-five years. His mother's name was Azubah daughter of Shilhi. <sup>32</sup>He walked in the ways of his father Asa and did not stray from them; he did what was right in the eyes of the LORD. <sup>33</sup>The high places, however, were not removed, and the people still had not set their hearts on the God of their fathers.

<sup>34</sup>The other events of Jehoshaphat's reign, from beginning to end, are written in the annals of Jehu son of Hanani, which are recorded in the book of the kings of Israel.

<sup>35</sup>Later, Jehoshaphat king of Judah made an alliance with Ahaziah king of Israel, who was guilty of wickedness. <sup>36</sup>He agreed with him to construct a fleet of trading ships. After these were built at Ezion Geber, <sup>37</sup>Eliezer son of Dodavahu of Mareshah prophesied against Jehoshaphat, saying, "Because you have made an alliance with Ahaziah, the LORD will destroy what you have made." The ships were wrecked and were not able to set sail to trade.

What is the Chronicler's final verdict on Jehoshaphat's life? As we have seen, there were tremendous high points in the king's pastoral care of his people, in his zeal for establishing the Lord's justice in the land and in his humble, inspiring leadership during the sneak attack from Judah's enemies. During all those times, the Lord had been his ally, and both king and people had prospered. But there was also that appalling lapse brought on by his marriage alliance with Ahab when he had made common cause in war with that wicked king. These verses make it clear that the pact he had made with evil had not ceased to get him tangled up in dubious ventures. It also would continue to give his descendants a lot of trouble.

After all that has happened, it seems nearly impossible for us to believe what our eyes see in verse 35: "Later, Jehoshaphat king of Judah made an alliance with Ahaziah king of Israel, who was guilty of wickedness." How could he, who had had a new beginning in the Spirit, again try to reach his goal by human effort (see Galatians 3:3)? One of our own synod's writers has put it so well: "Each child of God is both saint and sinner. And he is not only prone to sin, but capable of great, flagrant sins."[24]

Whenever the Lord gives us something, it is our tendency—so weak and prone to sin as we are—to regard it as safely stowed away and in our possession now by absolute right instead of by God's grace. We quickly lose our sense of grace and become jaded with what we have. So our eyes are drawn to something new, and our hearts begin to long for things we don't yet have. Apparently Jehoshaphat began to long for the gold of Ophir and the prestige of being a great trader-king like Solomon, even though the Lord had already given him great wealth and honor (see 1 Kings 22:48 and 2 Chronicles 17:5).

The example of Jehoshaphat can teach us that the problem is never with the way God has blessed us; our real problem is always the enemy within. We will never be content until God removes the idols from our hearts, establishes his peace there, and teaches us to find perfect rest in him. Sometimes the way God does this is by throwing our plans into confusion and wrecking all our ships. It is still his love at work, even when he's wounding us. He wants to help us die to sin and rely instead upon him. "Let me be your God," he is saying, "and find your joy in me."

In spite of Jehoshaphat's lapses, the Chronicler's verdict was that "he did what was right in the eyes of the LORD." When our judge and King looks at us, he sees more than the sin that calls for his wrath. He sees our Savior, who took that wrath upon himself and removed our guilt forever. Through him God evaluated a sinner-saint like Jehoshaphat as a king who did what was right. Only at the cross can we fully come to know the Lord, our judge, and understand how he can maintain both perfect justice and boundless mercy.

### God's kingdom under Jehoram

*A bleak summary of his reign:*
*"He walked in the ways . . . of Ahab"*

**21** Then Jehoshaphat rested with his fathers and was buried with them in the City of David. And Jehoram his son succeeded him as king. ²Jehoram's brothers, the sons of Jehoshaphat, were Azariah, Jehiel, Zechariah, Azariahu, Michael and Shephatiah. All these were sons of Jehoshaphat king of Israel. ³Their father had given them many gifts of silver and gold and articles of value, as well as fortified cities in Judah, but he had given the kingdom to Jehoram because he was his firstborn son.

⁴When Jehoram established himself firmly over his father's kingdom, he put all his brothers to the sword along with some

of the princes of Israel. ⁵Jehoram was thirty-two years old when he became king, and he reigned in Jerusalem eight years. ⁶He walked in the ways of the kings of Israel, as the house of Ahab had done, for he married a daughter of Ahab. He did evil in the eyes of the Lᴏʀᴅ. ⁷Nevertheless, because of the covenant the Lᴏʀᴅ had made with David, the Lᴏʀᴅ was not willing to destroy the house of David. He had promised to maintain a lamp for him and his descendants forever.

With this chapter the Chronicler begins an extended description of the decline and near fall of the house of David. This decline had originally been set in motion by Jehoshaphat's foolish decision to ally himself with the wicked house of Ahab through marriage. Now the poison tree was about to bear its fruit.

In spite of this one great error, Jehoshaphat had been a godly king and had enjoyed God's gift of many children. Following Rehoboam's example (11:23), Jehoshaphat had dispersed his sons throughout the kingdom, putting each in charge of one of his fortified cities. "But he [gave] the kingdom to Jehoram because he was his firstborn son." With so many sons, father Jehoshaphat wisely settled the matter of succession before his death. Jehoram, the son who had married Ahab's daughter, was to be the next king of Judah.

Jehoram's callous murder of his brothers and many of the princes of Judah must rank as one of the most evil acts done by any of the Judaic kings. Although we are not told why Jehoram felt the need to commit this unnatural act, we can come up with a pretty good guess. Judah up to this time had been largely shielded by its kings from the gross idolatry that had so thoroughly corrupted the Northern Kingdom. Asa and Jehoshaphat had made it their official policy to root out high place worship from their land (14:3; 17:6). While they had not entirely succeeded, their hearts were in the right place. As verse 11 from the next section makes clear, Jehoram reversed this policy and instead adopted his father-in-law's procedure of establishing high places among his people that were dedicated to the worship of the Tyrian god Baal. "He walked in the ways of the kings of Israel, as the house of Ahab had done." It is likely that such practices were part of a larger policy of close cooperation with the idolatrous kingdom to the north. When Jehoshaphat's other sons spoke out against what was happening, they were killed for their trouble, along with their supporters.

God's judgment was surely going to fall on such a wicked king. Yet "because of the covenant the LORD had made with David, the LORD was not willing to destroy the house of David. He had promised to maintain a lamp for him and his descendants forever." He does not annul his grace because of the evil that people do. God had promised David that his house and his kingdom would endure (1 Chronicles 17). Even if the world were full of Jehorams, the Lord would not renege on what he had said.

Concrete examples like this from history must have been a great comfort to those Jews who had returned from exile. Humanly speaking, the fortunes of the house of David were hanging by a slender thread in the days of Jehoram. As we are about to see, the royal house would soon be reduced to a single male offspring, while a usurper occupied the throne. Yet from this "stump of Jesse" (Isaiah 11:1), God would restore David's house to power. The returned exiles could take courage from considering God's faithful grace as they observed it in this instance and receive the heart to believe that God's mercies still endured ever faithful, ever sure. God *would* send his Messiah, even though there was no earthly cause for hope.

## God judges Jehoram

*God whittles Jehoram down to size*

⁸**In the time of Jehoram, Edom rebelled against Judah and set up its own king. ⁹So Jehoram went there with his officers and all his chariots. The Edomites surrounded him and his chariot commanders, but he rose up and broke through by night. ¹⁰To this day Edom has been in rebellion against Judah.**

**Libnah revolted at the same time, because Jehoram had forsaken the LORD, the God of his fathers. ¹¹He had also built high places on the hills of Judah and had caused the people of Jerusalem to prostitute themselves and had led Judah astray.**

Having made clear that God's grace reigns supreme over all he does, the Chronicler now proceeds to demonstrate once again the way that a violation of God's law inevitably leads to disaster. For Jehoram that disaster came in the form of rebellion. First the Edomites and then the city of Libnah refused to serve a king who had refused to serve the Lord. Given the long-standing hostility between Edom and Israel, the revolt of the Edomites is not surprising; Libnah's rebellion, however, is more so.

Most scholars locate Libnah on the border between the lowland hills of Judah and the coastal plains of Philistia (see map on the next page). First having been conquered by Joshua (Joshua 10:29-32), the city was considered part of Judah's territory (Joshua 15:42) and had been assigned to the sons of Aaron (Joshua 21:13; 1 Chronicles 6:57). Though Libnah had originally been one of the ancient Canaanite cities, it had been under the rule of God's people for such a long time that its inhabitants could hardly have considered the rule of the house of David to be a domination by a foreign power, as was the case of Edom. Why, then, would these people of Judah revolt against their own king? This was the hand of God, now turned against the house he had

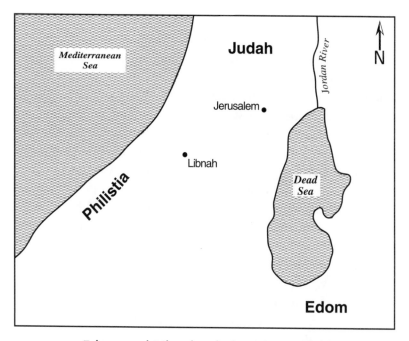

Edom and Libnah rebel against Judah

once upheld—all because Jehoram had "forsaken . . . the God of his fathers."

What Jesus once said about those who despise the Word helps us apply the solemn significance of Libnah's revolt to ourselves: "Whoever does not have, even what he has will be taken from him" (Matthew 13:12). Jehoram took Libnah for granted and assumed he could despise the Lord without consequence. He found out otherwise. Similarly, faith belongs to none of us by right of birth. If we take God's Word for granted or act as if Christ and his church will always be there for us no matter what we do, we might forever lose what we thought would always be ours.

As the Chronicler concludes this section, he describes Jehoram's sin in the starkest terms. By introducing such

247

gross idolatry and Baal worship into his kingdom, he had "caused the people of Jerusalem to prostitute themselves and had led Judah astray." The only other time our writer uses the expression "to prostitute themselves" is in his first book. There he chose it as the best way to characterize the sin of the northern tribes and gave it as the reason why God had abandoned them to their enemies (1 Chronicles 5:25,26). *Led astray* is also a highly charged expression in the vocabulary of biblical writers. Used in this sense by the Chronicler only here, we also find it in the book of Deuteronomy, where Moses warned the people against anyone who tried to entice them into following false gods, "gods you have not known" (Deuteronomy 13:13).

Such enticement was bad enough, whoever was responsible. But when kings were guilty of it—those who were charged with the responsibility of tending God's flock—the sin became far worse because of its impact on the whole Israelite society. As we have seen, Jehoram's father, Jehoshaphat, had taken his responsibilities as an undershepherd for the Lord seriously (see 19:4-11). But within the short reign of eight years, Jehoram was able to dismantle what his father had so carefully built up. The case against Jehoram is clear enough. We simply wait to hear the verdict. The one who will announce it is none other than Elijah, the great prophet of God.

*God pronounces judgment on Jehoram through Elijah*

¹²**Jehoram received a letter from Elijah the prophet, which said:**

> **"This is what the LORD, the God of your father David, says: 'You have not walked in the ways of your father Jehoshaphat or of Asa king of Judah. ¹³But you have walked in the ways of the kings of Israel, and you have led**

**Judah and the people of Jerusalem to prostitute them-
selves, just as the house of Ahab did. You have also
murdered your own brothers, members of your father's
house, men who were better than you. ¹⁴So now the
LORD is about to strike your people, your sons, your
wives and everything that is yours, with a heavy blow.
¹⁵You yourself will be very ill with a lingering disease of
the bowels, until the disease causes your bowels to
come out.'"**

A remarkable letter from a remarkable man! Elijah, as we
know from 1 Kings, conducted his ministry among the
northern tribes of Israel. The Lord had used him to prevent
his people from sliding into complete apostasy under Ahab
and Jezebel. As one of the last acts of Elijah's career, the
Lord used him to render his verdict over Jehoram.

In swift, sure strokes the prophet characterizes Jehoram
and his sin. In his disloyalty to the Lord, Jehoram had dis-
graced his own house. He had turned his back on his own
fathers, preferring the "ways of the kings of Israel." He murdered his own brothers, "members of [his] father's house,
men who were better than [him]." This last phrase provides
some support to the theory mentioned previously that Jehoram had murdered his brothers because they had been
opposed to his policies of Baal worship and close ties to
Israel. The name of David had been dragged through the
mud by his unworthy descendant.

Because Jehoram had so callously murdered his own
brothers and had despised the godly ways of his fathers,
God would pinpoint his judgment so that it primarily struck
down his own household. His people, his sons, his wives,
and all he possessed would feel the weight of God's wrath.
He himself would die of a loathsome and lingering disease.
God's punishment would fit the king's crime.

There are many who simply dismiss this prophecy as a rhetorical device and as a complete fabrication by the Chronicler. Since they doubt God's ability to intervene in history, they disbelieve any account that might imply either that God knows the future or that he controls it. They say that 2 Kings chapters 2 and 3 suggest the taking of Elijah to heaven as occurring around the year 853 B.C. This would have made it impossible for him to have written the letter to a king who began his sole rule around the year 848 B.C. To get around this, some conservative commentators have suggested that Elijah wrote this prophecy before he died—before Jehoram had even killed his brothers—and committed the manuscript to Elisha for sending along at the proper time. Others go so far as to say that this prophecy was a letter dropped from heaven—quite literally! They suggest that the Lord allowed Elijah to communicate from his state of bliss to people still living in this world of sin.

It is not necessary to go this far, however. Chapters 2 and 3 of 2 Kings do not explicitly state that they are to be read in chronological fashion, nor do they have to be read as if Elijah was gone before Elisha became active in his ministry. In 2 Kings we could well have a topical arrangement of material in which the holy writer first makes it clear that Elisha was Elijah's successor. No account would make this point better than Elijah's being taken into heaven. The writer of 2 Kings then goes on to give a few examples of what Elisha did and how he conducted himself during his prophetic work. At least some of these incidents must have occurred while Elijah was still alive. We should remember that the biblical accounts were written in order to work faith in the Lord; they were not written as exhaustive and complete histories.

Additionally, nothing would be more in keeping with Elijah's whole character than this blunt letter. We remember how firmly he had opposed Ahab in all his idolatrous ways.

What could be more like Elijah than for him to oppose Ahab's son-in-law once he saw that the idolatrous cancer was invading Judah? What would better fit the man who had told Ahab "Dogs will lick up your blood" (1 Kings 21:19) than the words "You yourself will be very ill with a lingering disease of the bowels, until [it] causes your bowels to come out"!

As to the matter of a prophet of the Lord and his ability to make such specific and detailed prophecies about the future, we only have to read these words from Isaiah to refresh our own faith: "Remember the former things, those of long ago; I am God, and there is no other; I am God, and there is none like me. I make known the end from the beginning, from ancient times, what is still to come. I say: My purpose will stand, and I will do all that I please" (Isaiah 46:9,10).

## God carries out his verdict

**¹⁶The LORD aroused against Jehoram the hostility of the Philistines and of the Arabs who lived near the Cushites. ¹⁷They attacked Judah, invaded it and carried off all the goods found in the king's palace, together with his sons and wives. Not a son was left to him except Ahaziah, the youngest.**

**¹⁸After all this, the LORD afflicted Jehoram with an incurable disease of the bowels. ¹⁹In the course of time, at the end of the second year, his bowels came out because of the disease, and he died in great pain. His people made no fire in his honor, as they had for his fathers.**

**²⁰Jehoram was thirty-two years old when he became king, and he reigned in Jerusalem eight years. He passed away, to no one's regret, and was buried in the City of David, but not in the tombs of the kings.**

Jehoram had tried to reverse the godly policies of his father, Jehoshaphat, and his grandfather Asa. So God reversed

Jehoram's plans and ruined all his hopes. God took from him not only everything he had tried to secure for himself but also many of the blessings given to his two predecessors. In so doing, God was making it clear to his Old Testament people that earthly blessings come to those whose lives are spiritually in order. But for those who would let their lives fall into spiritual disarray, trouble and sorrow would be all they could hope to find. For more on this subject, see "Immediate blessings and punishments" in the introduction.

By killing his brothers, Jehoram had tried to make his family secure from whatever threats they might have posed. When God was through with him, Jehoram's sons and wives were all dead, with the exception of young Ahaziah. Father Jehoshaphat had received tribute from the Philistines and the Arabs (17:11); son Jehoram was forced to give up his possessions to those same people when the Lord incited them to mount raids on his kingdom. His two predecessors had enjoyed relatively long reigns; Jehoram's was cut short after only eight years. He died a horrible death, his passing was mourned by none, and he was given none of the honors his predecessors had received. There was no ceremonial fire, and he was not buried in the family tombs. This shame to the house of David died in utter disgrace.

### God's kingdom under Ahaziah

*Listening to the counsel of the ungodly,*
*sitting in the seat of the scornful*

**22** **The people of Jerusalem made Ahaziah, Jehoram's youngest son, king in his place, since the raiders, who came with the Arabs into the camp, had killed all the older sons. So Ahaziah son of Jehoram king of Judah began to reign.**

²Ahaziah was twenty-two years old when he became king, and he reigned in Jerusalem one year. His mother's name was Athaliah, a granddaughter of Omri.

³He too walked in the ways of the house of Ahab, for his mother encouraged him in doing wrong. ⁴He did evil in the eyes of the LORD, as the house of Ahab had done, for after his father's death they became his advisers, to his undoing. ⁵He also followed their counsel when he went with Joram son of Ahab king of Israel to war against Hazael king of Aram at Ramoth Gilead. The Arameans wounded Joram; ⁶so he returned to Jezreel to recover from the wounds they had inflicted on him at Ramoth in his battle with Hazael king of Aram.

Then Ahaziah son of Jehoram king of Judah went down to Jezreel to see Joram son of Ahab because he had been wounded.

As bad as things are, they're about to grow much worse. The first verse gives us some additional information on the raiding parties we heard about in the last chapter and how it was that they had managed to kill most of the king's sons. Although the Hebrew is somewhat difficult to understand, it seems that these raiding parties of Philistines and Arabs (21:16) had managed to catch the members of the king's family while they were with him on campaign and living in the military camp of Judah. Ahaziah, being the youngest, had probably been left at home, perhaps to maintain a royal presence in Jerusalem. So it was that, on the death of his father, he alone had survived to ascend the throne.

Instead of the usual closing formula "*A* rested with his fathers and *B* succeeded him as king," here we are told that the people of Jerusalem united to put Ahaziah on the throne. It is difficult for us to know the exact significance of this expression. Were these the leading citizens of Jerusalem? the common people? This much we do know: the expression implies that a state of confusion and disorder existed in the kingdom, no doubt because of the raiding parties and the deaths of so many in the royal family at one time. The regular handing over of power from one king to the next was impossible. Wherever similar expressions occur (see 26:1; 33:25; 36:1), this seems to be the case. Palace intrigue, military defeat, assassination—good order is threatened in some way, and the people themselves have to step in to restore it.

Only 22 years old, Ahaziah was heavily influenced by the counsel of Ahab's family. Because of his mother, Athaliah, and his cousins from Ahab's side of the family, it seemed as if little Judah's spiritual and political fortunes were to become more and more intertwined with those of the North. We remember how at one time King Abijah had staunchly stood up for the legitimacy of the dynasty of David and for the true worship of God at the temple (see chapter 13). But now the ruinous marriage of Jehoram to Ahab's daughter Athaliah had brought David's house to its knees. Judah had become little more than Israel's vassal, militarily and religiously.

Completely under his mother's sway, Ahaziah "walked in the ways of the house of Ahab" and not in the ways of David. This undoubtedly means that the worship of foreign gods and idols continued to pollute the South, with the king's own blessing. And the house of Ahab advised him well—in the best way to ensure his own destruction, that is. He joined with Joram, Ahab's son, in Joram's military adventure against the rising power of Hazael, the new king of Aram (Israel's neighbor to the north). Joram had hoped to check Aram at Ramoth Gilead. Instead he was wounded and forced to retire to his summer palace at Jezreel, seeking to recover from his wounds. It is there that Ahaziah went to visit him.

The Chronicler gives us only a very compressed account of events described much more fully in 2 Kings chapter 9, an account he clearly assumes his readers are familiar with. His interest here is simply to sketch in again the rough outlines of the account, selecting and supplementing the material so as to drive home the spiritual lessons to be learned from it. Psalm 1 comes to mind again as being very close to the Chronicler's point in retelling this story here:

> Blessed is the man
> who does not walk in the counsel of the
> wicked
> or stand in the way of sinners
> or sit in the seat of mockers.
> Not so the wicked! (verses 1,4)

## *Becoming like chaff that the wind drives away*

⁷**Through Ahaziah's visit to Joram, God brought about Ahaziah's downfall. When Ahaziah arrived, he went out with Joram to meet Jehu son of Nimshi, whom the LORD had anointed to destroy the house of Ahab. ⁸While Jehu was executing judgment on the house of Ahab, he found the princes of Judah and the sons of Ahaziah's relatives, who had been attending Ahaziah, and he killed them. ⁹He then went in search of Ahaziah, and his men captured him while he was hiding in Samaria. He was brought to Jehu and put to death. They buried him, for they said, "He was a son of Jehoshaphat, who sought the LORD with all his heart." So there was no one in the house of Ahaziah powerful enough to retain the kingdom.**

There are a number of differences between this brief account and its parallel in 2 Kings chapter 9. Most of these can be easily explained by what was previously said: (a) the Chronicler is giving us a compressed version to bring out the theological truth, and (b) he assumes that his readers are familiar with 2 Kings. The most difficult difference to understand is the location of Ahaziah's death. Second Kings tells us that Ahaziah tried to escape while Jehu and his men were

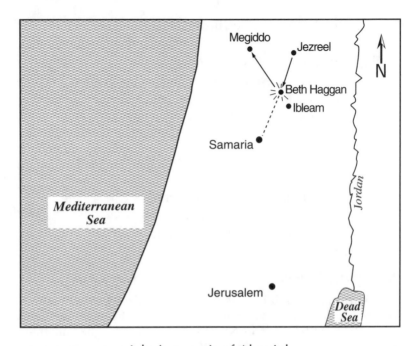

Jehu's pursuit of Ahaziah

putting Joram to the sword. From Jezreel, Ahaziah succeeded in reaching Beth Haggan, near Ibleam, on the road to Samaria. There Jehu got close enough to Ahaziah to be able to wound him, but with the help of his servants, Ahaziah still managed to struggle up to Megiddo, where he finally died (2 Kings 9:27). The Chronicler seems to be telling us that Ahaziah escaped to the city of Samaria, where he tried to find a hiding place. There Jehu's men captured him and brought him back to their master, who then carried out his execution.

We might explain this difference in the following way. In his compressed retelling of the story, the Chronicler chose to emphasize the place where Ahaziah was planning to seek refuge in his headlong flight. That Ahaziah never reached Samaria, he does not mention. He assumes that his readers can fill in that fact for themselves. His theological purpose in mentioning Ahaziah's goal is more obvious. Judah's king seeks refuge in a city that is inextricably linked with the house of Ahab, Jezebel, and Baal worship. He does not find it. There is no safe place left to hide for a son of David who cannot sing with David, "Keep me safe, O God, for in you I take refuge" (Psalm 16:1).

The Chronicler also lays great emphasis on the point that Ahaziah's ruin was the Lord's doing. "God brought about Ahaziah's downfall," he says, and continues by declaring that Jehu, in destroying Ahab's house, was the Lord's anointed. In other words, Jehu did what he did under the Lord's direction and with the Lord's blessing. Finally, Jehu's actions are described as "executing judgment." God had heard the cries of his oppressed people, had responded to the prayers and sighs of faithful prophets like Elijah and Elisha, and had raised up Jehu to work out his wrath on Ahab's perverted family.

Today we look out at a world becoming ever more brazen and provocative in the ways it devises to defy God. What the theologians call "natural law"—humanity's inbred sense of right and wrong—people these days seem to be able to shrug off more casually than a coat. We may wonder sometimes, Where is the God of justice when killers walk out of courtrooms unpunished or when depravity parades through the streets to show off its pride? But even more vile are the preachers and teachers we sometimes see in the visible Christian church, men and women who pollute the holy name of God with their outright denial of clear, biblical teachings. The story of Jehu and Ahaziah reminds us that our God is a jealous God, and he will take personally every ungodly act of sinful people. Sooner or later there comes a day when people must give an account for what they have done. For some God's judgment begins in this life and continues forever in the next. "We must all appear before the judgment seat of Christ" (2 Corinthians 5:10). Only those who trust in the deliverance won by our Savior will escape God's just and terrible wrath.

> For the LORD watches over the way of the
> righteous,
> but the way of the wicked will perish.
>
> (Psalm 1:6)

In death the only difference between Ahaziah of Judah and Joram of Israel was in the condition of their remains. Joram's body was left to rot on that same plot of ground for which his father Ahab had murdered Naboth (see 1 Kings 21 and 2 Kings 9:24-26). Ahaziah, though he belonged to the house of Ahab in spirit, was allowed a proper burial by Jehu and his men. They remembered that he was at least a physical son of godly Jehoshaphat.

As bleak as the next statement may sound, there is a gospel message at the heart of it. "There was no one in the house of Ahaziah powerful enough to retain the kingdom," the Chronicler concludes. Jehoram had murdered his brothers, and Jehu had killed not only Ahaziah but also many other princes of Judah who had been Northern sympathizers. And this would not be the end of the slaughter among the princes of Judah, as the Chronicler's readers well knew. No one in Ahaziah's family, the royal family of David, possessed the power to take over the kingdom at his death. Had the people of Judah considered the matter only on the basis of what they could perceive with their senses, it would have seemed to them as if the lamp of David had at last been snuffed out.

The Chronicler's original readers must have seen their own circumstances as being very similar. To them too it must have seemed as if no one in David's family could ever be strong enough to ascend the throne of Judah again. But what man cannot do, that God will most certainly do, whenever he has given his word. He had promised to preserve "a lamp for [David] . . . forever" (21:7). He was able to fulfill that word when all seemed so dark in the days following Ahaziah's death; he could do it again in the dark days following the return from exile. The royal line of David would be restored to the throne. As for us, we can see how God kept that promise in the person of Jesus. So we have even more assurance that however dark it gets for us, God's great day of love and glory will dawn over us and our Savior will return to bring us home.

## God's kingdom under the usurper—Queen Athaliah

### A direct assault on the kingdom

¹⁰**When Athaliah the mother of Ahaziah saw that her son was dead, she proceeded to destroy the whole royal family of the house of Judah. ¹¹But Jehosheba, the daughter of King Jehoram, took Joash son of Ahaziah and stole him away from among the royal princes who were about to be murdered and put him and his nurse in a bedroom. Because Jehosheba, the daughter of King Jehoram and wife of the priest Jehoiada, was Ahaziah's sister, she hid the child from Athaliah so she could not kill him. ¹²He remained hidden with them at the temple of God for six years while Athaliah ruled the land.**

On the one hand, what queen mother Athaliah did was perfectly normal, if considered only within the context of power politics in the ancient world. Her son the king was dead. Jehu had been wiping out her family in the North, so there was little hope of refuge for her there. Her only hope was to consolidate power for herself in the South while she still possessed some control over events. The greatest threat to her staying in power were any sons in the line of David who might be considered legitimate claimants to the throne. They could easily serve as focal points around which opposition could rally. Under the circumstances the only hope left for her was to destroy them before they could destroy her.

Faith in God, however, views this as a direct assault on God's ruling power and on the kingdom of God itself. It was God, after all, who had decreed that David and his successors were to occupy the throne. The promise made to David in 1 Chronicles chapter 17 was not only his way of ensuring stable rule over his people but was also his means of saving the entire world.

Athaliah therefore joins the ranks of people like Caiaphas, Judas, Pontius Pilate, and others, all those who—whether motivated by fear, greed, or cynicism—set themselves up against the Lord and against his anointed. In short, she was an antichrist, one of the many that must come as signs of the end (see 1 John 2:18).

It is probably worth the time to pause here and note the exact nature of Athaliah's other spiritual crimes. In addition to her direct assault on the promise of the Savior, she also took an active role in promoting Baal worship among her southern subjects. A true daughter of Jezebel and a worthy offspring of Ahab! In the city of God itself, she had enthroned Baal as lord, complete with his own temple, altars, and high priest (see 23:17). As if this weren't bad enough, she and her sons (or perhaps better, her followers) had broken into the temple of God itself so that, in honor of Baal, they could make unholy use of those holy objects set apart for the worship of the Lord (24:7). What could be worse than this? The throne of God's kingdom had been taken over by a usurper, and the temple where God's glory dwelt had been desecrated. Satan seemed to have triumphed in the land.

### God preserves his kingdom by the decisive actions of Jehoiada and Jehosheba

In every evil hour, it seems, there are at least one or two heroes of faith to whom God gives the courage and the will to stand up against the kingdom of darkness. At the time of Athaliah, there was Jehosheba, one of Jehoram's daughters[25] and the wife of Jehoiada, a priest about whom we will be hearing more shortly. This brave woman took young prince Joash from the group of children whom Athaliah had marked for slaughter, right out from under her nose. The child was still nursing, so Jehosheba hid him away in one of the inner bed chambers of the temple complex, along with his wet nurse. What she did took considerable courage, since palace and temple were located side by side, and no doubt there were few people she could trust, at least in the beginning. For the six long and terrible years of Athaliah's reign, Jehosheba and her husband protected the little prince from harm, until the time was right for declaring themselves.

**23** **In the seventh year Jehoiada showed his strength. He made a covenant with the commanders of units of a hundred: Azariah son of Jeroham, Ishmael son of Jehohanan, Azariah son of Obed, Maaseiah son of Adaiah, and Elishaphat son of Zicri. ²They went throughout Judah and gathered the Levites and the heads of Israelite families from all the towns. When they came to Jerusalem, ³the whole assembly made a covenant with the king at the temple of God.**

Jehoiada the priest had been in full agreement with what his wife had done. Along with her, he must have spent many anxious days and nights concealing the growing young prince from prying eyes. After seven years the time came at last to restore God's order. Jehoiada moved swiftly and decisively. First he secured the allegiance of the military by entering into a pact with five key leaders of the palace guard. Their names are supplied in verse 1 as a roll call of honor. These men were to go out on a secret mission and secure the support of the Levites and the heads of families throughout the kingdom of Judah. At an agreed-upon time, all were to present themselves at the temple of the Lord.

Some have questioned the veracity of the Chronicler here. They argue that such a wide-ranging conspiracy would have had to arouse the suspicions of Athaliah. This can be answered, however, by pointing out that the success of the plot against Athaliah was a pretty good indicator of the lack of love felt by her subjects for this foreign queen. The people of Judah were so united in their hatred of her that there was virtually no one left to inform her of what was about to happen. In addition, Jehoiada demonstrated a remarkable shrewdness in his plan. He was, as we shall see, able to time the little boy's acclamation as king in such a way as to provide him with maximum protection. No doubt he was also able to plan the exact date of the *coup d'etat* so that it coincided with one of the three great festivals of God's people. At a time like this, when all Israel was required to present itself before the Lord, the influx of great numbers of people into Jerusalem would have been nothing remarkable. Athaliah must have assumed that they were simply there to worship their God as he had commanded.

The concluding verse of this section is probably best understood as a general summary of what comes next. The entire assembly made a covenant with the new king in the following way:

Jehoiada said to them, "The king's son shall reign, as the LORD promised concerning the descendants of David. ⁴Now this is what you are to do: A third of you priests and Levites who are going on duty on the Sabbath are to keep watch at the doors, ⁵a third of you at the royal palace and a third at the Foundation Gate, and all the other men are to be in the courtyards of the temple of the LORD. ⁶No one is to enter the temple of the LORD except the priests and Levites on duty; they may enter because they are consecrated, but all the other men are to guard what the LORD has assigned to them. ⁷The Levites are to station themselves around the king, each man with his weapons in his hand. Anyone who enters the temple must be put to death. Stay close to the king wherever he goes."

⁸The Levites and all the men of Judah did just as Jehoiada the priest ordered. Each one took his men—those who were going on duty on the Sabbath and those who were going off duty—for Jehoiada the priest had not released any of the divisions. ⁹Then he gave the commanders of units of a hundred the spears and the large and small shields that had belonged to King David and that were in the temple of God. ¹⁰He stationed all the men, each with his weapon in his hand, around the king—near the altar and the temple, from the south side to the north side of the temple.

This is one of the more difficult sections of Scripture to understand, not because the main point of the passage is in any way unclear nor because its individual parts would be unclear if taken by themselves. When careful Bible students consider this section side by side with the account of these same events in 2 Kings, however, they are likely to come away scratching their heads a bit. Hopefully what follows will clear up at least some of that confusion.

We begin with the familiar thoughts that our writer is well acquainted with the account in 2 Kings and that he assumes it is known to his readers as well. To some degree the Chronicler sees his telling of the story as supplemental to that earlier version. He chooses to emphasize certain aspects of the story passed over in silence by the writer of 2 Kings, particularly when those aspects would have special impact on his original readers, the exiles returned from Babylon.

For example, if we only had 2 Kings, we would not know how great and decisive a role the priests and Levites played in the unfolding of events. We might even think that Jehoiada's takeover was more in the nature of palace intrigue or a military coup than being the widespread and popular uprising that it was. Naturally then, in his telling of the story, the Chronicler would bring to the forefront the work of the priests and Levites, especially since the priests and Levites of his own day were questioning the value of their ministries. He wanted to inspire them to rededicate themselves to their high callings.

Particularly confusing is the task of sorting out all the various groupings of men along with their various stations as described for us both here and in 2 Kings. We will try to stick with what we know and leave what is in doubt for others to sort out. First of all, simply because 2 Kings speaks of military men being involved in the coup, that does not in any way exclude the participation of the priests and Levites as described in 2 Chronicles. In fact, the writer of 2 Kings gives clear recognition to the pivotal role played by Jehoiada the priest. One could fairly conclude from this that other priests were involved as well. Similarly, the emphasis given to the role of the priests and Levites in 2 Chronicles is not intended to rule out the role of the military. Quite the opposite: the Chronicler even mentions the five key military men by name, facts omitted by the writer of 2 Kings.

When the Chronicler therefore spoke of Jehoiada's dividing the assembled priests and Levites into thirds, he did not intend to be understood as excluding the military men from those divisions. We know from 2 Kings 11:4-8 that troops from the regular army were included in the makeup of all three groups. Only through combining the two accounts does the full picture emerge. Armed Levites and armed soldiers stood side by side to protect the king. Since the group guarding the boy in the temple precincts was a mixture of Levites and regular soldiers, Jehoiada hastened to add the instruction, "No one is to enter the temple of the LORD except the priests and Levites." No matter how the situation played itself out, Jehoiada did not want anyone not a priest, in an excess of zeal, running into the Lord's temple itself.

Also clearly evident is Jehoiada's clever stratagem of timing the takeover so that it would coincide with the shift change on the temple mount (compare verse 8 with 2 Kings 11:7). In asking the shift of priests going off duty to remain and guard the king, Jehoiada was able to double the total number of men available for deployment without arousing Queen Athaliah's suspicions.

Another brilliant move by the priest was his use of the weapons and shields that King David had left in the temple treasury. Temples in the ancient world were repositories for all manner of dedicated gifts. There is nothing surprising in David's having dedicated some weapons to the Lord. They could have been captured from the enemy in one of his many campaigns, or they could have been left over after his fighting days were done. The fact that the arms were already in place made it possible for the troops of the new king to assemble themselves on the temple grounds without first having to walk through the streets of Jerusalem heavily armed. In this way secrecy could be maintained. More than that, the symbolism of using David's weapons to restore a son of David to the throne could not have been lost on the fighting men. Receiving those arms from the Lord's own priest in the Lord's own temple signified that the struggle against Athaliah was a holy war.

In conclusion, whether we are reading the account in Kings or in Chronicles, the picture emerges of a carefully crafted plan, carried out in several stages. Jehoiada was able to maintain secrecy throughout, with the result that Athaliah was taken by complete surprise. From the Chronicler's telling of the story, we learn in addition that all Israel, represented by the heads of families and any others who happened to be present on that Sabbath, joined together wholeheartedly in restoring the young prince to his rightful throne (see 23:2,3,13,17,21). The Chronicler brings the work of the priests and the Levites into particular focus for us. This was not merely a change in a political administration; Jehoiada had planned nothing less than the reformation of the people of God.

**¹¹Jehoiada and his sons brought out the king's son and put the crown on him; they presented him with a copy of the covenant and proclaimed him king. They anointed him and shouted, "Long live the king!"**

**¹²When Athaliah heard the noise of the people running and cheering the king, she went to them at the temple of the LORD. ¹³She looked, and there was the king, standing by his pillar at the entrance. The officers and the trumpeters were beside the king, and all the people of the land were rejoicing and blowing trumpets, and singers with musical instruments were leading the praises. Then Athaliah tore her robes and shouted, "Treason! Treason!"**

**¹⁴Jehoiada the priest sent out the commanders of units of a hundred, who were in charge of the troops, and said to them:**

"Bring her out between the ranks and put to the sword anyone who follows her." For the priest had said, "Do not put her to death at the temple of the Lord." ¹⁵So they seized her as she reached the entrance of the Horse Gate on the palace grounds, and there they put her to death.

¹⁶Jehoiada then made a covenant that he and the people and the king would be the Lord's people. ¹⁷All the people went to the temple of Baal and tore it down. They smashed the altars and idols and killed Mattan the priest of Baal in front of the altars.

¹⁸Then Jehoiada placed the oversight of the temple of the Lord in the hands of the priests, who were Levites, to whom David had made assignments in the temple, to present the burnt offerings of the Lord as written in the Law of Moses, with rejoicing and singing, as David had ordered. ¹⁹He also stationed doorkeepers at the gates of the Lord's temple so that no one who was in any way unclean might enter.

²⁰He took with him the commanders of hundreds, the nobles, the rulers of the people and all the people of the land and brought the king down from the temple of the Lord. They went into the palace through the Upper Gate and seated the king on the royal throne, ²¹and all the people of the land rejoiced. And the city was quiet, because Athaliah had been slain with the sword.

Jehoiada's plan worked flawlessly. Once his men were at their stations, the priest brought the young king out from his hiding place and presented him to the assembled throng. We are told that his sons helped their father at this dramatic moment. This was a godly family, united in their ambition to do the Lord's will. As far as they were concerned, the Lord had made a promise concerning David's descendants (23:3), and that was the end of the matter. May God give us faithful pastors and teachers like these, whose steps are guided by God's Word and will alone. As we will see later, the new king would not be as faithful to Jehoiada's sons as they were to him.

But on that day there seemed to be no cloud on the horizon. For the faithful this must have been like receiving someone back from the dead. Most of them no doubt had believed that the royal line of David had been utterly wiped out. Surprised by joy, they must have watched in wonder as they saw Jehoiada bring out the little prince, place the crown on his head, and anoint him with the holy anointing oil. Certainly after six long years of suffering under the rule of a usurper, it was more than mere ritual that led Jehoiada to cry out, "Here is your king, O Israel!" and for the people to respond, "Long live the king!" In a similar way, but with far greater joy, we receive our King back from the dead on Easter Sunday. Our pastor says, "He is risen!" and we respond, "He is risen indeed!" God's power is such that right where death seems to reign supreme, it is swallowed up in Christ's victorious and everlasting life.

We dare not miss the remark that "they presented him with a copy of the covenant." Judah was not a kingdom like all the other nations of the world, where the king ruled alone and where his word was law. It was the kingdom where God's Word was paramount. The copy of the covenant, therefore, was most likely a copy of Deuteronomy, where God had clearly spelled out what it meant for a people to be chosen as his very own. In that same book, God had instructed his people on what basis any future king of theirs had to rule: "When he takes the throne of his kingdom, he is to write for himself on a scroll a copy of this law, taken from that of the priests" (Deuteronomy 17:18).

The next portion of the events contains high drama indeed. Unsuspecting of anything amiss, Athaliah walks over to the temple grounds, attracted by all the noise and shouting. Like

a camera panning the scene, her eyes take it all in with growing horror—first the king, then her own officers, and finally
the people dancing, the trumpets blaring, and the singers
singing. The significance of what she sees sweeps over her in
a rush, and she tears her robes in grief and dismay. "Treason!
Treason!" she cries, revealing something interesting to us
about the psychology of evildoers.

We may at times naively suppose that the wicked are
fully aware of, and take pride in, the evil that they do. On the
contrary, however, as the case of Athaliah shows, they may
feel themselves to be perfectly in the right and may see any
act against themselves to be treachery and mayhem. "Surely
you place [the wicked] on slippery ground; you cast them
down to ruin. How suddenly are they destroyed, completely
swept away by terrors! As a dream when one awakes, so
when you arise, O Lord, you will despise them as fantasies"
(Psalm 73:18-20). Athaliah's judgment day had come. For all
her idolatries, murders, and blasphemies against the Lord and
against his anointed, she was justly put to death in accordance with God's decree (Deuteronomy 13:9). Anyone who
dared follow her would suffer a similar fate.

The land had been defiled by idolatry and the throne
desecrated by a pretender. All this had been contrary to specific commands and promises of God. The covenant, therefore, had been broken, and it was necessary to reestablish
it. That is why we read, "Jehoiada then made a covenant
that he and the people and the king would be the LORD's
people." It is a testament to God's grace that he was willing
to have them back! In their zeal for the Lord, the people
went en masse to the temple of Baal, destroying it with all
its altars and images and killing the priest who served there.

Part of the appeal of idolatry is its easy tolerance of other
religious points of view. "Oh, so you're a follower of the

Lord? That's great! I'm a devotee of Baal myself, but there have been times when I've offered a sacrifice or two to the Lord, I don't mind telling you." Athaliah had not destroyed the temple of the true God. She had just built a temple of Baal alongside it. We see this same principle in operation in much of what passes for spirituality in America today. Religion is seen to be this vast tent under which there should be many displays, enough to suit anyone's taste. Jehoiada had no such tolerance. There was no middle ground. Baal worship was destructive to the exclusive relationship that the Lord wanted to enjoy with his people. Similarly we are not to be fooled whenever a tolerance of evil masquerades as a broad-minded and compassionate love. God's people can have no fellowship with what is false and with that which, if clung to, will destroy spiritual life.

After years of neglect and indifference, it was necessary for Jehoiada also to reestablish the proper order in Judah's worship life. The priests were once again to offer the regular burnt offerings, as Moses had commanded. The Levites were to sing the psalms in solemn choruses of praise as David had decreed. Doorkeepers were once again set as guardians to the gates of God's house "so that no one who was in any way unclean might enter" (verse 19; see also 1 Chronicles 23–26). Since the Davidic king was so closely associated with the temple and with the one true faith in the hearts of the faithful, it was no less an act of worship for the assembly of God's people to escort him to the palace and to seat him on the throne.

"All the people of the land rejoiced. And the city was quiet, because Athaliah had been slain with the sword." In that city from which evil has been finally removed, where God's king rules, and where God himself lives among his people, there is bound to be peace, and God's people will know perfect joy. We see the peace foreshadowed here being fulfilled in the city that John later saw: "The city does not need the sun or the moon to shine on it, for the glory of God gives it light, and the Lamb is its lamp. On no day will its gates ever be shut, for there will be no night there. Nothing impure will ever enter it, nor will anyone who does what is shameful or deceitful, but only those whose names are written in the Lamb's book of life" (Revelation 21:23,25,27).

## God's kingdom under Joash

### A good beginning: the temple restored

**24** Joash was seven years old when he became king, and he reigned in Jerusalem forty years. His mother's name was Zibiah; she was from Beersheba. ²Joash did what was right in the eyes of the LORD all the years of Jehoiada the priest. ³Jehoiada chose two wives for him, and he had sons and daughters.

⁴Some time later Joash decided to restore the temple of the LORD. ⁵He called together the priests and Levites and said to them, "Go to the towns of Judah and collect the money due annually from all Israel, to repair the temple of your God. Do it now." But the Levites did not act at once.

⁶Therefore the king summoned Jehoiada the chief priest and said to him, "Why haven't you required the Levites to bring in from Judah and Jerusalem the tax imposed by Moses the servant of the LORD and by the assembly of Israel for the Tent of the Testimony?"

⁷Now the sons of that wicked woman Athaliah had broken into the temple of God and had used even its sacred objects for the Baals.

⁸At the king's command, a chest was made and placed outside, at the gate of the temple of the LORD. ⁹A proclamation was then issued in Judah and Jerusalem that they should bring to the LORD the tax that Moses the servant of God had required of

Israel in the desert. ¹⁰All the officials and all the people brought their contributions gladly, dropping them into the chest until it was full. ¹¹Whenever the chest was brought in by the Levites to the king's officials and they saw that there was a large amount of money, the royal secretary and the officer of the chief priest would come and empty the chest and carry it back to its place. They did this regularly and collected a great amount of money. ¹²The king and Jehoiada gave it to the men who carried out the work required for the temple of the LORD. They hired masons and carpenters to restore the LORD's temple, and also workers in iron and bronze to repair the temple.

¹³The men in charge of the work were diligent, and the repairs progressed under them. They rebuilt the temple of God according to its original design and reinforced it. ¹⁴When they had finished, they brought the rest of the money to the king and Jehoiada, and with it were made articles for the LORD's temple: articles for the service and for the burnt offerings, and also dishes and other objects of gold and silver. As long as Jehoiada lived, burnt offerings were presented continually in the temple of the LORD.

¹⁵Now Jehoiada was old and full of years, and he died at the age of a hundred and thirty. ¹⁶He was buried with the kings in the City of David, because of the good he had done in Israel for God and his temple.

Again, it may be hard for us to understand how a king could have begun so well yet ended so badly. But such is the story of King Joash. He was high priest Jehoiada's star pupil, and in some ways he even outshone his teacher in his zeal and dedication to God's Word and God's house. They say even the Roman emperor Nero had his good years before the madness of power gripped him. In Joash's case, his early years turned out so well because he was willing to accept the advice and counsel of a godly man. What is implied here in verse 2 is made explicit in 2 Kings, "Joash did what was right . . . all the years Jehoiada the priest instructed him" (12:2).

The remark in verse 3 is hardly incidental, in view of Judah's recent history. Jehoiada chose wives for Joash both to ensure the continuation of the house of David after its recent near destruction and to avoid the kind of disaster Jehoshaphat had brought on the kingdom in marrying off his son to an ungodly spouse. The Lord blessed David's house with sons and daughters. This little verse also makes clear to us how closely associated Joash and Jehoiada must have been in those early years and how great an influence the priest had upon the crown.

As Joash grew older, he began to assert himself more independently as king. And in the beginning, this was all to the good. Like David and Solomon, he saw as one of his chief concerns the spiritual welfare of his people, and that meant he needed to attend to the physical condition of God's house, where the Lord had promised to meet his people. By this time the temple had fallen into disrepair. It had suffered the indifference and neglect of rulers who cared more for their idols than for the house of the living God. But more than this, it had suffered the plunderings of Athaliah, "that wicked woman," and her followers. From the book of Kings, we get the impression that the walls themselves had become so deeply fissured and cracked that a full-scale renovation was in order.

At first Joash was content to delegate the matter into the hands of the priests and Levites. It was there that the building project ran into a snag, and as is so often the case, that snag developed over where the money to fund the project would come from. Joash's first proposal was that the priests and Levites should collect the money due them "annually from all Israel" and use that to repair the temple.

Perhaps his urging them to collect the money contains the implication that this had not been done regularly in the recent past.

We know from other places in Scripture that the priests and Levites enjoyed several sources of income, which were to be used not only to fund the upkeep of the temple but also to see to the physical needs of these called workers and their families. There was money coming in from the redemption of personal vows (Leviticus 27:1-25), from freewill offerings (Leviticus 22:23), and from the census tax (Exodus 30:12-16). It seems likely that the king's request raised the anxiety level a bit for the house of Levi. After all, if these funds were to be used for a massive project of repair and restoration, what would be left for them to buy their daily bread? Also, just the fact that the king was ordering them to use these funds must have seemed threatening to the Levites. If they obeyed him, they would be conceding the right to oversee fiscal matters in the temple. Then, as now, there were no prerogatives so jealously guarded as those that had to do with money.

In any case, the priests and Levites attended the meeting with the king, listened to his command to move quickly, and then proceeded to drag their feet. How many projects fail because their movers and shakers assume a consensus that is not there! After a long while, it must have become embarrassingly clear to everyone that the commands of the king were not being carried out. The king, therefore, summoned Jehoiada the chief priest and said to him, "Why haven't you required the Levites to bring in from Judah and Jerusalem the tax imposed by Moses the servant of the LORD and by the assembly of Israel for the Tent of the Testimony?"

As the man in charge of the temple and its establishment, Jehoiada was, of course, the one directly responsible for carrying out the king's commission. In his defense we should note that Jehoiada was very old at this time and perhaps not as active in temple affairs as he might have been earlier in life. Nevertheless, the king held him accountable. From 2 Kings we learn that other priests were also present at this meeting.

In making his case to the priests, the king focuses on that portion of the temple income which, by law and tradition, would most clearly be seen as connected with the upkeep of the house. In the wilderness Moses had imposed the census tax "for the service of the Tent of Meeting" (Exodus 30:16). Later in that same book, it becomes clear that the service mentioned included the actual building of the tabernacle itself (Exodus 38:25-28). Joash refers to this as "the tax imposed by Moses the servant of the LORD and by the assembly of Israel." In other words, the king is arguing, "Look, I have not asked you for anything arbitrarily, nor am I trying to impose my own will on you. I am only asking what Moses asked of Israel—and what Israel readily agreed to give for the building of the tabernacle. Is it out of line, then, for me to expect that the same money be used today for the house of God?"

If we combine the account here with information gleaned from its parallel in 2 Kings chapter 12, we learn that the king and the priests came to a compromise of sorts at this meeting. The king took the direct burden of responsibility for the restoration of God's house off the priests' shoulders. In turn, the priests conceded the king's right to work with the chief priest in collecting the census tax for the project. By the king's decree, a chest was set up for that purpose in the gateway to the Lord's temple. The people's response was immediate and gratifying. The box was regularly filled, an accounting for the precious metals was carefully kept, and the restoration project went forward. The workmen were diligent and were soon able to rebuild the temple of God "according to its original design." This last remark is meant to remind us of the divine origin of the temple plan (1 Chronicles 28:11,12). This was a spiritually sensitive restoration.

Even after the workmen had completed the bricks and mortar part of the project, there was still money left over. Joash and Jehoiada used it to answer another pressing need. As we learned from verse 7, Athaliah and her followers had plundered the Lord's house and had used many of the sacred vessels in her worship of Baal. No doubt these defiled vessels had been destroyed along with the heathen sanctuary. The money left over, then, was used to make "articles for the LORD's temple." In this way we can easily resolve what to some is a contradiction between this account and 2 Kings. There it is said that the money collected was not spent "for making silver basins, wick trimmers, sprinkling bowls, trumpets or any other articles of gold or silver for the temple of the LORD" (2 Kings 12:13). We understand this verse to mean that the king gave strict instructions that the project be carried out under a no-frills policy until the large-scale and necessary work of structural repair had been completed. Once it was, however, the Chronicler adds that there was enough money left over to take care of the temple furnishings as well.

The God-pleasing result of all this is stated in the final phrase of the paragraph: "As long as Jehoiada lived, burnt offerings were presented continually in the temple of the LORD." Under Jehoiada's watch the true worship of God remained constant and consistent. This faithful old priest died at the great age of 130—well beyond the standard "three score and ten"—and received an unusual honor at his funeral. We note first that his is the only nonroyal death that the Chronicler records in this formal way. Because of his vital work in restoring the house of David to the throne and for his efforts in reestablishing the true faith in Israel, he was given the great privilege of being buried with the kings. We are not saved by our good works, but it is certainly God-pleasing to recognize and praise good works when we see them. And even if the good we do escapes the notice of others, it will not be overlooked by our Savior on the Last Day. Every cup of cold water given in his name he will recognize and praise.

This section provides food for thought and a good example for any congregation involved in a building project. There will be snags, no doubt, just as there were snags in this project. Different groups within a congregation may well have interests that appear to conflict, just as they did here. What is important is the way those differences were not allowed to stand in the way of completing the work. They were ironed out; compromises were made; people communicated with one another. For this we have to give credit where credit is due. King Joash could have pouted, he could have stormed and raged, he could have acted in a much more high-handed way. Instead, he talked it out. He made the first move. If there's something God-pleasing to be done, it's worth putting aside petty differences to see a project through.

We also notice God's grace at work here. Just as in David's original "fund-raiser" for the house of God (1 Chronicles 29:1-9), the people were eager to give likewise here for its renovation. Hearts kindled with God's love, everyone gave willingly and abundantly. When it comes to funding major projects, we tend to focus on bottom-line issues and to ask repeatedly, How much? Far more important for leaders is to pose the question, Why? When congregational leaders concern themselves with gospel motivation and with pointing members to the one who for our sakes became poor, God's people will give abundantly to projects whose purpose is to proclaim God's love.

### A bad ending: Joash "[does] not remember" the kindness of Jehoiada

¹⁷After the death of Jehoiada, the officials of Judah came and paid homage to the king, and he listened to them. ¹⁸They abandoned the temple of the LORD, the God of their fathers, and worshiped Asherah poles and idols. Because of their guilt, God's anger came upon Judah and Jerusalem. ¹⁹Although the LORD sent prophets to the people to bring them back to him, and though they testified against them, they would not listen.

²⁰Then the Spirit of God came upon Zechariah son of Jehoiada the priest. He stood before the people and said, "This is what God says: 'Why do you disobey the LORD's commands? You will not prosper. Because you have forsaken the LORD, he has forsaken you.'"

²¹But they plotted against him, and by order of the king they stoned him to death in the courtyard of the LORD's temple. ²²King Joash did not remember the kindness Zechariah's father Jehoiada had shown him but killed his son, who said as he lay dying, "May the LORD see this and call you to account."

There have been times when faithful parents, anguished over a child gone wrong, have asked their pastor about the passage, "Train a child in the way he should go, and when he is old he will not turn from it" (Proverbs 22:6). They wonder what they did wrong in their child's training to cause such bad behavior. The proverb is, of course, a statement of a general truth, not an ironclad guarantee of what will always and in every case be true of a child raised in the fear and admonition of the Lord. That much is certain from Joash's case. No one could have had greater spiritual advantages than he. It is inconceivable that a priest as faithful as Jehoiada would have left anything undone in the young king's spiritual training. In addition the king also had Jehoiada's counsel and advice to guide him well into his adult life. Yet he came to a bad end.

Once Jehoiada had passed from the scene, Joash quickly sank into idolatry. It appears that his own officials were the ones who led him astray, although that is no excuse. The Chronicler says that his officials "paid homage" to him, a very unusual expression for our author to use. As the Chronicler normally employs it, the Hebrew word refers to the flat-on-the-face reverence a worshiper shows toward God. This is the only instance where the Chronicler makes use of it for the homage of subjects toward their human king. Perhaps he means to suggest that Joash's officials were able to influence him by exaggerated acts of devotion and by shameless flattery. Those who hold power are vulnerable to things like this, and we can readily see why it might have been a particular inducement to Joash for doing evil. After all, he had been under Jehoiada's tutelage for a very long time. Now he was free from it. What better time to slyly suggest to him that he assert his new freedom by doing something his old teacher never could have tolerated?

Whatever the psychological explanation for it, sin remains sin. "[Joash] listened to them" serves as the Chronicler's accusation against the king, not as an excuse for his behavior. "They abandoned the temple of the LORD" need not be read as an absolute leaving of the temple and all its services. No doubt the king and his officials continued to participate in temple festivals and sacrifices from time to time. However, they also saw no problem in worshiping at the high places and in offering to Asherah poles and idols the kind of reverence due only to the Lord. As far as the Chronicler is concerned, any false worship—however small a step it may seem to be in accommodating other points of view—is in principle an abandoning of the one true God and of Israel's only Savior. Thus it leads to God's righteous anger. In his reply to Solomon's prayer of dedication, God had solemnly warned his people, "If you . . . go off to serve other gods and worship them, then I will uproot Israel from my land" (7:19,20). The glory of God's name was at stake; he would most surely respond to the king's apostasy.

The next verse demonstrates at once both the grace of God and the willfulness of Judah's sin. God did not simply rain down fire and brimstone upon his people, although they certainly deserved it for spurning his love. "The LORD sent prophets to the people to bring them back to him." Here we see at work the same great heart that opens up its deepest recesses to us in the well-known Bible verse: "As surely as I live, declares the Sovereign LORD, I take no pleasure in the death of the wicked, but rather that they turn from their ways and live. Turn! Turn from your evil ways! Why will you die, O house of Israel?" (Ezekiel 33:11). Although the prophets were faithful in their warning, the people were unfaithful in their listening.

To make the matter crystal clear, the Chronicler describes for us an incident that our Lord himself would later use as an example of faithful witness being greeted by heartless murder. The Spirit suddenly seized Zechariah, the son of Jehoiada, so that he cried out before all the people: "This is what God says: 'Why do you disobey the LORD's commands? You will not prosper. Because you have forsaken the LORD, he has forsaken you.'" Apparently Joash was so thin-skinned (perhaps because his own conscience was accusing him) that he was unable to tolerate any rebuke, even one that had been stated in such general terms as Zechariah's. As the prophet Amos would later say (no doubt ironically), during certain periods the days are so evil that a prudent man keeps quiet (Amos 5:13). Zechariah, that faithful witness, had not learned that lesson yet, and he paid for it with his life. He became one more fool for the sake of Christ (1 Corinthians 4:10).

By the king's own command, various people joined together in a plot against the priest, and when the opportunity presented itself, they stoned him to death. The responsibility for the evil deed belonged to Joash, however, prompting the Chronicler to condemn him with the words, "King Joash did not remember the kindness Zechariah's father Jehoiada had shown him but killed his son."

This verse has a stronger flavor in the original language than one would gather from the way it sounds to us in English. Read literally, it tells us that Joash did not bear in mind the *chesed* that Jehoiada had practiced with him. Chesed (pronounced KE-sed) is one of those Hebrew words with a dozen possible translations, depending upon the context. Its basic meaning is loving-kindness, or mercy. But since words like *love* in our own language have become mushy, it's worth noting that chesed has connotations of commitment, loyalty, and steadfastness. It's a love that demonstrates itself in actions. It's the kind of faithful love the Lord continually showed to his people, remaining steadfast and true to his promise even though they had so often spurned him and provoked him to anger.

Jehoiada's actions toward Joash were aptly described as a practice of chesed. No one else knew or cared about this last descendant of David. Anyone who did him a kindness would have incurred the wrath of Athaliah if discovered. But Jehoiada and his wife did not react with the normal response of fear nor with a desire to win the favor of the powerful. They considered the promises of God that had been attached so firmly to the house and lineage of David. Then they lived by them, producing faithful, constant, loyal deeds of love. More than courage, more than decisiveness, what Jehoiada and Jehosheba had done required faith—the kind of faith that does not act on the basis of what one sees but rather reasons and lives from the promises of God. It is hard to understand how anyone could forget such chesed. But Joash casually put it all out of his mind and calmly gave the order for Zechariah to die.

As he lay dying, Zechariah said, "May the Lord see this and call you to account" (verse 22). He knew he had not spoken his own word but God's. He could commit his righteous cause into God's hands and trust that God would repay the king for despising his Word and for killing his prophet. Some commentators act as if this shows a somewhat lesser morality than that of Christ, who prayed for his enemies as he was dying. These writers act as if a New Testament Christian would never have such a deathbed prayer, whatever the provocation. Here we ought to remember what Jesus said to the high priest and the others who were searching for a legal way to murder him: "You will see the Son of Man sitting at the right hand of the Mighty One and coming on the clouds of heaven" (Matthew 26:64). This is the same as saying: "Right now I stand in your courtroom to be judged. But there is another court and another time for judgment. In it you will stand in front of me and receive your just condemnation."

It is certainly true that we live from the promises of God and that the gospel should predominate in all our speaking, preaching, and teaching. Nevertheless, God's wrath must still be proclaimed to the ungodly and to those who suppress the truth in their wickedness. It is in that same spirit that

Zechariah spoke his dying words. In that same spirit Jesus declared to hardened sinners who rejected him, "Upon you will come all the righteous blood that has been shed on earth, from the blood of righteous Abel to the blood of Zechariah" (Matthew 23:35). There is a day when God will call everyone to account. Our only hope and refuge is for the blood of Christ to cover us on that day.

The Lord's response to his people's unfaithfulness and to his prophet's murder was not long in coming.

**²³At the turn of the year, the army of Aram marched against Joash; it invaded Judah and Jerusalem and killed all the leaders of the people. They sent all the plunder to their king in Damascus. ²⁴Although the Aramean army had come with only a few men, the LORD delivered into their hands a much larger army. Because Judah had forsaken the LORD, the God of their fathers, judgment was executed on Joash. ²⁵When the Arameans withdrew, they left Joash severely wounded. His officials conspired against him for murdering the son of Jehoiada the priest, and they killed him in his bed. So he died and was buried in the City of David, but not in the tombs of the kings.**

**²⁶Those who conspired against him were Zabad, son of Shimeath an Ammonite woman, and Jehozabad, son of Shimrith a Moabite woman. ²⁷The account of his sons, the many prophecies about him, and the record of the restoration of the temple of God are written in the annotations on the book of the kings. And Amaziah his son succeeded him as king.**

In most respects the account of the Aramean invasion of Judah is given in greater detail in 2 Kings chapter 12. For example, from 2 Kings we learn that the plunder mentioned here in verse 23 consisted of the temple treasures that David and Solomon had dedicated to the Lord. No doubt they even included some of those silver and gold vessels that Joash had recently made as part of his temple restoration project. We also learn from 2 Kings that the Arameans did not gain the plunder so much from battle as they received it in tribute. Joash turned it over to Hazael to persuade him to cease and desist from his invasion. It is to the Chronicler, however, that we owe the information that there *was* a battle between the Arameans and the Judeans and that in the battle the leaders who had enticed the king into idolatry were killed and the king himself was severely wounded.

The Chronicler's chief contribution is to make explicit something that is only implicit in the 2 Kings account. He wants no one to be in any doubt that this battle was an act of God's judgment on Judah and on her king. The leading officials had led their king into idolatry. The consequence? They were all killed. The people had allowed themselves to be led into idolatry by their evil leaders. The consequence? In the past God's people had learned that the Lord helps the weak overcome the strong (see 14:11; 20:15-17). Now they discovered that this same principle could also work against them when they abandoned the Lord. "Although the Aramean army had come with only a few men, the LORD delivered into their hands a much larger army." Finally, Joash had given his blessing to a plot to kill God's prophet. The consequence? Joash's own palace officials conspired against him and murdered him while he lay in bed help-lessly wounded.

The king's disobedience led to disgrace in life and to dis-honor in death. Jehoiada the priest had received the distinc-tion of being buried with the kings of Judah, a distinction his erring pupil did not enjoy. Instead, Joash "was buried in the City of David, but not in the tombs of the kings."

In some ways a person could regard chapters 22 to 24 as being the Chronicler's meditation on keeping faith and on breaking it. It is apparent that he intended the three chapters to be read as a unit. We can tell this not only from the subject matter itself but also from the way a certain word recurs. That word first appeared in the mouth of Athaliah. "Treason! Treason!" she cried when she realized that her sin had caught up with her at last. Literally the word means "conspiracy," and it is most commonly used when people plot against their rightful government. We also observe the Chronicler using it in verse 21 of this chapter, where it refers to the people plotting against Zechariah the priest, and again in verses 25 and 26 to round out the entire section.

When we compare these three uses, something interesting comes to light: there's an edge to the way our author uses the word. Athaliah, that murderous woman, had no right to cry "Treason!" There is no treachery involved when God's people refuse to follow a spiritual leader who leads them astray. On the other hand, the plot against Zechariah was clearly treacherous. Some might call it treason when a prophet speaks out against a king and consider it the act of a loyal subject to kill such a prophet. But Zechariah was far more loyal to Joash than any of his fawning subjects could have been. He told his king the truth, a truth his king would have done well to listen to.

Finally, the end of Joash came about by a plot of his own palace officials. This was the first time a legitimate ruler in Judah had died because of a conspiracy against him. But was this treason, or was it God's justice? Without sanctioning violent revolution, the Chronicler still makes it plain that this was sin paying its wage. In a supreme act of treachery, Joash had murdered the son of Jehoiada, who in a supreme act of faithfulness had helped put Joash on the throne. Joash gave no thought to the way Jehoiada had kept faith with him. Therefore the Lord gave him measure for measure. He had once been kept safe in a bedroom (22:11), only to be murdered in his bed. There is no safe place for someone who has abandoned the Lord.

The Lord warns the faithful through Isaiah the prophet, "Do not call conspiracy everything that these people call conspiracy" (Isaiah 8:12). In other words, what looks like treachery in our own estimation may from God's perspective be great loyalty and faithfulness. Someone who stands on the Word of God will always be in the majority, even though the whole world may oppose him. This was as true at Worms, when Luther was asked to recant, as it was in the temple courts when Zechariah, filled with the Spirit, stood up to denounce the king. It will always be true. One doesn't need to be a prophet to be able to discern the nature of our own times and the need for bold confessors of God's truth. We must learn to be faithful to God and his Word or we will never succeed in keeping faith with anyone.

### God's kingdom under Amaziah

Amaziah is the second in a series of three kings to whom the Chronicler gives decidedly mixed reviews. All three started out well, but all three ended badly. For both Amaziah and Uzziah, the chief problem seems to have been pride. In Amaziah's case that pride was combined with idolatry; in Uzziah's it was combined with sacrilege.

### A good beginning: his heart is open to advice from the Lord

**25** **Amaziah was twenty-five years old when he became king, and he reigned in Jerusalem twenty-nine years. His mother's name was Jehoaddin; she was from Jerusalem. ²He did what was right in the eyes of the LORD, but not wholeheartedly. ³After the kingdom was firmly in his control, he executed the officials who had murdered his father the king. ⁴Yet he did not put their sons to death, but acted in accordance with**

what is written in the Law, in the Book of Moses, where the LORD commanded: "Fathers shall not be put to death for their children, nor children put to death for their fathers; each is to die for his own sins."

⁵Amaziah called the people of Judah together and assigned them according to their families to commanders of thousands and commanders of hundreds for all Judah and Benjamin. He then mustered those twenty years old or more and found that there were three hundred thousand men ready for military service, able to handle the spear and shield. ⁶He also hired a hundred thousand fighting men from Israel for a hundred talents of silver.

⁷But a man of God came to him and said, "O king, these troops from Israel must not march with you, for the LORD is not with Israel—not with any of the people of Ephraim. ⁸Even if you go and fight courageously in battle, God will overthrow you before the enemy, for God has the power to help or to overthrow."

⁹Amaziah asked the man of God, "But what about the hundred talents I paid for these Israelite troops?"

The man of God replied, "The LORD can give you much more than that."

¹⁰So Amaziah dismissed the troops who had come to him from Ephraim and sent them home. They were furious with Judah and left for home in a great rage.

¹¹Amaziah then marshaled his strength and led his army to the Valley of Salt, where he killed ten thousand men of Seir. ¹²The army of Judah also captured ten thousand men alive, took them to the top of a cliff and threw them down so that all were dashed to pieces.

Once he had consolidated his power, Amaziah's first order of business was to punish those who had killed his father. Even though their motive had been to avenge Zechariah's murder, they were still assassins who had taken up arms against the legitimate ruler of God's people. They deserved to die. The Chronicler, however, commends Amaziah for his restraint in carrying out the death sentence. Instead of wiping out their entire families, as many ancient monarchs might have done, the new king simply punished the ones who actually had blood on their hands. In doing so, he obeyed the particular law of Moses that had set a limit on those whom the state could hold accountable for a crime: "Fathers shall not be put to death for their children, nor children put to death for their fathers; each is to die for his own sin" (compare verse 4 with Deuteronomy 24:16).

The key description of Amaziah is found in verse 2: "He did what was right in the eyes of the LORD, but not wholeheartedly." His character and behavior may not have been subject to dramatic reversals—from good to bad or from bad to good—but his discipleship, if we can even call it that, was halfhearted throughout his life, with the good and the bad mixed together. As we take a look at his campaign against Edom, we will see that the Chronicler presents it to us as an example of a period in Amaziah's life when the good outweighed the bad.

First Amaziah called up and organized the fighting men at his disposal, much as king David had done (see 1 Chronicles 27). After counting all those 20 years old or more, he discovered that his army consisted of 300,000 fighting men, a disappointing total when compared to some of the numbers available to other kings who had gone before him. We remember Asa, for example, who could take to the field with 580,000 men, or Jehoshaphat's troops, which topped the million mark (14:8; 17:14-18). It was, perhaps, because of his disappointment with the numbers that he decided to hire 100,000 fighting men from Israel.

One would think—after all the grief the kingdom had suffered because of Jehoshaphat's disastrous alliance with Ahab—that Amaziah would have known enough to steer clear of making any connections with the North. A lukewarm faith, however, is bound to result in a listless love, and the visible advantage of larger numbers is bound to seem more important than the invisible (yet far more real) advantage of a faithful and powerful God, who makes a believer's battles his own. Perhaps Amaziah was able to justify his actions by telling himself that it was purely a financial arrangement and not an alliance. A man of God had to set him straight. "O king, these troops from Israel must not march with you, for the LORD is not with Israel," the man of God began.

Once again we hear the truth expressed by a prophet of God: that even though the Israelites were still part of God's covenant people, they were a people who had cut themselves off from God's true king and God's true worship (see commentary on 13:4-12). That is why God was not with them nor with any who made common cause with them. Any joint venture would go down in defeat. But we also understand the prophet as meaning something more basic: for the people of God the real issue in *any* battle was not the size of their army nor the courage with which they fought but whether God was with them. If he was, God's people would prevail. If he was not, God's people would fall flat on their faces. "For God has the power to help or to overthrow."

It is here that we see Amaziah's halfhearted faith trip him up. He began to calculate the financial losses he would incur if he dismissed the Israelite troops. "What about the hundred talents I paid for these Israelite troops?" he asks. The prophet's reply was, "The LORD can give you much more than that." To Amaziah's credit in this instance, confidence in the Lord's word triumphed over his calculating instincts. He dismissed the men he had hired. The Israelites stormed off in a rage. They were not deprived of their wages, perhaps, but they had lost out on whatever spoils of war might have come their way had they been allowed to take part in a successful campaign. For most soldiers in the ancient world, that was always the fattest part of their paycheck. Even more than that, they had been humiliated. The king of little Judah had summoned them, but the mighty men of Israel weren't good enough for him. Thoughts like these fueled a rage that was bound to burn itself out on something. We will see later how it did.

As for Amaziah's hostile intentions against Edom and the men of Mount Seir, these succeeded beyond all expectation. Not only were ten thousand of the enemy killed in battle, but the men of Judah also destroyed ten thousand more Edomites whom they had captured, hurling them down from a cliff. The sheer brutality of ancient war may sometimes take our breath away, particularly when we see it in campaigns conducted by the people of God. Part of what is troubling about this may be relieved if we remember the ancient enmity that existed between these two related peoples (see, for example, chapter 20). The most important thing to keep in mind, however, is the truth that there is also a spiritual battle being conducted under these physical forms. In Judah versus Edom we have one more skirmish in the never-ending conflict between believer and unbeliever, light and darkness, flesh and spirit, good and evil. There can be no quarter given in that conflict, and we do well to remind ourselves of that. Our sinful nature cannot be coaxed into doing good, nor will it be held captive by our good intentions. It must be drowned in the water of Baptism as we daily count ourselves dead to sin and alive to God in Christ.

For the Chronicler the account serves as an example of what happens when even a halfhearted king listens in faith to advice from a man of God. The Lord gave Amaziah strength beyond anything he naturally possessed and the power to overcome obstacles he would not have dared hope he could surmount.

Before considering the downward spiral of Amaziah's life, it might be worth pausing a few moments to consider what was happening in the larger political context of the ancient Middle East at this time. We recall from the last chapter how Hazael, king of Aram, had served as the Lord's instrument in punishing Joash and the people of Judah for their apostasy (24:23-25). Not only had Aram (sometimes called Syria in older texts and commentaries) been able to turn Judah into a client state, but it had also stripped Israel of much of its strength. It was during those dark days that the prophet Elisha had stood out as a pillar of strength, bolstering the courage of the faithful in Israel and throwing terror into the hearts of God's enemies (see 2 Kings 5–9).

By the time of Amaziah of Judah and Jehoash of Israel, however, a shift in power had occurred in the region. In 803 B.C. King Adadnirari III of Assyria raided the Arameans and succeeded in turning them into a tributary state. Jehoash and Amaziah were then able to move into the vacuum created by Aram's weakness. Jehoash further checked the power of the Arameans by defeating them several times in battle (2 Kings 13:22-25), while Amaziah was able to begin the process of reasserting Judah's control over Edom, a process later completed by Uzziah, his son. This would reestablish Judah's economic power as the country in charge of the port of Elath on the Red Sea, a vital link in the ancient trading network of the Near East (26:2).

Viewed from an entirely political and economic perspective, Judah and Israel stood at the beginning of an era in which their glory would be restored to a luster comparable to the golden days of David and Solomon. Political success and economic prosperity do not yield spiritual dividends, however. And it was the spiritual side of things that most concerned writers like the Chronicler.

### A bad ending: his heart is led away to idols and closed to the good words of God

¹³Meanwhile the troops that Amaziah had sent back and had not allowed to take part in the war raided Judean towns from Samaria to Beth Horon. They killed three thousand people and carried off great quantities of plunder.

¹⁴When Amaziah returned from slaughtering the Edomites, he brought back the gods of the people of Seir. He set them up as his own gods, bowed down to them and burned sacrifices to them. ¹⁵The anger of the LORD burned against Amaziah, and he sent a prophet to him, who said, "Why do you consult this people's gods, which could not save their own people from your hand?"

¹⁶While he was still speaking, the king said to him, "Have we appointed you an adviser to the king? Stop! Why be struck down?"

So the prophet stopped but said, "I know that God has determined to destroy you, because you have done this and have not listened to my counsel."

¹⁷After Amaziah king of Judah consulted his advisers, he sent this challenge to Jehoash son of Jehoahaz, the son of Jehu, king of Israel: "Come, meet me face to face."

¹⁸But Jehoash king of Israel replied to Amaziah king of Judah: "A thistle in Lebanon sent a message to a cedar in Lebanon, 'Give your daughter to my son in marriage.' Then a wild beast in Lebanon came along and trampled the thistle

underfoot. ¹⁹You say to yourself that you have defeated Edom, and now you are arrogant and proud. But stay at home! Why ask for trouble and cause your own downfall and that of Judah also?"

²⁰Amaziah, however, would not listen, for God so worked that he might hand them over to Jehoash, because they sought the gods of Edom. ²¹So Jehoash king of Israel attacked. He and Amaziah king of Judah faced each other at Beth Shemesh in Judah. ²²Judah was routed by Israel, and every man fled to his home. ²³Jehoash king of Israel captured Amaziah king of Judah, the son of Joash, the son of Ahaziah, at Beth Shemesh. Then Jehoash brought him to Jerusalem and broke down the wall of Jerusalem from the Ephraim Gate to the Corner Gate—a section about six hundred feet long. ²⁴He took all the gold and silver and all the articles found in the temple of God that had been in the care of Obed-Edom, together with the palace treasures and the hostages, and returned to Samaria.

²⁵Amaziah son of Joash king of Judah lived for fifteen years after the death of Jehoash son of Jehoahaz king of Israel. ²⁶As for the other events of Amaziah's reign, from beginning to end, are they not written in the book of the kings of Judah and Israel? ²⁷From the time that Amaziah turned away from following the LORD, they conspired against him in Jerusalem and he fled to Lachish, but they sent men after him to Lachish and killed him there. ²⁸He was brought back by horse and was buried with his fathers in the City of Judah.

The Chronicler picks up a thread of the story again in verse 13 that he had temporarily dropped in verse 10. The Israelite troops who had been dismissed from Amaziah's army went back to Samaria to lick their wounds for a bit before finding a way to give vent to their rage against Judah for humiliating them. It is probable that they saw an ideal opportunity present itself when Amaziah was off on his Edomite campaign. Seizing it, they launched raids against the now unprotected Judean towns along the border between

Israel and Judah, killing three thousand people and carrying off great quantities of plunder. Human pride must find a way to assert itself.

What is interesting about the placement of this incident is the way it seems to run counter to what the man of God had said to Amaziah when the king had wondered about the money he was going to lose in dismissing the men of Israel (25:9). Amaziah had obeyed the word of the Lord, but not only had the Lord not replaced the money Amaziah had lost, it appeared as if he had determined that Amaziah should lose even more. Clearly this was a test from the Lord to Amaziah, a challenge to see whether this halfhearted man could learn under cross and trial to grasp the Word and to walk by faith, not by sight.

We have often taken note of the almost indefatigable way in which the Chronicler points out that obedience leads to blessing while disobedience brings disaster. Our writer certainly wrote as a child of the old covenant, where physical blessings and afflictions played a key role in God's training program. Nevertheless, the inclusion of this incident demonstrates that he did not believe that God was conditioned to respond in an automatic way for every deed of man. God was and is absolutely free in all his actions. The paths he takes in history are always beyond our ability to fully trace.

The Chronicler's next paragraph demonstrates just how halfhearted Amaziah's commitment to the Lord was. After he had crushed the Edomites, he brought their captured gods back to Jerusalem and set them up for worship. Had he served the Lord wholeheartedly, he would have burned the idols as David had done (1 Chronicles 14:12; see also Deuteronomy 7:25; 12:3). Amaziah's idolatry may have been due to a logic common among superstitious and heathen rulers of that time. If a nation or tribe suffered defeat, the idea followed that their gods had turned against them and had smiled upon their enemies. And if a nation's gods had helped that nation's conqueror, it only made sense for the conqueror to acknowledge their help and to keep them contented. So ancient rulers would often carry off the idols of vanquished people and worship them, just as Amaziah did here.

But what makes perfect sense to a pagan mind-set is perfect nonsense to the eyes of faith. God's anger burned against Amaziah. Instead of punishing him immediately, God gave him fair warning through a prophet who exposed the true nature of the king's actions: "Why do you consult this people's gods, which could not save their own people from your hand?" The victory over Edom was from the Lord. It did not demonstrate the favorable attitude of Edom's gods toward Amaziah; instead it proved convincingly that they did not exist. They were gods that could not save.

Amaziah would have none of it. Before the prophet had even finished speaking his message, the king said sarcastically: "Hmmm, I don't recall appointing you as one of my advisers. Best keep quiet! Why get yourself hurt?" The prophet complied but bravely reserved for himself and God the final word, "I know that God has determined to destroy you, because you have done this and have not listened to my counsel." We have encountered similar judgments of God in the past. Those who refuse to hear the truth are abandoned by God to believe only lies.

Blinded by conceit, Amaziah was open to listen to some bad advice. His counselors encouraged their conquering hero to try his luck with Jehoash, the king of Israel. As already mentioned, Jehoash was himself a conquering hero and mighty warrior, with plenty of victories chalked up against Aram, a far more impressive foe than Amaziah had ever faced.

Full of himself, Amaziah issued Jehoash what amounted to a summons to fight: "Come, meet me face to face." As we know from 2 Kings, Jehoash was hardly successful as a believer, however adept in battle he might have been. All the same, he was inspired to offer his southern neighbor a not-so-friendly but well-intentioned warning.

"Let me tell you a story," said Jehoash, in effect. "Once upon a time there were two plants: a little thistle and a great big cedar tree. The thistle had the gall to propose a marriage alliance with the cedar. 'Give your daughter to my son in marriage,' he said. But before the cedar had even a chance to laugh off the proposal, along came a wild beast who made a permanent end to the thistle's outrageous ambitions." Then, just in case Amaziah failed to grasp the point, Jehoash added, "You say to yourself that you have defeated Edom, and now you are arrogant and proud. But stay at home! Why ask for trouble and cause your own downfall and that of Judah also?"

Amaziah didn't listen. More than that—the Chronicler tells us he *couldn't* listen. "For God so worked that he might hand [Judah] over to Jehoash, because they sought the gods of Edom." Judah suffered a crushing defeat, and Amaziah was captured. We notice how our writer identifies the captured king with the royal title "the son of Joash, the son of Ahaziah." But Amaziah is clearly not a worthy claimant to the title "son of David." He sought honor for himself in victory, but he wound up distinguished only by the completeness of his defeat. To put an end to any further ambitions Judah might have for military adventures into the North, the king of Israel broke down a large portion of the side of Jerusalem's wall that faced toward his kingdom. Jerusalem would not be too keen on wars of offense if her defenses were so weak.

Not content with this, King Jehoash added a final flourish as if to underline his victory. All the gold and silver articles in God's temple he appropriated for himself and took back to his capital along with some hostages. It is possible that we have a play on words in verse 24. Obed-Edom was a well-known Levitical name. It also happens to mean "servant of Edom." Perhaps the Chronicler uses the fact that the temple treasures were in the charge of a man with such a name to make a point. Amaziah had made Edom his servant but had become enslaved to their gods. Thus he lost everything he had gained.

The description of Amaziah's death marks the final stage in the king's degradation. His life under threat from conspiracy, the king of Judah was hunted down like a dog and killed by the conspirators' agents in Lachish, a town about 26 miles southwest of Jerusalem. The Chronicler clarifies for his readers the reason for this pathetic end to a once-proud king. The league against him began to form itself "from the time that Amaziah turned away from following the LORD." As it says in the book of Proverbs, "The LORD works out everything for his own ends—even the wicked for a day of disaster" (Proverbs 16:4).

From his repetition of the word *advise* in verses 16 and 17 (the root occurs four times in that brief space), we can easily detect the chief point the Chronicler wants to make in retelling the story of Amaziah. Amaziah's was a case in which all the good he had accomplished came about from listening to good and godly advice. Similarly, all the evil he suffered resulted from his closing his ears to God's Word. Once he had done that, he couldn't recognize the voice of wisdom anymore when he heard it. And so he was condemned to follow and suffer from the counsel of fools.

Even pagan nations have long been aware of the corrupting effect of power and success on a person's character. They say that the ancient Roman generals in their triumph parades had a slave continually whisper in their ear, "Remember, you must die!" More than one Greek tragedy was founded on the principle that a man who succeeds too much is liable to incur the jealousy and wrath of a god. From our own experience, we understand how easily power becomes blinded by itself. It quickly comes to believe that whatever it can do, it has a perfect *right* to do, and that is why it blusters and threatens anyone who by word or deed tries to check its purposes. We see the Chronicler draw these same lessons for us in the accounts of Amaziah and Uzziah.

The Chronicler, however, goes beyond these natural insights that even a serious-minded unbeliever might conclude on the strength of his own reason. There is more here, he suggests, than simply a matter of someone who can no longer recognize his mortality or his human limitations. There is also the matter of sin, which so infects our race that even believers (particularly halfhearted ones) can stumble and fall.

And there is the matter of God's judgment, which hardens the sinner who first hardens himself against the truth. Far from reacting out of petty jealousy or envy, the Lord's jealousy is born out of a pure and exclusive love for his own. He is the husband, and the company of believers is his beloved bride. He soothes, he comforts, he coaxes his people again and again in his Word. Sometimes he even pleads, "Listen to me! Why will you die?" Finally he sternly warns, thundering down from Sinai with fearful threats and wrath. But there comes a time when talk is at an end. There's nothing more to be said. In spite of all, the person spurns God's love and rejects his Word. Then God hardens, saying to the obstinate sinner: "You don't want to listen? Then you will not listen!"

All this is said not to discourage those believers who are already troubled by their own failure, who daily struggle with their flesh, who pray daily for the strength to become better, and who hunger and thirst for the sweet consolation that only the gospel message can give. It is rather aimed at those believers who have become puffed up by their own knowledge and spiritual successes, those who began with the Spirit—beggars like all the rest of us—but who now suppose that they can become perfect through their own efforts. It is to complacent Christians such as these that the Chronicler would say, "So, if you think you are standing firm, be careful that you don't fall!" (1 Corinthians 10:12).

### God's kingdom under Uzziah

**26** **Then all the people of Judah took Uzziah, who was sixteen years old, and made him king in place of his father Amaziah. ²He was the one who rebuilt Elath and restored it to Judah after Amaziah rested with his fathers.**

It is time, once again, to take a brief side journey to consider the matter of the chronology of the Hebrew kings, since the subject is suggested by these two verses. A careful Bible reader encounters some special difficulties in harmonizing all the data the Bible gives us on the reigns of Amaziah and Uzziah of Judah, particularly in how they are to be fit in with the reigns of Jehoash and Jeroboam II of Israel. The reader whose eyes glaze over at the mere mention of numbers can easily be forgiven if he or she wishes to skip to the next section.

First, from the regnal synchronizations in 2 Kings chapters 14 and 15, it appears that there must have been considerable overlap in the reigns of Amaziah and Uzziah of Judah. The same is true of the reigns of Jehoash and Jeroboam II.

As we noted already in our earlier discussion of this subject (page 185), the best way of understanding some of the numbers we are presented with in 1 and 2 Kings is to think in terms of co-regencies, that is, a situation in which a king and his son ruled jointly for a time. Biblical evidence for this appears in the section we are now considering.

We are told that "the people of Judah took Uzziah . . . and made him king in place of his father." The phrasing suggests that the transition from one king to the next was less than smooth. Thus the people themselves were forced to take matters into their own hands. We have come across a similar phrase before, in similarly unsettled circumstances (see 2 Chronicles 22:1). Because of Judah's defeat by Israel, Amaziah's capture, and the ruin of Jerusalem's defenses, there was no small amount of unrest and confusion in the Southern Kingdom. To restore order and perhaps also because they had lost confidence in Amaziah, the people demanded that 16-year-old Uzziah become king at once, alongside his father.

Some have even suggested that Amaziah remained a captive in Samaria until Jehoash's death, at which time the captive king was released. According to this theory, he then came back to Jerusalem and ruled jointly with his son for a time before finally meeting his end at the hands of conspirators. This idea is partially based on the Chronicler's remark in verse 25 of the last chapter: "Amaziah . . . lived for fifteen years *after the death of Jehoash.*" Although the writer of Kings often expresses major events in *one* kingdom in terms of the regnal years of the king who presided over the *other* kingdom, it is not the regular practice of the Chronicler to do so. Since his focus is the Southern Kingdom, he ignores the kings of Israel entirely, except when their paths would intersect with the house of David. Second Chronicles 25:25, then,

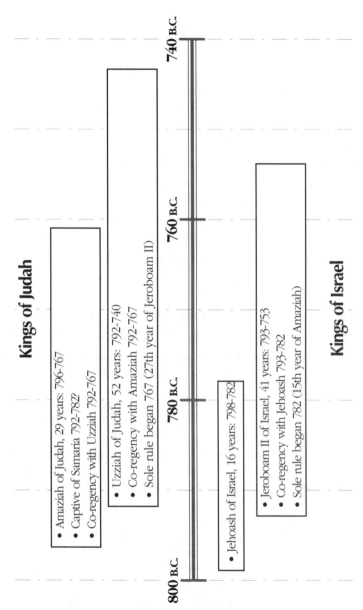

**Kings of Judah**

- Amaziah of Judah, 29 years: 796-767
- Captive of Samaria 792-782?
- Co-regency with Uzziah 792-767

- Uzziah of Judah, 52 years: 792-740
- Co-regency with Amaziah 792-767
- Sole rule began 767 (27th year of Jeroboam II)

- Jehoash of Israel, 16 years: 798-782

**Kings of Israel**

- Jeroboam II of Israel, 41 years: 793-753
- Co-regency with Jehoash 793-782
- Sole rule began 782 (15th year of Amaziah)

740 B.C.

760 B.C.

780 B.C.

800 B.C.

Co-regencies among the kings

would be an exception to that rule. The unusual comment would make perfect sense, however, if Amaziah's fortunes had been bound up with Jehoash's for many years.

Finally, verse 2 also contains a phrase that seems out of place. We were just told that the people had made Uzziah king "in place of his father Amaziah," and then we read that Uzziah rebuilt Elath "after Amaziah rested with his fathers." What appears at first to be mere repetition becomes perfectly understandable if we suppose both that Uzziah ruled together with his father and that he had only rebuilt Elath when he had begun to occupy the throne by himself after his father had died.

To help summarize the biblical data and place it neatly in our minds, the chart on the previous page is offered.

### *Uzziah remembers his name ("The Lord is my strength") and becomes powerful and prosperous*

³Uzziah was sixteen years old when he became king, and he reigned in Jerusalem fifty-two years. His mother's name was Jecoliah; she was from Jerusalem. ⁴He did what was right in the eyes of the Lord, just as his father Amaziah had done. ⁵He sought God during the days of Zechariah, who instructed him in the fear of God. As long as he sought the Lord, God gave him success.

⁶He went to war against the Philistines and broke down the walls of Gath, Jabneh and Ashdod. He then rebuilt towns near Ashdod and elsewhere among the Philistines. ⁷God helped him against the Philistines and against the Arabs who lived in Gur Baal and against the Meunites. ⁸The Ammonites brought tribute to Uzziah, and his fame spread as far as the border of Egypt, because he had become very powerful.

⁹Uzziah built towers in Jerusalem at the Corner Gate, at the Valley Gate and at the angle of the wall, and he fortified them. ¹⁰He also built towers in the desert and dug many cisterns, because he had much livestock in the foothills and in the plain.

He had people working his fields and vineyards in the hills and in the fertile lands, for he loved the soil.

¹¹Uzziah had a well-trained army, ready to go out by divisions according to their numbers as mustered by Jeiel the secretary and Maaseiah the officer under the direction of Hananiah, one of the royal officials. ¹²The total number of family leaders over the fighting men was 2,600. ¹³Under their command was an army of 307,500 men trained for war, a powerful force to support the king against his enemies. ¹⁴Uzziah provided shields, spears, helmets, coats of armor, bows and slingstones for the entire army. ¹⁵In Jerusalem he made machines designed by skillful men for use on the towers and on the corner defenses to shoot arrows and hurl large stones. His fame spread far and wide, for he was greatly helped until he became powerful.

One might consider the era of King Uzziah in Judah and King Jeroboam II in Israel to be a kind of silver age for the monarchy. True, the whole Land of Promise was no longer under the sway of a single ruler descended from great King David. But through the efforts of Uzziah and Jeroboam II, the borders of Judah and Israel were restored almost to the same boundaries once controlled by Solomon. The picture of material prosperity and physical well-being we see here seems to agree perfectly with the archaeological evidence that has been unearthed. Diggings in the south and southeast of Judah appear to indicate that the Hebrew settlement reached its greatest extent during this time frame. At one location a seal has even been discovered with Uzziah's name on it.

A brief glance at the Chronicler's presentation of the positive side of Uzziah's reign leads us to conclude that the king must have been an early prototype of a Renaissance man. Concerning his earthly successes, we are told that he enjoyed military victories, engaged in building projects, and farmed extensively. His interest in these matters was by no means superficial. Under his administration the army was well-organized and well-equipped. He kept his defenses up-to-date by the acquisition of the latest military hardware. His construction projects ran the gamut from the founding of settlements to the rebuilding of Jerusalem's shattered fortifications. In his spare time, he built defensive towers in the desert and dug cisterns for his livestock. As far as his farming was concerned, he was so adept at it that he earned for himself a title. He was called "Lover of the soil."

The extremely detailed section on the military—with its lists rolling on so endlessly—has about the same verbal impact as the visual effect the communist party faithfuls must have gotten when they watched the old May Day parades in Moscow's Red Square. And in reading the sections describing Uzziah's efforts in agriculture, a person can almost hear Beethoven's "Pastoral Symphony" playing in the background. It is no small wonder that "his fame spread far and wide" (verse 15). Even once-hostile nations brought him tribute.

The Chronicler does not leave us in any doubt as to the cause of Uzziah's success. "He was greatly helped" it says in verse 15, according to the NIV translation. This is a somewhat milk-and-water rendition of the Hebrew's "he was *wondrously* helped" or even "*miraculously* helped." In case we have any doubt as to *who* precisely came to his aid, we need only glance back to the statements "God gave him success" and "God helped him." In other words, whatever natural gifts or talents Uzziah might have possessed, they all came down from the Father of the heavenly lights (James 1:17). He was no self-made man; his success was given by God.

God granted this success because Uzziah had been faithful in seeking him. The Chronicler mentions the name of the teacher who had instructed Uzziah. This Zechariah is otherwise unknown to us, but he evidently made a great impact upon the king. He taught the young man the basic truths concerning the God of Abraham, the God who had freely made a covenant of pure grace with the man of faith and with all his descendants: "Through your offspring all nations on earth will be blessed" (Genesis 22:18). This same God had brought Israel to himself at Sinai, where he carved in stone the mighty precepts of the Law. Following that, he had settled his chosen people in a spacious and good land and had given them rest from all their enemies. He had attached his gracious promise of a Savior to the house of David and had enabled David's son Solomon to build a glorious temple, where the Lord was pleased to meet with his own. There he answered their prayers and pardoned their sins. Through Zechariah's careful instruction in law and gospel, God struck the spark of faith in the young king's heart and fanned it into flames so that "he aimed at seeking God" (verse 5, literal translation).

This message is reinforced by the Chronicler's technique of playing on the name of Uzziah throughout this passage. This king, in fact, is known to us by two names: Uzziah ("the Lord is my strength") and—the one preferred by the writer of 2 Kings—Azariah ("the Lord is my help"). The Chronicler plays upon both of these names, using words like *help* and *strength* no less than seven times. As a man is named, so is he. As long as Uzziah/Azariah remembered his name—remembered his true identity in the Lord—he prospered. Similarly, all those who continue in faith by remembering whose name they bear by virtue of their baptisms will prosper as well. In Baptism we draw our strength and consolation from Christ's power, Christ's grace, and Christ's glory. Because his strength is perfect, we are unshakably confident in him, knowing that we will prosper eternally.

This entire section is so positively focused that we are almost unprepared for what comes next. The only hints the Chronicler gives that something might go wrong are embedded in verses 4 and 5: "He did what was right in the eyes of the LORD, *just as his father Amaziah had done.* He sought God *during the days of Zechariah. . . . As long as he sought the LORD,* God gave him success." The first sentence makes us wonder. He did what was right—just like Amaziah? Considering how Amaziah ended up, we're not quite sure what the Chronicler means. In the following verse, the time references seem to imply—without exactly saying in so many words—that there might come a day when Uzziah would *no longer* seek the Lord and when he would for that same reason *no longer* enjoy success.

Whatever suspicions these few words might have aroused in our minds, the Chronicler quickly lays them to rest by the great delight he takes in describing the many things Uzziah was able to accomplish through the Lord's help. His praises of Uzziah roll on like a flooded river. It's as if the Chronicler is setting us up for a shock. And he is. When the change comes, it is abrupt, it is swift, and it is terrible. "Pride goes before destruction, a haughty spirit before a fall," the Scriptures say (Proverbs 16:18). The Chronicler has told the story in such a way to mirror the way it was for Uzziah. With the shocking fall of Uzziah, the Chronicler hopes to alert us to the danger of pride in ourselves *before* it sweeps us off a cliff.

### *He forgets who he is, and pride leads to his destruction*

**¹⁶But after Uzziah became powerful, his pride led to his downfall. He was unfaithful to the LORD his God, and entered**

the temple of the Lord to burn incense on the altar of incense. ¹⁷Azariah the priest with eighty other courageous priests of the Lord followed him in. ¹⁸They confronted him and said, "It is not right for you, Uzziah, to burn incense to the Lord. That is for the priests, the descendants of Aaron, who have been consecrated to burn incense. Leave the sanctuary, for you have been unfaithful; and you will not be honored by the Lord God."

¹⁹Uzziah, who had a censer in his hand ready to burn incense, became angry. While he was raging at the priests in their presence before the incense altar in the Lord's temple, leprosy broke out on his forehead. ²⁰When Azariah the chief priest and all the other priests looked at him, they saw that he had leprosy on his forehead, so they hurried him out. Indeed, he himself was eager to leave, because the Lord had afflicted him.

²¹King Uzziah had leprosy until the day he died. He lived in a separate house—leprous, and excluded from the temple of the Lord. Jotham his son had charge of the palace and governed the people of the land.

²²The other events of Uzziah's reign, from beginning to end, are recorded by the prophet Isaiah son of Amoz. ²³Uzziah rested with his fathers and was buried near them in a field for burial that belonged to the kings, for people said, "He had leprosy." And Jotham his son succeeded him as king.

Pride is such a deadly sin because it is so symptomatic of our basic mind-set since Adam's fall. We are born egocentric—"turned in upon ourselves," as Luther would say. And while we have received the new birth in Christ by Baptism, we still have to struggle against this enemy within as long as we live. Pride is a powerfully destructive force in all relationships. It can lead us into blind self-assertion over our neighbor, as it did in the case of Amaziah. Not content with his station, Amaziah had to be better than Jehoash. But even more serious is the way pride can destroy our relationship with God, as we see in the case of Uzziah.

We have already noted how gifted Uzziah was. His restless and venturesome mind led him to master many different facets of life. What a pity that it also led him into an attempt to master his relationship with God! Not content to go to the temple and to meet God there in the prescribed way, Uzziah wanted to set up his own way, his own worship. Doubtless he saw himself as one of the super-pious in this: "See how I—a king—go beyond any of my predecessors in my devotion to the Lord. I go before him and burn incense in his house." But whatever justification Uzziah may have used for his action, the Chronicler labels this act correctly as being unfaithful, a deed contrary to the clear Word of God. Azariah and his band of courageous priests followed the king into the sanctuary to confront their rebellious ruler: "It is not right for you, Uzziah, to burn incense to the LORD. That is for the priests, the descendants of Aaron, who have been consecrated to burn incense. Leave the sanctuary, for you have been unfaithful; and you will not be honored by the LORD God."

The king's response was rage—rage against those who would question his intentions, rage against those who would question his right to do as he saw fit. God's response was judgment. "While [Uzziah] was raging at the priests in their presence before the incense altar in the LORD's temple, leprosy broke out on his forehead." What a shock it must have been to both king and priests. In the midst of Uzziah's bellowing, there on his forehead—where no one could possibly miss seeing it—the white patches of a skin disease began to glisten in the dim light. We know from the gospels and from Old Testament books like Leviticus that leprosy rendered a person unclean. Until declared clean again by God's priest, a leper had to shun society. He was also unfit to worship together with God's people. There in the holy place stood an unclean leper! God had struck Uzziah with a physical disease to match his spiritual condition.

Azariah and the other priests immediately hustled the king out of the temple. Humbled and frightened, Uzziah meekly complied. He recognized his leprosy as the Lord's affliction. A co-regency was immediately set up with his son Jotham, while Uzziah himself vacated the palace to live out his days as a leper "in a separate house." Literally that last phrase reads "in a house of freedom," a euphemistic expression if ever there was one. The king was free all right—free from all the tasks of daily life that had once occupied his active mind, free from all normal human contact, free from joining with God's people to bask in God's gracious presence. What a horrible kind of freedom that was! And it is the inevitable future for all those who, by self-assertion, want to free themselves from God's gracious rule. Left to themselves, they end up in a self-imposed prison, a "splendid" isolation—if not in this life, then certainly in the one to come.

If there is any light in this text as far as Uzziah is concerned, it is found in the final verse: "Uzziah rested with his fathers and was buried near them in a field for burial that belonged to the kings, for people said, 'He had leprosy.'" His physical separation from God's people did not end in death, since a leper was judged unfit to occupy the same tombs as the other sons of David. Instead, he was buried in a royal burial field nearby. But we note again the first words, "Uzziah rested with his fathers." Is this simply a more pleasant way of saying he died? It cannot mean he was buried with his royal predecessors, because the next words make it clear that he wasn't. In the spirit of that charity which believes all things, we choose to interpret the words to mean that Uzziah rested with father Abraham, with Isaac, and with Jacob. He rested with David in the heavenly rest that remains for the people of God after the afflictions of this sad life come to an end. We choose to see again the matchless gleam of God's grace, which used the affliction of leprosy to bring the king back to himself, to a repentant faith that relied again on God's help and God's strength.

Christians might also derive some profit by observing the contrast between a king like Uzziah and our gracious King Jesus. Uzziah rose high, and when he reached the heights, he was not content to be what God made him. He wanted even more. God, therefore, brought him low, cutting him off from human contact, cutting him off from temple worship, cutting him off from the exercise of power he once had enjoyed. Our Lord Jesus, however, was God himself in the flesh. Even though he was the incarnate God, he did not consider his equality with God a prize to put on display. Instead, he made himself nothing, putting off the constant exercise of his divine power, allowing himself to be viewed as a great and terrible sinner, and even permitting himself to be cut off from God's people in the slavish manner of his death. He was at the heights, and he willingly plunged himself into the depths for our sakes. He wanted to heal our stubborn pride by the power of his sacrificial love.

### God's kingdom under Jotham

*He begins well—and sticks to it!*

**27** Jotham was twenty-five years old when he became king, and he reigned in Jerusalem sixteen years. His mother's name was Jerusha daughter of Zadok. ²He did what was right in the eyes of the Lord, just as his father Uzziah had done, but unlike him he did not enter the temple of the Lord. The people, however, continued their corrupt practices. ³Jotham rebuilt the

Upper Gate of the temple of the LORD and did extensive work on the wall at the hill of Ophel. ⁴He built towns in the Judean hills and forts and towers in the wooded areas.

⁵Jotham made war on the king of the Ammonites and conquered them. That year the Ammonites paid him a hundred talents of silver, ten thousand cors of wheat and ten thousand cors of barley. The Ammonites brought him the same amount also in the second and third years.

⁶Jotham grew powerful because he walked steadfastly before the LORD his God.

⁷The other events in Jotham's reign, including all his wars and the other things he did, are written in the book of the kings of Israel and Judah. ⁸He was twenty-five years old when he became king, and he reigned in Jerusalem sixteen years. ⁹Jotham rested with his fathers and was buried in the City of David. And Ahaz his son succeeded him as king.

By now, perhaps, we have grown used to reading about kings who begin well and in the fear of the Lord. As a result they enjoy the Lord's blessings for a time. But then pride or some other sin gets the better of them, and their reigns come to a ruinous end. In king Jotham we finally have a break in the pattern that has become tragic in its predictability. Here at last is a king who does what is right—and sticks with it to the end.

We note some close parallels between Jotham's reign and Uzziah's, so close in fact that the Chronicler seems to have intended us to see Jotham's rule as a comparison and contrast to Uzziah's. He states his main theme in verse 2: "He did what was right in the eyes of the LORD, just as his father Uzziah had done, but unlike him he did not enter the temple of the LORD." Here was a son who took the same godly course his father had but avoided the ungodly detour his father later took.

Like his father, he engaged in building activities. The father began the renovation of Jerusalem's wall (26:9); the son continued the project. The father built towers in the desert (26:10); the son built towers in the woodlands. The father achieved notable victories, with the Ammonites bringing him tribute (26:6-8); the son also won a victory in war over the Ammonites and received tribute from them. At the same time, we notice a lack in Jotham's account of the richness of detail we had observed in the Chronicler's account of Uzziah's reign. Jotham was a good king, but he was not as impressive as Uzziah had been. People found less to remember about him.

We should also note in passing that Jotham's godliness did not result in any major religious renewal among the people. They continued in their self-destructive ways. Prosperity can be toxic to faith, as we in America know only too well, and the prosperity that the people of Judah enjoyed under kings Uzziah and Jotham had built up their own sense of self-sufficiency to the point of ceasing to feel any real need for God. For a picture of the kind of corruption that prevailed at this time, a reader need only glance at Isaiah's first chapter or at Micah's third. Both of these prophets were active during Jotham's reign.

However corrupt the people may have been, their shepherd at least was faithful and true. No finer words could have been said of Jotham than the ones that point out the chief difference between him and his father: "Jotham grew powerful because he walked steadfastly before the LORD his God." Jotham's power did not lead to his downfall, because he fought against the pride that had ruined his father (26:16). He remembered where all his power came from and resolved to do his boasting in the Lord. His faith was settled and steadfast.

When we put all of the evidence together, we see what the Chronicler is trying to tell us. The overall impression we get of Jotham is of a son who labored in the shadow of a more brilliant father. He had no smashing victories to his credit. In fact, the rather short three-year span of Ammonite tribute seems to indicate that his rule over them was relatively limited. He could not claim to have reorganized the army, nor was his name to be inscribed in the annals of foreigners, as his father's had been. It is not for every generation to be trailblazers, but it is certainly enough from God's point of view to be faithful.

Only the spirit of pride and competition within us leads us to see such a life as dull. On occasion one hears people say (perhaps of a pastor with less than stellar gifts), "Oh, he's *just* a faithful guy"—as if that were no miracle in itself nor any great gift of God's grace. In some people's opinion, Jotham may well have been rather ordinary. His godliness, apparently, was not the sort that inspired others. He was "merely" faithful with the gifts God had given him, "merely" faithful in the way he gave God glory his whole life long. Of course, there's nothing mere at all about faithfulness like that. It's one of the most precious gifts God has to give.

### God's kingdom under Ahaz—a promoter of evil

As we continue our study of the kings of Judah, we can never forget that the Chronicler was preaching a sermon with history as his text. God's rule over his people in the past had a direct bearing, the Chronicler firmly believed, on God's kingdom in the present. The past sins that had brought God's people low still threatened them. The grace that had preserved them in the past still ruled over all. The Lord's mercy endures forever.

In particular we know that the people who had returned from Babylon were struggling with issues of identity. In a world filled with so many gods and lords, was the God of Abraham *really* the one and only God? Among so many tribes and tongues and nations, could they still be God's *chosen* people? If so, what made them so? Was their temple still that one place where God had placed his name? Was the Messiah still coming to redeem them? The records of the next two kings—Ahaz and Hezekiah—speak directly to that issue of identity. Being a true child of Abraham is more than a matter of bloodlines. Being a true son of David is more than a matter of sitting on a golden throne in Jerusalem.

### He leads the way into idolatry

**28** Ahaz was twenty years old when he became king, and he reigned in Jerusalem sixteen years. Unlike David his father, he did not do what was right in the eyes of the LORD. ²He walked in the ways of the kings of Israel and also made cast idols for worshiping the Baals. ³He burned sacrifices in the Valley of Ben Hinnom and sacrificed his sons in the fire, following the detestable ways of the nations the LORD had driven out before the Israelites. ⁴He offered sacrifices and burned incense at the high places, on the hilltops and under every spreading tree.

Ahaz stands within a select group, a contender for the prize as "Worst of the worst," as far as the kings of Judah are concerned. While his grandson Manasseh might have excelled him in his devotion to the more unsavory aspects of idol worship, Manasseh at least came to repentance later in life. For Ahaz, we see no shaft of light whatsoever to relieve the gloom. His sins were so great that, in the end, Judah was unable to recover from them. As a promoter of evil among his people (28:19), he had produced a wound Jeremiah the prophet would later pronounce "incurable" (Jeremiah 30:12). Despite reform efforts of successors like Hezekiah and

Josiah, the idolatrous practices fostered under Ahaz would prove to be Judah's final undoing.

"Unlike David his father, he did not do what was right in the eyes of the LORD." Ahaz could not make the godly boast, as his ancestor Abijah had once done to Jeroboam and the Israelites that "the LORD is our God, and we have not forsaken him" (13:10). Instead, he was guilty of all the same things for which Abijah had long ago reproved his brothers to the north. He made cast idols just as Jeroboam had done (verse 2; compare with 13:8). He sold his soul into the service of gods that were not gods (verses 3,4,23-25; compare with 13:9). He practiced and promoted idolatrous worship on the high places (verse 4; compare with 1 Kings 13:33,34). Worst of all, just like Jeroboam, Ahaz prevented his people from finding God in the temple, the only place where the true God could be found (28:24,25; compare with 1 Kings 12:26-30).

All the things that had made God's people in the South a people set apart—the temple, the priesthood, the throne—Ahaz defiled and corrupted. He was David's physical heir, but he was Jeroboam's spiritual kin, since he acted much more like a king of Israel than a king of Judah (verse 2; see also 28:19, where he is named outright as a "king of Israel"). In fact, to label him as being like the kings of Israel would be almost to praise him. In his pagan impulses he was more like "the nations the LORD had driven out before the Israelites." In short, under Ahaz, Judah became guilty of all the sins for which the prophets had called Israel to repentance and then some.

The Chronicler makes particular mention of the way Ahaz "sacrificed his sons in the fire" in the Valley of Ben Hinnom. Strictly forbidden by the law (Deuteronomy 18:10), this horrible practice was apparently a special way of appeasing the

Ammonite god Molech (Jeremiah 32:35). Located near Jerusalem, the valley in which this took place later gave its name (appropriately enough) to the place of final torment. *Geh* ("valley of") *Hinnom* was shortened by the time of Jesus simply to *gehenna,* one of the biblical names for hell. The abomination of sacrificing one's own children would later resurface during the reign of Manasseh and, sad to say, would persist in Judah until the days of Josiah's reform (2 Kings 23:10).

### God hands him over to Aram and Israel

⁵Therefore the LORD his God handed him over to the king of Aram. The Arameans defeated him and took many of his people as prisoners and brought them to Damascus.

He was also given into the hands of the king of Israel, who inflicted heavy casualties on him. ⁶In one day Pekah son of Remaliah killed a hundred and twenty thousand soldiers in Judah—because Judah had forsaken the LORD, the God of their fathers. ⁷Zicri, an Ephraimite warrior, killed Maaseiah the king's son, Azrikam the officer in charge of the palace, and Elkanah, second to the king. ⁸The Israelites took captive from their kinsmen two hundred thousand wives, sons and daughters. They also took a great deal of plunder, which they carried back to Samaria.

From the prophet Isaiah and the book of Kings, it is clear that Pekah and Rezin, the king of Aram mentioned in verse 5, had formed an anti-Assyrian coalition in which they wanted Ahaz to participate. If he did not, Pekah and Rezin would replace him with a king who would. By the 730s B.C. the power of the Assyrian empire was again making itself felt in the region, to such an extent that Aram and Israel, once bitter enemies, were convinced that they had better cooperate with each other. Anyone who did not see it their way was considered hostile (see 2 Kings 16:5,6; Isaiah 7:1-6). The

writer of Kings notes that the two rulers failed in their ultimate objective of bringing Judah into their camp, although
they did manage to deal her a crippling blow.

The Chronicler is not so much interested in the power
politics of the region as he is in taking careful note of the
judgments of God. In the campaigns of the kings of Israel
and Aram against Judah, the Chronicler sees God's punishment on a king who had forsaken him. "Therefore the
LORD his God handed him over." The king and his people
suffered astounding losses. Not only were many Judahites
taken prisoner by the Arameans, but King Pekah slaughtered 120,000 of their soldiers in one day. Among them
were King Ahaz' son, his royal steward, and his second in
command. All this was Judah's just punishment because
the people "had forsaken the LORD, the God of their
fathers." To those in Judah who stubbornly refused to
honor him as their God, the Lord said, "You are not
my people."

The Chronicler also mentions a great quantity of plunder
and captives that Israel's army carted off from Judah. These
captives occupy center stage in the following story.

### The men of Israel act more justly than the men of Judah

⁹**But a prophet of the LORD named Oded was there, and he
went out to meet the army when it returned to Samaria. He said
to them, "Because the LORD, the God of your fathers, was angry
with Judah, he gave them into your hand. But you have slaughtered them in a rage that reaches to heaven. ¹⁰And now you
intend to make the men and women of Judah and Jerusalem
your slaves. But aren't you also guilty of sins against the LORD
your God? ¹¹Now listen to me! Send back your fellow countrymen you have taken as prisoners, for the LORD's fierce anger
rests on you."**

¹²Then some of the leaders in Ephraim—Azariah son of Jeho-hanan, Berekiah son of Meshillemoth, Jehizkiah son of Shallum, and Amasa son of Hadlai—confronted those who were arriving from the war. ¹³"You must not bring those prisoners here," they said, "or we will be guilty before the LORD. Do you intend to add to our sin and guilt? For our guilt is already great, and his fierce anger rests on Israel."

¹⁴So the soldiers gave up the prisoners and plunder in the presence of the officials and all the assembly. ¹⁵The men designated by name took the prisoners, and from the plunder they clothed all who were naked. They provided them with clothes and sandals, food and drink, and healing balm. All those who were weak they put on donkeys. So they took them back to their fellow countrymen at Jericho, the City of Palms, and returned to Samaria.

At this time the Northern Kingdom of Israel was on its last legs, spiritually speaking. The prophets all agree that the people were ripe for judgment. In 721 B.C.—less than 15 years after the events recorded here—Samaria would fall under the onslaught of Assyrian might. Nevertheless, we should interpret neither the prophets' statements nor God's judgments against them to mean that every single Israelite was beyond spiritual reclamation. Clearly this was not the case, as this remarkable story shows and as Hezekiah's Passover will later prove (30:11). There were still some in Israel who would respond to a prophet's call to repentance.

One man bravely marched out to confront a victorious host to reprove them for their sins. That man was Oded, a prophet of God. As far as Oded was concerned, the issue was the question, Who is my brother, and how should I treat him? (See verse 11, where "fellow countrymen" would better be translated "brothers." The same word is also found in verse 15, where the NIV translates it as fellow countrymen again, and in verse 8, where the NIV has "kinsmen.") It took great spiritual courage to stand before an army and tell them that the only reason they had won was not due to their prowess in battle but rather "because the LORD, the God of your fathers, was angry with Judah." The God of the covenant would not turn a blind eye to those who were so wicked as to slaughter their own brothers "in a rage that reach[ed] to heaven." Besides that, the Israelites had in mind to add sin upon sin by enslaving the men and women of Judah whom they had captured.

The question Oded posed next had much the same point to it as the one the repentant thief on the cross once put to his unrepentant brother when he said, "Don't you fear God, . . . since you are under the same sentence?" (Luke 23:40). "Can't you see the truth as you stand here crowing over your victory," Oded is saying, "as the wails and cries of your captive brothers and sisters are ringing in your ears? Don't you know that you too are just as guilty of sins against the Lord as any whom you killed? Don't you fear God's wrath?" If there was any possibility that they could recognize their sinful condition, if there was any hope that God's mercy for sinners could kindle a spark of love in their hearts, then there was only one thing for them to do. They must demonstrate that they knew the Lord. Since he was a merciful and faithful God, they should show themselves to be his own by "send[ing] back [their] fellow countrymen [they had] taken as prisoners."

At that key moment, some of the leaders in Israel stepped forward. Struck by the prophet's words and horrified by what they saw, they confronted their own army: "'You must not bring those prisoners here,' they said, 'or we will be guilty before the LORD.'" Clearly these were men who had heard the prophets' warnings—not only Oded's but also the warnings of all the prophets whom God had sent to Israel. They recognized that they were a nation out of plumb and ripe for judgment, just as the prophet Amos had said (Amos 7,8). "Our guilt is already great, and his fierce anger rests on Israel."

Remarkably, miraculously, "the soldiers gave up the prisoners and plunder in the presence of the officials and all the assembly." Even more remarkable is the love we witness next, love for brothers whom war had turned into enemies. What the English depicts in a series of nouns, the Hebrew expresses in an array of verbs: The men of Israel clothed the captives, put sandals on their feet, fed them, gave them water to drink, and anointed their wounds with oil; then they put all who were unable to stand upon their donkeys, and they brought them all to Jericho, near to where their brothers lived.

In Luke chapter 10 our Lord tells the parable of the Good Samaritan. That memorable story is rooted in this historical account. Both accounts speak to the lawyer's question, "And who is my neighbor?" (Luke 10:29). Both also answer the question, Who truly belongs to Israel? It was not simply the title "priest" or "Levite" that rendered one fit to be counted among the faithful. If a priest's lack of compassion for a brother in need led him to pass by on the other side, he showed that he had no sense of God's mercy in his heart. And if a Samaritan—someone who by birth had no right to be counted among God's people—should come along and demonstrate his faith, then he showed even to the most prejudiced observer that he was a true Israelite indeed. No one truly fears God and deals justly with his neighbor except those who know that their immense debt of sin has been graciously pardoned.

Similarly these men of Israel—precisely at that time when Judah was living out a godless life under a godless king—

showed themselves to be true God-fearers and genuine descendants of faithful Abraham. There is more to being a child of God, the Chronicler is telling his people, than simply having the name "child of Abraham" painted over the rock of an impenitent heart. There is more to being a son of David than simply sitting on his golden throne as Ahaz did, more to being in fellowship with the true God than simply going through the motions at his temple as the people of Judah did. God's grace is such that even when he is poised to pronounce judgment on the many, there will always be some whom he preserves as his own. There will always be some who are called his people, who are called to faith from among the mass that is not his own.

### *Ahaz seeks help that is no help*

¹⁶At that time King Ahaz sent to the king of Assyria for help. ¹⁷The Edomites had again come and attacked Judah and carried away prisoners, ¹⁸while the Philistines had raided towns in the foothills and in the Negev of Judah. They captured and occupied Beth Shemesh, Aijalon and Gederoth, as well as Soco, Timnah and Gimzo, with their surrounding villages. ¹⁹The LORD had humbled Judah because of Ahaz king of Israel, for he had promoted wickedness in Judah and had been most unfaithful to the LORD. ²⁰Tiglath-Pileser king of Assyria came to him, but he gave him trouble instead of help. ²¹Ahaz took some of the things from the temple of the LORD and from the royal palace and from the princes and presented them to the king of Assyria, but that did not help him.

King Ahaz now found himself set upon from all sides. In the north there was the menace of Israel. From the northeast King Rezin of Aram had put the king of Judah squarely in his sights. Sensing a golden opportunity, the Edomites in the south threw off the Davidic yoke that they had sporadically labored under for so many years (verse 17; see also 2 Kings

16:6). Even the Philistines were able to make territorial gains among the towns of Judah in the western foothills. Wicked King Ahaz had lost everything good King David had once gained. By his unfaithfulness Ahaz forfeited that great rest which God had once provided for the people through Ahaz's faithful ancestor (see 1 Chronicles 17). From now until they were taken into exile, God's people would be continually harassed by great and powerful enemies.

It's at this point that Ahaz committed the greatest political and spiritual blunder of his life. "King Ahaz sent to the king of Assyria for help." This demonstrated about the same intelligence as the chicken who invited the wolf into the henhouse because she was tired of all the other hens picking on her. Far more than being a politically inept move, however, this was an act of utter unfaithfulness. The Lord had specifically commissioned the prophet Isaiah to bring consolation to the beleaguered king. "Say to [Ahaz], 'Be careful, keep calm and don't be afraid. Do not lose heart because of these two smoldering stubs of firewood—because of the fierce anger of Rezin and Aram and of the son of Remaliah. The head of Ephraim is Samaria, and the head of Samaria is only Remaliah's son. If you do not stand firm in your faith, you will not stand at all. Ask the LORD your God for a sign, whether in the deepest depths or in the highest heights'" (Isaiah 7:4,9,11).

Hiding his lack of trust under a false mask of piety, Ahaz replied, "I will not ask; I will not put the LORD to the test" (Isaiah 7:12). His brothers in Israel had heard stern messages of hard judgment and had responded in repentance and faith (28:12-15). Ahaz, by contrast, heard a message full of comfort yet responded in rank unbelief. God invited him to ask for a sign to confirm the gracious promise of help.

When Ahaz refused, right across the face of his unbelief God wrote the greatest sign of all: the sign of the virgin-born Immanuel (Isaiah 7:14).

Never had a king received so much and done so little with it. Ahaz preferred the help of a vicious Assyrian tyrant to the help of a gracious God. He got what he asked for. "Tiglath-Pileser king of Assyria came to him, but he gave him trouble instead of help." The only way Ahaz was able to earn even a temporary reprieve from the Assyrian predator was by buying him off with whatever treasures were left in the various treasuries of Jerusalem. What else can one say about such a king, except that "he [was] most unfaithful to the LORD."

### All his troubles lead him to do more evil rather than repent

²²In his time of trouble King Ahaz became even more unfaithful to the LORD. ²³He offered sacrifices to the gods of Damascus, who had defeated him; for he thought, "Since the gods of the kings of Aram have helped them, I will sacrifice to them so they will help me." But they were his downfall and the downfall of all Israel.

²⁴Ahaz gathered together the furnishings from the temple of God and took them away. He shut the doors of the LORD's temple and set up altars at every street corner in Jerusalem. ²⁵In every town in Judah he built high places to burn sacrifices to other gods and provoked the LORD, the God of his fathers, to anger.

²⁶The other events of his reign and all his ways, from beginning to end, are written in the book of the kings of Judah and Israel. ²⁷Ahaz rested with his fathers and was buried in the city of Jerusalem, but he was not placed in the tombs of the kings of Israel. And Hezekiah his son succeeded him as king.

In such dire straits, one might think that King Ahaz would have come to his senses. As the saying goes, "When you're

flat on your back, there's no place to look but up." Not so
with King Ahaz. With some people the only effect trouble has
is to harden them still further in their unbelief. In a perfect
description of the pagan mind at work, we read, "He offered
sacrifices to the gods of Damascus, who had defeated him;
for he thought, 'Since the gods of the kings of Aram have
helped them, I will sacrifice to them so they will help me.'"

It seems unlikely that these verses refer to the same incident as that in 2 Kings 16:10-14. There we are told that King
Ahaz was summoned to Damascus to meet his overlord,
Tiglath-Pileser. While in that city, his faithless heart was cap-
tivated by a magnificent altar. He sent back plans of it to
Uzziah the priest so that a copy of it could be erected in the
temple of the Lord. The only point of similarity between the
two stories is the mention of Damascus. In 2 Chronicles we
seem to have an account of something that occurred just
after Aram had defeated Ahaz. Instead of a copy of a pagan
altar being used in the worship of the Lord, we see Ahaz
openly worshiping the gods of Damascus. Ahaz' logic is
similar to the kind we imagined Amaziah as using to justify
his worship of the captured gods of Edom (see commentary
under 25:14).

It may be worth pausing here a moment to consider again
the pagan worldview as we see it illustrated in Ahaz, especially since we also detect that America is coming more and
more under its influence. The pagan mind-set, at its foundation, is tolerant, inclusive, and accommodating toward every
point of view except that of the absolute claims made by the
one true faith. It feels perfectly free to set up all sorts of different altars on every street corner and in every town (verses
24,25; see also 28:4). At first it may even tolerate true religion
alongside the false, just as Ahaz went along with temple wor-

ship in the beginning. But this amounts to no more than a hedging of bets, and there eventually comes a time when the Lord's demands for exclusive worship become too tiresome to put up with. Then the temple doors have to be shut at last and the temple furnishings taken away.

Deeply calculating, the pagan mind-set wants to see immediate value for its worship dollar. If the gods of Aram seem to "work," then it will want to worship the gods of Aram. If they fail, it will try others. It is impatient with calls to walk by faith (Isaiah 7:9) and with mysterious signs that invite believers to put their hope in things unseen (Isaiah 7:14). It has no use for the glory of the cross, because the glory of the cross is not the kind that can be seen. Above all else the pagan mind must see, hear, or feel that the god it worships will give the required help.

As a result the pagan mind becomes ever more restless and increasingly driven to find its certainties by running down a thousand blind alleys. In the course of this search, it is capable of making tremendous sacrifices and performing great acts of self-denial. It is even capable of sacrificing its own children to the cause (28:3). But it finds no rest in its restless wandering, and it discovers no certainties in all its work-righteousness. It is unaware of even a fraction of the great joy and certainty that every believer has in the perfect victory Christ has won over all our enemies. Whatever truths the pagan mind-set manages to discover on its own were once summed up neatly in the little jingle that was a favorite of Luther's:

> I live. How long, I do not know;
> Must die, but know not when I'll go;
> Pass on, but know not where 'twill be.
> My cheerfulness surprises me.[26]

This is a chapter heavy with the storm clouds of God's wrath. They brood darkly over his people, and there is precious little sunshine to relieve the gloom. "Therefore the LORD his God handed him over. . . . The LORD had humbled Judah. . . . [Ahaz] provoked the LORD, the God of his fathers, to anger" (verses 5,19,25). Undescribed yet certainly not unknown to the Chronicler's readers was the fact that, during the reign of Ahaz, the Northern Kingdom of Israel as a kingdom ceased to exist. It may be a worthwhile effort at this point to read 2 Kings chapter 17 again, which gives an excellent review of the Northern Kingdom's downfall.

In this chapter we have seen that even the leaders of Israel had to acknowledge how much they had deserved God's punishment: "Our guilt is already great, and [God's] fierce anger rests on Israel." God had been like a husband to his people. He had loved them, cherished them, warned them, and chastised them. But they would not listen. They persisted in going their own way and in following other gods.

One of the great theologians of the Wisconsin Synod, August Pieper, once wrote about the wrath of God he saw lowering over his own nation. In commenting on Paul's proclamation of God's wrath in Romans chapters 1 and 2, he said, "God's judgment will be so much the more terrible than that passed on the ancient pagan world, since the world of today has not only resisted the testimony of creation and conscience, but, in addition, the *testimony of the Spirit of God in the Gospel of Christ.*"[27]

America has been privileged to hear the proclamation of God's grace in an unhindered fashion for several hundred years. Now we seem to be descending into a paganism undreamed of back in 1926 when Pieper wrote those words. We too must confess, "Our guilt is great." May God help us all to read the signs of the times, and may he continue to give us the gift of penitent hearts. It is vitally important for us also to remember the Chronicler's other point of emphasis in this chapter. If there were those in Israel who could respond to God's Word even at the eleventh hour, we can be confident that there will be some who will also hear and believe in our own gray and latter days. And so we continue to preach the Word, just like the Chronicler, whether it seems in season or out of season.

## God's kingdom under Hezekiah: reform and renewal

After great and violent storms, there are times when the sun breaks through the clouds with such brilliance that it takes our breath away. How can we explain in purely human terms the sudden appearance of a king like Hezekiah? Like the sun, he burst through the clouds of wickedness and caused God's light to shine. In the story of Hezekiah, we see so clearly once again that God's grace is a gift beyond all measure, something contrary to all human expectation or deserving.

In the last chapter, the Chronicler demonstrated how God had shut up both Israel and Judah under wrath so that he might have mercy on them both. We saw signs of that mercy already at work in the repentance he granted to some in Israel even at the eleventh hour, when they were ripe for judgment. Similarly, under Ahaz, Judah had broken the covenant and had forfeited all right to be called God's people. How could she dare hope for mercy? Certainly not by any human calculation of merit or guilt. But God's thoughts are not our thoughts. By grace he chose Israel to be his very own, and the result in history was that a king like Hezekiah came along.

## The first step: the temple is cleansed

*Hezekiah re-enlists the Levites and priests
into the Lord's service*

**29** Hezekiah was twenty-five years old when he became king, and he reigned in Jerusalem twenty-nine years. His mother's name was Abijah daughter of Zechariah. ²He did what was right in the eyes of the LORD, just as his father David had done.

³In the first month of the first year of his reign, he opened the doors of the temple of the LORD and repaired them. ⁴He brought in the priests and the Levites, assembled them in the square on the east side ⁵and said: "Listen to me, Levites! Consecrate yourselves now and consecrate the temple of the LORD, the God of your fathers. Remove all defilement from the sanctuary. ⁶Our fathers were unfaithful; they did evil in the eyes of the LORD our God and forsook him. They turned their faces away from the LORD's dwelling place and turned their backs on him. ⁷They also shut the doors of the portico and put out the lamps. They did not burn incense or present any burnt offerings at the sanctuary to the God of Israel. ⁸Therefore, the anger of the LORD has fallen on Judah and Jerusalem; he has made them an object of dread and horror and scorn, as you can see with your own eyes. ⁹This is why our fathers have fallen by the sword and why our sons and daughters and our wives are in captivity. ¹⁰Now I intend to make a covenant with the LORD, the God of Israel, so that his fierce anger will turn away from us. ¹¹My sons, do not be negligent now, for the LORD has chosen you to stand before him and serve him, to minister before him and to burn incense."

Before launching into a full discussion of Hezekiah's reign, we ought to mention in passing the chronological conundrums connected with his year of accession. Chief among these is the difficulty we have in harmonizing 2 Chronicles 29:1 with

328

2 Kings 18:1,9,10. In a nutshell these chapters in Chronicles seem to speak of a reign of Hezekiah that began well *after* Samaria had fallen to the Assyrians in 721 B.C. Second Kings chapter 18, however, synchronizes the *beginning* of Hezekiah's reign with Hoshea, the last king of Israel, and puts the fall of Samaria in the sixth year of Hezekiah's rule. In other words, Hezekiah was already on the throne well *before* the end of the Northern Kingdom. No one yet has advanced a completely satisfactory explanation for this difficulty.

If we regard 2 Kings as reckoning Hezekiah's reign from that time when he ruled jointly with his father, Ahaz, the pressure is relieved somewhat. We can then suppose the Chronicler to be speaking of Hezekiah's first year (29:1) in terms of his *first year of sole rule*. Thus the great reforms Hezekiah initiated would be dated to the year 716 B.C. We will assume this date in the interpretation that follows, even though we are well aware that some difficulties remain. By far the best solution in all circumstances like these is to speak of what we know and to commend what we don't know to God, whose Word is truth.

For someone familiar with 1 and 2 Chronicles, particularly with the portraits of David and Solomon, it is easy to see how the Chronicler tells Hezekiah's story in such a way as to highlight the similarities between Hezekiah and his great ancestors. "He did what was right in the eyes of the LORD, just as his father David had done." The Chronicler's point is hard to miss. Hezekiah led his people back to the Lord in repentance and in a full-scale renewal of the covenant that encompassed all Israel (see 29:24; 30:14). It was to begin at the temple, since God's house had been defiled and desecrated under Ahaz. In this work Hezekiah showed himself to be a true son of David, the temple planner, and of Solomon, the temple builder.

Like Solomon, Hezekiah showed his concern for the Lord's house from the start. His restoration efforts began "in the first month of the first year of his reign" (verse 3; compare with chapters 1 and 2). He turned first, naturally enough, to the doors of the temple, which his father had shut. By opening them up again, he was declaring his intentions. Next he summoned together the called ministers of the Lord, the priests and the Levites. He was determined to channel them into the ranks of the Lord's faithful and to press them back into the service of God's precious Old Testament means of grace.

In his address to them, we notice how Hezekiah saw his office as being more suited to evangelical persuasion than to lordly command. He began by recounting in detail the sins committed under the past king. In this way he showed how much God's people needed a renewal. "Our fathers were unfaithful. . . . They turned their faces away from the LORD's dwelling place and turned their backs on him." Their whole problem was a spiritual one, the king was saying. It had its roots in God's people irrationally turning away from living in the Lord's presence and from seeking the Lord in his earthly dwelling place. They showed their contempt for God's grace, preferring darkness to light. It was not surprising, then, that hearts weary of grace gave birth to deeds deserving death. We learn here that King Ahaz' shutting of the temple doors included a complete cessation of normal worship. No lamps had been lit, no incense had been burned, no sacrifices had been offered.

As a result, the king continued, the Lord's anger fell upon his people, and they experienced the just penalty of those who break the covenant. "[God] . . . made them an object of dread and horror and scorn" (verse 8; see also Deuteronomy 28:25,37; Jeremiah 24:9; 29:18; 34:17). God's anger was not something hypothetical, a threat of words only and not deeds.

They had experienced his wrath themselves, seeing with their own eyes the death and captivity caused by war.

"Now I intend to make a covenant with the LORD, the God of Israel, so that his fierce anger will turn away from us." We might ask, On what basis? The covenant of Sinai, the covenant of law, they had surely broken. No escape from God's wrath could be hoped for there. As a people they could not lay claim to any excellence of deeds or any fervor of love that might recommend them to the Almighty. They could not ask God for what they deserved, because they deserved only his wrath and punishment.

They could, however, take comfort in the covenant of grace the Lord had made with Abraham; they could find rest in the sure mercies of David (see 1 Chronicles 17; 2 Chronicles 6:42; Isaiah 55:3). This was the covenant that, in the final reckoning, made the Lord "the God of Israel." This covenant was founded purely on God's gracious choice and on his promise to send the world a Savior through the royal line of David. And God had located that grace in the temple. This was where he had placed his name and where he had promised to be found. We remember here, as Hezekiah must have remembered, the words Solomon once prayed at the dedication of the temple: "When your people Israel . . . have sinned against you and when they turn back and confess your name, praying and making supplication before you in this temple, then hear from heaven and forgive the sin of your people Israel" (6:24,25). Such broken and contrite hearts the Lord would not despise. On such a basis, Hezekiah could be absolutely certain that God would turn away his fierce anger.

Luther once remarked that God does not thunder in wrath to "perpetuate the fear of those who recognize their sin and are frightened."[28] There may be times in the lives of believers when they become guilty of great sin. There is no hope then to be found in running hither and yon or in trying to make it up to God by being especially good. No one will ever find comfort in that way because no deed of ours is ever good enough to atone for even one sin. At best we can say of the good we do, "We have only done our duty" (Luke 17:10). We have not erased the penalty for what we have done wrong.

When, however, we remember the grace of our baptisms, we have found a true hiding place. We've found the place where all sin has been washed away forever. In Baptism, God made a covenant with us that's as unshakable and certain as the ones he made with Abraham and David. No wonder they're equally ensured—it's the same covenant, founded on the blood of Christ. When we return to our baptisms in repentance and faith, we can be sure that God will not deal with us in wrath.

Deeply conscious of God's grace over all, Hezekiah addressed the assembled Levites as "my sons." He went on to remind them of that special calling they had received as full-time workers who were called by the Lord. True, priests like Uzziah had brought shame upon the house of Levi by striking their deals with the devil (see previous commentary under 28:22-27). But God's gifts and his call are irrevocable (Romans 11:29). They were still the Lord's servants, chosen "to minister before him and to burn incense" (verse 11).

This is where all ministers of Christ must find the certainty of who they really are. They have been called into the Lord's service through his church. If they derive their sense of self from how well they do, they are blithely walking into the devil's trap. He will either inflate them with pride or will torment them with a sense of their own guilty shortcomings.

Similarly, this is where all God's people must find the certainty that their pastors or teachers are God's men or women for them. We are not to consider the corrupt lives of those many around us who claim to be the Lord's servants but in reality are not. Nor are we to succumb to the ironic shrugs of the cynical, who say, "Who can show us any good?" It is not a matter to be judged by our teachers' purity of life (though we have every right to expect that they be upright in their dealings), nor is it decided by the electrifying qualities of our pastors' preaching (though we have every right to expect that they be faithful). If we wonder whether our pastors or our teachers are truly the Lord's servants, we are to arrive at our conclusion only on the basis of God's Word, as Hezekiah does here. Have they been properly called? Then they are certainly chosen!

*The temple is purified*

¹²Then these Levites set to work:
from the Kohathites,
    Mahath son of Amasai and Joel son of Azariah;
from the Merarites,
    Kish son of Abdi and Azariah son of Jehallelel;
from the Gershonites,
    Joah son of Zimmah and Eden son of Joah;
¹³from the descendants of Elizaphan,
    Shimri and Jeiel;
from the descendants of Asaph,
    Zechariah and Mattaniah;
¹⁴from the descendants of Heman,
    Jehiel and Shimei;
from the descendants of Jeduthun,
    Shemaiah and Uzziel.
¹⁵When they had assembled their brothers and consecrated themselves, they went in to purify the temple of the LORD, as

the king had ordered, following the word of the LORD. ¹⁶The priests went into the sanctuary of the LORD to purify it. They brought out to the courtyard of the LORD's temple everything unclean that they found in the temple of the LORD. The Levites took it and carried it out to the Kidron Valley. ¹⁷They began the consecration on the first day of the first month, and by the eighth day of the month they reached the portico of the LORD. For eight more days they consecrated the temple of the LORD itself, finishing on the sixteenth day of the first month.

¹⁸Then they went in to King Hezekiah and reported: "We have purified the entire temple of the LORD, the altar of burnt offering with all its utensils, and the table for setting out the consecrated bread, with all its articles. ¹⁹We have prepared and consecrated all the articles that King Ahaz removed in his unfaithfulness while he was king. They are now in front of the LORD's altar."

In verses 12 to 14 we have another of those lists of names for which the Chronicler is justly famous. And, as has been our usual practice, we will come to understand its meaning for ourselves by observing the Chronicler's reasons for putting it here. They are not hard to discover. The three major subclans of Levi—Kohath, Merari, and Gershon—are all represented, as well as those descended from the great Kohathite leader Elizaphan (verse 13; see also Numbers 3:30). The list tells us that great clans of the Davidic singers reported for duty, those descended from Asaph, Heman, and Jeduthun. Everyone was there. The Levites were fully represented.

This idea of completeness and fullness is reinforced in other ways. When we count the clans and subclans represented, we note that they come to seven in all. This might be sheer coincidence if we did not also observe the number seven repeated in other places. We see it in the number of offerings made in the service of rededication: seven bulls, seven rams, seven male lambs, and seven male goats (29:21). Possibly to be included here are the number of days it took to complete the work. They come to seven plus one for the courtyard and seven plus one for the sanctuary itself. Since, in Old Testament usage, the number seven was commonly considered to be a full number, we can be fairly sure that the Chronicler is saying, "The sanctuary was completely cleansed—and then some. A full atonement was made for sin." Far more certain is the repetition of the word *all* in verse 24. After the apostasy of Ahaz, and after the destruction of the Northern Kingdom, Hezekiah was rededicating not merely some but rather "all Israel" as the Lord's.

Finally, a list of names like this lends to the whole account a formal tone and an official style, like the solemn calling of the roll at the start of a meeting. We will talk about the reason for this in a moment. Before we do, however, we want to notice that the Chronicler follows through on these formal touches in other ways. For example, he supplies us with other lists (29:18,21,25,32,35). He dwells upon the various features of the temple ritual with loving repetition (see 29:22 for the most obvious example). In fact, we might almost call the entire manner of the Chronicler's writing here a sort of ritual in itself.

For us this may make for a dull read, but for a child of the Old Covenant, this was by no means a vain repetition. The Chronicler was familiar with the many rites and ceremonies of temple worship, and he knew that they all were instituted by God, with God's promise attached. The formal quality of the writer's style, therefore, served to assure these children of God that Hezekiah had done everything just as it should have been done and that all was in perfect harmony with God's Word. The Chronicler's readers had listened in horror to all the details of Ahaz' depredations. Now these details were being verbally cleansed, in a sense, by the enumeration of the distinct phases of the temple cleansing and covenant renewal.

The Levites set about their work and quickly got it done. First they consecrated themselves. Then they set about consecrating the entire temple enclosure. Priests did the work proper for priests, and Levites did what was proper for Levites. A nonpriestly Levite was not permitted to enter the sanctuary itself, but he could receive from the priest's hands every defiling thing that had been in the sanctuary, to take it outside the city for proper disposal in the Kidron Valley. They recovered the sacred utensils from their places of defilement, neglect, and misuse, and they placed them next to the altar for their final consecration in the ceremony of blood (verse 19 together with 29:22, which might more literally be translated, "the priests took the blood and sprinkled it toward the altar"). In the end, everything necessary for the proper worship of the true God had been purified of taint and reconsecrated for use.

Again this attention to the details of ritual may seem quite foreign to us who live in the informal "anything goes" atmosphere of 21st-century America. Certainly, as those who are free in Christ, we know that we are not bound to sacred spaces free from taint or to God-ordained holy days and rituals. But let us be on our guard against turning our freedom into license and against walking through life as if nothing were sacred. Just the opposite is true, in fact. We know that in Christ every aspect of our entire lives is now the sphere of the holy. God's name has been placed on us in Baptism; our bodies are temples of the Holy Spirit (1 Corinthians 6:19). Our whole lives have been turned into living sacrifices of praise for our Savior's mercy (Romans 12:1). Everything we do in them is consecrated by the Word of God and prayer, and everything we use is pure. This is so because Christ has made us pure (1 Timothy 4:4,5; Titus 1:15).

## *The service of rededication*

²⁰Early the next morning King Hezekiah gathered the city officials together and went up to the temple of the LORD. ²¹They brought seven bulls, seven rams, seven male lambs and seven male goats as a sin offering for the kingdom, for the sanctuary and for Judah. The king commanded the priests, the descendants of Aaron, to offer these on the altar of the LORD. ²²So they slaughtered the bulls, and the priests took the blood and sprinkled it on the altar; next they slaughtered the rams and sprinkled their blood on the altar; then they slaughtered the lambs and sprinkled their blood on the altar. ²³The goats for the sin offering were brought before the king and the assembly, and they laid their hands on them. ²⁴The priests then slaughtered the goats and presented their blood on the altar for a sin offering to atone for all Israel, because the king had ordered the burnt offering and the sin offering for all Israel.

²⁵He stationed the Levites in the temple of the LORD with cymbals, harps and lyres in the way prescribed by David and Gad the king's seer and Nathan the prophet; this was commanded by the LORD through his prophets. ²⁶So the Levites stood ready with David's instruments, and the priests with their trumpets.

²⁷Hezekiah gave the order to sacrifice the burnt offering on the altar. As the offering began, singing to the LORD began also, accompanied by trumpets and the instruments of David king of Israel. ²⁸The whole assembly bowed in worship, while the singers sang and the trumpeters played. All this continued until the sacrifice of the burnt offering was completed.

²⁹When the offerings were finished, the king and everyone present with him knelt down and worshiped. ³⁰King Hezekiah and his officials ordered the Levites to praise the LORD with

the words of David and of Asaph the seer. So they sang praises with gladness and bowed their heads and worshiped.

³¹Then Hezekiah said, "You have now dedicated yourselves to the LORD. Come and bring sacrifices and thank offerings to the temple of the LORD." So the assembly brought sacrifices and thank offerings, and all whose hearts were willing brought burnt offerings.

³²The number of burnt offerings the assembly brought was seventy bulls, a hundred rams and two hundred male lambs—all of them for burnt offerings to the LORD. ³³The animals consecrated as sacrifices amounted to six hundred bulls and three thousand sheep and goats. ³⁴The priests, however, were too few to skin all the burnt offerings; so their kinsmen the Levites helped them until the task was finished and until other priests had been consecrated, for the Levites had been more conscientious in consecrating themselves than the priests had been. ³⁵There were burnt offerings in abundance, together with the fat of the fellowship offerings and the drink offerings that accompanied the burnt offerings. So the service of the temple of the LORD was reestablished. ³⁶Hezekiah and all the people rejoiced at what God had brought about for his people, because it was done so quickly.

Once he had received word from the Levites that the work was done, Hezekiah got up early the very next morning to go to the newly-consecrated temple and offer sacrifices. The sin offering was traditional for services of dedication and ordination (see Exodus 29). In that context it served to express the fact that every priest was a sinner who needed to have his own sin removed before he was fit for God's service. The use of the sin offering with objects like the altar was a reminder to Israel that every gift of God had also been tainted by sin and its curse. There was simply nothing that sin left untouched. Before any object could be used in the worship of the holy God, sin's pollution had to be removed.

Sin destroys the relationship between God and man in a most fundamental way. It causes a deep chasm to exist between us and the Source of Life. It must be atoned for, or, as the Hebrew puts it, "covered." Blood must be spilled. The wages of sin is death, so a life must be offered to remove it. Hezekiah offered the blood of bulls and goats through priests who were themselves sinners. How much better then does Jesus "[meet] our need," as the writer to the Hebrews says. "He does not need to offer sacrifices . . . first for his own sins, and then for the sins of the people. He sacrificed for their sins once for all when he offered himself" (7:26,27).

At Hezekiah's time there was another far more pressing need for a sin offering than its general use at times of dedication. During the reign of Ahaz, the people had defiled themselves by idol worship, while King Ahaz had not only defiled the temple but also the throne of David with his corrupt ways. Hezekiah therefore brought a sin offering "for the kingdom, for the sanctuary and for Judah." We note how the principle of substitution—life for life—is reinforced by the king and people laying their hands on the goats for the sin offering. No Christian who hears this can forget how the Lord laid on his own Son "the iniquity of us all" (Isaiah 53:6) or how the blood of Jesus "purifies us from all sin" (1 John 1:7). Before there can be any renewal in our lives, sin has to be dealt with. And God did deal with it by offering Jesus in our place.

Besides the sin offerings on that day, the king commanded that burnt offerings be made "for all Israel." For a festival of rededication, this type of sacrifice would follow quite naturally after the sin offering, since it was the kind of sacrifice that expressed the believers' desire and commitment to offer their whole lives in service to the God who graciously pardons sins.

Hezekiah revealed himself to be a true son of David in the ceremonies connected with the burnt offering. "King Hezekiah and his officials ordered the Levites to praise the LORD with the words of David and of Asaph the seer." We recall that the guilds of the Levitical singers had originally been organized under David's rule. David had written many of their psalms, and he had supplied many of their instruments (verse 27; see also 1 Chronicles 6:31-47). King David's deep love for sacred music can hardly be exaggerated. Here in his second book, the Chronicler has already made special mention of the ministry of the Levitical musicians several times. He noted their prominence on the day that Solomon first dedicated the temple (7:6). He also spoke of their adding to the festal joy on the day that a son of David was restored to the throne (23:13).

On this occasion in chapter 29, a couple of matters are especially noteworthy. We observe how closely the playing of music was joined to the ritual of sacrifice. The Chronicler makes quite a point of saying that the singers sang and the trumpeters played from the time the burnt offering was begun until the time it was completed. What a dramatic scene it must have been! We can easily imagine the guild of Asaph singing one of the psalms their great ancestor had written, reviewing the mighty saving acts of God on behalf of a stubborn and faithless people:

> [Though] their hearts were not loyal to him,
>> [and] they were not faithful to his covenant.
> Yet he was merciful;
>> he forgave their iniquities. (Psalm 78:37,38)

Second, it's worth noticing how emphatically the Chronicler says that the Levitical singers were stationed in keeping with the words and commands of God. Hezekiah had them stand in the places "prescribed by David and Gad the king's seer and Nathan the prophet; this was commanded by the LORD through his prophets." The Chronicler could not have been more clear in declaring this to be more than a merely human arrangement, more than something that fit in with worldly ideas of beauty or order. True beauty in worship is on display when people are carrying out God's commands. This entire service had God's stamp of approval upon it. You could see it even in the way that the Levites were standing.

For the people of his own era, the Chronicler's words would have had a direct bearing on their own identity as true worshipers of the one true God. Since the people of the Chronicler's day could observe services in God's house ordered along similar lines, they too could be certain that they were offering a genuine worship. God himself had ordained it.

None of our orders of worship can lay similar claim to being directly inspired by God. We can't say, for example, "This rite came to us by the hands of Luther, the prophet of God." But we can say that God still takes a dim view of self-chosen worship. And we can say that all believers ought to be certain in their hearts that they are worshiping God according to his command and in keeping with his Word. When we go to a worship service, there are definite markers we should be looking for to assure ourselves that we are worshiping in the assembly of God's people.

God is pleased to come to us in the foolishness of preaching; Christ crucified should predominate in that preaching, above all. The sacraments are no less important. Jesus offered his disciples his body and his blood in a miraculous way and then said to them, "Do this in remembrance of me" (Luke 22:19). He told us that he wanted us to make disciples of others by baptizing in the name of the Father, Son, and Holy Spirit. Where we see these things taking place, we may be absolutely certain that God is there in a divine service of our deepest needs. On the other hand, in that gathering where the life-giving Word is absent, there is no church at all. The music may be wonderful, the architecture may be awe-inspiring, the speaker's words may be topical and riveting, and we may be greatly entertained, but we are not at worship.

Often it is not quite that obvious a choice. Let's say that we have found a gathering where the Word is preached but where the sacraments are treated as something less than vital. May we call this worship? Of course! We know that God's Word does not return to him empty. But we Lutherans have always confessed that the church is not only called into being through the Word; she is also born into her new life by the washing of Holy Baptism and is continually sustained on her journey by the Supper of her Lord. As long as there are people who hold each one of God's words to be equally precious, there will be those who see the sacraments as essential to the life of the church. And if the Chronicler could delight in the positioning of the Levites, finding in it an assurance of the authenticity of his own worship, how much more will we confess both Word *and* sacraments as being the vital signs of the body of Christ.

With his own sacrifices on their behalf completed, Hezekiah could say confidently to the group, "You have now dedicated yourselves to the LORD." He then invited them to bring their own sacrifices of commitment and thanksgiving. There were so many "whose hearts were willing" to offer sacrifices of various kinds that the number of priests was insufficient to serve them all. The Levites had to be called in to lend a hand.

The only response that seemed halfhearted in any way was that of the priests. We are not told why; we are only told,

"The priests, however, were too few. . . . The Levites had been more conscientious in consecrating themselves than the priests had been." We can only suppose that Ahaz' corruption of the priesthood (see 2 Kings 16:10-16) still had lingering effects on the morale and general character of the priestly sons of Aaron. Certainly it is true in any visible church organization that not all called workers show the same outward dedication to the Lord's work. Still, we have good reason to thank God that he always provides conscientious people who are willing to lend a hand so that all the work gets done.

The joy on that day, however, was too great to be overshadowed by a less than conscientious priesthood. Joy could be seen in the eager way Hezekiah got up to greet the day. It could be heard in the glad praises of the Levites. It was demonstrated in the way the king, his nobles, the Levites, and the entire assembly bowed low to the ground before the Lord their Savior. And it was visible in the tremendous outpouring of gifts and sacrifices that the people made at their king's invitation. All this had taken place without months and months of careful preparation. In just over two weeks' time—two weeks from the beginning of Hezekiah's reign, two weeks from the end of the reign of the worst king Judah had ever had—"the service of the temple of the LORD was reestablished."

As they reflected upon it, both king and people began to understand something important. This had all happened so suddenly and so flawlessly that it could not have come about by human effort. It wasn't the zeal of the king or the efforts of the Levites and priests that had caused this day to dawn. God had brought it about. God had rededicated his house. And that gave the king and people true cause for joy.

Such confidence and joy is also ours every day that we go back to the source of our strength and find our whole being renewed in the Savior. He is the one who gave himself up for his bride, the church. He cleanses her "by the washing with water through the word" (Ephesians 5:26) from anything that might defile her. In him we find ourselves free from sin's stain and radiant with love's bliss.

### *The second step: all Israel celebrates the Passover*

Some events stand out as defining moments for God's Old Testament people. Of these, none was more significant than Israel's deliverance from slavery in Egypt. The Passover was Israel's great festival for celebrating that defining moment. It reminded God's people of the way the Lord had once saved them from the angel of death by the blood of a lamb painted on their doorposts. Directly after this deliverance, God had helped them escape from their enemies by leading them through the heaped-up waters of the Red Sea. "By a mighty hand and an outstretched arm" (Deuteronomy 4:34), God had transformed death and destruction into life and salvation for his people. Later he commanded all Israel to appear before him to celebrate the Passover at his central place of worship. Every year each household was to come together at Jerusalem and remember how God had set them free and had adopted them to be his own.

The Chronicler has not spoken about a single Passover celebration in all his writing before now. In view of the feast's importance, this seems an extraordinary omission. It's as if he wanted to wait until such a time when the children of Abraham were almost too weak to be considered a people. The whole kingdom had been cut in two by rebellion and corrupted by idolatry. The Northern Kingdom was no more, and now little Judah was left all alone in a world filled with tyrants, barely clinging to its life. But what better time could there be to talk about a festival celebrating God's saving power? God's power is always made perfect in weakness. Hezekiah's Passover was a celebration of the way God gives life to the dead and calls into being that which has ceased to exist. What could be more comforting to a band of returned exiles who feared for their own survival in a hostile world? We again detect the Chronicler at work in his ministry of consolation to his people.

## *The invitation goes out, with mixed response*

**30** Hezekiah sent word to all Israel and Judah and also wrote letters to Ephraim and Manasseh, inviting them to come to the temple of the LORD in Jerusalem and celebrate the Passover to the LORD, the God of Israel. ²The king and his officials and the whole assembly in Jerusalem decided to celebrate the Passover in the second month. ³They had not been able to celebrate it at the regular time because not enough priests had consecrated themselves and the people had not assembled in Jerusalem. ⁴The plan seemed right both to the king and to the whole assembly. ⁵They decided to send a proclamation throughout Israel, from Beersheba to Dan, calling the people to come to Jerusalem and celebrate the Passover to the LORD, the God of Israel. It had not been celebrated in large numbers according to what was written.

With this first verse, the Chronicler summarizes his subject and sounds out the themes he will develop throughout the chapter. The king intended to knit back together again "all Israel and Judah," that is, the southern tribes and whatever was left of the northern tribes. To lend emphasis to his subject, the Chronicler adds the distinctive terms for the North, "Ephraim and Manasseh." There can be no doubt: Hezekiah wanted to reunite with brothers who had long been separated from their true king, from the true God, and from God's true place of worship. His goal was not political union but rather spiritual reconciliation. The king wanted to call the North back to Jerusalem and its temple so that North and South together could celebrate the Passover. From the addition of the words "to Jerusalem," it is clear that more was at stake in this invitation than the united celebration of a single festival. The king wanted to reunite all Israel around the worship of the one true God.

Normally the Passover was celebrated on the fourteenth day of the first month (Exodus 12:1-6). If the law of Moses was to be applied only according to the letter, this would have made a celebration in Hezekiah's first year impossible, since "not enough priests had consecrated themselves and the people had not assembled in Jerusalem." Like a drunkard's hangover, the effects of Ahaz' wicked rule were not to be dispelled quickly. We remember in the preceding chapter that the Chronicler had already mentioned the priests' lack of zeal (29:34). After consulting with his leaders and the assembly of his people in Jerusalem, Hezekiah decided to make the necessary preparations to hold the Passover "in the second month." To this end, an invitation would be sent "throughout Israel, from Beersheba to Dan" (verse 5; see also Judges 20:1; 1 Samuel 3:20; 1 Chronicles 21:2).

We notice a tension here between a literally strict adherence to the Law of Moses and an obedience according to the spirit of love. This subject will resurface later in the chapter. One should never imagine that the literal requirements of the law were unimportant to the Chronicler (see 1 Chronicles 13:9-14, for example). After all, what was written was not the word of man but the Word of God. However, the Chronicler here recognized that there were times when a picky literalism could stand in the way of God's clear intent overall. King Hezekiah and his counselors wanted to celebrate a real Passover, with great numbers of people flocking from all over Israel to the one place where God had placed his name. This is what God had commanded in the first place.

Such a celebration, however, had not taken place for a long, long time (compare verse 5 with Deuteronomy 16:16). At least there was an inference to a postponed celebration in the provisions God had made for individuals who were ceremonially unclean at the time of the proper Passover (Numbers 9:9-11). In any case, after thinking it over, the king and counselors decided to postpone the celebration for a month to make it possible for large numbers of people to participate "according to what was written."

We might go in two different directions in applying these verses to our current situation. First, we note in Hezekiah and his leaders that same restless love that moves in every Christian (2 Corinthians 5:14). Why was Hezekiah not content to reform only Judah? Why send out the call to Israel? He was taking quite a risk of being misunderstood and rejected. The answer must simply be that he did it because the heart that knows the most perfect peace in the forgiveness of sins is filled at the same time with a restless yearning to help others find this same peace. In other words, we can learn from the Chronicler not to limit our love to expressions of it that seem safe and comfortable.

Second, we can apply these words as the Chronicler's way of telling us to "make every effort to keep the unity of the Spirit through the bond of peace" (Ephesians 4:3). It is true that false teaching divides the body of Christ. Far too often, however, the visible church has shown itself quick to divide and slow to come together again. Anger and ego too easily become engaged in issues where we may differ, leading us to jump to judgment and to be dismissive of those we had once called brothers and sisters. Instead of trying to heal wounds, we rub salt in them. Let us learn from Hezekiah to make that extra effort and to work at peace. True harmony in the church is without a doubt a supernatural gift of God, created by the Spirit of truth who speaks in the Word. The Chronicler knew that too, as we shall soon see. All the same, we can impede or disrupt a true and godly harmony both by the loveless actions we take and by the loving deeds we fail to do.

> ⁶**At the king's command, couriers went throughout Israel and Judah with letters from the king and from his officials, which read:**
>
> > **"People of Israel, return to the LORD, the God of Abraham, Isaac and Israel, that he may return to you who are left, who have escaped from the hand of the kings of Assyria. ⁷Do not be like your fathers and brothers, who were unfaithful to the LORD, the God of their fathers, so that he made them an object of horror, as you see. ⁸Do not be stiff-necked, as your fathers were; submit to the LORD. Come to the sanctuary, which he has consecrated forever. Serve the LORD your God, so that his fierce anger will turn away from you. ⁹If you return to the LORD, then your brothers and your children will be shown compassion by their captors and will come back to this land, for the LORD your God is gracious and compassionate. He will not turn his face from you if you return to him."**

In this invitation King Hezekiah showed himself to be a genuinely spiritual king who exercised his authority through the Word (see also 30:12,22). The summons to come to Jerusalem was a call to repentance for those who had "escaped from the hand of the kings of Assyria." The king made no attempt to gloss over sin by giving it a better-sounding name. Israel was guilty and had been unfaithful "to the LORD, the God of their fathers"; that was why they had become an "object of horror." The king does not compromise the truth in any way. Just like his ancestor Abijah (13:10-12), Hezekiah declared that the temple at Jerusalem was the sanctuary God had "consecrated forever." We are reminded here of our Savior's words to the woman of Samaria: "We worship what we do know, for salvation is from the Jews" (John 4:22).

His entire sermon of repentance, however, was based on the certainty that the Lord is gracious and compassionate. How else could he be so sure that the Lord would not turn away if the people of the North repented? When we urge someone to turn back to God, we are presupposing that the foundational will of God is to pardon the sinner, to heal the wounded, to help the helpless. We who see our Father's heart revealed in Christ hold to this truth as something made even more certain. Under the old covenant, Hezekiah could also hold out to the Israelites the hope that if they returned to the Lord, their children would "be shown compassion by their captors and . . . come back to this land" (verse 9; compare with Solomon's prayer in 6:36-39). From this proclamation it is clear that Hezekiah had envisioned far more than a single Passover celebration. In fact, the Passover is not even mentioned anywhere in the invitation. Hezekiah's emphasis is entirely on returning to the Lord by worshiping him in his sanctuary. Hezekiah hoped that God's Word would work a complete repentance and renewal of those who were left in the North.

**¹⁰The couriers went from town to town in Ephraim and Manasseh, as far as Zebulun, but the people scorned and**

**ridiculed them. ¹¹Nevertheless, some men of Asher, Manasseh and Zebulun humbled themselves and went to Jerusalem. ¹²Also in Judah the hand of God was on the people to give them unity of mind to carry out what the king and his officials had ordered, following the word of the LORD.**

A pastor who was about to send his team out on a door-to-door canvass of a neighborhood once said, "Remember: some will, and some won't." Jesus had seen Satan fall like lightning from the sky through the efforts of the 72 disciples; yet Jesus had also made it clear before sending them out that not all would believe their message (Luke 10:16,18). The message of the gospel is such a gentle word that it may seem weak and powerless at times, even to Christians. To the unconverted person, it seems utterly foolish. The couriers went from town to town, but in general "the people scorned and ridiculed them. Nevertheless, some . . . humbled themselves and went to Jerusalem." What the pastor said remains true. Some will; some won't. "For the message of the cross is foolishness to those who are perishing, but to us who are being saved it is the power of God" (1 Corinthians 1:18).

Within Judah, however, it was a different story. There "the hand of God" had worked to create "unity of mind to carry out what the king and his officials had ordered, following the word of the LORD." Once again we begin to see not only reflections of David and Solomon but also the cast shadow of the promised Messiah. Hezekiah, a true shepherd of Israel, brought unity to his people through the Word. As such he served to encourage the people of the Chronicler's day to hope for the Messiah who would one day come to unite all God's people under his rule. Under him there would truly be "one flock and one shepherd" (John 10:16; see also Jeremiah 31:10; Ezekiel 34:12,23).

## *The people assemble—the king intercedes for Israel and is heard*

¹³**A very large crowd of people assembled in Jerusalem to celebrate th**e **Feast of Unleavened Bread in the second month.** ¹⁴**They removed the altars in Jerusalem and cleared away the incense altars and threw them into the Kidron Valley.**

¹⁵**They slaughtered the Passover lamb on the fourteenth day of the second month. The priests and the Levites were ashamed and consecrated themselves and brought burnt offerings to the temple of the LORD.** ¹⁶**Then they took up their regular positions as prescribed in the Law of Moses the man of God. The priests sprinkled the blood handed to them by the Levites.** ¹⁷**Since many in the crowd had not consecrated themselves, the Levites had to kill the Passover lambs for all those who were not ceremonially clean and could not consecrate their lambs to the LORD.** ¹⁸**Although most of the many people who came from Ephraim, Manasseh, Issachar and Zebulun had not purified themselves, yet they ate the Passover, contrary to what was written. But Hezekiah prayed for them, saying, "May the LORD, who is good, pardon everyone** ¹⁹**who sets his heart on seeking God—the LORD, the God of his fathers—even if he is not clean according to the rules of the sanctuary."** ²⁰**And the LORD heard Hezekiah and healed the people.**

God granted good King Hezekiah the desire of his heart. He had wanted to celebrate the Passover with all Israel gathering together at the Lord's temple "according to what was written" (30:5). Through the power of the Word, "a very large crowd of people assembled in Jerusalem." One of the features of the Old Testament Passover was its emphasis on purity. Yeast, or leaven, was a common symbol for the impurity of sin. To symbolize that his people had been set free from the guilt of sin and were now enabled to live free from sin's power, God commanded the Israelites to remove all the leaven in all the households throughout the land for the duration of the festival (Exodus 12:15). Any bread they ate during this time was to be baked without yeast, hence the alternate name for the Passover: the Feast of Unleavened Bread.

At Hezekiah's Passover the people saw the removal of leavened bread as more than a matter of ceremonial cleanliness. They understood the ceremony's spiritual intent and proceeded to remove the pagan sacrificial and incense altars that Ahaz had set up "at every street corner in Jerusalem" (28:24). What Hezekiah and the Levites had begun by purifying the temple, the people brought closer to completion by cleansing Jerusalem. We will see the process brought to its logical conclusion a little later. Here we simply pause to note that ever since the time of the early church, one of the emphases in the Easter festival has always been to encourage God's people to consider themselves raised with Christ to a new and holy life. In a world made foul by sexual immorality and idolatry of every kind, God wants his people to celebrate the feast by getting rid of the old yeast. "For Christ, our Passover lamb, has been sacrificed" (1 Corinthians 5:7).

In the actual slaughtering of the Passover lambs, the Chronicler alerts us to two problems that might have cast a pall over the entire festival. The first was the apparent reluctance of both the priests and Levites to consecrate themselves in sufficient numbers to serve the many pilgrims to Jerusalem. Here we might suppose that the Chronicler is speaking of the priests and Levites from the outlying areas of Judah. They were likely to have remained unaffected by the first stirrings of renewal among their Jerusalem brethren (29:34). But their services were all the more urgently required on the day of the Passover, because "many in the crowd had not consecrated themselves" and therefore would be unfit to slaughter the Passover lamb as the head of the household was expected to do (Exodus 12:3,6). The expression the Chronicler uses implies that the people had not undergone the ritual washings considered to be proper preparation for anyone who wanted to participate in a sacrifice to the Lord (see Exodus 19:14). Either that or they had not been too careful about avoiding things that might have defiled them (see Leviticus 11–16). In either case, the people's failure combined with the Levitical lack of zeal could have rendered a proper celebration of the festival impossible.

Disaster was averted by the priests and Levites literally being shamed into service by the earnestness of the common people. We remember that these same people had spontaneously gone about destroying the pagan altars in Jerusalem. For this reason we can detect an important difference between the failure of the priests and Levites to consecrate themselves and the failure of the people. It seems clear enough that the people's failure had come about by sheer ignorance. They were believers, and they had come to Jerusalem because they wanted to serve the Lord. That much they had already demonstrated. Considering the spiritual context from which they had come—the corrupt rule of Ahaz in the South, the religious chaos of the North—it was no wonder that they were not ritually clean and ready for the sacrifice. Priests and Levites, however, had no such excuse. Their only reason was spiritual laziness. Either they did not consider service to the Lord a high enough calling to be excited, or they did not consider his Word important enough to hold fast to it in every instance.

This was not the first time that the zeal of some served to shame those who should have known better into doing the right thing. It will not be the last time either. The overall outcome, at least, was a happy one. The priests and Levites took up their prescribed positions, and Levites took over from their unconsecrated brothers the solemn privilege of sacrificing the Passover lamb. There was, however, still one more problem to come. The majority of the people from the North went on to eat the Passover in a state of ritual uncleanness. Again we may well suppose that ignorance was far more to blame than a spirit of disobedience. Nevertheless, what they did was "contrary to what was written."

Disaster was averted in this case by the righteous king praying on behalf of his people. In words that seem to be an echo of Solomon's prayer on the day of the temple's dedication, Hezekiah said, "May the LORD, who is good, pardon everyone who sets his heart on seeking God—the LORD, the God of his fathers—even if he is not clean according to the rules of the sanctuary" (verses 18,19; see 6:21,25,27,29,30,39). Hezekiah was asking the Lord to consider the people's faith as more important in this case than their lack of outward, ceremonial purity. He was confident that the Lord, "who is good," would listen in heaven to prayer directed toward his sanctuary on earth. The king was not mistaken in his confidence. Just as the Lord had responded to Solomon, so likewise here he "heard Hezekiah and healed the people" (verse 20; see 7:14).

As we work and worship together, we know that we are not completely pure in heart nor completely pure in the way we act. Our motives are often mixed; we may be weak in our understanding. When we are a church active in outreach, there will no doubt be a few among us who don't always stand up or sit down in just the right places in worship or who manage to transgress long-cherished congregational traditions outside of worship. This is where we learn to let love cover over a multitude of sins (1 Peter 4:8). God's love will cover our own great shortcomings, making us eager to overlook the trifling faults of our fellow believers. And in everything, we have the great joy of knowing that Christ, our righteous King, is interceding for us always at God's right hand (Romans 8:34). God hears our King's prayer and heals us, keeping us united in his love.

### *The feast is celebrated—"'Tis good, Lord, to be here"*

²¹**The Israelites who were present in Jerusalem celebrated the Feast of Unleavened Bread for seven days with great rejoicing, while the Levites and priests sang to the LORD every day, accompanied by the LORD's instruments of praise.**

²²**Hezekiah spoke encouragingly to all the Levites, who showed good understanding of the service of the LORD. For the seven days they ate their assigned portion and offered fellowship offerings and praised the LORD, the God of their fathers.**

²³**The whole assembly then agreed to celebrate the festival seven more days; so for another seven days they celebrated joyfully. ²⁴Hezekiah king of Judah provided a thousand bulls and seven thousand sheep and goats for the assembly, and the officials provided them with a thousand bulls and ten thousand sheep and goats. A great number of priests consecrated themselves. ²⁵The entire assembly of Judah rejoiced, along with the priests and Levites and all who had assembled from Israel, including the aliens who had come from Israel and those who lived in Judah. ²⁶There was great joy in Jerusalem, for since the days of Solomon son of David king of Israel there had been nothing like this in Jerusalem. ²⁷The priests and the Levites stood to bless the people, and God heard them, for their prayer reached heaven, his holy dwelling place.**

Hezekiah's Passover stands out as one of the happiest occasions in the entire Old Testament. "There was great joy in Jerusalem, for since the days of Solomon son of David king of Israel there had been nothing like this in Jerusalem." Israel and Judah had come together again, uniting under

God's chosen king and worshiping as one before the Lord's own sanctuary. Just as in the days of Solomon when the temple was first dedicated, this celebration was so filled with joy that no one wanted it to end. The people agreed to celebrate together for seven more days (verse 23; see 7:8,9).

While not as stupendous as the sacrifices Solomon had offered at the dedication, Hezekiah and his princes had no cause to feel ashamed of those they had provided for the occasion. The Levitical singers and priests sang the Lord's praises constantly, making music on the sacred instruments of God. Even the problem of the priestly apathy seemed to have righted itself at last. Judahite and Israelite, priest and Levite, the alien from the North and the alien from the South all came together in a worship setting that was about as close to perfection as anyone will see this side of heaven. And all who had come could leave that place of worship assured of the Lord's own blessing from heaven.

In the center of this picture we see Hezekiah, the righteous king. Like David before him, his people stood solidly behind him (30:4,12; compare with 1 Chronicles 12:38; 13:4). Like David before him, he gave spiritual matters top priority (29:3; compare with 1 Chronicles 13). Like David and Solomon before him, he listened to the Word and ruled by the Word (30:6-9,12,22; compare with 1 Chronicles 15:13-15; 2 Chronicles 1:8-10). Like David and Solomon before him, he prayed on behalf of his people (30:18,19; compare with 1 Chronicles 21:17; 2 Chronicles 6:14-42). We have seen this often enough to know that here the Chronicler is building up the Messianic hopes of his people. Under the great mystery of history, those people with the eyes of faith can discern the rule of God, see the face of Christ, and observe that love at work which must bring all our godly hopes to perfect fulfillment (Ephesians 1:10; Romans 8:28).

## From worship to work: the land is cleansed

**31** When all this had ended, the Israelites who were there went out to the towns of Judah, smashed the sacred stones and cut down the Asherah poles. They destroyed the high places and the altars throughout Judah and Benjamin and in Ephraim and Manasseh. After they had destroyed all of them, the Israelites returned to their own towns and to their own property.

Peter, James, and John had all wanted to stay on the mountain with Jesus and Moses and Elijah (Matthew 17:4). It was good to be there. But they had to go down to the valley again. There were demons to cast out and God's work to be done. Here God had met with his people in their worship in Jerusalem and had blessed them with his love. In this case too, the people wanted to stay. But the time also came for them to leave the mountain of the Lord so that they could serve him throughout the land. The temple had been purified and Jerusalem had been cleansed of its pagan altars, but the land remained to be freed from the demonic hold of its sacred stones and its altars dedicated to false gods. All the Israelites united in this work. When they were done, they went home to serve the Lord in their everyday lives. The Chronicler's message here is not hard to read: the Lord serves us with Word and sacrament to give us the strength to live our lives for him.

### The final step: the permanent services of the temple are reestablished

Hezekiah had cleansed the temple and had celebrated the Passover with a reunited Israel, but he could not consider his reformation complete until he had made permanent arrangements for the temple and its services to continue.

## The priests and Levites are reorganized

**²Hezekiah assigned the priests and Levites to divisions—each of them according to their duties as priests or Levites—to offer burnt offerings and fellowship offerings, to minister, to give thanks and to sing praises at the gates of the LORD's dwelling.**

In this brief verse, the Chronicler once again makes the connection between Hezekiah and his illustrious ancestors David and Solomon. It was David who had provided the original blueprint for organizing the priests and Levites into divisions (1 Chronicles 23–26). He had done this to ensure that they would serve in a regular rotation, month by month. Solomon had transferred and applied these same divisions to the services at the temple (8:14,15). Hezekiah reestablished these ancient orders after they had fallen by the wayside during the reign of Ahaz. The men in each form of ministry were to do their work according to the assignments given to them by Moses. The priests were to "offer burnt offerings and fellowship offerings," while the Levites were to assist them by singing songs of praise and thanksgiving "at the gates of the LORD's dwelling."

Vital connections were being made here with the past, connections that also spoke to the Chronicler's original audience. These organizational divisions, along with their genealogies, would play an important role in assuring the returned exiles of the authenticity of their own priests and Levites (see Nehemiah 7:39-65). In demonstrating how things *were,* the Chronicler was often showing to his own people how things *ought to be.* We know very well that the genuineness of our own pastors and teachers does not depend on their tribal roots or their family names. But we might well pause a moment to reflect on the Chronicler's method of pointing to the past to validate the present. What does it teach us? First and foremost, it points us to the foundation stone of our faith, Jesus Christ, and to the apostolic testimony about Christ with which we have been entrusted. The church is built on this inspired tradition (1 Corinthians 3:11; Ephesians 2:20), and it is our duty to guard it, to cherish it, and to hand it down to the next generation (1 Timothy 6:20).

Even more than this, however, it would not be out of place to find in the Chronicler's message to his own people a gentle corrective to an attitude widely held in America today. Far from traditional, we Americans like to think of ourselves as being progressive. We are bombarded everywhere with messages declaring that old is bad and new is better. In some circles to label something as "traditional" is to condemn it as hopelessly old-fashioned. But for Christians, connections to the past are still important. If we don't know where we came from, how will we ever know who we are? Studying church history may not be the same thing as studying the Holy Scriptures, but it is a vital task all the same. One Lutheran writer said that the church which disregards church history is bound to become a sect.

*Regular offerings are resumed, bringing heaps of blessing*

³**The king contributed from his own possessions for the morning and evening burnt offerings and for the burnt offerings on the Sabbaths, New Moons and appointed feasts as written in the Law of the LORD. ⁴He ordered the people living in Jerusalem to give the portion due the priests and Levites so they could devote themselves to the Law of the LORD. ⁵As soon as the order went out, the Israelites generously gave the firstfruits of their grain, new wine, oil and honey and all that the fields produced. They brought a great amount, a tithe of everything. ⁶The men of Israel and Judah who lived in the towns of**

Judah also brought a tithe of their herds and flocks and a tithe of the holy things dedicated to the LORD their God, and they piled them in heaps. ⁷They began doing this in the third month and finished in the seventh month. ⁸When Hezekiah and his officials came and saw the heaps, they praised the LORD and blessed his people Israel.

⁹Hezekiah asked the priests and Levites about the heaps; ¹⁰and Azariah the chief priest, from the family of Zadok, answered, "Since the people began to bring their contributions to the temple of the LORD, we have had enough to eat and plenty to spare, because the LORD has blessed his people, and this great amount is left over."

Who paid for the regular sacrifices in the temple? And how were the priests and Levites to support themselves if they were engaged full-time in the Lord's service? The Chronicler answers these questions in the section above. King Hezekiah wanted to ensure that sacrifices in God's house would be regularly offered in accordance with the Law of Moses (see Numbers 28,29). We have already heard how Ahaz had allowed them to lapse (29:7). From his own possessions, Hezekiah saw to it that "the morning and evening burnt offerings and . . . the burnt offerings on the Sabbaths, New Moons and appointed feasts" would be adequately provided for. The Chronicler noted a similar kind of leadership in David's case when he dedicated his own personal fortune to the building of God's house (1 Chronicles 29:3).

Having led them by his own example, the king now ordered "the people living in Jerusalem" to begin making regular offerings again for the support of the priests and Levites. *Firstfruits* properly belonged to the priests (verse 5; Numbers 18:12). The Levites, in their turn, were to receive their support from the *tithes* that the people gave yearly of all they possessed (verse 5; Numbers 18:24). God wanted his servants to be free from earthly care so that they could "devote themselves to the Law of the LORD." We take this last expression in its broadest sense to include the studying and teaching of God's Word (see 15:3; 17:7-9), the judging of disputes according to the Word (see 19:5-11), and the carrying out of all the temple duties prescribed by the Word.

Both Old and New Testaments view the earthly support of God's servants as the full-time worker's right and as the people's obligation (Numbers 18; Luke 10:7; 1 Corinthians 9:3-12; Galatians 6:6). What makes the people in Hezekiah's day remarkable is that they also counted it as a privilege and a joy. We see the Chronicler carry out this theme in a number of ways. Not only did the inhabitants of Jerusalem—those with a direct command—contribute, but the people from all the towns of Judah also eagerly participated as soon as word of the king's command spread. They began with the offering of the firstfruits in the third month at the Feast of Pentecost and concluded it in the seventh month with the Feast of Gathering. Besides this, we see that the sheer abundance of the offering is emphasized over and over again, inspiring thanks and praise from king, official, and priest alike. The power to give in such quantities could only have come from God.

Azariah's reply to the king's inquiry is particularly interesting, approaching the poetic in both its rhythm and compressed composition. Literally the verse reads, "From the beginning of the contributions' coming in to the house of the LORD, there was eating, satiety, and remainder up to an abundance, because the LORD has blessed his people; and what is left over—this huge amount!" It is hard not to think here of the evangelist's similar sense of amazement as he recorded the aftermath of our Lord's feeding of the five thousand: "They all ate and were satisfied, and the disciples picked up twelve basketfuls of broken pieces that were left over" (Matthew 14:20).

Where God's King rules, the Lord will bless his people, and God will provide for his servants abundantly. This was the Chronicler's message of encouragement for his own people. We know from other biblical books that those who returned from exile were not always so eager to bring in their offerings (Malachi 3:8-10). There were even times when the Levites were forced back into farming to support themselves (Nehemiah 13:10-14). With this historical account, the Chronicler was reinforcing the promise God had also given to his people through Malachi, "'Test me in this,' says the LORD Almighty, 'and see if I will not throw open the floodgates of heaven and pour out so much blessing that you will not have room enough for it'" (Malachi 3:10).

In a similar way, the Lord Jesus promises us, "Give, and it will be given to you. A good measure, pressed down, shaken together and running over, will be poured into your lap. For with the measure you use, it will be measured to you" (Luke 6:38).

## *Hezekiah provides for proper storage and distribution of the offerings*

**¹¹Hezekiah gave orders to prepare storerooms in the temple of the LORD, and this was done. ¹²Then they faithfully brought in the contributions, tithes and dedicated gifts. Conaniah, a Levite, was in charge of these things, and his brother Shimei was next in rank. ¹³Jehiel, Azaziah, Nahath, Asahel, Jerimoth, Jozabad, Eliel, Ismakiah, Mahath and Benaiah were supervisors under Conaniah and Shimei his brother, by appointment of King Hezekiah and Azariah the official in charge of the temple of God.**

¹⁴Kore son of Imnah the Levite, keeper of the East Gate, was in charge of the freewill offerings given to God, distributing the contributions made to the LORD and also the consecrated gifts. ¹⁵Eden, Miniamin, Jeshua, Shemaiah, Amariah and Shecaniah assisted him faithfully in the towns of the priests, distributing to their fellow priests according to their divisions, old and young alike.

¹⁶In addition, they distributed to the males three years old or more whose names were in the genealogical records—all who would enter the temple of the LORD to perform the daily duties of their various tasks, according to their responsibilities and their divisions. ¹⁷And they distributed to the priests enrolled by their families in the genealogical records and likewise to the Levites twenty years old or more, according to their responsibilities and their divisions. ¹⁸They included all the little ones, the wives, and the sons and daughters of the whole community listed in these genealogical records. For they were faithful in consecrating themselves.

¹⁹As for the priests, the descendants of Aaron, who lived on the farm lands around their towns or in any other towns, men were designated by name to distribute portions to every male among them and to all who were recorded in the genealogies of the Levites.

²⁰This is what Hezekiah did throughout Judah, doing what was good and right and faithful before the LORD his God. ²¹In everything that he undertook in the service of God's temple and in obedience to the law and the commands, he sought his God and worked wholeheartedly. And so he prospered.

The key words to remember about this section of Scripture are *orderliness* and *faithfulness*. The lack of either one can cause God's abundance to be wasted by people. The lack of either one can also sow seeds of suspicion and envy among even the most peaceful group. After he saw the offerings piled up in the temple courts, the king knew that he had to do something about preserving it, so he "gave orders to prepare storerooms in the temple of the LORD."

The king also saw to it that the storerooms were used for their intended purpose. The "faithfully" of verse 12 may well be intended to make a pointed contrast between the way the storage rooms were used in Hezekiah's day and the way they had once been used during the Chronicler's own era. While the Jews were under Persian rule, Eliashib the high priest had acted unfaithfully in setting aside a temple storeroom as living quarters for Tobiah, the Ammonite (Nehemiah 13:7-9).

The Chronicler picks up the theme of faithfulness again in verses 15 and 18. Kore's men were faithful in the way they distributed the contributions among the priests. Faithful as well were the Levites in preparing themselves for the Lord's service. Of all the virtues, faithfulness is the least remarkable, since by its nature it so seldom calls attention to itself. It just does what it does, day in and day out, with no great trumpeting to announce its presence. Only when it is lacking do people take notice. And of all the virtues necessary for putting his gifts to their proper use, do we have to guess which one the Lord considers to be the most important? Faithfulness!

Paul refers to it as the standard by which Christ's ministers are to be judged (1 Corinthians 4:2). Peter uses it as the benchmark of all Christian service (1 Peter 4:10; see also Romans 12:6-8). We see it in the student who carries out his daily assignments and in the pastor who prepares his weekly sermons. We see it in the mother who cares for her young children through days that sometimes seem endless and which never have enough hours in them. We observe it in the father who reads to his son every night. We notice it on Sunday mornings when the church pews are filled with the same people that they held last week.

We can see it also in the way people give to the Lord not in spasms of guilt or in sudden spurts of generosity but "on the first day of every week" (1 Corinthians 16:2). And we can identify it in the way the apostle Paul gathered in the offerings for the saints in Jerusalem. Men from all the areas participating in the offering accompanied Paul to Jerusalem as he brought their gifts there (Acts 20:4). Paul wanted "to avoid any criticism" of the way he took care of the believers' gifts (2 Corinthians 8:20).

Orderliness is the other hallmark of Hezekiah's distribution system. A number of these verses are written in a different style from the other narrative sections of 2 Chronicles. They are extremely condensed, as if they were written as some sort of official list of specifications. This has led some commentators to ask if the Chronicler might simply have copied them directly into his manuscript from another ancient document, perhaps even the official palace documents of Hezekiah's day. Whether or not this is true, we can see that Hezekiah followed all the steps necessary to ensure that a proper organization was set up for collection and distribution.

Conaniah and his men were in charge of receiving the various contributions. They numbered 12 in all—a fairly standard unit in the Hebrew organizational structure. They served under the dual leadership of the king and the official in charge of the temple. Conaniah himself shared responsibilities with Shimei, his second in command. Somehow it has always seemed to make sense to pair up when counting the offerings. Kore and his men had the task of distributing the gifts. Just as congregations today often have both a financial secretary and a treasurer, so also Hezekiah wanted to see to it that the hand that wrote the checks was different from the hand that took in the money.

The method of distribution was also open, above-board, and set out for all to see. Priests were provided for from the time they were weaned (three years old and up), while the Levites had their needs taken care of from the time they entered into active service (20 years old and up). In order for this to happen, the priests and the Levites had to be registered—"enrolled . . . in the genealogical records," as the Chronicler puts it. Distinctions were also made between the priests who would be serving regularly in Jerusalem and the ones who would be called up only for occasional temple service. Since the latter could spend most of their days "on the farm lands around their towns" in Judah, it seemed only fair that there be some distinction in the way they were provided for.

With all this emphasis on order and faithfulness, we must never forget the motivation underlying it all. These were a people who had found joy in the presence of their gracious God (see 30:21-26, where a form of the word *joy* is repeated four times). That kind of joy would just naturally spill over into deeds of love. Remember too that this was a nation that had been reunited under God's anointed king, a king who was "good and right and faithful before the LORD his God. In everything that [Hezekiah] undertook in the service of God's temple and in obedience to the law and the commands, he sought his God and worked wholeheartedly." The Chronicler gives no other ruler after Solomon such a positive evaluation, not even good King Josiah. Certainly he is not unaware of Hezekiah's faults (see 32:24-26). But these are not in focus here, since the Chronicler wants to lift up his readers' hearts once again with a foreshadowing of the Ideal King.

How much more blessed must we count ourselves, who can trace our Savior's face not only in shadows and types but also in his full glory as the only begotten Son of the Father, full of grace and truth (John 1:14). To him the apostle can point us directly, encouraging us to spend our own lives in loving service to such a King: "You know the grace of our Lord Jesus Christ, that though he was rich, yet for your sakes he became poor, so that you through his poverty might become rich" (2 Corinthians 8:9).

## God's king tested

Before entering into the full discussion of the next chapter, it's well worth pausing again to make a few observations about the Chronicler's overall method in composing his history. We can discern his manner of working in a particularly clear way here because we have not one but two parallel accounts in Scripture informing us about these same events (see 2 Kings 18–20 and Isaiah 36–39). As we note the differences, we can draw a number of conclusions. In some places the Chronicler simply assumes that his readers are familiar with the parallel accounts. Verses 24 to 26 of chapter 32 are extremely general compared to the richly textured accounts of these same matters in Kings and Isaiah. His readers would almost certainly have had difficulty understanding the verses if they had not already been familiar with the stories. But if the Chronicler could assume such knowledge, his simple allusions would lend great impact in a brief space.

This compression of material also has the effect at times of making truths more generally applicable and timeless or of making contrasts more dramatic in their force. For example, in the invasion of Sennacherib, the Chronicler's 21 verses cover the same basic ground as the 57 verses the writer of Kings requires to tell the same story. The Chronicler does not give us all the names of Sennacherib's generals, nor does he inform us about Hezekiah's revolt against the king of Assyria, as the writer of Kings does (2 Kings 18:7). In the Chronicler's description, however, we receive a more stark portrayal of the confrontation between good and evil, between God's kingdom of light and the kingdom of darkness.

Finally, we have noted more than once the way that the Chronicler shapes the accounts he finds in the books of Samuel and Kings and how he often supplements them with new material found nowhere else in Scripture. Sometimes the overall effect of this shaping and filling in gives us an almost entirely different impression of a particular king than that which we previously had. It's helpful to remember again that truth is rarely two-dimensional. Two people can describe the same event and make entirely different points. Neither one is distorting the truth; each speaker simply chooses to focus upon a particular facet of the truth that the other does not emphasize in quite the same way. The writer of Kings chooses to underscore some of Hezekiah's faults, such as the way he used the temple treasures in an attempt to buy off Sennacherib or his initial despairing reaction to the Assyrian commander's taunting (2 Kings 18:15,16; 19:1-3). The Chronicler, still interested in showing us Hezekiah as a foreshadowing of the Ideal King, presents the invasion as a test of faithfulness, a test that Hezekiah passed with the Lord's strength.

*Sennacherib invades Judah; Hezekiah fortifies Jerusalem and its people*

**32** After all that Hezekiah had so faithfully done, Sennacherib king of Assyria came and invaded Judah. He laid siege to the fortified cities, thinking to conquer them for himself. ²When Hezekiah saw that Sennacherib had come and that he intended to make war on Jerusalem, ³he consulted with his officials and military staff about blocking off the water from the springs outside the city, and they helped him. ⁴A large force of men assembled, and they blocked all the springs and the stream that flowed through the land. "Why should the kings of Assyria come and find plenty of water?" they said. ⁵Then he worked hard repairing all the broken sections of the wall and building towers on it. He built another wall outside that one and reinforced the supporting terraces of the City of David. He also made large numbers of weapons and shields.

⁶He appointed military officers over the people and assembled them before him in the square at the city gate and encouraged them with these words: ⁷"Be strong and courageous. Do not be afraid or discouraged because of the king of Assyria and the vast army with him, for there is a greater power with us than with him. ⁸With him is only the arm of flesh, but with us is the LORD our God to help us and to fight our battles." And the people gained confidence from what Hezekiah the king of Judah said.

As we have said, the Chronicler forcefully sets the invasion of Sennacherib within the context of Hezekiah's faithfulness, a faithfulness our writer so lovingly described in the previous chapters. Was this invasion a test from the Lord? It seems so. This one he would pass; a later one he would not (see 32:31). "Sennacherib king of Assyria came and invaded"—by this time (about 701 B.C.) merely the report of the Assyrian king's arrival would have been enough to turn most near-eastern kings into quivering bowls of gelatin. The Assyrians were ruthless empire builders. They had great military power, and they were not shy about using it. As Luther often remarked, it is precisely when God seems hidden that people have the greatest opportunity to exercise faith in his promise.

That is exactly what God's faithful king did. The faith in Hezekiah's heart was revealed by the actions he took in his life. Realizing that he was no match for the Assyrians in the open field of combat, Hezekiah immediately set about strengthening the defenses of Jerusalem. To hold off a more powerful enemy for any length of time, ancient cities required a few basics. Among these were water to drink, food to eat, walls to defend, and willing defenders to patrol. In addition, the more a defending city could deny its adversary these same resources, the better its chances of survival were.

With this in mind, Hezekiah dealt first with Jerusalem's water supply. He "blocked all" springs outside the city to deny their use to his enemy. These may well have included a number of channels and conduits in the Kidron Valley that distributed water from the Gihon spring. It is likely that the project mentioned later in verse 30 is also to be dated to this same period of time: "Hezekiah . . . blocked the upper outlet of the Gihon spring and channeled the water down to the west side of the City of David." Many interpreters feel that because the king wanted to ensure a steady water supply for his city if besieged, he rerouted waters from the spring. When he had finished, the waters from the spring flowed through a tunnel carved out of the rock and emptied themselves into a reservoir located *within* the city walls. Over a hundred years ago, bathers in the pool of Siloam discovered an ancient Hebrew inscription at the entrance to such a tunnel giving details of how the workers had finally broken through the last few yards of rock. Many scholars date this Siloam inscription to Hezekiah's time. The Gihon spring became a river that refreshed the city of God (see Psalm 46:4).

Not content with simply securing the water supply, the king proceeded to tackle the matter of Jerusalem's walls, working hard to repair all the broken sections and erecting towers at strategic points. Verse 6 informs us that, as a final step, he organized and equipped his military forces like other great kings before him (most notably David). Thus he had met most of his city's requirements to withstand a siege. Water, walls, and defenders were all present and accounted for. We can only assume that he had not neglected to acquire an adequate amount of food as well.

The rhetorical question asked by his men when blocking off the springs pretty much sums up the spirit of the first five verses: "Why should the kings of Assyria come and find plenty of water?" In other words, Why should we make it any easier for the enemy? Here we might take up the discussion of a question posed by the comparison of this crisis with a similar one from the life of king Jehoshaphat. Hezekiah worked diligently to get ready for the siege he knew was coming. When the lives of Jehoshaphat and his people were under the threat of imminent attack, the king made no physical preparations at all to defend himself. All he did was gather the congregation of Israel, go to the temple, and express in prayer his utter dependence on God (chapter 20). We might well want to ask the Chronicler, Which is the better response to trouble: prayer or work?

His answer is, of course, Both. Depending on the circumstances and the personalities involved, sometimes a king might throw himself into a whirl of activity, praying all the while. At other times another king might simply wait for the Lord to accomplish the victory. Either way, the chief thing is to depend on the Lord's mighty power. By his preparations Hezekiah had no intention of denying the Lord. In fact, as a true, evangelical king, he later prepared the hearts of his people for combat by telling them, "Be strong and courageous. . . . There is a greater power with us than with him. With him is only the arm of flesh, but with us is the LORD our God to help us and to fight our battles." Hezekiah realized, just like Jehoshaphat before him, that the battle was the Lord's.

371

Our problem is that we sometimes fall into the habit of thinking there is only one form for piety to take. The idealist looks at the pragmatist and says, "You have no faith!" The pragmatist looks at the idealist and says, "You're tempting God!" Is it possible that the Lord has placed both the idealist and the pragmatist into one body of faith so that each one might learn from the other? The Chronicler says, "Of course!" Both must find rest for their souls in the words and promises of God. The pragmatist must be on his guard so that he doesn't start to depend on all his actions and practicality to save him. God can win the victory with or without his work. The idealist must be on his guard so that he doesn't grow carelessly confident and think that his sinful flesh has somehow disappeared and therefore requires no further discipline (see 1 Corinthians 9:25-27). After all, why make it easy for the enemy?

Hezekiah's sermon and stirring declaration of faith to his people on the brink of war deserve a closer look. Other generals through the centuries have encouraged their troops by pointing them toward glories to be won or toward the proud traditions of their people that they should want to emulate. Some might minimize the strength of the enemy while magnifying their own army's skill and power. "Be strong and courageous. Do not be afraid or discouraged," Hezekiah says, just like any earthly general would. With almost the exact same words, Moses also encouraged his people when they were poised to enter the Promised Land (Deuteronomy 31:6). So also Joshua spoke to his troops and David to his son (Joshua 10:25; 1 Chronicles 22:13, 1 Chronicles 28:20).

But the basis of Israel's courage was entirely different, just as its objective in battle was different. In every case the Israelites were encouraged to be strong because the Lord was with them (Deuteronomy 31:8,23; Joshua 1:9; 1 Chronicles 28:20).

He had chosen them as his people and had promised to glorify his saving name in them. Therefore, the objective of Israel's troops in battle was never to win glory for themselves but rather to carry out God's commands (Joshua 1:7,18; 1 Chronicles 22:13; 28:20).

Knowing that the Lord was with them, Israel had every reason to be confident. It came down to a simple comparison. On the one hand, there was the king of Assyria and the "vast army" accompanying him (no minimizing of the enemy's strength here: the Hebrew word for Assyria's army might just as well be translated "horde"). On the other hand, there was "the LORD our God to help us." In a masterful understatement, the king reminded his troops what this meant: "There is a greater power with us than with [the Assyrian king]." Why? Because no matter how numerous, no matter how terrifying and bloodthirsty the Assyrians might be, they were and would remain "the arm of flesh," while Israel was protected by the Lord's mighty hand and his outstretched arm (see Deuteronomy 5:15). There simply was no comparison between the two powers.

Apart from Christ, we lie under the compulsion of many furious tyrants. We are hounded by our sinful flesh and harassed by the unbelieving world. We must constantly be on guard against either the devil's enticements to sin or his accusations of guilt. If we or our enemy should ever fail to take the Lord's power into account, we would be trapped like a bird in a cage (a proud boast Sennacherib once made regarding Hezekiah). But Christ has trampled our enemy underfoot, carried everything that condemns us to the cross, and overcome all the world's fierce enmity. By depending on his strength, we win the victory over everything that threatens.

This leaves one key question to be answered. How can believers who are under attack know for certain that the Lord is with them? The Lord himself has given us a sign: "'The virgin will be with child and will give birth to a son, and they will call him Immanuel'—which means, 'God with us.'" (Matthew 1:23; see also Isaiah 7:14). God himself became a human being to rescue us. That is why we who live in the city of God always enjoy the most perfect peace, even though the entire world may explode into chaos around us.

> God is our refuge and strength,
>> an ever-present help in trouble.
> Therefore we will not fear, though the earth
>> give way
> and the mountains fall into the heart of the sea,
> though its waters roar and foam
> and the mountains quake with their surging.
> There is a river whose streams make glad the
>> city of God,
> the holy place where the Most High dwells.
> God is within her, she will not fall;
>> God will help her at break of day.
> Nations are in uproar, kingdoms fall;
>> he lifts his voice, the earth melts.
> The LORD Almighty is with us;
>> the God of Jacob is our fortress. (Psalm 46:1-7)

As did the people of Jerusalem, so we also find comfort from the words of our King.

### Sennacherib mocks God and his Word

**⁹Later, when Sennacherib king of Assyria and all his forces were laying siege to Lachish, he sent his officers to Jerusalem with this message for Hezekiah king of Judah and for all the people of Judah who were there:**

**¹⁰"This is what Sennacherib king of Assyria says: On what are you basing your confidence, that you remain in**

Jerusalem under siege? ¹¹When Hezekiah says, 'The Lord our God will save us from the hand of the king of Assyria,' he is misleading you, to let you die of hunger and thirst. ¹²Did not Hezekiah himself remove this god's high places and altars, saying to Judah and Jerusalem, 'You must worship before one altar and burn sacrifices on it'?

¹³"Do you not know what I and my fathers have done to all the peoples of the other lands? Were the gods of those nations ever able to deliver their land from my hand? ¹⁴Who of all the gods of these nations that my fathers destroyed has been able to save his people from me? How then can your god deliver you from my hand? ¹⁵Now do not let Hezekiah deceive you and mislead you like this. Do not believe him, for no god of any nation or kingdom has been able to deliver his people from my hand or the hand of my fathers. How much less will your god deliver you from my hand!"

¹⁶Sennacherib's officers spoke further against the Lord God and against his servant Hezekiah. ¹⁷The king also wrote letters insulting the Lord, the God of Israel, and saying this against him: "Just as the gods of the peoples of the other lands did not rescue their people from my hand, so the god of Hezekiah will not rescue his people from my hand." ¹⁸Then they called out in Hebrew to the people of Jerusalem who were on the wall, to terrify them and make them afraid in order to capture the city. ¹⁹They spoke about the God of Jerusalem as they did about the gods of the other peoples of the world—the work of men's hands.

The proud king of Assyria sent his messengers to Hezekiah, while he himself was occupied with the siege of Lachish. A busy man indeed! No doubt his sending of messengers was all part of his campaign of psychological warfare, useful for sapping the enemy's will to resist. He, the great Assyrian king, did not need to come in person. His lackeys were good enough. Nazi Germany's Josef Goebbels did not invent propaganda; a glance at the king's message here tells us that Goebbels couldn't even claim to have perfected it. Sennacherib had managed to do that long before him. It's all here: the distortions, the half-truths, and the big lie.

"On what are you basing your confidence?" the king asked the people of Jerusalem, "Hezekiah's little sermon? He's lying to you when he says that the LORD will protect you." Sennacherib then goes on to try to drive a wedge between the Lord's people and their king. His words in verse 12 are saying, in effect, "Why should the LORD have any special regard for Hezekiah? Didn't I hear somewhere that he was the fellow who pulled down all the LORD's altars on the high places and who insisted that the LORD must be worshiped in one place and in one place only?" As an idolater himself, he found it impossible to believe that the Lord would have insisted on such a thing. After all, from his perspective the more altars there are, the merrier any god must be. By this same logic it would follow that Hezekiah had offended the Lord, the God of Israel, in pulling down those altars and hence could make no special claim to speak for him. Given Judah's unholy habit of putting up those altars in the first place, we can see how this argument might have carried some weight with a people under siege. Under pressure, people often revert to the old ways, the old superstitions.

"Besides," the king goes on, "don't you read the papers? Aren't you aware of who you're dealing with? We Assyrians have pretty much mopped up the place, and none of the other gods of the other nations has ever done them any good. Why should you think your god is any different?" The Chronicler briefly alludes to events described more fully in 2 Kings (compare verses 17-19 with 2 Kings 18:26-37 and 2 Kings 19:9-13). As far as the Chronicler is concerned, however, the issue is already crystal clear: the king of Assyria had lumped the God of Jerusalem together with all the rest of the earth's gods. It was the worst kind of blasphemy to put the living God into the same category as "the work of men's hands."

Sennacherib had taken his stand against the Lord and against his anointed one. That's the way it is in every conflict between the forces of light and the forces of darkness. We can expect that the devil will try to drive a wedge between us and our King. He does this by mocking God's Word, by ridiculing God's promises, and by heaping up our sins so high above our heads that we cannot see the Savior who died for them all. The devil also tries to separate our King from God himself. He insinuates that the God we worship is really no different from the god anyone else worships. "Many ways, many paths—Christian, Muslim, Jew, Hindu, Animist—we all get there in the end. Why be so strict about the one Name and the one Way?" We might let Luther give the answer, both to Sennacherib and to anyone else who speaks such proud blasphemies against our God and King:

> I will hear and know of no other God, but I will [instead] look and listen solely to this Christ. And if I hear Him, I already know on what terms I am with God; and I need no longer torment myself, as I did before, with any anxiety about atonement and reconciliation with God. For in this picture all wrath and terror vanish, and only grace and comfort shine forth.[29]

## God answers at break of day

**[20]King Hezekiah and the prophet Isaiah son of Amoz cried out in prayer to heaven about this. [21]And the LORD sent an angel, who annihilated all the fighting men and the leaders and**

officers in the camp of the Assyrian king. So he withdrew to his own land in disgrace. And when he went into the temple of his god, some of his sons cut him down with the sword.

²²So the LORD saved Hezekiah and the people of Jerusalem from the hand of Sennacherib king of Assyria and from the hand of all others. He took care of them on every side. ²³Many brought offerings to Jerusalem for the LORD and valuable gifts for Hezekiah king of Judah. From then on he was highly regarded by all the nations.

From the nature of our discussions up to this point, a victorious outcome seems assured. The Chronicler has previously given us examples of God's people being faced with overwhelming odds and still gaining the victory (see 20:1-30). When the Lord's name as the Savior-God has been called into question, he has acted to vindicate the trust his people had placed in him. "I will be exalted among the nations, I will be exalted in the earth," the Lord says (Psalm 46:10). But that does not make prayer something superfluous. From 2 Kings we know that Hezekiah had asked Isaiah to intercede in prayer for Jerusalem (2 Kings 19:4). The Chronicler tells us here that Hezekiah prayed as well. In his own forceful way, Luther once told his congregation, "God's order or command and the prayers of Christians . . . are the two pillars that support the entire world."[30] He specifically mentions how intercessory prayers were the weapons that "defeated the hosts of the Assyrian emperor."[31]

God answered those prayers decisively: "The LORD sent an angel, who annihilated all the fighting men and the leaders and officers in the camp of the Assyrian king. So he withdrew to his own land in disgrace. And when he went into the temple of his god, some of his sons cut him down with the sword." There have been many theories advanced as to exactly what happened. Some have suggested that

Sennacherib's forces were struck down with bubonic plague; other speculations range from the miraculous to the ridiculous. What the Chronicler emphasizes here is the reversal of every single one of Sennacherib's boasts: the Lord *did* deliver his city, as Hezekiah had said he would and as Sennacherib denied that he could. On the other hand, Sennacherib's god could not save Sennacherib even when his devotee was praying in his own temple. There the proud Assyrian who had boasted in his fathers (verse 13) was cut down by his own sons. The Assyrian had also mocked the temple as the central place of worship (verse 12). By defeating Sennacherib, God increased the glory of his house by inspiring many to bring gifts to him at Jerusalem. Finally, Sennacherib claimed to be the terror of the nations (verses 13,14). God replaced that terror with high regard for his anointed king Hezekiah.

### Treasure in clay pots: Hezekiah's pride, success, and death

²⁴In those days Hezekiah became ill and was at the point of death. He prayed to the LORD, who answered him and gave him a miraculous sign. ²⁵But Hezekiah's heart was proud and he did not respond to the kindness shown him; therefore the LORD's wrath was on him and on Judah and Jerusalem. ²⁶Then Hezekiah repented of the pride of his heart, as did the people of Jerusalem; therefore the LORD's wrath did not come upon them during the days of Hezekiah.

²⁷Hezekiah had very great riches and honor, and he made treasuries for his silver and gold and for his precious stones, spices, shields and all kinds of valuables. ²⁸He also made buildings to store the harvest of grain, new wine and oil; and he made stalls for various kinds of cattle, and pens for the flocks. ²⁹He built villages and acquired great numbers of flocks and herds, for God had given him very great riches.

³⁰**It was Hezekiah who blocked the upper outlet of the Gihon spring and channeled the water down to the west side of the City of David. He succeeded in everything he undertook. ³¹But when envoys were sent by the rulers of Babylon to ask him about the miraculous sign that had occurred in the land, God left him to test him and to know everything that was in his heart.**

³²**The other events of Hezekiah's reign and his acts of devotion are written in the vision of the prophet Isaiah son of Amoz in the book of the kings of Judah and Israel. ³³Hezekiah rested with his fathers and was buried on the hill where the tombs of David's descendants are. All Judah and the people of Jerusalem honored him when he died. And Manasseh his son succeeded him as king.**

Hezekiah was a good king and a godly king. Throughout his account of Hezekiah's rule, the Chronicler has spared us nothing in singing his praises. Continuing here in the same vein, he tells us that Hezekiah enjoyed great wealth, engaged in many different kinds of building projects, and even shared great-grandfather Uzziah's flair for farming and animal husbandry. He was a success at everything he did, leaving behind a reputation for "acts of devotion." Upon his death, he was greatly honored, receiving a burial in the tombs of the kings.

Hezekiah was a good king, a godly king, but not a perfect king. In his day of trouble and sickness, he had called upon the Lord. Though the Lord had delivered him and had even given him a miraculous sign, Hezekiah did not honor him as God. Instead, when put to the test, the innate pride of Hezekiah's sinful nature sprang to life. Hezekiah gloried in all his wealth by showing it to the envoys of Babylon when they came calling. We get all the details from the more complete telling of the story in 2 Kings chapter 20. Though he merely alludes to the 2 Kings account, the

Chronicler is by no means minimizing the sin. If anything, the Chronicler highlights it by splitting it up into two separate references. The first reference shows in starkest contrast God's great mercy and Hezekiah's sinful pride. The Chronicler uses the second reference to cap off his description of the many blessings Hezekiah had received. In punctuating God's goodness with another reference to man's ingratitude, the Chronicler is showing us how God's rich blessings are often set within the frame of man's pride.

What are we to make of this? Besides the obvious warning to his people of how easily they could forget God's benefits, the Chronicler is telling Israel that they had to keep waiting for another king, a righteous King who would never fail and would never disappoint either God or man by falling into sin. Hezekiah was at best a shadow of him, a shadow whose very imperfections were meant to stir in his people a longing for someone better to come along. And someone better *would* come. As we know, one day that righteous King came riding into Jerusalem. He was gentle, sitting on a donkey's back. No pride was there to mar the view of his perfect grace. He came bringing salvation; he came to preach peace to the nations (Zechariah 9:9,10).

### God's kingdom under Manasseh and Amon: reform undone

Whatever spiritual gains God had enabled Hezekiah to win for his people, Manasseh and his son Amon managed to lose them. The kingdom of God as we perceive it with our senses is the church militant. The thrusts of the godly are matched by the counterthrusts of the ungodly. The true beauty of the church is so hidden in this world that only the grace of Christ can give us the eyes to see it. Again we observe in these two kings a period of great darkness, reminding us never to take our own spiritual heritage for granted. Each generation must win anew for itself the eternal, saving truths of God's holy Word. If we become complacent, misreading the nature of the battle we're engaged in, we risk losing everything.

Ahaz had built Judah's spiritual coffin; Manasseh and Amon put the lid on it and drove in the nails. The Chronicler and the author of Kings completely agree on this point. What is striking about the Chronicler's account of Manasseh's reign is his description of Manasseh's repentance, a matter that the author of Kings leaves unmentioned. The reason for this must simply be that the author of Kings chose to use the text of history to preach the law in all its severity. His audience needed to sober up and understand why the King had rejected his kings. We have often spoken about the needs of the Chronicler's audience. Their spiritual depression called for liberal applications of the healing balm of the gospel. This is why the Chronicler chose to use the facts of Manasseh's history to preach both severest law *and* sweetest gospel. We will note some of his specific methods as we discuss the text.

### Manasseh leads Judah astray

**33** Manasseh was twelve years old when he became king, and he reigned in Jerusalem fifty-five years. [2]He did evil in the eyes of the LORD, following the detestable practices of the nations the LORD had driven out before the Israelites. [3]He rebuilt the high places his father Hezekiah had demolished; he also erected altars to the Baals and made Asherah poles. He bowed down to all the starry hosts and worshiped them. [4]He built altars in the temple of the LORD, of which the LORD had said, "My Name will remain in Jerusalem forever." [5]In both courts of the temple of the LORD, he built altars to all the starry hosts. ⁶He sacrificed his sons in the fire in the Valley of Ben Hinnom, practiced sorcery, divination and witchcraft, and consulted mediums and spiritists. He did much evil in the eyes of the LORD, provoking him to anger.

⁷He took the carved image he had made and put it in God's temple, of which God had said to David and to his son Solomon, "In this temple and in Jerusalem, which I have chosen out of all the tribes of Israel, I will put my Name forever. ⁸I will not again make the feet of the Israelites leave the land I assigned to your forefathers, if only they will be careful to do everything I commanded them concerning all the laws, decrees and ordinances given through Moses." ⁹But Manasseh led Judah and the people of Jerusalem astray, so that they did more evil than the nations the LORD had destroyed before the Israelites.

Manasseh's goal from the beginning was to mount a counter-reformation. Every good thing his father had done, Manasseh tried to ruin. His sins read like a catalog of all the possible wickedness an evil king might do (see Deuteronomy 12:5–13:9; 18:9-14). The Chronicler structures his listing in such a way so that at both the beginning and the end there are references to the nations the Lord had driven out from the Land of Promise before the Israelites. Ominously, our writer foreshadows not only the punishment the Lord was about to inflict on Manasseh but also the punishment his own people were about to receive. They had joined in the king's sin and had incurred the same guilt. God was about to drive them from his land.

Jesus spoke the same message to his disciples, using slightly different terms: "You are the salt of the earth. But if the salt loses its saltiness, how can it be made salty again? It is no longer good for anything, except to be thrown out and trampled by men" (Matthew 5:13). Once there is no longer anything distinctive about Christians, once we start looking, talking, and acting just like everybody else, we have ceased to carry out the purpose for which God created us in Christ. When we make ourselves unfit for godly uses and become common, God treats us as common and casts us out into the street to be trampled underfoot. These are Christ's solemn words of warning to any who trifle with grace.

We might make one more observation about the masterful way the Chronicler has structured this section. Notice how skillfully he has juxtaposed the vilest sins with the most precious of the Lord's promises. Instead of preserving the central sanctuary undefiled, Manasseh built altars in its courts to all the starry hosts of heaven—right in the place where the Lord had said, "My Name will remain . . . forever." In God's temple, Manasseh put a carved image—in the sanctuary and in the city where the Lord had chosen to reveal himself to Israel. The effect of the contrast works the sheer horror of the sins into the reader. God displayed his sweet grace in the temple and city, and this was the thanks he got for it! In this country today, we like to think that we're becoming more sophisticated about things. Maybe all we're becoming is more shameless. Maybe the sheer volume of horrific acts to which we're exposed daily has simply rendered us incapable of shock. May God give us a true horror of sin; may he help us see it in all its loathsome reality!

We might as well take a brief look at Manasseh's sins to better grasp their significance for our own times. First there was his idolatry in which he went even further than his grandfather Ahaz. Ahaz had founded what we might call opposition altars: other places where God's people could worship besides the house of God. Those places of Ahaz might be dedicated to the Lord, or they might be dedicated outright to a false god. Either way, they were forbidden.

Ahaz had also corrupted the true worship of God at the temple with his new altar of sacrifice, copied from the one he had seen in Damascus. Finally, he simply had closed the doors to God's house, preventing any worship of any kind.

A person might ask, What could be worse than that? The answer is what Manasseh did by setting up pagan altars and worshiping false gods and idols *right inside* the temple itself. The Lord, who had loved his people as a husband loves his wife, was now being asked to tolerate rivals inside his own house (Jeremiah 31:32). Surely he whose name is Jealous (Exodus 34:14) wouldn't put up with this! Manasseh's actions are roughly equivalent to the practice some Christians have today of incorporating pagan practices into their worship. They might try to justify it by calling it inclusivity or celebrations of diversity. But God has a different name for it. And his label of "detestable" will stick!

In verses 3 and 5, the starry hosts referred to are all the heavenly bodies—sun, stars, planets—that we see in our physical skies. Many ancient societies, from the Chaldeans to the Romans, believed that the lights they saw in the heavens were either gods or closely associated with the gods. Keeping them friendly through worship was always a good idea; tracking their movements was also a way of predicting the future. "In the beginning God created the heavens and the earth" (Genesis 1:1) may not sound like a very earthshaking statement to you and me, but the fundamental differentiation it makes between God and his physical creation was not always grasped so well in the past. That is why the Scriptures never tire of saying that *God made* the heavenly hosts (Psalm 33:6; Isaiah 45:12); they are therefore not to be worshiped.

Similarly, Scripture teaches that God alone knows the future and can accurately predict it (Psalm 33:8-11; Isaiah 41:26-29). Scripture lumps together astrologers and stargazers with other false prophets and practitioners of abominable things (verses 5,6; Deuteronomy 17:3-5). All of this would not be worth talking about were it not for the fact that our society seems to be returning to the same rank forms of paganism. We see horoscopes in every newspaper, astrologers listed by the score in the Yellow Pages, and many people so befuddled that they cannot tell the difference between God and his creation anymore.

The same thing is true for some of the other abominations practiced by Manasseh. In connection with Ahaz, we have already discussed the matter of child sacrifices (see commentary under 28:3). They sacrificed their children as the supreme act of devotion to their false god. Many in our nation abort their babies as a sign of their supreme indifference to both God and his gift of life. Which nation bears the greater guilt?

There is also food for thought in looking at the various types of superstition mentioned in verse 6. The "black arts" all have a lack of trust in God at their roots. Powers greater than human are conceived as having to be manipulated, appeased, cajoled, and sometimes even fooled into doing whatever human beings want them to do. Instead of trusting in God's promises, a diviner wants to get special "inside information" about the future. Instead of depending on the Lord's help, the sorcerer uses magical charms—some that work passively to protect their wearer from harm, others that work actively to influence others. Still other charms supposedly give their users special abilities not enjoyed by the average person. It matters little whether someone is consulting the dead, mixing potions, watching the flight of birds, or running in superstitious awe from an omen. As far as the Lord is concerned, these are all "detestable practices" that provoke his anger.

From its infancy the church of God was composed of people called out from many tribes, and it grew to embrace many different cultures. As our own church body moves away from its rural, European origins, we certainly welcome and encourage a greater sensitivity to the customs and the cultures of others among us. As we reach out more and more with the saving gospel, we will want to be on our guard against imposing our own way of doing things upon others out of some mistaken sense of superiority. After all, our faith is founded on God's eternal Word, not on the cultural container by which it came to us. We will want to listen to and learn from Christians born in other cultures and allow their insights to enrich our own understandings of God's Word. But at the same time, let's not forget that Christians as a group are meant to stand out from their cultures. There is no expiration date on Paul's admonition, "You must no longer live *as the Gentiles do,* in the futility of their thinking" (Ephesians 4:17). God still wants us to put off the old self and to put on the new self, created in the image of Christ (Ephesians 4:21-24). As the example of Manasseh makes clear, not everything in a given culture is worth preserving.

### The Lord leads Manasseh into exile

¹⁰**The Lᴏʀᴅ spoke to Manasseh and his people, but they paid no attention. ¹¹So the Lᴏʀᴅ brought against them the army commanders of the king of Assyria, who took Manasseh prisoner, put a hook in his nose, bound him with bronze shackles and took him to Babylon.**

The faithful God sent his prophets to warn his faithless people, "but they paid no attention." So the Lord gave Manasseh up to the tender mercies of the Assyrian king. Modern historians suggest that this is likely to have happened in connection with a revolt of the Babylonian king Shamash-shum-ukin (652–648 B.C.).[32] While this theory may be of historical interest, far more important for us to note is the Chronicler's purpose in recounting this incident in the first place. Manasseh was unfaithful to the Lord; he led Judah astray along with him (33:9). Together they flagrantly violated the law of God and broke his covenant. Instead of living holy lives as God's people, they made themselves even more impure than those nations the Lord had originally dispossessed (33:9). They were both ripe for judgment, but only Manasseh was led off into exile. Was it just an accident that the king was exiled to Babylon? God dealt with Manasseh in such a way that the king might serve as an example of the Lord's intentions toward his people—both of his impending wrath in uprooting them from their land and of his amazing grace in restoring them.

### *Manasseh's repentance and restoration*

¹²In his distress he sought the favor of the Lord his God and humbled himself greatly before the God of his fathers. ¹³And when he prayed to him, the Lord was moved by his entreaty and listened to his plea; so he brought him back to Jerusalem and to his kingdom. Then Manasseh knew that the Lord is God.

¹⁴Afterward he rebuilt the outer wall of the City of David, west of the Gihon spring in the valley, as far as the entrance of the Fish Gate and encircling the hill of Ophel; he also made it much higher. He stationed military commanders in all the fortified cities in Judah.

¹⁵He got rid of the foreign gods and removed the image from the temple of the Lord, as well as all the altars he had built on the temple hill and in Jerusalem; and he threw them out of the city. ¹⁶Then he restored the altar of the Lord and sacrificed fellowship offerings and thank offerings on it, and

told Judah to serve the Lᴏʀᴅ, the God of Israel. ¹⁷The people, however, continued to sacrifice at the high places, but only to the Lᴏʀᴅ their God.

¹⁸The other events of Manasseh's reign, including his prayer to his God and the words the seers spoke to him in the name of the Lᴏʀᴅ, the God of Israel, are written in the annals of the kings of Israel. ¹⁹His prayer and how God was moved by his entreaty, as well as all his sins and unfaithfulness, and the sites where he built high places and set up Asherah poles and idols before he humbled himself—all are written in the records of the seers. ²⁰Manasseh rested with his fathers and was buried in his palace. And Amon his son succeeded him as king.

A strict moralist would have trouble with this account. After all Manasseh had done, how could the Lord receive him back into favor, bring him back to Jerusalem, and put him back on his throne? If we are honest, we might confess that even we are tempted to question the kind of grace that could forgive a person like Manasseh. To play devil's advocate, God's grace seems so unfair—even immoral—in lumping the good with the evil, in forgiving the deserving and the undeserving alike. It's one thing to offer God's forgiveness to the outwardly pious. It seems quite another to offer it to people whose actions make them the equivalent of spiritual mass murderers. How many spiritual lives had Manasseh ruined by his idolatrous ways? Thousands upon thousands seems a conservative estimate. Yet he "humbled himself," and the Lord "listened to his plea." Where's the justice in this?

For the Chronicler it was a simple matter of the Lord's promise. In answer to Solomon's prayer, the Lord had said, "If my people, who are called by my name, will humble themselves and pray and seek my face and turn from their wicked ways, then will I hear from heaven and will forgive their sin and will heal their land" (7:14). King Manasseh had humbled himself, and the Lord heard him and forgave him, just as the Lord had said he would. Because of this same promise, the people of Judah, who themselves were later taken into exile, could have the sure hope that the Lord would bring them back again. It was this same comfort that could brighten the days of the exiles who had returned and were struggling to survive. So many of their people remained in exile. Would the Lord gather his people? Would Israel ever be whole again? God had made his promise, and what he had promised, he would do. He would answer his people when they cried out, "Save us, O God our Savior; gather us and deliver us from the nations" (1 Chronicles 16:35).

Either grace is grace for all or there is no grace at all. In the New Testament we might point to people like Peter, Paul, or any of the disciples during the passion of our Lord. They were all spiritual kin to Manasseh. All the disciples forsook Jesus and fled. They all turned their backs on him when he needed them most. Peter spoke for them all in his threefold denial of Jesus. They had been too full of themselves and their own strength and too empty of God's power. Which of them could say, "I *deserve* my Lord's forgiveness; I *deserve* better than a Judas or a Caiaphas"? Not one!

Maybe the Lord has spared us the anguish of having committed a great outward sin. Perhaps we don't come from a background of sinful turmoil and chaos. There are no obvious pagan high places in our past and no idol altars out in the open for all to see. But what about the high places in our hearts? the idol altars right within the Spirit's temple, which no one sees except the Lord? the pride, the ego, the selfishness, and the willfulness? the secret, the shameful, and the base—all the wantonness of our restless spirits? Who will atone for these, and how will we stand before the judgment seat of God?

Martin Franzmann once wrote about the significance of Jesus' resurrection for the disciples. His words are very much to the point:

> The grace which they experienced in the res- urrection was a whole grace which spoke of a total forgiveness . . . [one which] does not degrade and grind down the sinner but restores him instantly and fully to the brother- hood. Jesus was turning the other cheek when He called these bankrupted and faith- less men His disciples and brethren. He was risking anew their betrayal of Him, their flight from Him, their denial of Him. But He took the risk of forgiving love, the love which insures its risk only with its own gift.[33]

In the end we must all describe ourselves with the words of Paul, "By the grace of God I am what I am" (1 Corinthians 15:10). It is that same grace we see displayed in the life of Manasseh.

After his own fall into sin and subsequent repentance, King David wrote of what God's grace would prompt him to do: "Then I will teach transgressors your ways, and sinners will turn back to you" (Psalm 51:13). In other words, grace does not lead us to be soft on sin; it rather moves us to witness in word and deed to the Lord, who showed such kindness to us. This is exactly what Man- asseh did. In Babylon he had learned the truth that "the LORD is God." Once back in Jerusalem, he did his best to get rid of the foreign gods and to remove the images he had set up in the Lord's temple. That he did not perfectly succeed we can deduce from passages like 2 Kings 23:12, where we are told that Josiah was forced to remove some of Manasseh's altars again from the temple in his own reformation. Perhaps Manasseh's son Amon had put them back. In any case, even the Chronicler makes it clear that Manasseh's reformation was nothing like Hezekiah's. "The people, however, continued to sacrifice at the high places."

### Amon's unfaithfulness and death

**²¹Amon was twenty-two years old when he became king, and he reigned in Jerusalem two years. ²²He did evil in the eyes of the LORD, as his father Manasseh had done. Amon worshiped and offered sacrifices to all the idols Manasseh had made. ²³But unlike his father Manasseh, he did not humble himself before the LORD; Amon increased his guilt.**

**²⁴Amon's officials conspired against him and assassinated him in his palace. ²⁵Then the people of the land killed all who had plotted against King Amon, and they made Josiah his son king in his place.**

The description of the reign of Manasseh's son Amon is kept mercifully short. He was the perfect image of his father in depravity, "worship[ing] and offer[ing] sacrifices to all the idols Manasseh had made." The only difference was that "he did not humble himself before the LORD." Quite the opposite, in fact: he only grew worse. Amon ruled only two years, losing his life in a palace conspiracy. The people of the land elevated his son Josiah to his place as king. Josiah was the last king to mount any sort of spiritual reformation. It is his story the Chronicler wants us to consider next.

### God's kingdom under Josiah—one last reform

All along in our reading of 2 Chronicles, we have tried to remain aware of our own author's distinctiveness. Certainly he covers the same material we find in Samuel and Kings, but he has his own concerns, his own areas of emphasis, and his own unique voice. This is all for the good. After all, the Holy Spirit could have inspired a single human author to cover the entire period, but he chose instead to inspire more than one, and we do well to respect his choice.

At the same time, we should be aware of some scholars who are so concerned with preserving a biblical writer's distinctive voice that they do damage to the unity of Scripture. We have a case in point in these chapters. The writer of Kings chose to highlight the ministry of Josiah the king and to treat his reign in a thematic fashion. In the interests of emphasizing Josiah's complete repentance—his wholehearted response to the law of the Lord—the writer of Kings put his entire description of Josiah's reforms after the discovery of the Book of the Law in the temple. If we had only his account, we might think that the Book of the Law's discovery prompted the reformation instead of causing it to gain momentum and directing it along specific paths. From the Chronicler we learn that Josiah's reforms were well under way before the Book of the Law was brought into the picture. There are some negative Bible critics who will simply label this as a contradiction, since they don't share our high view of Scripture's verbal inspiration.

We let them go their way. We simply praise our God for giving us biblical writers who help us, each in his own way, to understand the different facets of a single account. We note the freedom they had to emphasize or downplay various features of a familiar story according to the particular needs of those who were to receive their message. And we come away with a better idea of what it means to faithfully teach God's Word to the next generation.

Teaching faithfully means more than a mechanical recitation of every single word we've heard in the exact same order in which we've heard them. True, we want to be faithful to the details, but we want to be faithful also to the gospel essence of an account. If we fail to detect in Scripture God's earnest call to repentance and his offer—without condition or hidden costs—of pardon in the precious blood of Christ, we fail to hear Scripture at all. Teaching faithfully involves helping each generation realize that its own sins are being called to account, not the sins of a generation dead and gone. Much more than that, each generation must hear its teacher applying God's grace to its own struggles and heartaches, not to problems suffered in far-off times or in distant lands.

## *A faithful king purges land and temple*

**34** Josiah was eight years old when he became king, and he reigned in Jerusalem thirty-one years. ²He did what was right in the eyes of the LORD and walked in the ways of his father David, not turning aside to the right or to the left.

³In the eighth year of his reign, while he was still young, he began to seek the God of his father David. In his twelfth year he began to purge Judah and Jerusalem of high places, Asherah poles, carved idols and cast images. ⁴Under his direction the altars of the Baals were torn down; he cut to pieces the incense altars that were above them, and smashed the Asherah poles, the idols and the images. These he broke to pieces and scattered over the graves of those who had sacrificed to them. ⁵He burned the bones of the priests on their altars, and so he purged Judah and Jerusalem. ⁶In the towns of Manasseh, Ephraim and Simeon, as far as Naphtali, and in the ruins around them, ⁷he tore down the altars and the Asherah poles and crushed the idols to powder and cut to pieces all the incense altars throughout Israel. Then he went back to Jerusalem.

⁸In the eighteenth year of Josiah's reign, to purify the land and the temple, he sent Shaphan son of Azaliah and Maaseiah the ruler of the city, with Joah son of Joahaz, the recorder, to repair the temple of the LORD his God.

⁹They went to Hilkiah the high priest and gave him the money that had been brought into the temple of God, which the Levites who were the doorkeepers had collected from the people of Manasseh, Ephraim and the entire remnant of Israel and from all the people of Judah and Benjamin and the inhabitants of Jerusalem. ¹⁰Then they entrusted it to the men appointed to supervise the work on the LORD's temple. These men paid the workers who repaired and restored the temple. ¹¹They also gave money to the carpenters and builders to purchase dressed stone, and timber for joists and beams for the buildings that the kings of Judah had allowed to fall into ruin.

¹²The men did the work faithfully. Over them to direct them were Jahath and Obadiah, Levites descended from Merari, and Zechariah and Meshullam, descended from Kohath. The Levites—all who were skilled in playing musical instruments—¹³had charge of the laborers and supervised all the workers from job to job. Some of the Levites were secretaries, scribes and doorkeepers.

There are times when the whole world seems muffled in a dull, gray cloud, when the beauty of an upright life appears to lose its luster. People begin to see life not as something founded on a set of bedrock verities but as a grab bag of choices, all equally good. There are ages when God's truths are greeted not so much with anger as with a cynical shrug and an eyebrow raised in irony. Who can doubt the effect upon Judah that 50 years under the spiritual rule of Manasseh had, especially since his entire era was rounded off by the unabashed sinfulness of Amon? Yet out of those gray and latter days there arose one more good king, one more shaft of light to pierce the gloom. His name was Josiah.

There are many remarkable things about him one could mention, not least of which was his very existence. From where did he come? In such a fallen society, what produced a king who, from the age of 16, made it clear that he would be a follower of the Lord? Showing his hand at such a tender age, before he had reached his majority, was certainly not without its risks. By this time Judah had grown used to her idols. By this time Judah had seen reformers come and go. Yet precisely in that place from which it seemed no good could ever come again, God supplied someone whose courage, faithfulness, and piety were without equal. "He did what was right in the eyes of the LORD and walked in the ways of his father David, not turning aside to the right or to the left." It is particularly that last remark on the undeviating nature of Josiah's faithfulness that makes him stand out from all the other kings before him. Without a doubt, it distinguished him from his own perverse and crooked generation. To no other king does the Chronicler give so high an accolade.

At age 20, the age at which the Hebrews considered a boy to be ready to take over a man's work (see Numbers 1:3; 26:2; 2 Chronicles 25:5), King Josiah went to war against the idols in his kingdom. The truth of God had consequences; Josiah saw that seeking "the God of his father David" entailed the destruction of all rival altars and objects of worship. While it bore similarities to previous purges under previous kings, Josiah's reformation seems noteworthy for its systematic and thorough nature. Beginning in Judah and Jerusalem, he proceeded to the "towns of Manasseh, Ephraim and Simeon, as far as Naphtali."

Down went the high places, the Asherah poles, the idols, and the images (concerning the latter three, the Hebrew says literally: he smashed them and pulverized them). Josiah tore down the altars for sacrifice to Baal and cut to pieces Baal's altars of incense. As if that weren't enough, he made sure that no one would ever want to use the old altars or images again by defiling them all with the pollution of the dead (Numbers 5:2). He spread the idols' ashes over the graves of those who had worshiped them, and he polluted the places sacred to the idols' worship with the bones of those who had served them as priests. In this too it seems he went further than any king before him.

Students of history may want to know how it was possible that Josiah was able to extend his reformation so far to the north. Hadn't all of these areas been incorporated into the Assyrian empire? Ashurbanipal, the last significant Assyrian ruler, died in 627 B.C., throwing the empire into a tailspin from which it never recovered. Because of the rapid disintegration of Assyria, northern Palestine rather quickly became a kind of no-man's-land. We can readily see how Josiah would have had a much freer hand to work for change in the North if we assume that he began his purge north of Judah's frontier somewhere around 625 B.C. From the Chronicler's point of view, Josiah's work served as one more piece of evidence to prove that the one who sat on the throne of David was the legitimate king over *all* Israel.

The Chronicler makes a similar point with respect to the temple repairs. In his 18th year (622 B.C.), Josiah sent high-ranking officers to initiate a renovation project for the temple. It had been thoroughly trashed during the reigns of Manasseh and Amon. Josiah's desire in this project was to purify the entire country, since a temple still bearing the marks of idolatrous neglect was a spiritual pollutant not merely for Jerusalem but for the whole land of Israel. The king had taken up an offering for the work, and the money had come in not only from Judah but also from "the people of Manasseh, Ephraim and the entire remnant of Israel." God had intended his house to be the sanctuary for *all* Israel; *all* Israel took part in repairing it.

We almost would consider verses 12 and 13 as throwaway lines if we didn't recognize by now the way they reiterate some of our writer's common themes. Once more the Chronicler pauses to highlight the workers' faithfulness in carrying out their duties. In addition, it seems he would never pass up a single opportunity to mention the names of a few Levites. In this case, surprisingly, only the clans of Kohath and Merari are represented. We don't know why Gershon was omitted.

Perhaps even more surprising are the backgrounds of these Levitical supervisors. Under normal circumstances they worked as musicians, scribes, secretaries, and doorkeepers—posts that seem a long way removed from serving as supervisors on a construction crew. There is evidence to suggest that musicians may have played a musical accompaniment to the workers on some ancient construction sites.[34] It could be that the Chronicler has something like this in mind here. On the other hand, he might simply want to point out the Levites' flexibility in being willing to take on different kinds of work instead of exclaiming, "That's not in my call!" We cannot tell for sure.

What *is* clear is that the Chronicler never considers it superfluous to give recognition to the faithful work done by faithful people. Their names are recorded in Scripture. More important, their names are recorded in God's heart, along with the names of countless others who may never have made it into Scripture nor rated so much as a line in their church's bulletin. But the Lord knows those who are his, and he knows what they have done for him.

## The Book of the Law is found; the king's repentance

¹⁴While they were bringing out the money that had been taken into the temple of the LORD, Hilkiah the priest found the Book of the Law of the LORD that had been given through Moses. ¹⁵Hilkiah said to Shaphan the secretary, "I have found the Book of the Law in the temple of the LORD." He gave it to Shaphan.

¹⁶Then Shaphan took the book to the king and reported to him: "Your officials are doing everything that has been committed to them. ¹⁷They have paid out the money that was in the temple of the LORD and have entrusted it to the supervisors and workers." ¹⁸Then Shaphan the secretary informed the king, "Hilkiah the priest has given me a book." And Shaphan read from it in the presence of the king.

¹⁹When the king heard the words of the Law, he tore his robes. ²⁰He gave these orders to Hilkiah, Ahikam son of Shaphan, Abdon son of Micah, Shaphan the secretary and Asaiah the king's attendant: ²¹"Go and inquire of the LORD for me and for the remnant in Israel and Judah about what is written in this book that has been found. Great is the LORD's anger that is poured out on us because our fathers have not kept the word of the LORD; they have not acted in accordance with all that is written in this book."

Think of what this event tells us about the faithlessness of God's people during the reigns of Manasseh and Amon: a great portion of God's Word had been entirely lost! The famine of God's Word that had been predicted by Amos had come to pass (Amos 8:11). Some have aptly named this judgment "the awful silence of God." It was more than being a matter of the people's unwillingness to hear what God had to say. They had lost all knowledge of the Book of the Law's existence. Some have ventured the opinion that the book Hilkiah discovered was the book of Deuteronomy, basing this idea on the striking parallels between King Josiah's reforms and the content

of that book. Others maintain it was the entire Penta-
teuch, the five books of Moses, the first five books of the
Bible. It doesn't matter either way.

What matters is the king's reaction to hearing it. The
story is a dramatic one, complete with many details and
interesting touches. The temple project was near completion when the book was suddenly discovered somewhere
on the temple grounds. Hilkiah the high priest gave it to
Shaphan, who was apparently chief among those whom
the king had sent to head up the temple restoration project (verses 8,15). Shaphan must have had some inkling
of the book's significance, but it was not until after he
had given a full report on the temple project that he said,
"Hilkiah the priest has given me a book." Then he read it
out loud "in the presence of the king."

In various ways and at various times in the past, the
Lord had communicated with his kings. He had appeared
to them in visions and had made his powerful presence
felt in acts of mercy and judgment. Often he had spoken
to them directly through a prophet or a priest, uttering
words of praise or rebuke. Just as often the kings had
reacted in anger and defiance when told about things
they did not want to hear (16:10; 25:16; 26:19). No living
prophet had to come to see Josiah; Josiah simply listened
to God's Law being read to him by one of his servants.
He heard what God had to say about the kind of behavior he expected from his people. He heard God's message for his people when they stubbornly refused to
obey him:

> Cursed is the man who does not uphold the
> words of this law by carrying them out. . . .
> The LORD will drive you and the king you set
> over you to a nation unknown to you or your

fathers. There you will worship other gods, gods of wood and stone. You will become a thing of horror and an object of scorn and ridicule to all the nations where the LORD will drive you. (Deuteronomy 27:26; 28:36,37)

What was Josiah's reaction? Not anger, not defiance. He attributed to the book the absolute authority of the Word of God, and he applied its message to himself. "He tore his robes" in grief and anguish. He knew very well that God's people had broken the covenant. There was no fig leaf of human righteousness to hide behind. The only thing left for a nation that had proven to be so stubborn and persistent in its rebellion was "a fearful expectation of judgment and of raging fire that will consume the enemies of God" (Hebrews 10:27).

Human society measures people by what they can make of themselves, what they are and have and do. In the judgment of God, what we are is sinful, what we do is wickedness, and what we possess is a gift from God for which we fail to return proper thanks to him. Through his law God measures us and finds us wanting. He makes us nothing, teaching us to humble ourselves before him in heartfelt repentance. Before God, the ultimate measure of all people is how they hear and heed his Word. King Josiah humbly heard God's message and then sent some of the top men in his kingdom on a delegation to the prophetess Huldah in order to find out from her what the Lord's intentions were toward "the remnant in Israel and Judah."

### God's response through Huldah: peace for Josiah's time, but after him, the deluge

<sup>22</sup>**Hilkiah and those the king had sent with him went to speak to the prophetess Huldah, who was the wife of Shallum son of**

Tokhath, the son of Hasrah, keeper of the wardrobe. She lived in Jerusalem, in the Second District.

²³She said to them, "This is what the LORD, the God of Israel, says: Tell the man who sent you to me, ²⁴'This is what the LORD says: I am going to bring disaster on this place and its people—all the curses written in the book that has been read in the presence of the king of Judah. ²⁵Because they have forsaken me and burned incense to other gods and provoked me to anger by all that their hands have made, my anger will be poured out on this place and will not be quenched.' ²⁶Tell the king of Judah, who sent you to inquire of the LORD, 'This is what the LORD, the God of Israel, says concerning the words you heard: ²⁷Because your heart was responsive and you humbled yourself before God when you heard what he spoke against this place and its people, and because you humbled yourself before me and tore your robes and wept in my presence, I have heard you, declares the LORD. ²⁸Now I will gather you to your fathers, and you will be buried in peace. Your eyes will not see all the disaster I am going to bring on this place and on those who live here.'"

So they took her answer back to the king.

There is a certain solemnity about this story we would do well to consider. The delegation that went to Huldah was an official one. The men are referred to by their full names (including their fathers' names) or by their titles. We can already recognize Hilkiah as the high priest (verse 9). Similarly, Huldah the prophetess is identified in an extremely formal way by giving her husband's full name and title and her place of residence. The solemnity is that of a courtroom in which the verdict of a capital case is about to be announced. The key players were all there. Representatives of the king, representatives of the people, and representatives of the temple all stood before Huldah to hear her give the Lord's reply. What would be his decree regarding Israel?

"Tell the man who sent you"—an ominous beginning. Striking is the absence of any reference to Josiah either by his personal name, his family, or his title. As far as the Lord was concerned, he had no more tender words to speak to the house of David and no more comfort to offer his people Israel. Josiah's piety could not alter the settled purpose of the Lord. "I am going to bring disaster on this place and its people—all the curses written in the book that has been read in the presence of the king of Judah. Because they have forsaken me and burned incense to other gods and provoked me to anger by all that their hands have made, my anger will be poured out on this place and will not be quenched."

The Lord made this announcement not to Josiah as an individual but to Josiah as a man who had asked about the fate of his people. God would not consider the personal piety of the one interceding for Israel anymore. Things had gone too far for that. It was just as the Lord once said to Jeremiah: "Even if Moses and Samuel were to stand before me, my heart would not go out to this people. Send them away from my presence! Let them go!" (Jeremiah 15:1). The sentence had already been passed. It could not be repealed.

The sentence, however, would not come about while Josiah was alive. This was the substance of the Lord's message to "the king of Judah" (notice in verse 26 how the prophetess switches to using the king's title) "who sent you to inquire of the LORD" (and thereby showed himself to be a true spiritual kin to David). God was not forgetful of his own, as his people had been forgetful of him. The Lord would always listen to the sighs and tears of a penitent sinner. "I have heard you, declares the LORD. Now I will gather you to your fathers, and you will be buried in peace. Your eyes will not see all the disaster I am going to bring on this place and on those who live here." The meaning of the phrase "you will be buried in peace" is defined by the following phrase: "Your eyes will not see all the disaster I am going to bring on this place." King Josiah would be killed in battle at Megiddo, but he would not have to witness the destruction of his kingdom or see the temple laid to waste.

Jesus' disciples were once cut to the heart by some stern words of judgment he spoke regarding the rich: "It is easier for a camel to go through the eye of a needle than for a rich man to enter the kingdom of God" (Matthew 19:24). Astonished, they asked if any person at all could hope to be saved. When we hear words of judgment—whether the ones Jesus announced or the ones we read here in 2 Chronicles—we ought to pay close attention to the reply Jesus gave to his chosen band. "Jesus looked at them and said, 'With man this is impossible, but with God all things are possible'" (Matthew 19:26). God insists upon reserving the name *Savior* for himself. With his law he breaks us down, emptying our hearts of any reason to boast in ourselves, so that we are ready to take in a message only sinners are glad to hear.

### The covenant is once more renewed

²⁹**Then the king called together all the elders of Judah and Jerusalem. ³⁰He went up to the temple of the LORD with the men of Judah, the people of Jerusalem, the priests and the Levites—all the people from the least to the greatest. He read in their hearing all the words of the Book of the Covenant, which had been found in the temple of the LORD. ³¹The king stood by his pillar and renewed the covenant in the presence of the LORD—to follow the LORD and keep his commands, regulations and decrees with all his heart and all his soul, and to obey the words of the covenant written in this book.**

³²Then he had everyone in Jerusalem and Benjamin pledge themselves to it; the people of Jerusalem did this in accordance with the covenant of God, the God of their fathers.

³³Josiah removed all the detestable idols from all the territory belonging to the Israelites, and he had all who were present in Israel serve the LORD their God. As long as he lived, they did not fail to follow the LORD, the God of their fathers.

The genuineness of Josiah's repentance is demonstrated in the fruits of faith we see here. He did not quibble or argue with God's judgment on his people. He did not question God's justice or complain about God's lack of mercy. He resolved to press ahead and renew the covenant once more in the presence of the Lord. He had all the people gather together in solemn assembly. He read aloud the book that had been found, and before them all he pledged himself "with all his heart and all his soul . . . to obey the words of the covenant written in this book." What is more, "he had everyone in Jerusalem and Benjamin pledge themselves to it." As their king he had the power to compel his people to be obedient to the Lord. He continued to root out every trace of idolatry he came across and, as long as he was alive, his people "did not fail to follow the LORD, the God of their fathers."

The genuineness of Josiah's repentance is not in question. But what about the repentance of his people? We notice that the universal joy—a characteristic of Hezekiah's reformation—is missing. The people apparently did what they did because they had to. As Jeremiah once said of them, the name of the Lord was on their lips but not in their hearts (Jeremiah 12:2). Their worship, for the most part, was an act of pretense (Jeremiah 3:10). This is not to say that no one listened. Certainly the Levites were enthusiastic participants during Josiah's Passover, at which time Josiah's high officials also showed their faith by willingly contributing a great number of sacrificial animals. But those two groups were merely exceptions to the rule, and the prophet's overall assessment remains unchanged. In spite of the response of some, the people's repentance was only skin deep and not one that engaged their hearts and minds.

In the book of Jeremiah, there is a stirring passage in which the prophet mirrors in his own life the actions of Josiah here. Jeremiah is told by the Lord to stand before the people, read the terms of the covenant, and urge them on toward heartfelt obedience (Jeremiah 11:1-7). But it is all hopeless. The people pay no attention (Jeremiah 11:7). The single, solitary voice of assent is that of the prophet himself saying, "Amen, LORD" (Jeremiah 11:5). The sad truth is that the Word of God can be rejected, and though there will always be a remnant of the faithful wherever God's means of grace are in use, many in the visible church are merely hypocrites, going through the motions for the sake of propriety. Once, at a dark and frustrating time in his own reformation, Luther remarked, "I can get no farther than [the people's] ears; their heart I cannot reach."[35]

Concerning our own Savior and King, we know that he has done far more for us than simply point out the path to righteousness. He has also done far more than provide us with a good example. He has gone to death and back in one perfect act of devotion and obedience that counts for us all, just as if we had done it ourselves. In his blood he has made an entirely new covenant for us, a completely unconditional covenant in which God promises to forgive our wickedness and remember our sins no more (Jeremiah 31:34).

Yet even Jesus was deeply conscious of how the still, small voice of the gospel could be ignored, rejected, and despised by humanity. He promised that he would come soon to put all things right, but at the same time he lamented, "When the Son of Man comes, will he find faith on the earth?" (Luke 18:8). And so in these days of gray—when people believe in something, nothing, everything—we humbly ask: "Dear Savior, keep faith alive! Preserve a remnant of your people until you come. We trust your promise. Amen."

### *A celebration of the Passover without equal*

After the discovery of the Book of the Law, King Josiah immediately began to make preparations to celebrate the Passover (compare 34:8 with 35:19). Again, the dominant presence throughout this entire celebration is the king himself. He initiated the celebration. He organized and encouraged the priests and the Levites, giving them specific instructions so that a great crowd of people could be accommodated. Finally, he provided all the sacrificial animals that were necessary for the lay people. All they had to do was arrive and participate.

### *Preparations are made*

**35** Josiah celebrated the Passover to the LORD in Jerusalem, and the Passover lamb was slaughtered on the fourteenth day of the first month. ²He appointed the priests to their duties and encouraged them in the service of the LORD's temple. ³He said to the Levites, who instructed all Israel and who had been consecrated to the LORD: "Put the sacred ark in the temple that Solomon son of David king of Israel built. It is not to be carried about on your shoulders. Now serve the LORD your God and his people Israel. ⁴Prepare yourselves by families in your divisions, according to the directions written by David king of Israel and by his son Solomon.**

**⁵"Stand in the holy place with a group of Levites for each subdivision of the families of your fellow countrymen, the lay**

people. ⁶Slaughter the Passover lambs, consecrate yourselves and prepare the lambs for your fellow countrymen, doing what the LORD commanded through Moses."

⁷Josiah provided for all the lay people who were there a total of thirty thousand sheep and goats for the Passover offerings, and also three thousand cattle—all from the king's own possessions.

⁸His officials also contributed voluntarily to the people and the priests and Levites. Hilkiah, Zechariah and Jehiel, the administrators of God's temple, gave the priests twenty-six hundred Passover offerings and three hundred cattle. ⁹Also Conaniah along with Shemaiah and Nethanel, his brothers, and Hashabiah, Jeiel and Jozabad, the leaders of the Levites, provided five thousand Passover offerings and five hundred head of cattle for the Levites.

Josiah wanted things to be done right. Unlike Hezekiah's great Passover celebration, Josiah wanted the Passover lambs to be slaughtered on the fourteenth day of the first month (verse 1; see also Exodus 12:6). Perhaps verse 2 implies some lack of zeal on the part of the priests; more likely it is simply a summary statement telling us that Josiah organized and encouraged the priests in a manner similar to the following description in the case of the Levites. Because of the Chronicler's special interest in the Levites, he wishes to describe the king's words of encouragement to them in greater detail.

We are not exactly certain how the king's words in verse 3 are to be understood. Some have suggested that faithful Levites had hidden the ark of God during the days of Manasseh and Amon. According to this interpretation, Josiah is telling them to put it back where it belongs and to busy themselves with more current needs. Others say that the words are capable of being construed as follows: "Leave the sacred ark where it is; you don't have to carry it on your shoulders as you did in the old days. God has new ministries, new services for you to render for his people Israel." Either way, the basic thrust of the king's remarks is to point the Levites away from the old forms of service—useful in the past but now no longer required—so that they may devote themselves to the new forms of service required in the present.

A case in point was the need on the day of the Passover. The king wanted all Israel to be present. Huge numbers of goats and lambs had to be slaughtered and prepared for sacrifice and for eating. Who would coordinate all this and make it possible for all Israel to come together at one central sanctuary yet still celebrate the Passover in their individual family groupings, as prescribed by the Law of Moses (see Deuteronomy 16:5-7; Exodus 12:3)? The king's answer was to ask the Levites to do this, following the example of Hezekiah's Passover and turning those emergency measures into a regular arrangement (verse 6; see also 30:17). Therefore Josiah had them arrange themselves in their regular Levitical divisions and then subdivide themselves so that a group of Levites would be responsible for each lay family in Israel. They would take care of slaughtering and preparing the lambs for their fellow countrymen.

But who would provide the lamb? On this occasion the answer was King Josiah! In a lavish outlay of his personal wealth, the king provided 30,000 sheep and goats for the Passover offerings themselves and an additional 3,000 cattle for the fellowship offerings that had long been associated with the Passover (Leviticus 3:16). Inspired by his example, the chief priest and other top administrators of God's temple voluntarily contributed a sufficient number of animals for the priests in Israel, while the Levites mentioned in verse 9 took care of the sacrificial needs of all the Levites. Once again we notice one of the themes our writer loves to return to again and again: Look at how freely and lavishly hearts moved by God's love can give—provided that they serve under God's kind of king. No congregational leader need feel that talking about money for the support of God's work is an unspiritual matter.

### The Passover service is conducted

¹⁰**The service was arranged and the priests stood in their places with the Levites in their divisions as the king had ordered. ¹¹The Passover lambs were slaughtered, and the priests sprinkled the blood handed to them, while the Levites skinned the animals. ¹²They set aside the burnt offerings to give them to the subdivisions of the families of the people to offer to the LORD, as is written in the Book of Moses. They did the same with the cattle. ¹³They roasted the Passover animals over the fire as prescribed, and boiled the holy offerings in pots, caldrons and pans and served them quickly to all the people. ¹⁴After this, they made preparations for themselves and for the priests, because the priests, the descendants of Aaron, were sacrificing the burnt offerings and the fat portions until nightfall. So the Levites made preparations for themselves and for the Aaronic priests.**

¹⁵**The musicians, the descendants of Asaph, were in the places prescribed by David, Asaph, Heman and Jeduthun the king's seer. The gatekeepers at each gate did not need to leave their posts, because their fellow Levites made the preparations for them.**

The theme of willing service is continued in this section, in which the Chronicler describes for us the actual celebration of Josiah's great Passover. In particular he highlights the faithful service of the Levites on that day. Such a celebration was a massive and complex undertaking in which countless things could have gone wrong. But the king had asked the Levites to devote themselves to this new form of service, and the Levites responded wonderfully. The result? Everything went smoothly.

The Levites slaughtered the Passover lambs for the lay people and then brought the blood to the priests so that they could sprinkle it against the altar (see Leviticus 3:2). While the priests were busy with that, the Levites were skinning the animals and preparing them for eating and for sacrifice. Certain portions of the Passover lamb were to be burnt on God's altar. These portions the Levites set aside so that the heads of the household could offer them to God in a formal way by taking them to the priest. The rest of the lamb was to be roasted and eaten by the entire family. The Levites took care of this cooking chore too. As was mentioned before, there were a number of fellowship offerings closely associated with the Passover ritual. The Levites also took care of the slaughter, the preparation for sacrifice, and the cooking of these animals. Unlike the Passover lamb, which was to be roasted, these offerings could be prepared for the worshipers to eat by boiling the meat in pots and kettles (verses 12,13; see Deuteronomy 16:7).

Slaughtering animals, dividing the meat into portions, preparing it in various ways for eating—what else was there for the Levites to do? We read that they "served them quickly to all the people." They were not ashamed to serve as waiters, running the heaping platters of food out to where the people were waiting. One would think that would have been enough. But after all that was done, they still attended to the needs of the priests and of their own company. The priests had their hands more than full with all the work of offering the Lord's portions on the altar of sacrifice "until nightfall." Some of their fellow Levites had other duties to carry out on that day. The singers had to remain at their posts, and the gatekeepers had to attend to the overall security of God's house. But no one had to leave his assigned duties in order to celebrate the feast because "their fellow Levites made the preparations for them."

What a beautiful picture of service this is! The king had called the Levites "teachers of all Israel," and indeed they were. They demonstrated the kind of spirit that God expects to see in all those who serve him—in the holy ministry above all, but also in each one of our holy callings. We remember that we serve a King who was willing to hitch up his own garments and wash his disciples' feet. And he did this as he was taking on his shoulders the weight of their sins and was about to give up his life for them all. He told them, "I've left you an example and an infallible sign by which you might identify true ministry." True ministry is not about amassing titles; it is not found in the heaping up of power for show. It is rather seen in taking all our gifts and using all our powers to love our brothers and our sisters. Ministry is about laying our lives down at our fellow Christians' feet.

### The greatest ever

**¹⁶So at that time the entire service of the LORD was carried out for the celebration of the Passover and the offering of burnt offerings on the altar of the LORD, as King Josiah had ordered. ¹⁷The Israelites who were present celebrated the Passover at that time and observed the Feast of Unleavened Bread for seven days. ¹⁸The Passover had not been observed like this in Israel since the days of the prophet Samuel; and none of the kings of Israel had ever celebrated such a Passover as did Josiah, with the priests, the Levites and all Judah and Israel who were there with the people of Jerusalem. ¹⁹This Passover was celebrated in the eighteenth year of Josiah's reign.**

The Chronicler joins the writer of Kings in calling Josiah's Passover the greatest ever. It was better even than Hezekiah's celebration. What made it so great? No doubt part of the reason was the turnout. "The priests, the Levites and all Judah and Israel . . . were there with the people of Jerusalem." In part it was also due to the proper way it had been observed: "on the fourteenth day of the first month . . . 'doing what the LORD commanded through Moses' . . . as is written in the Book of Moses . . . as prescribed" (verses 1,6,12,13).

It was the greatest ever, and yet it was celebrated on the eve of Judah's destruction. It was the greatest ever, and yet there were some things missing. We miss the happy songs so prominent in the descriptions of other great celebrations of this book. Here we read nothing but a terse "the musicians . . . were in the places prescribed by David" (35:15). All the people were there, in numbers that were greater than at any other Passover, and yet we miss the descriptions of the wholehearted joy and the universal willingness to unite under God's kind of king that we read of in so many other places. Much of this Passover had to be done for the people. All they had to do was show up. Is it reading too much into the text to hear in these omissions the Chronicler gently saying: "It was the greatest ever—in an outward way. But the people's spiritual core remained untouched."

We can see why Josiah would have celebrated such a Passover, and we can understand the Chronicler's purpose in emphasizing the positive aspects of it as much as possible. One writer, in speaking about the Chronicler's point of view, gives a good summary of God's wisdom in giving his people the Passover festival:

> [At the Passover] the Israelite began to see, or saw
> again, what it was to be Israel. . . . Israel must

be drawn constantly back to its roots, to know again and again its true identity, to be delivered from the delusion that comes from the normal preoccupation with the routine, the menial, and the material, that the sum of life is no more than this.[36]

Under Hezekiah's celebration we've discussed the significance of the Passover as a memorial of the Lord's great constituting act of salvation for his ancient people—their deliverance from Egypt. We've probed the festivities' emphasis on purity. In Josiah's Passover we see some other features of the celebration come more sharply into focus.

There is no escaping the sacrificial aspects of the day. Blood must be shed. Sin costs a life, the pure life of an unblemished lamb. We also notice the meal of fellowship. Israel ate the Passover as individual families, knit together on that one day into a much greater family. For all these reasons, we can understand why our Lord, on the eve of his own death, said to his own disciples: "I have eagerly desired to eat this Passover with you before I suffer. For I tell you, I will not eat it again until it finds fulfillment in the kingdom of God" (Luke 22:15,16).

Everything came together that night on which our Lord was betrayed. The Lord's disciples ate the Passover together with the Lamb who was shortly going to fulfill it. In its place Jesus gave his own another meal to celebrate, a meal that reminds us all of the sacrifice he made to set us free, a meal that unites us all into one body as we join together to eat his body and drink his blood. Every celebration of the Lord's Supper and every ancient celebration of the Passover will finally reach its goal when all God's people join together in that great feast of joy "in the kingdom of God" (Luke 22:16). As the world's time grows short and the days become more evil, we celebrate the feast in holy anticipation of that day, yearning for our Lord's return.

### A lament over King Josiah's untimely death

²⁰After all this, when Josiah had set the temple in order, Neco king of Egypt went up to fight at Carchemish on the Euphrates, and Josiah marched out to meet him in battle. ²¹But Neco sent messengers to him, saying, "What quarrel is there between you and me, O king of Judah? It is not you I am attacking at this time, but the house with which I am at war. God has told me to hurry; so stop opposing God, who is with me, or he will destroy you."

²²Josiah, however, would not turn away from him, but disguised himself to engage him in battle. He would not listen to what Neco had said at God's command but went to fight him on the plain of Megiddo.

²³Archers shot King Josiah, and he told his officers, "Take me away; I am badly wounded." ²⁴So they took him out of his chariot, put him in the other chariot he had and brought him to Jerusalem, where he died. He was buried in the tombs of his fathers, and all Judah and Jerusalem mourned for him.

²⁵Jeremiah composed laments for Josiah, and to this day all the men and women singers commemorate Josiah in the laments. These became a tradition in Israel and are written in the Laments.

²⁶The other events of Josiah's reign and his acts of devotion, according to what is written in the Law of the LORD—²⁷all the events, from beginning to end, are written in the book of the kings of Israel and Judah.

The Chronicler wants to make a clear connection between this tragic episode and the far happier one preceding it: "After all this, *when Josiah had set the temple in order,* Neco king of Egypt went up to fight at Carchemish." The map of the Middle East was changing again, and the alignments of the great powers were shifting dramatically. The Assyrians had been driven from all their traditional centers of power by a coalition of Medes and Babylonians. The Assyrians' last king, Ashuruballit, was trying to hold on to the last vestiges of power at Carchemish, a city on the Euphrates River. Surprisingly, Neco, the king of Egypt, went to his aid against the Babylonians. Josiah, king of Judah, tried to stop him.

A number of motives have been suggested for this. Some say that Josiah wanted to continue the policies of a Babylonian party within Judah, which had aligned itself with the rising power of Babylon ever since the days of King Hezekiah. Others less fancifully suggest that he did not want to concede to the Egyptians the right to pass through territory he had so recently reclaimed for the crown from Assyria. If he allowed the Egyptian king to pass through without a fight, theoretically he would soon have been drawn into Egypt's sphere of influence, and Judah's independence would have been lost. The battleground was Megiddo, notable in biblical lore as the place where Deborah and Barak had defeated Jabin in the days of the judges (Judges 5:19). Megiddo is also notable for being the scene where, according to the book of Revelation, the final conflict is to occur between the kings of the earth and the kingdom of God. There we know it by its Greek spelling, "Armageddon" (Revelation 16:16).

Whatever Josiah's political motives were, the Chronicler laments his lack of theological insight in taking on this fight. There is something plaintive in the way he writes, "After all this, when Josiah had set the temple in order . . ." The year is 610 B.C., and about 13 years have passed since the Book of the Law was found and the great Passover was celebrated. Nevertheless, as far as the Chronicler is concerned, Josiah's actions have to be considered within the spiritual context of the temple restoration. It's as if he were saying, "Once again, after displaying such devotion, after demonstrating such great spiritual power and perception, the king from the house of David fell into great sin." God could not have made it more plain to Josiah than he had through Huldah the prophetess. Judah would not long survive Josiah's death (see 34:24-28). Yet here was Josiah, trying to preserve God's kingdom with physical, coercive means when it could be built and strengthened only by spiritual means.

Not only this but God also added a prophetic warning against Josiah's fighting. "Neco sent messengers to him, saying, 'What quarrel is there between you and me, O king of Judah? It is not you I am attacking at this time, but the house with which I am at war. God has told me to hurry; so stop opposing God, who is with me, or he will destroy you.'" The Chronicler labeled this message "God's command," which Josiah stubbornly refused to heed. Many have asked, "How was Josiah supposed to know that the message of a heathen king was truly from the Lord? Hadn't even Sennacherib claimed—without justification—to have had the support of Israel's God?" The answer seems quite simple: they were words perfectly consistent with the earlier prophecies of Huldah. They also agreed with what the prophets had all been saying for quite some time: Judah was going to fall. Finally, God's ongoing admonition to all of his kings had always been to avoid entangling themselves in foreign conflicts and alliances. Given that background, it was no great stretch to expect Josiah to have recognized in Neco's words the voice of his own God.

"He would not listen . . . but went to fight." This was truly a great error in a king who had otherwise ranked among Judah's greatest. Just as King Ahab had done

417

before him—a king who had been evil through and through—Josiah "disguised himself" (verse 22; see 18:29). As with King Ahab, this was a rebellious attempt to evade the piercing truth of God's Word and a foolish bid to hide away from his guilty fears. And it would not succeed any more than Ahab's had: "Archers shot King Josiah, and he told his officers, 'Take me away; I am badly wounded.'"

The NIV's translation of Josiah's final moments, particularly its rendering "[they] brought him to Jerusalem, *where he died*," is not the best. It appears needlessly to set up a contradiction with the parallel account in 2 Kings, where we read, "Neco faced [Josiah] and killed him at Megiddo. Josiah's servants *brought his body in a chariot* . . . to Jerusalem" (2 Kings 23:29,30). The Chronicler's Hebrew simply says, "They brought him to Jerusalem, *and he died*." It could even be translated "and so he died" without violating the laws of language. The point is that Scripture is not very specific about where the king breathed his last. He could have died at Megiddo. He might have died on the journey back. It is doubtful, in view of the way the writer of Kings expresses it, that he died in Jerusalem.

"All who draw the sword will die by the sword," our Lord once said to Peter (Matthew 26:52). The words are an apt commentary on the endless and cyclical nature of human conflict. No nation stays on top forever. Someone always comes along to push down the king of the hill. But it goes much deeper than that. Jesus' words make clear to us the spiritual nature of the forces arrayed against the kingdom of God and the spiritual way power is to be exercised in his church. Jesus calmly accepted being put under arrest in the garden. He knew that what was happening was all taking place under the will of God, which governs all, and under the

Word of God, which had expressly predicted these events. No one may exercise power in God's kingdom contrary to God's Word. That is why the Lamb did not complain as he was led away. He placed his life into the hands of God, saying, "Thy will be done." And so he won the victory. All who try to exercise power in God's kingdom by using the weapons of the world—force, coercion, politics—must expect that similar weapons will be used against them and that their attempts ultimately will fail.

Josiah's untimely death came as a great shock to Judah. He was greatly mourned by all. Jeremiah even composed formal laments to commemorate his death (not the book of Lamentations), which became part of Israel's repertoire of traditional music. It is easy to see why this would be so. The storm clouds threatening God's wrath and Judah's destruction had been growing dark on the horizon for some time. Under this young, vigorous, and pious king, Judah had known a brief resurgence, as miraculous as if a tree were to bud and bloom in late October just ahead of the winter's blast.

This flowering did not last; it *could* not last. The leaves would soon fall, and the tree would become dry and lifeless. One day Jeremiah himself would simply forbid further mourning of this kind, no doubt because it was simply a wallowing in earthly emotions in such a way that avoided waking up to spiritual reality (Jeremiah 22:10). For similar reasons Jesus once turned to some women bewailing his impending crucifixion and told them, "Daughters of Jerusalem, do not weep for me; weep for yourselves and for your children. For if men do these things when the tree is green, what will happen when it is dry?" (Luke 23:28,31).

This lamentation over Josiah probably forms the ground of comparison in Zechariah's message concerning the way the godly would one day mourn over the slain Messiah: "On that day the weeping in Jerusalem will be great, like the weeping of Hadad Rimmon in the plain of Megiddo" (Zechariah 12:11). Many interpreters see Hadad Rimmon as being that place near Megiddo where Josiah finally died, and hence they view the entire verse as a reference to the same tradition of which the Chronicler speaks here. God's people would one day mourn Jesus as they had mourned Josiah.

We think of Christ's words to his disciples just before his death: "I tell you the truth, you will weep and mourn while the world rejoices. You will grieve, but your grief will turn to joy" (John 16:20). He could say that to them because he could make them a promise Josiah could have never made: "I will see you again and you will rejoice, and no one will take away your joy" (John 16:22).

### God's kingdom under wrath and grace

The Chronicler's final chapter is once again a jewel of composition. First, he makes extensive use of his technique of compression, reducing to 23 verses a story that required 57 verses in 2 Kings. This has that same generalizing effect we observed earlier, rendering the account of human rebelliousness and God's response to it more timeless and applicable to all generations. As an example of this from our own chapter, we might simply consider the almost bewildering array of kings and empires that pass before our eyes in this brief space. First Egypt, then Babylon, and finally Persia. First Neco, then Nebuchadnezzar, and finally Cyrus. Kingdoms rise; kingdoms fall. The kingdom of God endures over all.

Second, there is a pattern in the way that the Chronicler quickly disposes of the reigns of the last four kings. All four were faithless. All four experienced the pain of exile—either impending (as in Jehoiakim's case) or actual (as in the case of all the others). All four were forced to pay tribute to a foreign king. At first it involved merely paying a fine of a certain weight of gold and silver. In the end it involved submitting to successive plunderings of the sacred vessels in the Lord's house and to the stripping away of the accumulated wealth of the entire kingdom.

We see then how his presentation works itself up to a climax. The sins of Jehoahaz, the first king in this series, are barely mentioned. They must be inferred from the fine that was levied by King Neco and from the knowledge we have of him from the book of Kings (2 Kings 23:32). King Zedekiah's indictment, however, is much more complete and leads into the description of God's formal charges against all levels of Judean society. Similarly, in the cases of Jehoahaz, Jehoiakim, and Jehoiachin, the Chronicler zeroes in on the *kings'* exile. We know that, beginning with Jehoiachin, a large number of the people of Judah were taken into captivity as well. But the Chronicler does not mention this, reserving his description of the *people's* exile until the end of Zedekiah's reign.

The effect of all this is similar to that of watching a large tree being chopped down. Each blow with the ax cuts deeper until, finally, the entire tree comes crashing to the ground. The ax of God's judgment was being laid at the root of David's royal house. In the end there was nothing left of the monarchy but a stump, to show where it once had been (Isaiah 11:1; Matthew 3:10).

We should, however, not suppose that death and destruction are going to be God's last words to his people in this book. The Chronicler concludes his massive work with a song of hope in the Lord, who rules over all and who promises us the victory by his grace.

## Increasing defiance to the Lord and the Lord's response

### King Jehoahaz

**36** And the people of the land took Jehoahaz son of Josiah and made him king in Jerusalem in place of his father.
²Jehoahaz was twenty-three years old when he became king, and he reigned in Jerusalem three months. ³The king of Egypt dethroned him in Jerusalem and imposed on Judah a levy of a hundred talents of silver and a talent of gold. ⁴The king of Egypt made Eliakim, a brother of Jehoahaz, king over Judah and Jerusalem and changed Eliakim's name to Jehoiakim. But Neco took Eliakim's brother Jehoahaz and carried him off to Egypt.

Following Josiah's death, the people of the land elevated Jehoahaz to power. Scripture also refers to him as Shallum (1 Chronicles 3:15; Jeremiah 22:11). This undoubtedly was his personal name, with Jehoahaz being the name he took when he ascended to the throne. Jehoahaz was the fourth son of Josiah, so it is somewhat unusual to see him assume power ahead of his brothers. Some commentators put forth an interesting opinion to explain this. They assert that the people of the land supported Josiah's desire to remain free from Egyptian influence, so the Israelites put a son of his on the throne who they knew would continue his father's policies. Certainly it is true that the choice of Jehoahaz was not at all pleasing to the Egyptians, since Neco replaced him with his brother while on the way back to Egypt from Carchemish (see 35:20; 2 Kings 23:31,34). The Chronicler also gives us one piece of information that might lend more credibility to the idea. Not only did Neco depose Jehoahaz, he also imposed a fine (the word translated "levy" in verse 3 means "money due as a penalty") on the land of Judah. A punishing fine makes perfect sense if the Egyptian king saw the act of the people of Judah as one of rebellion against himself. Neco's changing of Eliakim's name to Jehoiakim was a not-so-subtle way of letting everyone know who was boss. "This man is my creature," he was saying.

## King Jehoiakim

⁵Jehoiakim was twenty-five years old when he became king, and he reigned in Jerusalem eleven years. He did evil in the eyes of the Lᴏʀᴅ his God. ⁶Nebuchadnezzar king of Babylon attacked him and bound him with bronze shackles to take him to Babylon. ⁷Nebuchadnezzar also took to Babylon articles from the temple of the Lᴏʀᴅ and put them in his temple there.

⁸The other events of Jehoiakim's reign, the detestable things he did and all that was found against him, are written in the book of the kings of Israel and Judah. And Jehoiachin his son succeeded him as king.

Jehoiakim is probably best known to us as the king who showed his contempt for God's Word by cutting up a scroll on which Jeremiah had written his prophecies and methodically feeding the pieces to the fire (Jeremiah 36:23-25). Jeremiah had predicted that his wickedness would earn for him the "burial of a donkey" (Jeremiah 22:19). That prophecy might have had something to do with the burning of the scroll.

In 605 B.C., the third year of Jehoiakim's reign (Daniel 1:1,2), Nebuchadnezzar of Babylon put an end to Egyptian power in Palestine by defeating King Neco at the battle of Carchemish. As Nebuchadnezzar pursued the Egyptian king back to his homeland, he stopped off at Jerusalem to collect some tribute from "the temple of the Lᴏʀᴅ." From now on Nebuchadnezzar wanted Jehoiakim to acknowledge Babylon's power as supreme. At the same time, the Babylonian strong man took some hostages to ensure the loyalty of his new vassal. Among these was a bright young nobleman by the name of Daniel (Daniel 1:1-6).

For a while Jehoiakim submitted to the Babylonian yoke, but his delusions of grandeur led him to try to be something more. His misguided rebellion against King Nebuchadnezzar (2 Kings 24:1) eventually led to his being bound with bronze shackles for a trip to Babylon. But for some reason, he never had to go.[37] Following his death, his son Jehoiachin took his place.

### King Jehoiachin

⁹**Jehoiachin was eighteen years old when he became king, and he reigned in Jerusalem three months and ten days. He did evil in the eyes of the Lᴏʀᴅ. ¹⁰In the spring, King Nebuchadnezzar sent for him and brought him to Babylon, together with articles of value from the temple of the Lᴏʀᴅ, and he made Jehoiachin's uncle, Zedekiah, king over Judah and Jerusalem.**

If we go by the genealogy given in the first book (1 Chronicles 3:17-24), Jehoiachin was considered the last legitimate ruler over Judah in the line of David. It was through him that the royal house was traced throughout the years of exile and return. He also had the bitter distinction of being the presiding monarch in 597 ʙ.ᴄ., when Nebuchadnezzar deported the first large group of Judahites to Babylon (see 2 Kings 24:13-16). His father Jehoiakim's rebellion had been a complete fiasco, leading to the imposition of a Babylonian siege upon Jerusalem. During those worst of times, Jehoiachin came to power, and he enjoyed an evil reign of only three months before capitulating to Nebuchadnezzar. Jehoiachin was brought as a captive to Babylon, along with many articles of value from the temple of the Lord. But because Nebuchadnezzar did not yet want to make a permanent end of Judah, he installed his own puppet-king on Judah's throne: Jehoiachin's uncle Zedekiah. And just to be on the safe side, the Babylonian ruler made Zedekiah swear loyalty to him before he left for home.

## *King Zedekiah ushers in the end*

¹¹Zedekiah was twenty-one years old when he became king, and he reigned in Jerusalem eleven years. ¹²He did evil in the eyes of the LORD his God and did not humble himself before Jeremiah the prophet, who spoke the word of the LORD. ¹³He also rebelled against King Nebuchadnezzar, who had made him take an oath in God's name. He became stiff-necked and hardened his heart and would not turn to the LORD, the God of Israel. ¹⁴Furthermore, all the leaders of the priests and the people became more and more unfaithful, following all the detestable practices of the nations and defiling the temple of the LORD, which he had consecrated in Jerusalem.

¹⁵The LORD, the God of their fathers, sent word to them through his messengers again and again, because he had pity on his people and on his dwelling place. ¹⁶But they mocked God's messengers, despised his words and scoffed at his prophets until the wrath of the LORD was aroused against his people and there was no remedy. ¹⁷He brought up against them the king of the Babylonians, who killed their young men with the sword in the sanctuary, and spared neither young man nor young woman, old man or aged. God handed all of them over to Nebuchadnezzar. ¹⁸He carried to Babylon all the articles from the temple of God, both large and small, and the treasures of the LORD's temple and the treasures of the king and his officials. ¹⁹They set fire to God's temple and broke down the wall of Jerusalem; they burned all the palaces and destroyed everything of value there.

The climax of the Chronicler's presentation of the last four kings comes with Zedekiah. He evaluates the spiritual state of both king and people to sum up what had been developing in the heart of the kingdom for some time. With Zedekiah the people had reached the final stage of hardening themselves against the Lord's message. Spurning God's Word, they made themselves fit only for judgment.

Zedekiah reminds us of another hardened sinner—Herod the tetrarch. Weak, vacillating, and easily influenced by others, both rulers were intensely curious about what the prophets had to say and yet were unwilling to put it into practice (Jeremiah 37:16,17; 38:14; Mark 6:20). The Chronicler characterizes Zedekiah by reading off a bill of indictment containing all the Lord's charges against him. "He . . . did not humble himself"—with this phrase the Chronicler again recalls God's promise once made to Solomon: "If my people . . . humble themselves . . . , then will I hear" (7:14). This was a king who trifled with grace and who despised God's promises. He obstinately refused to listen to Jeremiah's warnings, which were the Lord's own words to him. Furthermore, he "rebelled against King Nebuchadnezzar, who had made him take an oath in God's name" (verse 13; see also Ezekiel 17:19). Thus, in one act of rebellion, he broke not only the Fourth Commandment but also the Second. This constant, willful despising of God's Word led inevitably to a settled state of impenitence. "He became stiff-necked and hardened his heart and would not turn to the LORD, the God of Israel."

How sad that this should be the last word spoken about the house of David in the Chronicler's book! But perhaps the author intended for us to view it differently. From this point on, there is no more mention of Zedekiah. He simply drops from the narrative. What is even more striking is that no mention is made of his death. And this is true not only in Zedekiah's case but of all four kings whose reigns are described for us in this chapter. Interpretations drawn from silence are, of course, inconclusive. But it does make a person wonder when the Chronicler suddenly abandons what has been his regular practice and allows the deaths of the last four kings to pass by without a single word. We have noticed throughout how our writer has shaped his presentation so as to engender hope in the reader's heart that Israel's Ideal King would one day come. With this lack of finality, this refusal to come to closure in his final chapter, could it be that the Chronicler is saying, "The final chapter on David's house is yet to be written"?

As he continues, the holy writer shows us how the people of Judah in their own ungodly lives perfectly reflected the obstinacy of their king. They "became more and more unfaithful"—the Hebrew here is very emphatic. Literally we might render it, "They did much in respect to faithlessly committing faithless acts." In other words, their sins were more than mere slips or momentary lapses. For them sin became a consistent way of life, with their acts of unfaithfulness being repeated over and over again. They were also flagrant—"detestable practices of the [heathen] nations." Viewed by their actions, God's people were no longer God's people. They had even "defil[ed] the temple of the LORD, which he had consecrated in Jerusalem" (verse 14; see also Jeremiah 7:30; 32:34). All levels of society were involved in this, both "the leaders of the priests and the people."

God's response? At first "he had pity on his people and on his dwelling place." He sent word to them repeatedly through his messengers, the prophets, "but they mocked God's messengers, despised his words and scoffed at his prophets." The final stage of hardening has arrived when people not only refuse to listen to God's Word but also

427

show their utter contempt for it by laughing at it. This is a sin for which there is no remedy, because its essence is to despise the only remedy God has provided. God has determined to save mankind through the "foolishness" of preaching. When we willfully, persistently, and flagrantly despise preaching and God's Word, there comes a point when there is no hope left.

In the destruction of Jerusalem, we observe God's fierce anger at work. King Nebuchadnezzar had his own reasons for going against Judah and its king. But he was nevertheless under the Lord's direction, and his power was under God's command. "[The LORD] brought up against them the king of the Babylonians," the Chronicler says. He goes on to stress the completeness of God's act of judgment. God himself caused his own sanctuary to be defiled with the pollution of the dead. Nebuchadnezzar spared no one, making no distinctions on the basis of sex or age. All the treasure troves in all the city's treasure houses were taken away. Nebuchadnezzar picked the place clean, and after he did that, he burned the rest down.

Verse 19 emphasizes the finality of God's judgment in a stylistic way as well. We may observe in it the Chronicler's use of another chiasm (see page 197 for definition and discussion). Since its features do not come out very clearly in the English, we will look at it in a diagrammatic form:

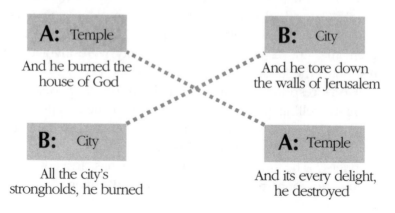

**A:** Temple

And he burned the house of God

**B:** City

And he tore down the walls of Jerusalem

**B:** City

All the city's strongholds, he burned

**A:** Temple

And its every delight, he destroyed

The last phrase, "its every delight, he destroyed," the NIV interprets as referring to the valuable contents of the palaces. We prefer to see it as a poetic reference to the temple itself (compare Isaiah 64:11). God had warned his people. They would not listen. So God carried out his sentence upon his people through Nebuchadnezzar.

### "*Yours, O Lord, is the kingdom*"

*God graciously preserves a remnant of his people*

²⁰**He carried into exile to Babylon the remnant, who escaped from the sword, and they became servants to him and his sons until the kingdom of Persia came to power.**

Even God's judgments serve the interests of his grace. Out of death and destruction, he brings life and salvation. The dramatic turning point of the chapter comes at this verse. God set a limit to the destructive force of his anger against his people. As he had promised through Jeremiah, a "remnant" survived, escaping the sword (Jeremiah 23:3). They were kept in captivity "until the kingdom of Persia came to power."

### *The land enjoys its sabbath rests*

²¹**The land enjoyed its sabbath rests; all the time of its desolation it rested, until the seventy years were completed in fulfillment of the word of the Lord spoken by Jeremiah.**

In the meantime, God gave rest to his land, the land he had promised to Abraham, Isaac, and Jacob, the land so dear to each believer's heart as a foreshadowing of our heavenly home. God himself was purifying the land "all the time of its desolation," making it ready for the return of his people by allowing it to enjoy its sabbath rests (see Leviticus 26:34,35).

He freed the land from man's constant digging in its dirt and searching to amass its store of treasure, which had taken precedence over thought for God. He gave it a rest from the tramping of man's restless, sinful feet, which roamed in a futile quest to find comfort in idols. Through his prophet God had predicted all this: "seventy years," Jeremiah had said—the span of one person's life (Jeremiah 25:11,12; 29:10). For 70 years the land would enjoy its rest until it was ready to serve as home once more to God's people. God's promise through Jeremiah did not fail.

How much more sure we can be of our Savior's promise! He said, "I am going . . . to prepare a place for you. And if I go and prepare a place for you, I will come back and take you to be with me that you also may be where I am" (John 14:2,3). The way to that land he has promised us also leads through the dying of all our earthly hopes until our hearts rest secure in his promise alone. He went the way of suffering before us, the way of God's wrath and of hell's destruction. He went the way of the cross and rose again to make his promise to us absolutely certain: "I am the way and the truth and the life. No one comes to the Father except through me" (John 14:6).

### God moves Cyrus to issue a proclamation: "Return and rebuild!"

[22]In the first year of Cyrus king of Persia, in order to fulfill the word of the LORD spoken by Jeremiah, the LORD moved the heart of Cyrus king of Persia to make a proclamation throughout his realm and to put it in writing:

[23]"This is what Cyrus king of Persia says:

"'The LORD, the God of heaven, has given me all the kingdoms of the earth and he has appointed me to build a temple for him at Jerusalem in Judah. Anyone of his

**people among you—may the LORD his God be with him, and let him go up.'"**

God rules over all! Or, as David once put it, "Yours, O LORD, is the kingdom" (1 Chronicles 29:11). A decree goes out from Cyrus king of Persia, but it comes in fulfillment of the Lord's Word through his prophet. A decree goes out from Cyrus king of Persia, but it was the Lord who stirred up his heart in the first place to issue it. At the ending of his first volume, the Chronicler recorded David's confession of faith, from which we read the above excerpt. At the end of his second volume, the Chronicler reproduces what is essentially the same confession, only this time coming from the mouth of a gentile king. "The LORD, the God of heaven, has given me all the kingdoms of the earth and he has appointed me to build a temple for him at Jerusalem in Judah." God rules over all to make his saving ways known to every nation and to gather his people together from every place.

The Chronicler thus joins all the threads of his history together in a masterful way. He has made the connections necessary for building up the hearts of his fellow believers. The Israelites had gone off into exile, but they had not ceased to be God's people in that foreign land. The king's proclamation clearly had identified them as the Lord's own and had spoken his blessing upon them, "May the LORD [their] God be with [them]." The temple and city had been destroyed but were not to remain so forever. As he did with David and Solomon, God had clearly put it in the heart of this Persian king to say, "The LORD . . . has appointed me to build a temple for him at Jerusalem." And so God reversed the exile's calamity. Temple, city, and people had been restored. "Give thanks to the LORD, for he is good; his love endures forever" (1 Chronicles 16:34; see 2 Chronicles 5:13; 7:3; 20:21).

In his last verse, the Chronicler has given us the goal of God's rule. God works in history to restore his people to the Land of Promise, where they may live a life centered around his dwelling place and bask in the joy of his presence. We recall how he began his account with Adam (1 Chronicles 1:1), walking us through the ages in the genealogies, leading us through all of David's preparations to build, and describing in loving detail the temple's construction and dedication under Solomon. The Chronicler has shown us how God, through weal and woe, through good kings and bad, graciously preserved his house and his people. Earlier in this final chapter, he noted the temple's destruction because of his people's obstinate faithlessness. Now he has closed the circle. The people may go back, fully assured that they *are* God's people. They may go back to Jerusalem and rebuild God's house. The Chronicler permits the words of the Persian king to serve as his final words of encouragement and so ends his book on this note of hope and new beginnings.

We see all these things come to their completion in Christ. He is the Ideal King, who was born in fulfillment of his people's yearnings (Luke 1:31-33). He is the true Temple, the incarnate God come to live among us (John 1:14; 2:19). He is the one who gathers all the exiles scattered throughout the nations into one people that belong to God forever (Ephesians 2:19-21). Through preaching, through Baptism, and through his Holy Supper, he makes us his own and keeps us his own.

But just as we have this sense of hope and of something yet unfinished when we come to the end of the Chronicler's work, so we also know that though God has kept his ancient Word by sending Christ, its ultimate fulfillment is yet to be. As things are now, we see only in part, "through a glass, darkly," as the King James Version puts it (1 Corinthians 13:12). The final restoration of all things has not yet happened, and the last chapter of God's kingdom work is still to be written. And so we wait for our Lord to come back, faithfully gathering around Word and sacrament in the meantime, so that we can continue to perceive all things from the sure, firm center of God's gracious will. Our exile too one day will end. What joy will then be ours!

# ENDNOTES

[1] Adapted and abridged from Raymond B. Dillard's comments on literary structure in *2 Chronicles* of the Word Biblical Commentary series (Waco: Word Books, 1987), pp. 5,6.

[2] Martin Luther, *Luther's Works,* edited by Jaroslav Pelikan and Helmut T. Lehmann, American Edition, Vol. 24 (St. Louis: Concordia Publishing House; Philadelphia: Fortress Press, 1955–1986), p. 90.

[3] Small Catechism, Article V:16, *The Book of Concord: The Confessions of the Evangelical Lutheran Church,* translated and edited by Theodore G. Tappert (Philadelphia: Fortress Press, 1959), p. 350.

[4] Translation of quote in August Pieper, "The Glory of the LORD," *The Wauwatosa Theology,* Vol. 2, edited by Curtis A. Jahn (Milwaukee: Northwestern Publishing House, 1997), p. 419.

[5] Pieper, p. 419.

[6] Dillard, p. 28.

[7] "Simple Instructions for Prayer," in *Luther's Prayers,* H. Brokering, editor (Minneapolis: Augsburg Publishing House, 1967), p. 41.

[8] Most notably Sara Japhet, *I and II Chronicles: A Commentary* (Louisville: Westminster/John Knox Press, 1993), p. 610.

[9] Brokering, p. 18.

[10] First pointed out by Williamson, *Oudtestamentische Studiën* 21 [1981], as quoted in Dillard, p. 87.

[11] J. Goldingray, "The Chronicler as a Theologian," *Biblical Theology Bulletin,* 5, 1975, pp. 102-104; as quoted in Japhet, p. 663.

[12] Japhet, p. 667.

[13] Dillard, pp. 99,100.

[14] *Confessions* 2:10.

[15] Brokering, p. 23.

[16] Japhet, p. 706.

[17] *D. Martin Luther's Werke. Kritische Gesamtausgabe* [WA] (Weimar, Hermann Böhlau und Nachfolger, 1883–1948), Vol. 52, pp. 24ff.

[18]Japhet, p. 747.

[19]Again I consider myself in Sara Japhet's debt for this idea (p. 762).

[20]Susan Howatch, *Scandalous Risks*, p. 373.

[21]*Notes on the State of Virginia*, query 18 (1784).

[22]Luther, WA Vol. 31, pp. 95ff.

[23]*Luther's Works*, Erlangen Edition, Vol. 37, pp. 423,424.

[24]Werner H. Franzmann, *Bible History Commentary: Old Testament* (Milwaukee: Board for Parish Education, Wisconsin Ev. Lutheran Synod, 1980), p. 484.

[25]Jehosheba, besides being King Jehoram's *daughter,* was also Ahaziah's *sister* (see 2 Kings 11:2). Perhaps this means Queen Athaliah was her *mother,* which would make Jehosheba's loyalty to the house of David all the more remarkable. While this is possible, it is by no means certain, since Jehosheba and Ahaziah would still have been brother and sister with the same father (Jehoram) even if they had been born from different mothers.

[26]*Luther's Works*, American Edition, Vol. 24, p. 44.

[27]August Pieper, "The Judgment of God on the Ungodly." An essay read before the meeting of the Western Wisconsin District of the Ev. Lutheran Joint Synod of Wisconsin and Other States, held at Beaver Dam, Wisconsin, June 15–22, 1926. From Pastor Thomas Jeske's recent update of Pieper's own translation. Italics in the original.

[28]*Luther's Works*, American Edition, Vol. 24, p. 61.

[29]*Luther's Works*, American Edition, Vol. 24, p. 98.

[30]*Luther's Works*, American Edition, Vol. 24, p. 81.

[31]*Luther's Works*, American Edition, Vol. 24, p. 80.

[32]Dillard, p. 264.

[33]Martin Franzmann, *Follow Me: Discipleship According to Saint Matthew* (St. Louis: Concordia Publishing House, 1961), pp. 217,218.

[34]Dillard, quoting Rudolph, p. 280.

[35]*Luther's Works*, American Edition, Vol. 51, p. 76.

[36]J. G. McConville, *I and II Chronicles* (Philadelphia: The Westminster Press, 1984), pp. 260,261.

[37]There is considerable mystery surrounding Jehoiakim's final years and death. What scriptural evidence we do have is fragmentary and hard to piece together into a coherent whole. Werner Franzmann's evaluation of Nebuchadnezzar's intention to take Jehoiakim to Babylon remains the best. This intention, he says, "almost certainly was never carried out" (*Bible History Commentary: Old Testament,* p. 528).